Conceiving the Inconceivable

Conceiving the Inconceivable

PART 2

A Scientific Commentary on
Vedānta Sūtras

Original Text Composed by
Sage Vyāsa

Ashish Dalela

SHABDA PRESS

Conceiving the Inconceivable Part 2—A Scientific Commentary on
Vedānta Sūtras
by Ashish Dalela
www.shabda.co

Published by Shabda Press
press.shabda.co
ISBN 978-93-85384-33-2
v1.2(06/2021)

SHABDA
PRESS

CONTENTS

Chapter 3

This is the longest chapter in the text, and it establishes the doctrine of difference and non-difference in many ways. First, it states that consistency of claims is not a goal because the soul moves through conflicts and its choices are made to resolve these conflicts. Second, it undertakes a detailed discussion about the difference and non-difference between various scriptures, various methods of spiritual upliftment, and how they are different and yet non-different. Third, it describes how even for the perfected soul, the difference between truth, right, good vs. false, wrong, and bad exists, and yet these are also reconciled in the Absolute Truth. Fourth, it describes how this process of difference and non-difference is the cause of the manifestation of the material and spiritual worlds and the scriptures. Fifth, it describes how freedom and regulations are intertwined: as people act more individualistically and independently, they are bound by a greater number of laws and regulations; but as they act more cooperatively and unselfishly, the laws and regulations are eliminated for them.

Section 1: This section introduces the idea of movement by inner conflict. It is said that the soul evolves by a succession of questions and answers, and the conflicts between them lead to progression. It also says that inner conflict is resolved by choices, which are controlled by prāṇa. It then answers questions about the soul's free will, which seems to be lost in the world, and how that free will is recovered upon the dissolution of karma. Then follows a detailed discussion around the nature of sin, why the soul must suffer the consequences of sin, the nature of hell, and the type of rebirth that occurs after enduring the results of karma in hell. A discussion about various kinds of species, and how they appear and disappear suddenly, is then undertaken. The text states that children need not have similarities to their parents, and new species can be created by a mother and father who are quite different from their children.

Section 2: This section discusses how the transcendental state is beyond the conventional opposites of attachment and renunciation, bondage and liberation, etc. It then describes that despite the dissolution of such opposites, the distinction between truth and false, good and bad, right and wrong doesn't disappear. Thus, the liberated soul exists in the world, makes a distinction between true and false, good and bad, right and wrong, and also remains equanimous to all such distinctions. Hence, the existence in the material world is not considered bondage, and liberation is not getting out of the material body. Rather, the devotee lives in the world for the Lord's pleasure and tolerates everything. Then the section propounds the whole-part doctrine of the Lord being the whole and the soul being the part and explains how the whole divides into parts. This division is said to follow a logical or rational process. Thus, the world is created by a rational process, the production of karma or consequences of actions are also created rationally, and even scriptures are produced rationally. This sets up the motivation for the scientific study of the world and the scriptures.

Section 3: This section discusses the different processes of attaining the Absolute Truth. While earlier many methods had been rejected as unsuitable, they are now accepted as being useful complements aiding in the understanding of the Absolute Truth. Thus, many forms of yoga, the study of scriptures, and the pursuit of philosophical understanding are recognized as valid methods. And yet, it is established that all these methods work correctly when the devotion to the Lord is accepted as the supreme goal. It is also said that sometimes one path doesn't deliver the complete result, and the missing results can be obtained by the alternative paths. Thus, the hard and fast distinctions between the various paths are dissolved, and these paths are described as various methods available to the spiritual aspirant to overcome different problems in their journey. The understanding of the whole-part relation is modified, and it is said that just as the part is within the whole, similarly, the whole is within the part. This idea is now extended to the relation between the masculine and feminine aspects of the Absolute Truth, and they are described to be distinct, and yet inseparable. This further rejects the absolute separation of different methods, because each method is sufficient in one sense, and all the methods are collectively necessary in another sense. In this way, the doctrine of non-difference is established.

Section 4: This section takes the discussion of morality and compares it to the process of sacrifice in which a lower good must be sacrificed for a higher good, however, in this sacrifice, the least amount of good must be sacrificed. The text now discusses the three systems of social organization—egalitarian, hierarchical, and distributed. In the egalitarian system of society, everyone has the right to make the best decision of what can be sacrificed for which good. Since this system doesn't work unless the people are enlightened, a hierarchical system of organization is discussed in which the higher sections of society (determined by their higher morality) have greater freedom of choosing than the lower sections (determined by their lower morality). Then, when the upper sections of society go missing, then a distributed system of morality is described in which people are equally bound by rules and regulations and nobody has greater or lesser freedom. Finally, the nature of spiritual society is discussed in which nobody has any rights or duties, although everyone acts voluntarily.

SECTION 1

Topic 1

QUESTION

You are explaining the process of change through guna and karma, but the explanation is difficult to understand due to many inherent complexities. Is there a simpler and easier way to understand this process of change?

3.1.1 (293)

तदन्तरप्रतिपित्तौ रंहति संपरिष्विक्तः प्रश्ननिरूपणाभ्याम्

tadantarapratipattau raṃhati sampariṣvaktaḥ
praśnanirūpaṇābhyām

tadantarapratipattau—upon a change toward a new conclusion; raṃhati—goes; sampariṣvaktaḥ—enveloped by many types of statements; praśnanirūpaṇābhyām—by the dual process of questioning and answering.

TRANSLATION

The (soul) enveloped by many kinds of statements goes upon a change toward a new conclusion by the dual process of questioning and answering.

COMMENTARY

This sūtra describes the evolution of the soul occurring by the same process as the evolution of knowledge. Knowledge is described as *sampariṣvaktaḥ* or the covering of many statements. These statements are the facts, axioms, beliefs, and convictions we carry at present.

However, nobody is fully satisfied with their belief system because they know that something is missing. Unless perfect happiness is attained, the doubts about one's beliefs remain. And under these doubts, one naturally develops the tendency to ask questions. These questions appear as different kinds of desires, pursuits, and quests, and present themselves as problems to us. The problems created from the current belief system conflict with the beliefs—so long as something is missing from the beliefs—and this conflict then leads to the need for conflict resolution. Thus, the incompleteness of our beliefs leads to inconsistency between beliefs and questions.

In most modern thinking, we suppose that nature moves from premises to conclusion by recursively applying a certain type of logic to the premises. For example, in classical physics, the current state of a particle is the premise. The application of some natural laws (such as the law of gravitation) pushes the particle to a new state, which then becomes the new premise, to which the same logic (e.g., the mathematical law of gravitation) is reapplied, to get another conclusion. But this process of successive change begs a question: When did it begin? What was the primordial initial state of reality upon which the laws of nature were applied to obtain conclusions? In short, when and in what state did the universe begin? Aristotle during Greek times had formulated an 'Unmoved Mover' argument to illustrate the problem: if everything is moving because of being pushed by something else, then the original cause which got the universe rolling could not have itself been caused (because that would lead to infinite regress) and the movement is due to an 'Unmoved Mover'. The thesis of the 'Unmoved Mover' paralyzed Western thinking for two millennia because the mechanism of movement involved a contradiction—something that wasn't being pushed was the cause of the original push. And yet, this thesis was necessary to answer all fundamental questions of philosophy of that time: namely, that the world has an origin, that it was caused by an uncaused agent, and therefore, the meaning and purpose of this existence rested in that first cause.

Western science began when Newton discarded the idea of an Unmoved Mover. His first law of motion states: Things keep moving unless hindered by a force. In short, we don't have to ask how motion started; we just take it for granted and only study the changes to the motion. Implicit in this view of the world was the idea of logic as something that leads us from premises to conclusions. So, if motion is given as a premise, then the laws of motion (e.g., the theory of gravitation) are only needed to find a conclusion (i.e., the next state of motion) based on the premise. This logical conclusion then led to determinism: If you fix the initial state of a system, all subsequent states are logically fixed. There was hence no role for choice, which subsequently became the problems of morality, the responsibility for our actions, and why we even seek happiness.

Now, contrast this idea of change by the one being described here: we have several beliefs, axioms, or facts, which constitute the premises. However, premises don't lead to conclusions; they first give rise to a question, a problem, or a doubt. This doubt then creates a conflict with the premises, and a new conclusion must be drawn to resolve that conflict. The difference now is that these premises and conclusions aren't merely physical states; they can also be semantic states, such as ideas, theories, and data. So, reasoning doesn't merely move a particle to its new state. Rather, in the evolution of knowledge, our theories, premises, and axioms can change along with the observations of the world. Ideally, you want to be able to explain both the earlier and the new data. But in real life, we might discard the assumptions of our childhood as we grow into adulthood, because we may think that childhood is never coming back.

In we apply the Western model of inference to the development of new ideas, then the problem is that reasoning can never change the axioms. So, if we began with wrong assumptions, we will forever be restricted to conclusions that are consistent with our previous beliefs—an echo chamber of self-reinforcing ideas. The only way experience changes our assumptions is if it is not following the process of logical inference—i.e., presenting us with problems incongruous with our previous assumptions. This forces us to choose between two undesirable extremes: (1) nature is illogical, but we can improve our ideas by experience; we don't know what the destination is, because there are no logical-mathematical laws governing nature, or (2) nature is logical, there is no choice in improving our knowledge, so either we are already in perfect knowledge, or we can never obtain perfect knowledge even if there were infinite time.

This sūtra offers a resolution of this conundrum: there are perfect laws of nature, but the process of change alternates between solutions and problems. These problems can arise within us due to perceived inconsistencies in our axiom system, or they can arise because we are compelled to observe things inconsistent with our prior formed beliefs. The genesis of questions involves a choice: (1) you may not develop an internal problem if you don't want to rethink your assumptions, and (2) you may selectively process the data that fits your assumptions and ignore the rest of the data or interpret it differently. By and large, change is slow because we either reject the data incompatible with our assumptions or we try to explain it based on preexisting assumptions. It is rare that choice is involved, namely, when we must decide to stop ignoring the new data or trying to explain it away using the preexisting beliefs.

We can simplify this issue by saying our beliefs are the answer to the problem posed by the world, and these answers are used to solve the problems of the external world. These beliefs are changed only when they fail to solve the problems. The soul covered by beliefs is the internal world that tries to determine the answers to the externally posed questions. The soul can decide whether a problem needs a new premise or the reuse of a previous premise. This dialectical process of knowledge evolution is here generalized to define the evolution of the soul: the soul evolves through alternating questions and answers; the covering of beliefs changes to address the emerging questions.

QUESTION

You are saying that the soul evolves due to inner and outer conflicts. But how is that possible if the soul is one? How can the soul have conflicts?

3.1.2 (294)
तर्यात्मकत्वात्तु भूयसत्वात्
tryātmakatvāttu bhūyastvāt

tryātmakatvāt—due to having a three-fold nature of the self; tu—but; bhūyastvāt—on account of the preponderance of one of the aspects.

TRANSLATION

Owing to the soul having a three-fold nature (conflicts can develop) but due to the preponderance of one of the aspects (the conflict is resolved).

COMMENTARY

As discussed in previous chapters, the soul has three aspects, *sat*, *chit*, and *ānanda*. *Sat* is responsible for our relation to something (including ourselves), which we call consciousness or awareness (of the object). Following a relation there is a cognition (of the self or the object of awareness), which is called *chit*. Finally, the cognition either fulfills a desire or contradicts it; due to the satisfaction or dissatisfaction, there is ānanda or happiness and distress. This causal sequence from relation to cognition to emotion can also be reversed, when we begin with a desire for something (emotion), form a relation to something to fulfill that desire, and then cognizing that thing which fulfills the desire. Likewise, we can also begin in cognition—e.g., innate beliefs—and infer that these beliefs imply that some desires can be fulfilled through some relationships.

Of course, our desires can be incompatible with our cognition and relation—e.g., when we are not seeing what we want to see. This incompatibility between our cognition, emotion, and relation creates a conflict. The resolution of this conflict can involve a change to either of these three aspects. For instance, we can suppress our desires to comply with the current cognition and relation. Or, we can change our relation and cognition to comply to the desires. All conflict thus results in a resolution, and the resolution is that one of three aspects of the soul becomes dominant, while the other aspects are subordinated.

In this sūtra this dominance is called *bhūyastvāt* or the preponderance of an aspect. The preponderance can be a problem or a solution. If, for instance, our desires are constantly being suppressed to comply to the current relation and cognition, then the suppression of the desire produces a problem. The resolution of that problem is that relation and cognition are subordinated to emotion, and the force of emotion compels a change to the relation and cognition.

After stating that change occurs due to the conflict between the questions and answers in the previous sūtra, this sūtra states that both questions and answers can be modeled in the same way—i.e., as the dominant-subordinate structure of the three aspects. If some aspect is consistently dominant, then it presents a problem to be solved, and the solution is the reversal of the dominant-subordinate structure. The reversed structure is again temporary and becomes a problem after some time and must be reversed after a while. Thus, sometimes we work according to our desires, and sometimes we compromise our desires to adapt to the situation. Sometimes the situation creates a desire in us, and sometimes the generated desire causes a change to the present situation.

While we have discussed the effects of such dominant-subordinate structures in the previous purports, this the first time Vedānta Sūtra itself mentions this dynamic. I have employed this idea in earlier sūtras because we have noted at the outset that nature is self-contradictory, the soul is self-contradictory, and even God as the source of all contradictory ideas is self-contradictory. There is no universalist system of reasoning or logic that can explain how these contradictions co-exist. Such existence requires us to say that these contradictions are possibilities, which manifest in three modes. If they manifest at the same time, then they must manifest in different places. This manifestation can also be enjoyed by different persons. But if they are in the same person and place, then they must manifest one after another. Hence, the modalities of space, time, and persons resolve these contradictions. Even though everything is self-contradictory, these contradictions don't manifest at the same person, in the same place, at the same time. Each of these modalities prevents the contradiction.

But since one or more modalities can avoid these contradictions, one of the three modes must be the dominant reason for avoiding the contradiction, while other modes remain subordinate. The flipping of these modes allows us to say that the same person can exhibit different qualities at different places and times, and while these qualities are in the person as possibilities, their coexistence doesn't produce a contradiction. In short, we cannot do logic without space, time, and persons. The universal truth is simply a possibility. The experienced truth is always at some time, place, and for some person. The flipping of these modes constitutes the mechanism for change, evolution, and logical progression, but it is radically different from modern notions of change. The idea of the tripartite nature of the soul, which then reflects in the three modes of nature, and how both the modes and the self are often self-contradictory, and how this contradiction then results in change is central to understanding Vedānta.

QUESTION

But if there is a change in the preponderance of the three aspects, then what is the cause of this change? How do we decide which aspect has to be dominant or subordinate? Isn't there a choice involved in this change?

3.1.3 (295)
पूराणगतेश्च

prāṇagateśca

prāṇagateḥ—due to the movement of the prāṇa; ca—also.

TRANSLATION

(The selection of one of the three aspects of the soul, which constitutes a choice is) due to the movement of the prāṇa also (aside from the three aspects).

COMMENTARY

We discussed earlier how knowledge evolves through the accumulation of data if the data becomes incompatible with our understanding or beliefs. But this change in beliefs doesn't come about with the first encounter with a discrepancy. Rather, even as contradictory data accumulates, we try to explain away the discrepancies, until we reach a tipping point. At this tipping point, suddenly the data (and the discrepancies) become more important and the beliefs become subordinate to the data. This causes a change in our beliefs.

Thomas Kuhn—an American physicist and philosopher—described the process of scientific evolution as comprising two parts. He called large-scale changes a 'paradigm shift', when old ideas are suddenly discarded and replaced by radical new ideas. He also called the accumulation of small changes 'normal science', where the previous paradigm shift is validated and any inconsistencies are ignored. Kuhn's main argument was that science doesn't progress linearly—i.e., adapting our theories to every new emerging data. Rather, science tries to explain the new data using existing theories until the discrepancies between the data and the theory reach a tipping point and the process is reversed—we now use the data to change theories rather than theories to explain the data. Thus, according to Kuhn, the evolution of knowledge involves a distinction between 'normal science', which explains the emerging data based on current theories with little to no modification to the basic ideas (which Kuhn calls a 'paradigm'), and a 'scientific revolution' that involves the overturning of existing theories and beliefs (which he describes as 'paradigm shift').

Clearly, there is a role for the accumulated data in causing a paradigm shift. We cannot overthrow a belief system because of a few discrepancies, and the resistance to change creates some stability in knowledge. However, the stability is peppered by occasional drastic changes. The point at which we bring that change is a choice. We can choose to ignore the accumulated discrepancies because our beliefs work quite well for other things. This belief in the current powers of science is called 'scientism' and it claims that science is always right even if it cannot explain the accumulating discrepancies. Scientism stands for what Kuhn calls 'normal science' that ignores all the discrepancies. Under scientism, even alternative ideas, which satisfy the conditions of rational and empirical verification—but which violate the established dogmas—are rejected as 'pseudoscience'. The greater the accumulated discrepancies, the greater is the force of change, and the change—when it comes—causes serious disruptions to our thinking. Ideally, we don't want to accumulate many discrepancies because the resulting change would be enormously disruptive. In the interest of stability, we should aim to continuously evolve our beliefs to resolve the conflicts. But whether one makes continuous changes or is forced to adapt to disruptive changes is a choice. Choices are forced when discrepancies accumulate; but we can avoid this force by voluntarily changing while there is still time.

When this dynamic of knowledge evolution is applied to the evolution of the soul, then we can see a role for choice, apart from the three aspects. If one aspect is subordinated for a long time, a disruptive change will be forced, and that change will be caused by the subordinated aspect. But before such a drastic change is forced upon us, we can choose to voluntarily change gradually.

This process of gradual change is called prāṇa. It represents our choices by which we prevent the creation of serious imbalances, which eventually lead to disruptive and drastic changes. We rather evolve by balancing between the forces generated by the three aspects—each pulling in a different direction—allowing each aspect to dominate alternately to prevent the creation of serious imbalances. The action of prāṇa thus contrasts the ideas of 'normal science', which explains without changing itself, and 'paradigm shift' which creates drastic disruptions when the old belief system is replaced by a new one. The action of prāṇa is continuous change in which our theories and ideas co-evolve with the data. All living beings possess this ability for gradual evolution. Societies and organizations also have this ability for gradual evolution—if the people managing the society and organization are themselves prepared to evolve. However, since such evolution involves a conscious intervention into resolving a conflict, and becoming responsible for that choice, most people, societies, and organizations tend not to make the choice and own the responsibility. They wait for the situation itself to force a drastic and dramatic change. A person, society, or organization that delays the changes to avoid the responsibility emerging from that choice has surrendered their choice to the circumstances. They are effectively not living because they are not making the correct choices.

A non-living system will be naturally disrupted by the accumulating discrepancies. A living system can change itself to avoid the disruption. Thus, the term *ca* in this sūtra refers to the fact that evolution can be both conscious and non-conscious. Non-conscious evolution is forced by the accumulated discrepancies reaching a tipping point. Conscious evolution—caused by prāṇa—is the ability to prevent disruptive change and maintain the stability and longevity of the system through smaller, balanced, and incremental adaptive choices.

QUESTION

In the everyday world, we see changes occurring due to transfer of energy. For example, food gets cooked by fire, machines run by burning fuel, and even the human body generates heat as long as it is living. It is said that the sun powers this planet and the life on it. So, if change is seen when there is heat and energy, then why do we say that the soul's choices are the cause of change?

3.1.4 (296)

अग्न्यादिगतिश्रुतेरिति चेत् न भाक्तत्वात्

agnyādigatiśruteriti cet na bhāktatvāt

agnyādigatiḥ—due to the movement of fire etc.; śruteḥ—as it has been stated in the scriptures; iti cet—if it be said; na—not so; bhāktatvāt—because (notion of the movement of fire etc.) is only said in a secondary sense.

TRANSLATION

If it is said that the śrutī attributes the cause of motion to fire etc. (then we say) not so; such statements are only made in a secondary sense.

COMMENTARY

The term *bhāktatvāt* used in this sūtra has many meanings, apart from the secondary sense, which I have used here. All these meanings are relevant to this discussion. For instance, *bhāktatvāt* also means 'due to fit for eating', 'due to fed by something else', 'due to control of something else', the 'devoted', etc. To understand all these meanings, let's look at the different kinds of causes.

It is true that the world changes due to heat and light. But what causes the transfer of heat and light? We know from atomic theory that the emission and absorption of light is indeterministic—(a) we don't know when the light particle will be emitted, (b) we don't know which object will emit the light, and (c) once the light is emitted, we don't know where it will be absorbed. These three kinds of uncertainties in atomic theory correspond to the three modes of nature. We only know that matter exists as a possibility and its conversion into an observation requires another agency. This agency decides when a particle is emitted, where it is emitted, and where it is absorbed. The von Neumann interpretation of quantum theory calls this agency 'choice' or 'consciousness'.

In Vedic philosophy, the agency is called prāṇa. The prāṇa itself has five types, which are called ingestion, digestion, circulation, elimination, and expression. Therefore, the cause of change is not one.

Sometimes, an atomic object moves because the destination of information wants to absorb it—this is called 'ingestion'. At other times the atomic object moves because it is adapting to its environment—this is called 'digestion'. Then sometimes the atomic object moves because it is unable to adapt within an environment—this is called 'elimination'. If the information has adapted in an environment, then it spreads within that environment—this spreading is called 'circulation'. And once it has spread within an environment, it crosses the boundaries of the environment—this crossover from one environment to another is called 'expression'.

The problem in modern science is the legacy of classical physics in which change was caused by a material force. In atomic theory we know that force is not always exerted toward everything. It is exerted sometimes, by some particles, toward some other particles. Therefore, there are three types of uncertainties. And yet, to fit this uncertain model of atomic into the certainty of classical physics, we say that the emission of light is uncertain, but the change resulting from this emission is deterministic. In short, even when choice is involved in the emission of the light, the effects are due to light, rather than choice. This too is false. The cause of emission can decide which particle emits light, and when it emits it. But it cannot decide where this light particle ends up eventually. To make the latter claim, we must say that the causality is bidirectional.

For instance, we can say that we are able to see because the sun is shining. But what causes the sun to shine? The short answer is that there is a person—the sun god—who controls the emission of light, and the sun globe is merely the possibility of that emission. But the sun may be shining, and yet its light may be covered by the clouds. Alternately, we may sit in a dark room and not receive the sun's light. Therefore, the causality is not merely in the sun; it is also in our desiring and deserving. We may desire not to receive the sun's light, and we can avoid it by desiring. But sometimes, we may be forced to receive the sun's light even though we desire to sit in a cool and shady place. Our desiring and deserving are also governed by the prāṇa as much the sun's light is.

Thus, the Vedic texts draw a distinction between the sun god, the sun globe, and the sun light. The sun-god represents the choice to emit light. This choice acts on the possibility of the emission of light represented by the sun globe. And the effect of the choice is the sun light.

When we see sun's light, we attribute this seeing to the sun globe, and not to the person—i.e., the sun-god. Then, we claim that the sun has risen instead of saying that the sun-god has come.

In many Vedic texts, the sun god is worshipped via the sun globe; for example, the worshipper can offer water to the sun-god by looking in the direction of the sun globe. But this sūtra clarifies that anything attributed to the sun- globe—i.e., the ball of fire—is only in a secondary sense. The primary cause is the sun-god under whose supervision the sun globe emits the light. We have seen the rejection of impersonalism earlier where matter is itself the cause of changes in the world, and this is another clear example of this rejection. The impersonal reality is not rejected, and its causality is not denied. However, this causality is said to be the inferior or secondary type of cause, which we have called 'possibility' earlier. This possibility is described variously as 'something fit for eating', 'controlled by something else', etc. Therefore, all these meanings of *bhāktatvāt* are simultaneously true one we realize that the sun-globe is the material cause, and the sun-god is the efficient cause, while sun-light is the effect of the combination of the material and efficient causes. The nuclear reactions in the sun are not the sole cause of the sun-light, because all such nuclear reactions are only possibilities, which may never happen. The real cause is that the sun-god's prāṇa controls these nuclear reactions through a choice.

QUESTION

But what you call the appearance, or a secondary cause, is the first thing we perceive. And what you call the real cause remains invisible. We measure the world by the effects that we can perceive because we cannot see the cause itself. Isn't it natural to explain the world by the effects rather than causes?

3.1.5 (297)

प्रथमेऽश्रवणादिति चेत् न ता एव हि उपपत्तेः

prathame'śravaṇāditi cet na tā eva hi upapatteḥ

prathame—primary; aśravanāt—because not heard; iti cet—if it be said; na—not so; tāḥ eva—that only; hi—because; upapatteḥ—the conclusion.

TRANSLATION

If it is said that because (the prāṇa is) not heard to be primary (therefore it cannot be called primary) (then we say) not so; it is only because (the primary cause) is the derived conclusion (and not directly found from the effects).

COMMENTARY

This sūtra uses contrasting words to the previous sūtra—instead of the term 'secondary', this sūtra uses the term 'primary'. Instead of the term śrutī (or that which is heard authoritatively), this sūtra used the term śravaṇāt (or that which is heard commonly). Beyond these contrasting words, the point of the sūtra is that we never arrive at the cause by the effects, the *pratyakṣa* or the observation because there are potentially numerous explanations of the same effect. Rather, the effect is derived from the cause, which is called *upapatti* or the inference of the cause into effect. In modern language, we can distinguish these two as *truth* and *proof.* The effect we perceive is the truth, but it is not the cause. The cause is the proof underlying the truth—because truth is arrived at via the proof.

This is a rejection of empirical truth as knowledge. At least, it is knowledge only in a secondary or inferior sense. The real knowledge pertains to the reality which creates the effect, and that effect can be proved logically from the premise or the reality. The claim is that what we observe is heat and light, but that is merely the truth. We must generate this truth using a proof, and that proof—e.g., why, when, and how a possibility becomes a reality—is the real cause. The existence of prāṇa entails the existence of the soul, since prāṇa represents the choices. Thus, impersonalism arising from the idea that the cause of observations is light or heat is rejected here as only being as a secondary cause. The real causation is attributed to a person whose choices generate heat and light.

QUESTION

But many impersonalists argue that choice or free will is an illusion. They cite Bhagavad-Gita 3.27 (The bewildered spirit soul, under the influence of the three modes of material nature, thinks himself to be the doer of activities, which are in actuality carried out by nature) to suggest that the soul is not doing anything; it is merely caught in the observation of material changes, but falsely considers itself to be the doer or controller. In short, there is no choice, and things are moving automatically due to matter. So whatever personalism we attribute to nature—e.g., that nature is controlled by demigods—must factually be an illusion because nature is said to be the cause according to scriptures.

3.1.6 (298)

अश्रुतत्वादिति चेत् न इष्टादिकारिणां प्रतीतेः

aśrutatvāditi cet na iṣṭādikāriṇām pratīteḥ

aśrutatvāt—due to being against the claims made in śrutī; iti cet—if it be said; na—not so; iṣṭādikāriṇām—the numerous controllers (e.g., soul and God) in the śrutī; pratīteḥ—becoming merely imaginary entities.

TRANSLATION

If it is said that due to (the claims of personal causality being) against śrutī (we cannot accept them), (then we say) not so (such a conclusion will entail that) the numerous controllers (e.g., soul and God) in the śrutī are imaginary.

COMMENTARY

In the beginning of this chapter, it was stated that the progression of the soul is due to the succession of questions and answers, and this progression involves a choice. The seeker is now rallying against the existence of choice from a different viewpoint than before, arguing for the determinism of material nature. Note that the soul has been held responsible for its fall in earlier chapters, and any attempt to shift the blame for one's choices to God or the circumstances has been refuted. But one can attack the idea using a different argument: namely, that matter is working deterministically and hence I have no choice. If I have no choice, then the succession of questions and answers doesn't involve a choice, and if that is the case, then I'm not responsible for my evolution.

The sūtra however counterargues and says that we have already acknowledged the existence of ātmā and Paramātma as the secondary and primary controllers of material nature. So, now saying that material nature is working automatically—i.e., without the intervention of conscious choices—would result in a contradiction. To solve this contradiction, we would have to say that the ātmā and Paramātma are imaginary entities, concocted by us. And such a claim then goes against the grain of previous statements and śrutī in general.

We can note here that some philosophers such as Hegel have described a dialectical model of change that involved thesis, antithesis, and synthesis. The trouble with this doctrine is its determinism. If the thesis is defined, then antithesis is just its logical opposite. And once both thesis and antithesis are defined, then the synthesis is also predetermined. Yes, the generation of the antithesis may seem a little counterintuitive under the notions of classical logic—How can X become not-X?—but this doesn't change the fact that the evolution is deterministic. Under this determinism, we have no choice; we are simply driven by the historical flow of thesis and antithesis, and if the thesis was fixed to begin with, then everything subsequently is predetermined. In short, we can argue that this dialectical model of change in the sequence of question and answer eliminates choices, which then eliminates the personalism and leads to a new kind of impersonalism—which has come to be known as 'dialectical materialism'.

The key point of inflexion in this argument is that asking a question is not stating an antithesis. Yes, the question presents a conflict with the premise or the thesis, and the answer to that question resolves the conflict to present a new answer which then becomes the thesis. However, the generation of the question from the thesis is not predetermined like the generation of antithesis from the thesis. For instance, if the thesis is that "I'm rich", then the questions can be "How do I become richer?" or "How do I spend my riches?". The antithesis on the other hand would be that "I'm poor", which will then lead to the synthesis that "I am moderately rich—neither rich nor poor". The opposition to that claim would again be "I'm not moderately rich" which could be interpreted in two ways—"I'm extremely rich" or "I'm extremely poor". How do you decide which of these two types of interpretations constitute the antithesis? And unless we can make that decision, the subsequent evolution will come to a halt. Therefore, even if we stick to the thesis-antithesis-synthesis model, we cannot escape choices because the model—while presented as determinism—is not so.

If choices are inevitable, then personalism cannot be avoided even if we adopt a dialectical model of material change. If there are choices, then there must be judgments—i.e., how do decide between the alternatives? These decisions must be rational, and the rationality involves truth, right, and good. Due to rightness, the choices have consequences, and due to goodness, these consequences may be painful, forcing us to revise our judgments and choices.

One can ask: if there are choices, then why is nature said to be governed by prakriti rather than the soul? The short answer is that there is a difference between the doer and the approver. Material nature puts up a proposal for approval, and executes that proposal, provided it is approved by the soul. Nature is therefore doing the grunt work of creating proposals and executing them. And yet, the soul is still the executive decision-maker who accepts and rejects these proposals. The false ego of the soul is not just that it is the decision maker, but that it is the doer. This claim is false because when a person goes to sleep, the body is still working even though we are not making choices. So, if the body can work on its own, the soul's decisions are unnecessary for nature. And yet, just because nature can work independently doesn't mean that is always so.

As we have noted earlier, if we don't make a choice to bring about a change, changes will be forced upon us. Choices can precede these forces and can be used to make a change before the change is imminently forced. So, the determinism of nature is not contrary to our choices; nature gives us an opportunity to make the right decisions and forces a change if we remain inert. It rewards good decisions, and punishes bad ones, but is not dependent upon us to bring a change. Thus, nature can work automatically *if* we don't act. Due to this action, the world will evolve regardless of our choices. Our choices are simply opportunities by which we can act correctly or incorrectly and enjoy or suffer as a consequence of the right or wrong choices made in an opportunity.

QUESTION

But if the soul was indeed the controller of the material world, then why would it be forced to suffer against its choices? Why would it be bound to do things that it is not truly desirous of doing? Isn't that against free will?

3.1.7 (299)

भाक्तं वानात्मवित्त्वात् तथा हि दर्शयति

bhāktaṃ vānātmavittvāt tathā hi darśayati

bhāktaṃ—in a secondary sense; vā—but; anātmavittvāt—on account of lack of self-knowledge; tathā—so; hi—because; darśayati—so seen.

TRANSLATION

(The causality in material elements) is said to be secondary (to the causality in the soul) but due to the lack of self-knowledge (the soul is) thus (bound by the laws of matter) because it sees (itself as being covered up by matter).

COMMENTARY

The soul is the controller of the body (as stated above) but it comes under the control of the body due to lack of self-knowledge. What is self-knowledge? That the soul is full of pleasure, and it doesn't need the support of the body to be happy. But because the soul doesn't know that there is happiness within itself, he seeks happiness in the external world, through the body and the senses. Thus, the soul becomes dependent on the body for his happiness and starts serving the body's needs rather than being the controller of the body. If the body's necessities are not fulfilled, the soul considers itself unhappy. When the same necessities are fulfilled, then the soul considers itself very happy. So, the happiness of the body becomes the happiness of the soul, rather than the happiness of the soul becoming the happiness of the body. In short, the soul becomes the servant of the body, rather than being the master of the body.

Topic 2

QUESTION

Then how can the soul recover its free will and get freedom from matter?

3.1.8 (300)

कृतात्यये ऽनुशयवान् दृष्टस्मृतिभ्याम् यथेतमनेवं च

kṛtātyaye'nuśayavān dṛṣṭasmṛtibhyām yathetamanevaṃ ca

kṛta—acquired; atyaye—on the finishing; anuśayavān—possessed of the consequences of one's actions; dṛṣṭasmṛtibhyām—from the recollection or memory of the soul; yathā etam—just as it is; anevam—not so; ca—and.

TRANSLATION

Upon the finishing of the previously acquired consequences of one's actions that possess the soul, (the covering of matter is) also (finished) from the memory of the seer (the soul) just as if it was never there (to begin with).

COMMENTARY

Several important points are made in this sūtra. First, the consequences of one's past actions are compared to a smriti or memory. Normally, the term memory is reserved for the things that we can recollect from the past. We call this the 'conscious' memory. However, in addition to these facts—which are generally limited to the events of this life—there are also memories from the past lives, which remain unconscious. These unconscious memories have three parts—(a) the *chitta* or the unconscious imprints of past events, (b) the habits or proclivities of enjoyment, and (c) the consequences of previous actions.

First, the chitta creates thoughts in us. Due to the proclivities of the past, we like or dislike these thoughts and develop our plans for enjoyment. Due to the results of previous actions, these plans are fulfilled or disrupted. The unconscious constitutes our 'causal body' or *kārana sarīra* that covers the soul life after life, and the subtle and the gross bodies are developed from it. The subtle body constitutes our conscious memories, thoughts, moralities, etc. And the gross body comprises the senses of perception and the organs in the body. Often, we see things that we instantly recognize, although we cannot find a conscious memory in this life about encountering these things. This is because the chitta has these memories which remain unconscious and can be manifest into our experience either on their own or due to contact with the external world. Similarly, our desires or tendencies and consequences of previous actions are manifest from the unconscious. All these are manifest because of time.

Second, by the time karma is destroyed, the material desires and the impressions of the past are also destroyed. Of course, it is possible that some souls who have overcome the material desires and the impressions of past lives that create thoughts in us may still have some residual karma. As a result, some pure souls may also continue to suffer or enjoy in the material world, even though they have become enlightened. However, the reverse is generally false—i.e., by the time karma is destroyed, the soul becomes free of all desires and impressions. Thus, this sūtra states that the destruction of karma entails freedom from the material covering of desires and past impressions, which then lead to complete freedom both from the push exerted by the thoughts and desires, and the consequences one is compelled to face to fulfill these thoughts and desires. Thus, the freedom from karma entails the removal of material covering.

Third, once this material covering is removed, the soul loses all history of material existence. It is now said to be eternally liberated, because the history of past births and deaths, the experiences of many lifetimes, and the fulfilled or unfulfilled desires of the past are all destroyed. Even though the soul was previously born in a body, and may exist in a body at the present, such a soul is said to be *nitya-siddha* or eternally liberated. It is as if there was never a material birth or death, and the soul had never entered the material existence. Thus, upon liberation, there is no difference between those souls who had never entered material existence, and those who had entered and were liberated.

QUESTION

You are saying that freedom from karma leads to freedom from the material covering. Why not the reverse—i.e., freedom from the material covering leading to freedom from karma? Can we not say that if a person has developed good qualities and conduct, he should be free of the consequences of past actions? After all, he has now learned the lessons of life, and corrected himself?

3.1.9 (301)

चरणादिति चेत् न उपलक्षणार्थेति कार्ष्णाजिनिः

caraṇāditi cet na upalakṣaṇārtheti kārṣṇājiniḥ

caraṇāt—due to conduct; iti cet—if it be said; na—not so; upalakṣaṇārthā—for the purpose of secondary qualities of a person (also known as their roles or duties); iti—thus; kārṣṇājiniḥ—Kārṣṇājini (states).

TRANSLATION

If it is said that due to good conduct (a person can become free of karma) (then we say) not so (because) the secondary qualities of a person (the roles and responsibilities of past actions still must be borne); thus, says Kārṣṇājini.

COMMENTARY

There is a doctrine in modern law that states that a person sent to prison due to their misdeeds can be freed earlier if they exhibit good behavior. In this doctrine, the purpose of punishment is to correct a person, and if the person has been corrected, then there is no need for them to suffer. Thus, those exhibiting good behavior are let go earlier than their normal sentence. This sūtra refutes such doctrines. It states that if a person has committed crimes, there is due punishment regardless of their corrected behavior. If they haven't been corrected, then they will commit more crimes in the future, and there will be subsequent punishments for them. But just the fact that someone is behaving well now doesn't entail a reduction in their punishments. This is important because people often ask: Why do bad things happen to good people? Their assumption is that if people have become good, then their punishments must also be reduced or eliminated. This sūtra, however, cites Kārṣṇājini as saying that a person must suffer all the karma regardless of whether they have been purified or not. It also means that the consequences of good and bad actions don't cancel each other. So, we cannot perform good deeds and hope to nullify bad karma. The good and bad actions produce individual results which must be endured.

There can be a debate about the meaning of *upalakṣaṇārthā* in this sūtra. For instance, one can argue that it denotes "indirect meaning", "secondary meaning", "indirect purpose", etc. Based on this we can translate this *sūtra* as follows: "If it is said that due to good conduct (a person can become free of karma) (then we say) not so (because) the hidden/indirect/secondary purposes or meanings in a person; thus, says Kārṣṇājini". Such a translation would imply that unless a person has suffered the consequences of their deeds, they cannot be said to have fully learned their lessons. Since they have gotten off easily, they may believe that there are ways to escape the punishment of bad deeds—e.g., doing good deeds or exhibiting good behavior and thus it is all right to mix both good and bad deeds as these can cancel each other's effects. Such alternative meanings of *upalakṣaṇārthā* don't change the purport, namely, that a person must endure their previous karma regardless of good behavior. This endurance can be attributed to the fact that bad karma exists and cannot be nullified by good behavior. Or, it can be attributed to the notion that nullifying such karma due to good behavior would create the wrong conclusion—i.e., that good deeds can be used to cancel the outcomes of bad deeds—which is unacceptable. So, regardless of how we interpret *upalakṣaṇārthā*, the purport is the same.

QUESTION

But freedom from suffering is often an incentive for people to improve. If we say that good behavior doesn't cancel the bad deeds, then doesn't it take away the incentives for a person's improvement? Some people may not improve if they think that improvement doesn't reduce their present suffering.

3.1.10 (302)

आनर्थक्यमिति चेत् न तदपेक्षत्वात्

ānarthakyamiti cet na tadapekṣatvāt

ānarthakyam—resulting in counterproductive outcomes; iti cet—if it be said; na—not so; tadapekṣatvāt—due to in comparison/contrast to that.

TRANSLATION

If it is said that (good qualities don't immediately lead to freedom from suffering) will result in counterproductive outcomes (i.e., people not renouncing bad deeds) (we say) not so due to the comparison/contrast to that.

COMMENTARY

If you purchase something on a loan, and you start paying the premiums of those loans, your good behavior of repaying those premiums doesn't reduce the number of premiums you have to pay. If this were the case, nobody would buy anything by paying cash; everyone would purchase things on a loan, pay some premiums, and then ask for a reduction in the total payment. Karma, similarly, is a debt, which must be paid in full. If one argues that a person under debt will get an incentive to be debt-free if the lender forgave the debt, the counterargument is that if such debts were forgiven, more people would want to get into debts because they wouldn't have to pay the full price of things. They can just buy things on a loan, pay some premiums, and then ask for clemency. Thus, such an arrangement would not reduce the number of people under debt. In fact, it would increase their numbers, besides, of course, creating an unfavorable situation for those who pay the full cost of a thing upfront in cash. In fact, those who were paying their loans fully, might now argue: Why do I have to pay the loan fully when so many others are not paying their loans? This sūtra contrasts the two competing positions and states that the outcomes of forgiving are even more counterproductive than the outcomes of not forgiving.

QUESTION

This objective treatment of karma may lead people to say that natural laws on morality are not compassionate as they don't forgive a person's actions. Isn't that criticism justified given that you say that nature's laws are unforgiving?

3.1.11 (303)
सुकृतदुष्कृते एवेति तु बादरिः
sukṛtaduṣkṛte eveti tu bādariḥ

sukṛta—good activities; duṣkṛte—evil activities; eva—certainly; iti—thus; bādariḥ—says the sage Badari.

TRANSLATION

(This argument can be) certainly applied to both good and evil activities; thus, says the sage Bādari (i.e., if it were applied to good activities, then sometimes we may not get the good returns on the previous good activities).

COMMENTARY

If one argues that delivering the just punishment to one who has already suffered a lot is uncompassionate, then how about we reverse the argument and say that giving happiness to someone who's had a lot of it already is unjust? If too much of the outcome of evil actions is unjust, then too much of the outcome of good actions must also be unjust. So, by that measure, even if someone has performed several good deeds, nature should not deliver the good returns in proportion because giving too much good to one person would be unjust. The point of the sūtra is that people ask for a reduction in the bad outcomes but not a reduction in good outcomes. How can we accept one but not the other? If we started reducing the outcomes of bad actions, then we would also need to reduce the outcomes of good actions, which means that the evildoers will suffer less, and the good-doers will enjoy less. Would that be considered justice?

Topic 3

QUESTION

The scriptures are primarily devoted to the description of good deeds, including those that lead to salvation. How can a person know what sin is, and how to lead one's life, if the descriptions of sins are not very prominent?

3.1.12 (304)

अनष्टादिकारिणामपि च श्रुतम्

aniṣṭādikāriṇāmapi ca śrutam

anisṭādikāriṇām—the descriptions of sinful activities; api—even; ca—also; śrutam—is declared by the śrutī.

TRANSLATION

Even the descriptions of sinful activities are also given in the śrutī.

COMMENTARY

While the knowledge of Vedas is eternal and encompassing, its presentations may vary in emphasis based on time, place, and the type of persons. For example, if a society is not incestuous, then the scripture may not forbid incest, because it is considered unnecessary. They may instead, based on the lack of incest, instruct the people to treat other people's wives like their mothers and sisters. On the other hand, if incest was prominent in a society, then scripture would forbid incest, and not recommend other women to be treated like mothers and sisters (because the idea then would be that if incest is possible in the family, then even other women—who are like one's daughters and mothers—can also be enjoyed since they are just like our mothers and daughters).

Thus, what is present or absent in scriptures often depends on the people f the scripture is meant for. The descriptions of sinful activities are limited in the śrutī because society was almost sinless. Texts like Rig Veda don't describe hells. Atharva Veda describes places of suffering for sinful people, but these descriptions are not detailed. Yajur Veda provides more substantive descriptions about hells. Thus, this sūtra states that there are descriptions of sinful activities in the śrutī. The use of *api* and *ca* indicates that these are "also described". It is accepted that the emphasis is not on such descriptions, but they are present indicatively for those who might be interested in such guidance.

QUESTION

But there are many people who don't accept the descriptions of sin in scriptures. How can they be corrected from the performance of sinful actions?

3.1.13 (305)

संयमने त्वनुभूयेतरेषामारोहावरोहौ तद्गति दर्शनात्

saṃyamane tvanubhūyetareṣāmārohāvarohau tadgati darśanāt

samyamane—in the abode of Yama; tu—but; anubhūya—having experienced; ataresām—of others; ārohāvarohau—the ascent and descent; tadgati—the result of the actions; darśanāt—from the observation.

TRANSLATION

(A person can be corrected from sinful activities) in the abode of Yama; but having experienced the ascent and descent of others, resulting from their previous actions, one can (also) be corrected from such observation (of others).

COMMENTARY

There are three prominent methods of knowledge—*pratyakśa*, *anumāna*, and *śabda*, or direct experience, inference from experience, and scriptural knowledge. If someone doesn't accept the word of the scriptures, they can obtain the same knowledge by direct experience or inference from experience. These two methods are referred in this sūtra. The direct experience is provided in the planets of Yamarāja who administers the results of sinful activities by punishing the sinner. Otherwise, we can also observe how other people are going up and down in the lives and understand that their enjoyment or suffering is due to their previous actions. This is knowledge by inference—namely that if other people are suffering or enjoying, then the distinction must be due to their past activities, and hence one must avoid sinful activities. In short, we should not consider suffering and enjoyment to be accidents of life. We must try to explain them, and the logical inference is that enjoyment and suffering are due to one's past actions. Thus, the preferred method of knowledge is scriptural descriptions, but if one doesn't accept that, then there is knowledge by inference obtained when one learns from the experience of others. If a person is still not convinced (and regards these as accidents) then there is direct experience. Thus, like all other knowledge, the knowledge of sins is available in many ways.

QUESTION

But don't you think a detailed description of hells and their respective sufferings is important if people are to avoid various kinds of sufferings?

3.1.14 (306)

समरन्तचि

smaranti ca

smaranti—the smritis declare; ca—also.

TRANSLATION

(Those interested in a detailed understanding of the hells) can also refer to the smriti (such as the Purāṇa, or texts such as the Manu Smriti).

COMMENTARY

Detailed descriptions of hells are found in several Purāṇa such as the Śrīmad Bhāgavatam and the Devi-Bhāgavata Purāṇa. They are also found in Manu Smriti. Here is another instance in which the Vedānta Sūtra treats the śrutī and smriti as a continuum of texts providing different kinds of information. If the description of hells is not prominently found in the śrutī—because these were meant for the almost sinless souls—they are prominently found in the smriti which are meant for the common population. Thus, we can see that the different descriptions are relative to the kind of people. The knowledge is universal, but its presentation changes emphasis depending on the audience. The sinless souls don't need descriptions of hells, as they are already disinterested in such things. The sinful souls—which may be found among the common population—can easily benefit from such descriptions. Still, the description of hells is less than 1% of the content of the smriti. It means that even those reading the smriti were expected to be mostly sinless.

QUESTION

Is the suffering for all kinds of sinful activities the same? Or are there differences in the type of suffering endured for different kinds of sinful acts?

3.1.15 (307)
अपि च सप्त
api ca sapta

api ca—moreover; sapta—seven.

TRANSLATION

(The sinful activities and the hells) are moreover seven (distinct types).

COMMENTARY

The conscious experience of the soul is divided in Sāṅkhya into seven layers—morality, ego, intellect, mind, senses, properties, and objects. Based on this seven-fold layering of experience, the universe is divided into upper and lower halves, each with seven parts where the pleasure dominates in these seven layers of experience. The earth planetary system is the seventh in the upper half of the universe, and the primary pleasure here is derived from objects. In svarga, however, the senses themselves can create pleasure. In further higher planetary systems, pleasure is obtained through the actions of the mind, the intellect, the ego, and the moral sense. In all these seven planetary systems, there is morality tied to the existence of the Lord; that is, there is an understanding that the punishment of sinful activities is meant to uplift a person toward transcendence. But as one goes into lower planetary systems, this understanding gradually vanishes and is replaced by the fear of powerful authorities that govern these places. These lower realms are ruled by demons, and in this society the duties are performed not due to the desire for transcendence or spiritual upliftment but due to the fear of the rulers, government, etc. There is no inner desire for perfection; it is only the fear of punishment that controls the demonic.

Each of these fourteen planetary systems (seven above and seven below) are sometimes further divided into fourteen subparts. The bhūloka is, for instance, divided into seven 'islands' and 'oceans'. This method of division is often carried forward into subsequent subdivisions. Thus, depending on the level of detail, the same seven-fold method of division is employed many times. This method of division is referenced in this sūtra regarding the hells as well.

The Śrīmad Bhāgavatam and Devi-Bhāgavata Purāṇa describe the existence of 28 hells, mimicking the 28-fold division of the non-hellish regions. This sūtra shortens that description and refers only to a seven-fold division. We can infer that these divisions pertain to the suffering at various levels of experience ranging from the body, sensations, senses, mind, intellect, ego, and moral sense. A soul can suffer in many ways. For example, if someone doesn't receive justice in a society, the pain is experienced in their moral sense. The pain of being cheated is experienced through a person's ego. The pain of having accepted false information as true, is experienced in the intellect. The pain of misunderstanding is felt in the mind. The pain of ineptitude is felt in the senses. And the pain of hot and cold is felt through the sensations. Finally, the suffering of the body includes weakness, tiredness, and numerous kinds of illnesses. Everybody doesn't suffer in the same way. Depending on the source of their sinful actions, the results of sinful actions are also reaped in the same way.

QUESTION

When a person suffers a lot, he sometimes takes shelter of the Lord, begs for forgiveness, and promises a change in his attitude. Is this true for the hells, and can a person remember the Lord even in hell, just like the present life?

3.1.16 (308)

तत्रापि च तद्व्यापारादविरोधः

tatrāpi ca tadvyāpārādavirodhaḥ

tatra—there; api—even; ca—and; tat-vyāpārāt—due to the business of that (i.e., progressing in spiritual life); avirodhaḥ—is not impeded (by suffering).

TRANSLATION

Even there (in the hells) due to the business of that (i.e., progressing in spiritual life) not being impeded (by the suffering of the body and mind).

COMMENTARY

Abrahamic religions believe in an eternal hell; this idea is summarily rejected here. Not only is hell not eternal, but it doesn't forbid one from progressing in spiritual life. In fact, as people turn toward God during suffering, the soul can get purified of his sinful desires, even as he undergoes many types of suffering, thus preparing him for a better life after the hellish existence. Spiritual progress can never be impeded by any material circumstances—good or bad. When the situation is good, the spiritualist takes advantage of the comforts and diverts his attention toward spiritual practices. When the situation is bad, the spiritualist still takes advantage of the situation and learns to be detached from the material existence and focuses on transcendence. Thus, for the spiritualist, no situation is harmful, as all situations lead to spiritual progress.

QUESTION

How can a person who has seen hellish life (because they ignored the word of scriptures) prevent recurrence of this life? Also, how can one who wants to avoid going to hell prevent the occurrence of sinful activities in their life?

3.1.17 (309)
वदियाकर्मणोरतिति तु प्रकृतत्वात्
vidyākarmaṇoriti tu prakṛtatvāt

vidyākarmaṇoḥ—the knowledge of actions (and consequences); iti—thus; tu—but; prakṛtatvāt—from producing or creating (the body and life).

TRANSLATION

From the knowledge of actions (and consequences) as noted earlier (i.e., in the śrutī and smriti) but (also the knowledge of) how actions create (new life).

COMMENTARY

It is impossible to list all kinds of sinful activities just as it is impossible to list all kinds of good deeds. A partial list of good and evil deeds is present in the scriptures, subject to the time, place, and the type of persons involved. If one wants to ensure that he is not performing sinful deeds, one must learn the science of how our actions create future lives. This science involves three parts. First, every action leaves behind a memory in the *chitta*, which can become a thought, which can become a desire and lead to sinful activities. Thus, the purification of the *chitta* is the primary means of avoiding sinful actions. Second, every action we perform becomes a liking and habit at an unconscious level; if we have done something once, we have formed a habit, which can recur. These habits will then make us believe that it is all right to do sinful actions again—after all, we have done them once; what's the harm in doing it again? These habits lead to a new body; for example, a meat-eater will be born in a species where meat-eating is a natural habit or tendency. Third, the consequences of the actions leave behind karma which then puts the soul into a new type of circumstances where the soul is forced to suffer or enjoy; for instance, due to good karma a tiger will get to hunt and eat deer, but due to bad karma, the same tiger will either have to stay hungry or eat the leftovers of other tigers.

Thus, if one understands the science of how the present body leads to a new body, then the quality of future lives decides what we do right now. For instance, if we want to be born again in a human body, then we should avoid the tendencies of animals who hunt, kill, and eat other animals. We don't even have to understand the prescriptions of the scriptures that killing is bad; we just must know that if we act like animals, then we will be reborn as animals. Likewise, if we understand that by cheating and deceiving others, we would also be cheated and deceived in the future, then the numerous ways of cheating and deceiving don't have to be found in the scriptures. If we understand that every action creates an impression and forms a habit, which then produces subsequent thoughts and behaviors, then we would be careful about what we think and what habits we form. The cause of suffering is the lack of understanding of how a new life is created by the actions of the present life. If this knowledge was acquired, then the person who knows this would avoid all sinful actions.

QUESTION

But so many people are incapable of understanding the laws of karma and how it creates the body. They may not want to neglect

the word of scriptures or the process of reincarnation and karma. But they just don't understand it. What happens to people who are not intelligent and capable of knowledge?

3.1.18 (310)
न तृतीये तथोपलब्धेः
na tṛtīye tathopalabdheḥ

na—not; tṛtīye—in the third; tathā—so; upalabdheḥ—being found in.

TRANSLATION

(Those who are incapable of understanding the knowledge of karma and reincarnation) are not found in the third stage of existence (hellish planets).

COMMENTARY

The material universe is divided into three parts—heavenly planets, demonic planets, and the hellish planets. The entry into hellish planets is ascribed to those who are openly atheistic and disregardful of the scriptural injunctions. Those who are unintelligent, uneducated, or uninformed about these injunctions are treated just like animals who have no idea about morality, the purpose of human life, and how it is restricted by the laws of nature. Their ignorance is not punished by the experience of hellish planets according to this sūtra. They are just unfit to be humans, and they are hence reborn as animals. Animals too have some altruism, but that is not because of a moral sense of responsibility. It is only because of emotional attachment and kinship. Thus, many animals protect their own, not because of a sense of duty, but due to attachment. Animal society is not structured hierarchically in which the powerful are also aware of their responsibilities. Animal society is simply power without responsibility. Therefore, those who cannot understand responsibility are born as animals. If they have good karma, they also get power. If they have bad karma, they are born weak. They still suffer and enjoy, but they don't feel guilty about their bad actions, nor do they feel unhappy about the injustices by the powerful.

QUESTION

Many people may think of doing something bad but may not do it. Is the thought of sinful activities also punishable by the experience of hells?

3.1.19 (311)

स्मर्यतेऽपि च लोके

smaryate'pi ca loke

smaryate—thinking; api—also; ca—and; loke—in the world.

TRANSLATION

And those thinking (about sins) are also in the world (that is not hellish).

COMMENTARY

The succession of sūtras here is quite interesting because the previous sūtra asked if a person who performs actions unknowingly—i.e., has no conscious intention of being sinful—is sent to hell, and the answer was no. This sūtra responds to a different question—what if the person is consciously intending, but doesn't enact those intentions? The answer to that question is again no. In short, both the action and the intention are considered. If there is unintentional action, then there is some punishment, but it is not hell. Likewise, if there is intention without a corresponding action, then again there is no hell. However, a person who harbors evil thoughts is best suited to live a life where these thoughts may be fulfilled. This will be clarified in subsequent sūtras where people who possess sinful thoughts are born into lower forms of life. In short, those who harbor sinful thoughts, but don't act on them, are not sent to hell, but they don't continue in human life either. They are considered fit for animal life forms.

There is hence a distinction between guna and karma. Those who perform sinful actions produce adverse karma. But those who simply think sinful thoughts still create sinful guna. Such living entities change their bodies where they can fulfill their sinful desires, without incurring sin or hellish life.

Karma doesn't disable the mind, or the other subtle instruments such as intellect, ego, and morality. If karma disabled the mind, then one could claim that all subsequent misdeeds are caused by the mind not working properly, and one misdeed, therefore, leads to another misdeed, which then perpetuates an eternal cycle of misdeeds. However, if one constantly thinks of sinful activities, their morality, ego, intellect, mind, and senses become unfit for human life.

Such people may also perform sinful activities in this life. Thus, many people are too selfish to execute their responsibilities; they keep exploiting others but do not give in return on par with what they are taking from them. Some are extremely egoistic and insensitive to others. Some present false ideas as truth. And many are simply illusioned by the preponderance of false ideas. As one performs sins under various influences, the cause of the sin is traced back to the mind, the intellect, the ego, or the moral sense. Thus, if sinful reactions originate in a bad morality, then the punishment is also felt in the moral sense—e.g., others will behave selfishly with them. If the sins originate in the ego, then the punishment is also felt in the ego—e.g., they will be humiliated by others. If the sins originate in the intellect, then the punishment is also felt in the intellect—e.g., they will be cheated and deceived. If the sins originate in the mind, then the punishment is also felt in the mind—e.g., those who misinterpret others would be misinterpreted themselves. Thus, it must be understood that if things remain in the mind, the intellect, the ego, or the moral sense, then the soul simply changes the body appropriate for that type of mentality. But if the mental activity becomes the bodily activity, then the soul suffers not just bodily but is also hurt mentally, intellectually, emotionally, and morally. But this hurt doesn't disable the mind, the intellect, the ego, or the moral sense. Therefore, the working of karma is very nuanced and difficult to understand. There is no sin unless the body acts; if the body acts, then mental suffering is entailed by the sinful activity; and yet, despite this suffering, the mind can still prevent the recurrence of sinful activities and stop the cycle of action and reaction.

QUESTION

What about people who see criminal acts being performed but aren't doing those actions themselves? Does this silent observation lead one to hell?

3.1.20 (312)

दर्शनाच्च

darśanācca

darśanāt—on account of observation; ca—also.

TRANSLATION

On account of observation also (one doesn't go to hell).

COMMENTARY

Seeing a sinful activity is not the same as doing the sinful activity. This, however, holds true only when the person seeing these activities is not authorized to prevent its occurrence. For instance, leaders who are responsible for others' behavior cannot escape their responsibility by saying that I was only observing the sins, and I'm sinless because I did not perform the sins. Thus, the Kshatriya or the rulers are implicated if they neglect their duties silently. This statement applies only to those who are not expected to prevent others from sinful actions, and yet, they may be silent observers to others' sinful activities.

Inaction is also the action of endorsing the sinful actions when a person in authority is expected to prevent it. The person who is not in such a position to prevent the sinful actions cannot be said to be endorsing it. However, this doesn't mean that they go unpunished. There is still punishment, although the suffering is not as severe as those of the hellish planets. Conversely, those in the position of power, who do not prevent sinful actions, are destined to hell.

QUESTION

But many of these people—who watch the performance of sinful actions—may not protest them because they are enjoying their performance. They may not do such sins themselves, but they like to watch others do such sins. Doesn't karma punish them in some way? Or, are they considered totally sinless?

3.1.21 (313)

तृतीयशब्दावरोधःसंशोकजस्य

tṛtīyaśabdāvarodhaḥ saṃśokajasya

tṛtīya-śabda-avarodhaḥ—the third stage is said to be not advocated for them; saṃśokajasya—they are born into species that spring from sweat.

TRANSLATION

The third stage (the hellish planets) are said to be not advocated for them; they are born into species that spring from sweat (called *svedaja* species).

COMMENTARY

Vedic texts identify four kinds of births—*andaja* (born from eggs, like reptiles), *pindaja* (born from a womb, like humans), *svedaja* (born from sweat, like bacteria), *udbhija* (born from the seed, like plants). The *svedaja* body subsists on rotting materials. Among these four classes, they are the lowest type of birth, and this sūtra states that those living entities who enjoy watching the performance of sinful activities are born to subsist upon rotting materials. An example of such decadence is watching illicit sex, gambling, stealing, and murder in movies. People who watch such movies may not do these things as they know they are wrong. But they still like to watch others do it and perpetrate the performance of such activities in society by paying for such 'entertainment'.

The progression of these sūtras indicates successively greater types of sins, which are yet not sinful enough to take a person to hell. Thus, we first spoke about those who perform sins unknowingly. Then we spoke about people who know what is right and wrong, and they don't perform the sinful actions because of this knowledge, but they cannot stop thinking about doing these sins. Then we spoke about those who know the difference between right and wrong, but they might not have the courage to stop their occurrence even when they see it. Now we are speaking about those who don't perform such sins, but they still enjoy watching sinful actions and may pay others for doing them.

This decadent form of pleasure is condemned in this sūtra, and those enjoying such decadence are said to be born to subsist on rotting materials. They are not as sinful as those who perform such actions. But because of their tendencies to enjoy such decadent pleasure, they are born as bacteria and worms.

Topic 4

QUESTION

Are all sinful creatures reborn into the species produced from sweat?

3.1.22 (314)

तत्साभाव्यापत्तःउपपत्तेः

tatsābhāvyāpattiḥ upapatteḥ

tat-sābhāvya—according to their nature; āpattiḥ—misfortune or calamity; upapatteḥ—being the reasonable conclusion.

TRANSLATION

According to their nature, and whatever is a reasonable conclusion (based upon their activities), a misfortune or calamity (is assigned to them).

COMMENTARY

The previous sūtra described the qualification for entering the *svedaja* body. But we have previously spoken of other types of sinful activities, such as doing sins unknowingly, thinking about doing sinful activities, and watching sinful activities uncomfortably but not preventing their occurrence. Those who enjoy seeing others do sinful activities are condemned to be born out of rotting materials, but this is not the fate of every other sinful type of person. This sūtra states that there are many grades of life and one goes to them according to their nature. All these species are called a calamity or misfortune. However, the level of misfortune is decided by assigning whatever is a reasonable response.

Topic 5

QUESTION

Is the soul stuck in these lower species of life for a very long time? Or does he get a chance to get back to the human form of life after a short while?

3.1.23 (315)
नातचिरिण वशिेषात्
nāticireṇa viśeṣāt

na—not; aticireṇa—in a very long time; viśeṣāt—due to specialties.

TRANSLATION

(The soul) is not (in lower species of life) for a long time (if) there are special qualities (which entitle the soul to be reborn into the human form of life).

COMMENTARY

The entry into the animal species of life is contingent upon their guna. With this guna, they can enjoy or suffer their specific natures. Thus, some dogs remain street dogs, while other dogs get a comfortable home. Some cows are protected by their owners, while other cows are slaughtered by their owners. Enjoyment or suffering doesn't end even as the soul leaves one body and enters another. However, the nature of the enjoyment or suffering changes depending on the guna. Therefore, a soul who enters an animal body due to some animalistic qualities can come back to higher forms of life if their guna changes.

The animal form of life is obtained due to the dominance of tamo-guna. If the tamo-guna reduces, and rajo-guna increases, then the soul is reborn into the human life. This sūtra notes that life in the animal body is limited if tamo-guna is limited. Thus, one should not try to generalize all living entities born into a lower species as being equally sinful. Some of them are less sinful, and if their tendencies are corrected, then their existence in these species is shorter.

Topic 6

QUESTION

Can the soul be born without a mother or father from a species? In other words, can life be created out of material elements, without another life?

People often get tired of the difficulty in understanding the process of rebirth. There is a role for the body and the mind; when the mental activity manifests into the body, there is sin, but otherwise, there is simply change in the body. Whether or not there is sin, the suffering is not eternal. In fact, the soul can remember the Lord even in hell. And some bodies are long-lived while others are short-lived. Sometimes, the soul goes through many bodies before returning to human life. And sometimes the soul may return to human life after one animal birth. Troubled by these difficulties, some people have a knee-jerk reaction: Let's forget about all these complexities, and just say that all life is temporary; the birth into a specific type of species has no explanation, etc.

Such questions are found not just in atheists or materialists. Even many spiritual aspirants, who have practiced some form of spiritual process, can also fall into this trap if they are unable to understand the complex explanations. They now seek alternative explanations, including materialistic answers.

Even many religions are victims of such knee-jerk reactions. Faced with the difficulties in explaining rebirth, they claim that there are no demigods or demons, animals and trees have no life, the soul is born in a human life only once, and after this human life, there is eternal salvation or eternal hell.

3.1.24 (316)

अन्याधष्ठिते पूर्ववत् अभिलापात्

anyādhiṣṭhite pūrvavat abhilāpāt

anya-adhiṣṭhite—into what is ruled by another; pūrvavat—as in the previous cases; abhilāpāt—due to the manifestation.

TRANSLATION

(A soul is born) into a body that is ruled by another (soul), just like the previous soul (was born into a body ruled by another soul). (This birth into different bodies is) due to the manifestation (of their guna and karma).

COMMENTARY

Material scientists like to believe that life is created from matter, but in this sūtra, this idea is rejected. Life is always created by a previously existing living body, and that life too was produced from a previously living entity. So, there is never a point in which the living being is produced from non-living matter. We have already discussed that matter exists as a possibility and therefore all species of life are eternally possible. They are, however, manifest occasionally, and this sūtra states that the birth into a species is according to the process of this manifestation. The process of manifestation is based on the soul's desires and the consequences of their previous actions. The desires determine the type of mind and body, and the consequences of previous actions decide the kind of environment this body is placed into. Thus, the soul can be born not just into different bodies but also into different environments. These two are sometimes called nature and nurture in modern times. The nature is the soul's desires or guna, while the nurture is caused by the soul's actions or their karma.

This sūtra is testimony to the fact that even after discussing the nature of the Absolute Truth, devotion to the Lord, the nature of the soul's bondage and suffering, one is still prone to falling back into the trap of materialistic thinking. When such questions arise, scientific knowledge of rebirth, guna, and karma become essential. Therefore, one must not prematurely consider oneself advanced in spiritual life unless they have understood the process of rebirth. Such questions can arise at any time in anyone's mind, and they destroy a person's spiritual endeavors if left unaddressed. Unless a soul is situated in perfect bliss through the realization of the Lord and has completely transcended the cycle of repeated birth and death, the scientific knowledge of birth and death never ceases to be relevant. One neglects the philosophy at their own peril.

QUESTION

This process seems imperfect because there are so many species that aren't manifest at any time, and so many new species are created at different times. So, how can we say that a soul is born according to their desire and action?

The argument of the previous sūtra is continued here. Even though we have discussed the eternity of matter earlier, the same topics are revived again for a simple reason—the discussion of sin, death, rebirth, and entry into hell, generally makes a person atheistic. Who is God to judge my actions, and cause my repeated births, or punishment in hell? Everything that was learned previously is forgotten if we are assigned responsibility. Thus, we find many pseudo spiritualists who talk about happiness and liberation but never discuss sin and hell. They simply like to speak about all the good that can happen if someone follows some practice, but they don't like to discuss the fate of those who don't. But if these topics are somehow encountered, the pseudo spiritualist becomes a materialist. He starts saying: there is no hell or heaven; these are just our creations. All spiritual practices are then not for liberation from the cycle of birth and death; they are only to obtain greater peace and happiness in this life.

3.1.25 (317)
अशुद्धमिति चेत् न शब्दात्
aśuddhamiti cet, na, śabdāt

aśuddham—imperfect; iti cet—if it be said; na—not so; śabdāt—based on the statements in the scriptures (i.e., the descriptions of the various *yuga*).

TRANSLATION

If it is said that this process of manifestation is imperfect (because many species are not always present) (we say) not so; (these species are manifest in due course of time) based on the descriptions of the scriptures.

COMMENTARY

The manifestation of the possibilities involves two distinct tiers—cosmic and individual. Due to time, certain unmanifest things go into the 'about to manifest' state; what seemed impossible earlier becomes possible; this is the cosmic stage of manifestation. Subsequently, a living entity can convert this 'about to manifest' state of matter into a manifest state. The living entity enters a certain type of body based on their desires. And this body is placed in a certain kind of environment based on the consequences of their previous actions. Thus, even if a living entity wants to be born in a certain type of species, he must wait until the time for the manifestation of that species has arrived. Thus, the cosmic evolution of the species is predetermined by time, but the birth of a specific individual into that species is based on their desires and previous actions.

The influence of time is described in the scriptures as the cycles of *yuga* and *manavantara*. All things happen at their pre-appointed time, not before or after. The universe is completely deterministic in terms of what will happen when. However, the universe does not determine who will do what. Therefore, the soul's desires and actions determine their future body under the control of time. Due to time, not everything is possible at every moment. But due to the soul, not everybody will choose to be the instrument of every timely possibility.

QUESTION

But so many species are not present right now (such as dinosaurs). How can they be created if you insist that they are only created by living beings? How can these unmanifest species come into manifestation without parents?

The theory of evolution has become a standard doctrine for atheism. According to this doctrine, since some living bodies have ceased to exist, therefore, the species must be evolving. If the species are evolving, then we can say that even humans have evolved from other species. And if humans have evolved from previous species, then there was a time we did not exist. And if the human species is not eternal, therefore, the present life cannot be ascribed an eternal or transcendental purpose. If such eternity is not possible, then rebirth must also be an illusion. If rebirth is an illusion, then moral responsibility, eternal hell, or heaven, must be fictions of the human mind to enforce moral behavior on the humans. If people could create such fictions in the past, then we can also create another set of fictional moral principles— which evolve with time—now. Thus, we can be 'good' people without requiring God, but that good is either subjective, or collectively inter-subjective. It cannot be defined in an eternal way.

3.1.26 (318)
रेतःसगि्योगोऽथ
retaḥ sigyogo'tha

retaḥ sika-yogo—union of male and female procreative fluids; atha—then.

TRANSLATION
By the mixing of the male and female procreative fluids.

COMMENTARY
The atheistic reasoning of the theory of evolution can be arrested at the very first step by answering the question: How do species appear and disappear at different times? The answer is that material bodies are combinations of three modes—the universal, the individual, and the contextual. The dinosaur is a universal. It sometimes becomes an individual and is then born in some contexts or environments. The same universal can appear as many individuals, in different contexts. Therefore, the universal is separate from the individual and the contextual. When we study the fossils of the dinosaurs, we see the individual and the contextual. But we don't see the universal. And without the universal, it seems that the appearance of a species must be the accident of the environment. If the environment changes, then the species must be destroyed.

This kind of thinking is borne out of materialism in which ideas don't exist. Or if they exist, then they are simply epiphenomena of chemical reactions. However, we also know that if we take out modalities from a scientific description, then the theory is always incomplete. Evolutionary theory is also incomplete for several reasons. The first reason is that all scientific theories must provide predictions, but evolutionary theory cannot make predictions. The second reason is that scientific theories must provide explanations that are necessary and sufficient, but evolutionary explanations are neither necessary nor sufficient. For instance, the mechanism of evolution is random mutation, but since there is no cause of the random mutation, therefore, the explanation is insufficient. Similarly, the adaptation by natural selection doesn't indicate which direction the evolution could go—should the species adapt to the environment, or does the environment adapt to the species? Since the theory cannot say which adaption is preferred, therefore, the explanation is not necessary. If we consider the theory of evolution as a scientific theory, then by the same measure, we must also consider every other doctrine that doesn't predict and doesn't provide an explanation that is necessary and sufficient, as a scientific theory! That should mark the end of all scientific questions and rational inquiries.

However, refuting the random mutation and adaptation mechanisms of evolution is not the explanation of how the universals are instantiated. This sūtra provides an answer, which is—consistent with the previous claim that every new life is born out of previous life— that there is always a mother and a father. Does this mean that dinosaurs are always born out of previously existing dinosaur parents? Not necessarily. The mother and the father can belong to another species, although there must always be a mother and a father.

This viewpoint calls into question a very fundamental assumption in modern biology—genetic inheritance. The claim is that the genes of the child must be like the genes of the parents, and children can only have minor differences with their parents. The similarity between parents and children is not accepted in the Vedic texts. We already know of numerous ways in which children can differ from their parents. The children can be much taller than their parents, far more intelligent than their parents, or have talents that their parents did not. But biologists claim that these are merely phenotypical rather than genotypical differences. In short, the children of a human will always be humans. If at all there is a possibility of variation, then, they must also occur very slowly.

However, the Vedic texts describe how non-human species are born from humans. An example is Kadru and Vinita—two wives of sage Kaśyapa—giving birth to snakes and to the bird Garuda, respectively. Similarly, the demigods and demons are created from the wombs of Aditi and Diti, respectively—also wives of Kaśyapa. While the process by which the children differ so significantly from their parents is not discussed here, the Vedic texts mention that Kaśyapa was empowered by Brahma to broaden the population and the types of species in the universe. This sūtra only states that new species are born by the mixing of the male and female procreative fluids. What is uncommon, however, is that the parents of one species can create children of another species. The creation by sages such as Kaśyapa is detailed in the subsequent sūtras.

QUESTION

Then a materialist can argue that if they are able to create the male and female procreative fluids as chemicals and combine them, then they can also create new species. Doesn't this contradict your previous statement that all life comes from previously existing life, rather than from non-living matter?

3.1.27 (319)
योनेःशरीरम्
yoneḥ śarīram

yoneḥ—from the womb; śarīram—body.

TRANSLATION

The body (of the new species) must be built in the womb (of a mother).

COMMENTARY

Scientists can isolate the genetic material of a male and a female as chemicals and mix them outside a living body. However, a living body doesn't develop unless this mixture of genetic material is implanted back into the body of a living mother. As we have discussed before, matter doesn't move by itself; it is always moved by the influence of prāṇa. Thus, for instance, food cannot reach a fertilized egg without the presence of prāṇa. It is prāṇa that causes the ingestion, digestion, circulation, and excretion. Similarly, processes like cell division, the specialization of a cell into different kinds of cells uniquely suited for different functions in the body, the formation of a functional structure, etc. are all dependent on the presence of prāṇa. Life is therefore not identified with the material elements; it is rather identified with the presence of prāṇa. And prāṇa is always associated with the presence of a soul. A mother's body feeds and builds the body of a child, or the mother produces an egg which is imbued with the life force that can produce a child. Although chemicals can be mixed outside a living body, the life force cannot be created by these mixtures. Therefore, a living mother is essential to produce life, and the idea that because we can mix the genetic material in a test tube, we can also create new life, is false. Yes, we can produce new kinds of genetic materials, but we can't create new life if there wasn't already a type of life that can convert the genes into a living body.

SECTION 2

Topic 1

QUESTION

You are saying that the species are created in due course of time by the combination of some appropriate mother and father, according to the cycles of time described in the scriptures. Do these creations happen all throughout the ages, or is there a certain phase in which the species are dominantly produced?

3.2.1 (320)

संध्ये सृष्टिराह हि

samdhye sṛṣṭirāha hi

samdhye—in the sandhi stage (between the various ages); sṛṣṭih—(there is) creation (of the new species); āha—suddenly; hi—certainly.

TRANSLATION

(New species) are certainly suddenly produced during the *sandhi* (the joining between the different ages called the yuga and chatur-yugī).

COMMENTARY

Vedic cosmology describes time as comprising of cycles called *yuga*. These yuga are aggregated into cycles of four called a *chatur-yugī*. These chatur-yugī are aggregated into a cycle called *kalpa*, which are then aggregated into a cycle called *manavantara*. The periods between these successive yuga, chatur-yugī, kalpa, and manavantara are called *sandhi* (hyphenation or conjunction) or *sandhyā* (the evening of the previous phase of the cycle). The durations of these conjunctive periods vary depending on the type of cycle that is beginning or ending. Thus, longer cycles also have longer periods of sandhi, while shorter cycles have a shorter period of sandhi. All the sandhi, however, occur at pre-defined periods of time. This period of transition is said to destroy most of the previously existing life forms, in what seems like a partial annihilation. This sūtra states that the creation of most of the species also occurs during this stage. So, the period of sandhi destroys older species and creates new ones.

This idea goes against the notion of gradual evolution, where species are slowly created over a long period of time. This sūtra states that there is sudden creation of species (and elsewhere we can find descriptions of destruction at the end of each age). There is some empirical evidence of this sudden creation in what is today called the Cambrian Explosion where many species are known to have been suddenly manifest, counter to the notion of gradual evolution.

QUESTION

It is said in Vedic texts that Brahma is the creator of all the species, and so he should create all the species at the beginning of the universe. Then why are new species manifest at different stages (the sandhi) during the creation?

3.2.2 (321)

नरिमातारं चैके पुत्रादयश् च

nirmātāraṃ caike putrādayaś ca

nirmāta—well instructed; itāram—the others; ca—and; ike—some; putrādayaḥ—sons etc.; ca—also.

TRANSLATION

And well-instructed, the others are created by some of the sons as well.

COMMENTARY

The creation of the species is described in the Purāṇa, and it begins when Brahma creates four sons called the four Kumāra. He asks them to perform austerities before they begin producing further progeny.

However, these four sons become enlightened by their austerities and refuse to engage in the process of sexual creation. In fact, to never be enamored by sex, they refuse to grow up beyond the age of four. Brahma then very angry at their refusal to obey his orders, and as a result Rudra—the 'crying one'—is born. Brahma doesn't consider Rudra suitable for creating further progeny and considering the futility of anger, Brahma then creates more sons, and is finally successful in expanding the population and filling the universe with various kinds of species. Kaśyapa, as discussed above, is one such son, who creates demigods and demons, birds and snakes, etc. Thus, Brahma is the creator of the sons, who create further species. Thus, the term *ike putra* or some sons is used because other sons (like the four Kumāra) did not create further progeny. Likewise, the term *itara* or the others is used to indicate that Brahma created some sons who then created other species. Thus, the creation is primarily attributed to Brahma, and secondarily to his sons. But not all his sons are the cause of the subsequent creations.

QUESTION

In what way is Brahma and his sons said to be the creators when the material energy is said to be the real creative energy? You have previously mentioned that the Lord injects the soul into the material energy, just like a father impregnates a mother. Then how are Brahma and his sons the creators?

3.2.3 (322)

मायामात्रं तु कार्त्स्न्येनानभिव्यक्तस्वरूपत्वात्

māyāmātraṃ tu kārtsnyenānabhivyaktasvarūpatvāt

māyā—the illusory covering; mātraṃ—only; tu—but; kārtsnyena—in entirety; anabhivyakta-svarūpatvāt—by the unmanifest state of forms.

TRANSLATION

But the illusory covering only produces the forms in their entirety by creating the unmanifest forms (which are manifest by Brahma and his sons).

COMMENTARY

The various types of minds and senses are manifestations of the *chit*. In Sāṅkhya philosophy, the chit is moral sense, ego, intellect, mind, senses, their properties, and the different values of these properties. The root of all these elements is the unmanifest prakriti. Along with these elements constituting the chit, there is a parallel creation of various types of desires, which in the unmanifest stage is called māyā or 'that which is not'. As discussed before, māyā is an inferiority complex of the soul and all desires are produced to overcome this inferiority. Each creation of the prakriti is suited to fulfill some desires produced by māyā. Hence, Vedic texts distinguish between chit-śakti and māyā-śakti, as two different kinds of energies. Their creations, however, combine as each type of desire requires some instruments to fulfill the desire. The Lord injects the soul into māyā-śakti, and the soul acquires a personality of desires. To fulfill these desires, Brahma creates a body of instruments by employing the prakriti. Thus, chit-śakti is various body types and māyā-śakti is various desire types. Then, due to karma, these bodies are placed in different contexts.

If the soul thinks that "I am not knowledgeable" then knowledge becomes an ideal in the moral sense; then, the goal of acquiring knowledge using our own strength becomes a goal in the ego; then, some assumptions about this knowledge will be acquired or what constitutes knowledge are formulated as intellect; then based on these assumptions, speculative theories about the nature of the object of knowledge are produced in the mind; these speculations are then transformed into observational procedures in the senses; these procedures are then transformed into purported objective properties of reality; finally, these properties are converted into a world of material objects.

What we see is the objects and their properties. However, the observer, which employs senses, mind, intellect, ego, and a moral sense remains hidden. Even more hidden is the māyā or the inferiority complex of the soul. Thus, everyone pretends to be the Lord and master of the world, while suffering from the inferiority of not being able to become the Lord and master internally.

The creation of the elements of Sāṅkhya is called the primary creation, and the creation of bodies from these elements is called the secondary creation. Lord Viṣṇu creates the elements as universals at the beginning of the universe. Lord Brahma then creates these body and mind types. These body types are subdivisions of the various elements. For instance, the original or pure mind is represented by the form called Aniruddha. However, this mind gradually gets modified and contaminated and becomes the mind of individual living entities. These modified varieties of minds are produced by Lord Brahma. When these diversified forms are absent, the original and pure mind exists. However, because the living entities are influenced by varieties of inferiorities, these inferiorities combine with the original mind and create partial ignorant minds. These partial ignorant bodies and minds are like the trunks, branches, twigs, leaves, and fruits manifested from a root: the root is complete and unmanifest, but the byproducts of this root are incomplete and manifest as material bodies.

QUESTION

You earlier said that māyā is the cause of the material existence. You are now saying that there are many kinds of māyā—and māyā is not one thing?

3.2.4 (323)

सूचकश्च हि श्रुतेःआचक्षते च तद्वदिः

sūcakaśca hi śruteḥ ācakṣate ca tadvidaḥ

sūcakaḥ—the symptom; ca—also; hi—certainly; śruteḥ—from the śrutī; ācakṣate—say; ca—also; tadvidaḥ—those who are knowledge-able in that.

TRANSLATION

Also (the bodies and minds are) certainly the symbols or symptoms (of māyā); such is the opinion of the śrutī and those who know this subject.

COMMENTARY

If matter is viewed physically, then the parts are in the whole, but the whole is not in the parts. But if we understand the whole and part semantically, then the part is in the whole, and the whole is in the parts. The presence of the whole in the parts, makes these parts the symbols of the whole. Therefore, the various types of minds and senses are subdivisions of the whole as well as the symbols of the whole. Just as a cow is a subdivision of mammal, as well as a symbol of mammal, similarly, māyā also has subdivisions which are its symbols.

Māyā means aversion to the Lord. This basic desire for aversion divides into many parts, to create many kinds of aversions. But the whole—i.e., the māyā—is present in each part. Therefore, all these parts are symbols of māyā. In simple terms, we can find numerous kinds of desires in this world, but they are all symptoms or symbols of the aversion to the Lord. Anybody who has a desire to serve himself, his family, community, society, nation, etc. is expressing a portion of māyā, and that portion is the symbol of the aversion to the Lord.

The parts of chit, however, are not averse to the Lord. The chit that exists in this world is exactly like the chit in the spiritual world. This means that all that we can see, taste, smell, hear, or touch, all that we can think, judge, intend, or value, also exists in the spiritual world. The difference is simply that in the spiritual world, the chit is used to serve the Lord, and in the material world, it is used to fulfill the aversion to the Lord. Similarly, the relations in this world are exactly like those in the spiritual world. Thus, out of three components, two— the material bodies and their relations—are identical to their spiritual counterparts. Only the third—our desires—are averse to the Lord. For a devotee, therefore, the material and the spiritual worlds are not different because he doesn't see the material body and relations as being contrary to the Lord. He rather sees them as instruments and opportunities to satisfy the Lord's desires.

When desires are used to serve the Lord, the instruments and relations also become spiritual. Conversely, when the desires are averse to the Lord, the instruments and relations become material. Hence, the body of a devotee is spiritual, and the body of an atheist is material. The relationships of the devotee are spiritual, and the relationships of an atheist are material. All the knowledge, beauty, wealth, power, fame, and renunciation of this world are useless unless they are meant for serving the Lord, because they are all symbols of māyā. They are like a lot of 0's in which the first number is also a 0. When the first number is changed to 1, then all these 0's become collectively valuable. Similarly, when everything originates from māyā, then everything is worthless. And when the same māyā is transformed into devotion to the Lord, then it is valuable.

QUESTION

You have earlier said that by the meditation on the Supreme Lord māyā is destroyed, and the soul is liberated from material existence. But now you are indicating that the material world need not be considered bondage. How do we reconcile these opposites: Is the present world liberation or bondage?

3.2.5 (324)

पराभध्यिानात्तु तिरोहितिम् ततो ह्यस्य बन्धवपिर्ययौ

parābhidhyānāttu tirohitam tato hyasya bandhaviparyayau

parābhidhyānāt—by meditation on the Supreme Lord; tu—but; tirohitam—destroyed; tataḥ—thereafter; hi—certainly; asya—this; bandhaviparyayau—bondage and its opposite, i.e., liberation.

TRANSLATION

By meditation on the Supreme Lord (māyā) is certainly destroyed; but thereafter (one attains) a state beyond the opposites of bondage and liberation.

COMMENTARY

Liberation from the material world is taught as a preliminary idea, when we don't have a good understanding of matter and the nature of our bondage. The superficial cause of bondage is karma, but the deeper cause of bondage is our desires. The bodies and the relations used to fulfill these desires or karma are not material. Hence, the desire is the cause, and karma is the effect. And these two are the only material reality; everything else is spiritual. If the desires are corrected, then karma slowly dies out, and the soul is said to be liberated. Once the soul is liberated, he can choose to live in a body as long as he wants. He can choose to die whenever he so desires. He is neither forced to be born, nor forced to die. Both birth and death, and the bodies, become his choices.

As discussed previously, the manifested reality is divided into four parts, of which Brahman and the material world are just two parts. These are respectively the domains of liberation and bondage. Beyond these two realms are two further realms of Vaikuṇṭha and Goloka. In the realm of Vaikuṇṭha, the devotee associates with the Lord as His servant. But in the realm of Goloka, the devotee also associates with the Lord as His friend, elder, or lover. The bond of the friend, elder, or lover is stronger than the bond of the servant to the master. Thus, after the soul is liberated from material entanglement, the bondage doesn't go away; it rather increases further as one's love is deepened.

Therefore, 'beyond bondage and liberation' has many meanings. First, it can mean that the soul exists in this world but is not bound by the laws of birth and death. Second, it can mean that he transcends the material world and Brahman, which are the domains of bondage and liberation. Third, it can mean that the soul, even after liberation from this world, becomes bound again to the Lord in a relationship, but that bondage of love is neither painful nor temporary.

QUESTION

If liberation from this material body and mind is not the goal of meditation on the Supreme Lord, does it mean that the devotee of the Lord remains bound to the material body eternally? Or does he also get liberated from the body?

3.2.6 (325)
देहयोगाद्वा सोऽपि
dehayogādvā so'pi

dehayogāt—from its connection to the body; vā—moving or separated or detached; saḥ—that (the soul); api—also.

TRANSLATION

The soul is also detached from the connection to the body.

COMMENTARY

The non-devotees are always insecure, but the devotee has no insecurity because the Lord provides him with everything necessary. When the non-devotees compare themselves to the devotees and find them superior in some way, their insecurity manifests as enviousness. Instead of accepting that whatever the devotee has is only by the grace of the Lord, and it can never be taken away unless the Lord desires, the non-devotees mount their aggression on the devotee. When the devotee is troubled in this way, he may decide to leave. But whether the devotee stays or leaves, he is not bound to take rebirth. He may choose to be reborn to serve the Lord or may return to the Lord's abode.

Topic 2

QUESTION

You are saying that the devotee need not be freed from the material body, and yet he transcends the states of bondage and liberation. If he is said to be liberated while living in the body, what then happens to bodily maintenance?

3.2.7 (326)
तदभावो नाडीषु तच्छ्रुतेःआत्मनिच
tadabhāvo nāḍīṣu tacchruteḥ ātmani ca

tat-abhāvaḥ—the absence of that; nāḍīṣu—in the nerves; ātmani ca—and in the self-consciousness; tat-śruteḥ—upon hearing that (i.e., the Lord).

TRANSLATION

Upon hearing that (the names of the Lord), and feeling separated from that (the Lord), the devotee loses all consciousness of the body (obtained through the nerves) and even the sense of the self (i.e., concern about oneself).

COMMENTARY

Awareness of the material body is produced due to lust and fear. We are conscious of the body because we desire the enjoyment of the senses, or because we are afraid that we might lose this enjoyment and we act fervently through the body to protect the body and the things that give the body pleasure.

However, when the devotee becomes absorbed in the consciousness of the Lord, he simultaneously feels connected and separated from the

Lord. This is the nature of love: it makes the heart ache, and it delights the heart. The aching is the separation from the Lord, and the delight is the union with the Lord. In the material world, union and separation are contrary: you are either united or you are separated. However, the transcendental experience is beyond this duality. In this experience, there is simultaneous union and separation. The separation is the cause of the wakefulness, and the union is the cause of the unconsciousness. Thus, in the state of wakefulness, the devotee anxiously searches for the Lord, and if the Lord is found (through the process of hearing His name), then the devotee loses his consciousness and becomes unaware of his self. Thus, wakefulness means that I exist, but I'm devoid of the Lord. And unconscious ness means that I have found the Lord, and I have lost the sense of self. Through constant separation and meeting, the devotee loses consciousness again and again, only to wake up and search for the Lord almost like a madman.

QUESTION

If the devotee is losing consciousness of the body and the self, then how can this state be called the state of enlightenment, knowledge, self-awareness, etc.? Isn't self-realization contrary to the loss of awareness of the self?

3.2.8 (327)
अतःपरबोधोऽस्मात्
atah prabodho'smāt

atah—thereafter; prabodhah—full understanding; asmāt—from this.

TRANSLATION

From this (loss of the sense of self) follows the full understanding (of self).

COMMENTARY

We are constantly seeking the purpose of our existence. This purpose is the separation from the objective of our existence. When this purpose is found, we lose ourselves in fulfilling that purpose. But through this purpose, we also discover our true nature. So, finding the purpose means losing the self in that purpose and finding the true meaning of our existence. Finding the self and losing the self only seem to be contradictory ideas from a mundane perspective, and that is because we think that the self is the purpose of existence. Self-realization is thus touted to be full self-awareness. But what if we are not the purpose of our existence? In the material world, we are searching for mundane purposes, and even here we lose ourselves in these purposes, sometimes forgetting to take bath, eat food, sleep well, or take care of the near and dear ones. Since these purposes aren't completely fulfilling, we are frustrated, especially because by losing ourselves in these purposes we also destroy the sense of self. Then we go about seeking a new purpose of existence, where we can lose ourselves, and yet find ourselves through that purpose. When the Lord is the purpose of our existence, the goal is never frustrated. Thus, we lose ourselves in that purpose and forget the self-interest due to love. And yet, through this love of the Lord, we also find the real purpose of our existence. Thus, this sūtra states that the idea of finding the self by self-awareness is a flawed conception. The real self-discovery is the understanding of the purpose of existence that comes by losing the self in that purpose, and that loss is also the supreme gain.

Topic 3

QUESTION

If someone has not attained this supreme understanding of the self through the loss of the self into the purpose, what can he do to obtain it?

3.2.9 (328)

स एव तु कर्मानुस्मृति शब्दवधिभिय:

sa eva tu karmānusmṛti śabdavidhibhyaḥ

sa eva—Him certainly; tu—but; karma-anusmṛti—working and remembering (the Lord); śabda-vidhibhyaḥ—following the scriptural processes.

TRANSLATION

The Lord is certainly (the purpose); but (He should be worshipped) by remembering through regular duties, as prescribed in the Vedic scriptures.

COMMENTARY

In Bhagavad-Gita 8.7, Lord Kṛṣṇa tells the following to Arjuna:

tasmat sarvesu kalesu
mam anusmara yudhya ca
mayy arpita-mano-buddhir
mam evaisyasy asamsayah

Therefore, Arjuna, you should always think of Me and
at the same time carry out your prescribed duty of fighting.
With your activities dedicated to Me and your mind and
intelligence fixed on Me, you will attain Me without doubt.

When we perform our day-to-day activities, we keep thinking about the outcomes of these actions. For example, someone might think that they will get money out of their work, and the ways they will enjoy with that money. Or, they might think about their families and dear ones, and how this money would be used to make them happy, and their happiness will become our happiness. This meditation on the purpose, even as we do our day-to-day duties, is already present in everyone. This sūtra states that we should change this purpose to the Lord. By changing this purpose, we slowly become attached to the Lord.

A key symptom of this attachment is that all our choices only prioritize the Lord's happiness. For example, a person may be offered a job that gives him more money, but it will also take time away from the Lord's service. The non-devotee will choose the job over the Lord's service, and the devotee will choose the Lord's service over the job. Constantly remembering the Lord means that our choices at every moment are driven by what will please the Lord the most.

Topic 4

QUESTION

But if meditation on the Lord is the real purpose, then why do we even bother with material duties as prescribed in the Vedic scriptures? Why can't we renounce all such mundane duties and just focus upon the meditation?

3.2.10 (329)

मुग्धेऽर्धसंपत्तःपरिशेषात्

mugdhe'rdhasaṃpattiḥ pariśeṣāt

mugdhe—being engrossed in delight; ardhasaṃpattiḥ—half wealth or possession; pariśeṣāt—due to the only thing left in the material world.

TRANSLATION

Being engrossed in delight (in remembering the Lord) (the devotee considers the material body and its possessions) half-wealth (and that engrossment and delight) due to (the Lord) being the only thing left in the material world.

COMMENTARY

In this section we can see that many false contradictions are being refuted one by one. First, the contradiction of whether māyā is one or many was refuted. Then the contradiction between bondage and liberation was refuted. Then the idea of losing oneself as being contradictory to finding oneself was refuted. Now, the contradiction between association and renunciation is being refuted. Through these refutations, a transcendent reality that goes beyond the apparent opposites of this world is being established. These contradictions are found in impersonalist philosophy, and by refuting them, impersonalism is refuted.

The impersonalist believes that the material world is false; that it doesn't exist, or it exists as an illusion. The devotee doesn't reject the existence of the world but rejects the *purpose* of this existence as being the self. In the impersonalist interpretation, māyā being the source of the world, and māyā being that which doesn't exist, is taken to imply that the world doesn't exist. In the personalist interpretation, māyā is the source of the world, and is that which doesn't exist, but this māyā is the purpose of existence, from which existence springs. Accordingly, freedom from māyā is the freedom from the false purpose, rather than the freedom from the material body. Once the false purpose is discarded, whether the material body exists or not becomes immaterial. Instead, even the material body can be used for the Lord's purposes. Thus, freedom from the material body—or what is called liberation—isn't the goal of life. The goal is to revive the true purpose of our existence—namely, the Lord.

Māyā is the emotional or intentional cause of the world. From this purpose, springs the prakriti or the material cause of the world. The impersonalist believes that there is only a material cause, but why this material cause covers the soul—i.e., what purposes are fulfilled by this covering—remains unanswered. The root cause is the envy in the soul, but this envy then develops into an inferiority complex; the envy is in the soul, and is real; however, the inferiority is material and is false. And yet, when the inferiority covers the soul, the soul starts feeling inadequate, incomplete, and insufficient. It forgets its true nature, and this forgetfulness is then identified as that which doesn't exist. The impersonalist now concludes that since the root of material existence is the material cause, therefore, liberation from matter is the primary goal of life. But this sūtra refutes this understanding. It states that renunciation of the world is not the real answer, because the world is not false; the purposes we attribute to this world—i.e., that this world is meant for my enjoyment—is false. The devotee isn't interested in discarding the world. He is only interested in changing the purpose of his existence. In other words, change lies within the soul, rather than in the rejection of the world. Once this change has occurred, then whether the body is temporary, or eternal, doesn't matter. The devotee simply tries to please the Lord through all his efforts, and the world is employed in this service.

This sūtra also says that engrossed in the thoughts about the Lord, the devotee considers everything else insignificant. Whether it is there or not, doesn't matter. Thus, all these things are called half-wealth in this sūtra. This means if they are there, then the devotee performs his duties as necessary. But if they are not there, then he is not disturbed.

The real wealth is the unflinching devotion to the Lord. The materialistic wealth, family, fame, or love cease to be meaningful. The only meaningful thing in this world is remembrance of the Lord.

Topic 5

QUESTION

Some people say that this world is false, except for things like the holy places of worship, the scriptures describing the Lord, and the deities by which the Lord is worshipped. So, they don't reject the entire world, but they are also partially rejecting the world. Is their position acceptance or rejection?

3.2.11 (330)

न स्थानतोऽपि परस्योभयलिङ्गम् सर्वत्र हि

na sthānato'pi parasyobhayaliṅgam sarvatra hi

na—not; sthānataḥ—due to (the difference of) place; api—even; parasya—of the transcendental; ubhayaliṅgaṃ—the twofold deities; hi—because; sarvatra—present everywhere.

TRANSLATION

(For the devotee) it is not the differences of place, not even the twofold deities of the transcendent reality, because (the Lord is) present everywhere.

COMMENTARY

The neophyte devotees like to worship the deities, read the scriptures, and live in holy places. They might consider all other things, such as the performance of social duties, teaching the knowledge to others, or other kinds of services to the Lord—which seem to involve the material world—as inferior. The neophytes are prescribed these kinds of rules so that they don't get entangled in the material world and start using it for their enjoyment. Their life is limited in this way to help them advance in spiritual life. However, one who has advanced through such regulative practices, comes to the point where he sees that everything is meant for the satisfaction of the Lord. Everything is real, but the purposes for which we are using it may not necessarily be real. Such a devotee becomes qualified to engage everything in the service of the Lord, and the false dichotomy of material and spiritual, renunciation and attachment, etc. is destroyed. This sūtra states that such a devotee is not even attached to the holy places or the worship or the twofold deities (the masculine and feminine forms of the Absolute Truth) because he can see that these forms are everywhere.

This sūtra says that the Lord is everywhere. He is of course present in the deities, the scriptures, and the holy places. But He is not absent from the other places. In the deities, the scriptures, and the holy places, the Lord is more manifest, but only the devotees can see the Lord in these forms. The atheistic people consider scriptures 'mythology', deities as 'idols', and the holy places as being no different than any other place. Therefore, even to give greater regard to the holy places, scriptures, and deities, one must be a devotee. As this devotion advances, the Lord is seen everywhere. This 'everywhere' vision doesn't mean everything is the Lord. It only means that the Lord is the purpose of everything. The purpose exists in everything, but those things are not the purpose.

QUESTION

But if you say that the advanced devotees see the Lord present everywhere, does it mean that they lose the discrimination between good and bad, right and wrong, true and false? Because they see the Lord being present everywhere?

3.2.12 (331)

न भेदादिति चेत् न प्रत्येकमतद्वचनात्

na bhedāditi cet na pratyekamatadvacanāt

na—not; bhedāt—due to difference; iti cet—if it be said; na—not so; pratyekam—toward the One; atadvacanāt—due to the contrary declaration.

TRANSLATION

If it is said that (the devotees) cannot make the difference (between right and wrong, good and bad, true and false) (we say) not so; everything toward the One (is true, right, and good) since (non-discrimination is) rejected.

COMMENTARY

The impersonalist sometimes argues that since everything is Brahman, or the Lord is everywhere, so there is no high or low, nothing good or bad, nothing is right or wrong, etc. But this is a wrong idea because the meaning of the statement "the Lord is everywhere" is that the *purpose* of everything is the Lord. The Lord is in everything as its purpose; the purpose exists in everything, and it is the same purpose for everything—i.e., to serve the Lord. However, the purpose is also different from those individual things, and the Lord is hence also outside each of those things. Only the Lord is fully identical to Himself because He is His own purpose. He is also the purpose of everything else, and due to that purpose, He remains immanent in everything, even as He is transcendent to everything. If we don't distinguish between the existence and its purpose, then we equate the idea that "the Lord is everywhere" to existence, rather than purpose. Then we think that if the Lord is everywhere, then everything can be worshipped. This is a false claim. Everything cannot be worshipped, but everything can be used for worship. When this purpose of the existence is reestablished, then we can see that the Lord is present in everything as their purpose.

This sūtra states that the devotee knows how to judge things based on the purpose they are being used for. Elaborately cooked food that is not offered to the Lord is therefore inferior to uncooked fruits, flowers, leaves, or water, which are offered to the Lord. Elaborately cooked food can also be offered to the Lord, so there is potential for it to be superior. The devotee can see how everything can be used for the service of the Lord, but that doesn't mean everything is being used for the service of the Lord. The devotee thus discriminates between high and low, right and wrong, good and bad, true and false, in relation to the Lord. Everything that pleases the Lord is higher than things that don't please the Lord. Things that please Him more are superior to things that please Him less. Thus, the Lord is the single standard for all judgments, and the idea that if the Lord is everywhere then everything must be worshipped is rejected.

QUESTION

Does this mean that certain things that are considered wrong or bad or false from the mundane point of view (i.e., the viewpoint of the materially entangled souls) could also be considered spiritually superior by the Lord's devotees?

3.2.13 (332)
अपचैवमेके
apicaivameke

api ca—moreover; evam—thus; eke—some.

TRANSLATION

Moreover, by this criterion some (forbidden actions can be devotion too).

COMMENTARY

Living entities are prescribed dharma according to their social roles. Thus, a father must take of his children, a son must serve the parents, a citizen must defend the country, etc. But the service to the Lord takes precedence over various kinds of dharma and is called sanātana-dharma or eternal duty. When there is a contradiction between dharma and sanātana-dharma, then the latter takes precedence. However, such cases are generally rare, and the use of the term *eke* or some indicates that rarity. Quite often, when we reject dharma, thinking that we are performing sanātana-dharma, then we are in violation of both.

An example of such violation is the use of murder and mayhem to propagate religion. Innumerable crimes have been committed in the name of religion. All such actions are justified as sanātana-dharma (service of God) over dharma (moral principles such as peace, non-violence, and tolerance). Hence, a blind rejection of dharma to perform sanātana-dharma is a very treacherous path. The fact is that when people reject dharma, claiming to perform sanātana-dharma, most times they are in violation of both dharma and sanātana-dharma.

The general principle is that dharma must always be performed, and one must try to find all ways and means to do sanātana-dharma within their prescribed dharma. The rules and regulations of society have also been ordained by the Lord, as a countermeasure to religious upstarts using religion and God to create chaos. In general, if someone says that their religion requires changes to the basic principles of social organization, then their religion is wrong.

But this also means that we inquire into the nature of dharma. What is proper social organization? What are the correct principles of economy and government? What are the duties of citizens? How must different classes in society conduct themselves? Unless we know dharma, we will keep changing the ideas about society, economy, and government, and one dharma would be replaced by another. The study of dharma is a vast subject, and the basic principle of understanding dharma is karma—namely, that there are natural laws of morality, and social laws must be formulated to prevent sinful activities.

If dharma has been formulated by the understanding of karma, then there are only rare situations in which it can be superseded by sanātana-dharma.

What are those situations? These are situations in which dharma is itself not clear because there are contradictory principles at play. Such an example is provided in the Śrīmad Bhagavatam where King Bali is advised by his guru to ignore his promise to Lord Vāmana to donate three steps of land. This presents a dilemma: if King Bali broke his promise, he would have neglected dharma; similarly, if he rejected the order of his guru, he would have neglected dharma. When faced with such dilemmas, we can ask: which of these two principles would please the Lord? King Bali chose to reject his guru because he realized that Lord Vāmana was indeed the Lord Who had come to ask for his land. This principle is also enunciated in the Bhagavad-Gita where Arjuna is caught in a dilemma regarding his duty. He thinks that defending his honor is his duty. He also thinks that killing his relatives is against his duty. Since defending the honor contradicts the protection of his relatives, Arjuna is caught in a dilemma. He engages in a long discussion about the nature of dharma, but even as Lord Kṛṣṇa describes various paths, such as karma-yoga, jñāna-yoga, and dhyāna-yoga, they don't resolve the dilemma about whether he should fight or not. Either of these choices are equally consistent with all the above three paths. Therefore, Lord Kṛṣṇa provides the final answer: Do what pleases Me the most. This resolves the dilemma, and Arjuna fights because Lord Kṛṣṇa asks him to.

Therefore, we must always follow dharma unless there is a conflict in deciding what the dharma is. If a conflict in deciding dharma arises, then we must choose one dharma over another based on sanātana-dharma. If the law of karma is understood, then dharma is also understood, and the situations of dilemma are very rare. But when these dilemmas arise, and sanātana-dharma overrides dharma, it is not truly rejecting dharma. It is only preferring one kind of dharma over another. However, to the extent that one dharma may be rejected due to sanātana-dharma, it is noted here as *eke* or a rare situation. Finally, sanātana-dharma can be performed while performing dharma. As we have discussed above, one can remember the Lord, and wherever possible, make those choices that are suited for increasing our remembrance of the Lord.

QUESTION

But many people say that these social distinctions and duties that come with them only increase our entanglement to the world. We think we are father, mother, son, daughter, citizen, etc. and by these designations we get entangled. So, their recommendation is that we give up all these designations. Once these designations are discarded, then there is nothing higher or lower, nobody is superior or inferior. We are just spiritual particles who must give up our false identities. What would be your answer to this type of counterargument?

3.2.14 (333)

अरूपवदेव हि तत्प्रधानत्वात्

arūpavadeva hi tatpradhānatvāt

arūpavat—formless; eva—only; hi—certainly; tat-pradhānatvāt—from that being just like pradhāna (the unmanifest state of material nature).

TRANSLATION

Certainly (the attitude of giving up all kinds of designations), only leads to a formless state, just like from the primordial state of matter called pradhāna.

COMMENTARY

Brahman is a state in which the knower-known distinction is abolished. In this state, there is nothing other than the self, because the self is the only known. Thus, other individual souls are *believed* to not exist, because everyone is self-absorbed. From this self-absorbed state emerges pradhāna in which the soul can see that there are many other individuals, but they are of the same type as us. In Brahman, only "I" exist. In pradhāna, many "I" exist, but they are all the same type. This distinction indicates different kinds of impersonal philosophies. The spiritual impersonalist says that there is only one knower and that knower is the known, and hence all the individual knowers are illusions. The material impersonalist recognizes the individuality of different souls but says that we are all equal. The modern left-wing political ideology is derived from this material impersonalism, where society aims to drop all distinctions of gender, race, rich and poor, higher and lower, all in the name of 'equality'.

There is a charm in this ideology because it is in some sense anti-materialistic; it rejects superficial distinctions, gross materialism, and exploitation of others. But it has a mistaken idea about individuality; we are never the same type of individuals. We are all different, and the difference is qualitative. Some people have better qualities and they are expected to be higher; others have lower qualities and they are expected to be lower. The designations in society are supposed to be based on these qualities or guna. The problem of this material world is that people who don't have the right guna but have the right karma, get into powerful, influential, and affluent positions. They then exploit others and to avoid exploitation, society then conjures a state of equality.

The ideology in which we recognize many individuals but consider them to be of the same type is pradhāna. By pursuing this ideology, one cannot get liberated from the material existence. But one can still reach the primordial state of material reality of egalitarian equality. It is better than gross material existence but not as good as Brahman, and certainly not equal to personalistic transcendence where distinctions are based on a person's genuine qualities.

Karma is absent in the transcendent world, so an unqualified person can never become rich, powerful, famous, etc. Only people who have good qualities are in a superior position, and those with lesser qualities are in inferior positions. This is a stable situation because the distinctions of high and low remain, and yet everyone understands that this is a meritorious society. When merit is equated with karma rather than guna (as in the material world), then people with bad qualities also become powerful. This aberration of the material world is deliberate, and its rejection simply takes us to the primordial state of matter. To enter the transcendental world, we must distinguish by qualities, not karma.

QUESTION

But don't the Vedic scriptures say that the soul is sat-chit-ānanda and since all souls have this property, therefore, all the souls must be of the same type? They are only separate individuals, although they cannot be higher or lower? Some people say that we are all particles of effulgence, and this material body is simply a covering of these particles? Thus, if this material covering is discarded, then isn't what remains simply the sat-chit-ānanda nature of the soul?

3.2.15 (334)

परकाशवच्चावैयरथ्यात्

prakāśavaccāvaiyathyārt

prakāśavat—like light; ca—also; avaiyatharyāt—due to not meaningless.

TRANSLATION

Due to not being meaningless, (the souls) are also like light.

COMMENTARY

The *sat-chit*-ānanda of the soul is simply a potential—the potential to relate to other individuals (*sat*), the potential to know those individuals (*chit*), and the potential to desire and enjoy with other individuals (ānanda). We can also call these the capacities for relation, cognition, and emotion. However, these capacities don't become experience unless there is an actual relation, cognition, and emotion. The conversion of the potentials of cognition, relation, and emotion into an actual experience requires a choice. This choice produces a meaning, namely, a specific type of relation, emotion, and cognition. Hence, this sūtra says that the soul is light, namely, the potential to enlighten. But that light must also fall on something to enlighten that thing. What does it fall upon? That is up to the soul's choice, and such choices are made to produce meaning. So, the fact that the soul exists as the potential for relation, cognition, and emotion, doesn't entail that there are no differences; the difference is their choices.

QUESTION

If you are saying that the soul is a potential, then it means that it is incomplete without the reality that converts the potential into an experience?

3.2.16 (335)
आह च तन्मात्रम्
āha ca tanmātram

āha—declares; ca—and; tanmātram—form only.

TRANSLATION

(It is) also said that (the soul) is just like tanmātra or form alone.

COMMENTARY

To understand this sūtra, we must understand the meaning of *tanmātra*. In Sāñkhya philosophy, the term tanmātra is used to denote properties such as form, color, taste, shape, smell, size, pitch, tone, roughness, heat, etc. Each of these properties then divides into many types called bhūta, which represent the values of these properties. For example, if the property is color, then the values are red, green, and blue; if the property is shape, then the values are square, round, and triangle; if the property is taste, then the values are sour, bitter, sweet, pungent, etc. In modern terminology, the properties are called *dimensions* and their values are called *values*, which are present on these dimensions. For instance, if weight is a dimension, then 5kg is a value on that dimension; if temperature is the dimension, then 50 0C is the value on that dimension.

So, tanmātra or property is a dimension. However, these dimensions are incomplete without the values. The values on these dimensions are different kinds of relations (father, mother, child, etc.), cognitions (table, chair, red, hot, bitter, etc.), and emotions (fear, desire, greed, anger, confusion, etc.). These dimensions and values constitute a 'space' in which the soul acquires a position. This position is a choice, and by obtaining the position, each soul becomes different from other souls—as each soul obtains a different position. The soul and the Lord are identical in terms of their dimensions—each has three dimensions of relation, cognition, and emotion. But the Lord and His Śakti are the origin of this space, from this origin the rest of space expands, and the soul obtains a position in that space. These three dimensionalities of the Lord, His Śakti, and the soul are mistakenly interpreted as the identity between the soul, the Lord, and His Śakti. The correct understanding is that the Lord and His Śakti define the three dimensions and the complete value as the origin of space, and while the soul has the same three dimensions, and it can make a choice about the position in space, it can never become the origin of this space. It can also never obtain the experience of the complete value of these dimensions.

The soul is pure tanmātra or dimensionality and the Lord's Śakti is pure values. The soul is always incomplete unless it obtains a position—i.e., the dimension gets a value. This value represents the experience of the soul, and the experience is produced due to a choice. The soul is capable of a choice, but the possibilities from which he must choose are produced by the Lord's Śakti.

QUESTION

The term tanmātra is used in relation to sense perception. But the soul also has mental, intellectual, and subtle emotional experiences like happiness (beyond the sense pleasures). Are these also gained from the external reality?

3.2.17 (336)

दर्शयति च अथो अपि स्मर्यते

darśayati ca atho api smaryate

darśayati—sees; ca—and; atho—then; api—also; smaryate—remembers.

TRANSLATION

(The term tanmātra) can be applied to sense perception and then also to remembrance (or thought processes occurring in the mind and intellect).

COMMENTARY

The distinction between dimension and value is not unique to sense perception. The capacity to think and judge is also a dimension, and the meanings and the judgments are values on dimensions. Due to this distinction, concepts and judgments are also objective, rather than subjective. Thus, they can exist outside an individual's mind and intellect and due to this objectivity, we can attribute objective meanings to a sentence. Similarly, we can say that some meaning is true or false. If these were not objective values, then the meaning and judgment would only exist in a person's mind, and we could not say that the world is objectively a table or a chair, or that meaning is true or false. The distinction between the capacity to think and judge and the concepts and judgments is essential to maintain the objectivity of meanings and judgments.

When space is understood as a tree, then every node on that tree is both a dimension and an object. For example, color is a space because it contains shades like yellow and green. But color is an object in the space of seeing. And color is a property in relation to other properties like shape, size, distance, direction, etc. This means that when we speak of 'color', we must use three modalities. In the space modality, we look downward, and see many shades of color. In the object modality we look upward and see color as a part of seeing. Finally, in the property modality we look sideways and understand how color is one of the many properties. Thus, by looking upward, downward, and sideways, in a space of concepts, we understand an idea in different ways.

Now, the main point is that color manifests from seeing, and yellow manifests from color. Similarly, thoughts manifest from the mind, and the judgments manifest from the intellect. So, the senses, the mind, the intellect, etc. are considered tanmātra or spaces (or dimensions) that produce objects (or values). Hence, the term tanmātra is not limited to sense perception. Once we understand what it means, then tanmātra can be extended to thoughts, judgments, intentions, and morals. The context delineates what we mean by tanmātra.

QUESTION

But due to the possibility of hallucination, we also distinguish between the perception and the object of perception. If the soul is associating with a perception and mental reality, then that reality must be understood as the image or representation of the world. And this image must be different from the world being perceived or thought of. Does this mean there is a relation between the object being perceived and the perceptions—both of which are objective?

3.2.18 (337)
अत एव चोपमा सूर्यकादवित्
ata eva copamā sūryakādivat

ata eva—therefore; ca—also; upamā—comparison; sūryakādivat—like the images of the sun etc.

TRANSLATION

Therefore, we also draw a comparison to the images of the sun.

COMMENTARY

The image of the sun is different than the sun, and similarly, a distinction is drawn between a picture of the world in our senses and the mind as against the reality that is being pictured. Both the picture and the object being pictured are objective, but the picture also refers to its object. This reference may be true or false. For example, when a rope is perceived as a snake, then both the picture (of the snake) in the mind and the senses, as well as the object being perceived (the rope) are real. However, the referential connection between the picture and the object is false. Thus, the hallucination exists, but it is not considered true. The rejection doesn't reject the reality of a snake or a rope; both are real and eternal concepts. It just means that *this thing* that we are seeing is not a snake.

QUESTION

So, what happens when we close our eyes and stop perceiving the world? Do we still have the capacity for perception, or is this capacity also lost?

3.2.19 (338)
अम्बुवदग्रहणात् तु न तथात्वम्
ambuvadagrahaṇāt tu na tathātvam

ambuvat—like water; agrahaṇāt—from not being in a house; tu—but; na—no; tathātvam—similarly them.

TRANSLATION

But just like water from not being in a house (a pot for water); (the perceiver or the senses) don't have a house (or border), and they exist in that state.

COMMENTARY

In Yoga philosophy, the mind and the senses are compared to an ocean, with thoughts and sensations arising as waves in this ocean. To understand these waves, think of a vibrating string. For a string to vibrate, it must be clamped at the two ends. If the string is not clamped, and you push it, it will simply be displaced from one position to another; it will not vibrate. If the string is clamped at one end, then any push will cause it to rotate, rather than vibrate. All vibration, therefore, arises when there is a boundary exerted on a string. In physics, these are also called 'boundary conditions'. The senses and the mind are also described as water here, that is not in a pot. When the restrictions of the pot are removed, then the mind and the senses are like a non-vibrating membrane. This is the basic principle of mind and sense control: remove the restrictions of the boundary conditions. Since the world exerts a boundary condition on the senses and the mind, they start vibrating, and that vibration is called sensation and thought. But if the boundary condition is removed, then the mind and the senses become silent. So, perception is due to these boundaries.

A lot of impersonalist philosophy is based on this idea of sense and mind control. It says that this world exerts a boundary on the consciousness, and these boundaries then produce an individual consciousness (which we call the soul), and once the individual soul is produced by exerting a boundary, then the consciousness starts producing waves. If we remove these boundaries, then there are no longer individual souls, and they will not vibrate. Hence, the removal of these boundaries removes all perception and individuality. The impersonalist, therefore, talks about *ghatākash* and *mahākasha*. The *ghatākash* is space inside a pot, and *mahākasha* is space without the pot boundary. The claim is that māyā is the pot, and it divides space into potted spaces. These potted spaces then vibrate, and these vibrations produce perceptions. If the pots of māyā are removed, then the individual space will merge into the universal space, and as the individuality is lost, the vibrations will also cease. Thus, by removing these boundaries, we become devoid of sensation and thought, and that freedom from all perception is the transcendental state of the soul.

There is however another way to understand this description. In this understanding, the vibration is not a problem; the problem is the meaning of this vibration. What we call the boundary—which creates the vibration—is not physical. This boundary is created by a meaning, and this meaning is the relation between the whole and the part. For example, if the idea of mammal is the *mahākasha* then the *ghatākash* of the cow is created from this *mahākasha* by expanding the idea of mammal into a cow. Now, we must note that the idea of cow already existed in the idea of a mammal. It is not an external imposition on the mind. It is rather *avyakta* inside the mammal and it becomes *vyakta*.

In the impersonal philosophy, the boundary or māyā is an external imposition on the consciousness, and by exerting these boundaries potted spaces are created. But what if the pot was inside the space—like a cow is inside a mammal—and it only comes out of the space? This requires a different understanding of space which enfolds the complexity within itself and unfolds it gradually. The impersonal understanding of space is that it is like an infinite box. The personalist understanding of space is that it is like tree—expanded from the root. The root is the origin, but as trunks, branches, and twigs are manifest from the root, the space also expands. This expansion is the subdivision of space, and by this subdivision, the *ghatākash* is created from the *mahākasha*. So, the impersonal understanding is based on a physical notion of space. If this idea of space were revised to a semantic understanding—in which the root is an idea, which then divides into smaller ideas—then māyā will cease to be an external imposition. It will rather spring out of the consciousness as its innate property.

If this understanding of space is clarified, then a distinction can be drawn between an externally imposed boundary, and an internally springing out boundary. The externally imposed boundary is called *bahiranga śakti* or external energy, and the internally springing out boundary is called *antaranga śakti* or internal energy. The contention of the impersonalist that all boundaries are externally imposed is thus rejected. Yes, the material boundaries are externally imposed, but there is another kind of boundary that springs from within.

When a pure devotee chants the names of the Lord, the mind and the senses vibrate. The impersonalist thinks that this vibration is an external imposition on the mind—a boundary that was applied to create a vibration. But the devotee understands that this vibration was enfolded in the soul, and it is just being unfolded. This vibration springs out of the soul like a tree grows out of a seed. Devotion is therefore compared to a *bīja* that gives rise to a creeper.

This philosophy about the natural springing of sound was also expounded by stalwarts of Sanskrit like Bhartṛhari who speak about language as a *sphota*— a bursting out or an explosion. Vaishnavas also say that when the consciousness is purified, then the sound springs out automatically—*svyameva sphurati adah*. These terms like *sphota* and *sphurati* indicate the same idea—the vibration is not due an external boundary. It is rather innate and immanent in the soul in an unmanifest form. It is only manifest when the soul is purified.

Thus, in the physical analogy of vibrations, the boundary is applied externally. But in the semantic understanding of vibrations, the boundary springs out of the soul. It is like a spider producing a web that binds the spider. The web is not an unnatural thing; it is rather immanent in the soul, and manifest from the soul. Of course, the spider can keep the web within itself. And that control of the consciousness is Brahman, where the soul is *avyakta*. It rests like a seed which hasn't manifested the tree of devotion from within itself. The soul in this seed form is not considered the full-blown consciousness. However, because it has the potential for full-blown consciousness, it is always an individual. The destruction of boundaries—that are externally imposed by the material nature—brings the soul to a non-vibrating state or liberation. Upon further progress, the vibrations come out of the self and are not externally imposed.

In this sūtra, the externally forced boundaries are being described, and it is said that if the pots are broken, then the senses and the mind become silent. Since this often leads to an impersonal misunderstanding about the transcendent state beyond the state of complete silence, we must understand the difference between the externally imposed and the internally created boundaries. If we changed the analogies, then we can see that even the external imposition is ultimately the fulfillment of the soul's desires: we want to be entangled in material nature, and material nature simply fulfills our desires. The desire for entanglement, however, sprang from within; the material energy simply fulfilled that desire by providing the boundaries that cause the mind and the senses to vibrate. So, māyā is not forcing itself upon us. We are asking māyā to come to us. If we give up material desires, then these boundaries on the mind and senses will end. But another kind of boundary will spring from within. This new boundary will create new kinds of vibrations and hence perceptions.

QUESTION

But factually we cannot close our eyes forever. We must perceive, think, judge, and intend—even if we want to pursue spiritual life. So, how can someone who is unable to break the pot boundary become spiritually realized?

3.2.20 (339)

वृद्धिह्रासभाक्त्वमन्तर्भावाद् उभयसामञ्जस्यादेवम्

vṛddhihrāsabhāktvamantarbhāvād ubhayasāmañjasyādevam

vṛddhi-hrāsa-bhāktvam—enjoying growth and decline; antar-bhāvāt—from being within; ubhaya-sāmañjasyāt—from equanimity in both; evam—thus.

TRANSLATION

From being situated within, enjoying the growth and decline (i.e., the up and down of a vibration), being equanimous in both thus (leads to Brahman).

COMMENTARY

The root cause of material entanglement is material desire. Due to this desire, right or wrong actions are performed, and karma is produced. Even if we stop desiring, the fruits of the karma must be borne out. These fruits will automatically bring us in contact with the external world, and under this contact, the mind and the senses will start vibrating. This sūtra advises that when this happens, the soul must remain equanimous through the ups and downs. In short, end the process of liking and disliking of perception and bear out the fruits of the previously created karma. Once the karma has ended, and the soul has ceased in its desires, then the soul will automatically be liberated. The key, however, is remaining equanimous. How can we keep tolerating the pleasures and pains produced due to karma if there is nothing to look forward to? A simple praise makes us happy, and an insult makes us unhappy. A person can be equanimous only when there is innate happiness, and the happiness or sadness provided by the external world become insignificant in comparison. If the solution to the problem of entanglement asks us to become equanimous before we can become happy, then the solution is easily stated, but very difficult to practice. The converse solution where we become happy first, and that leads to equanimity is more practical. Therefore, this solution—while not impossible—is difficult to practice and often doesn't result in the intended outcomes.

QUESTION

But how can one become equanimous in this turbulent world? We are tossed by the waves of changes, and some make us happy, while others make us sad. It is very hard to maintain equanimity in the face of these changes.

3.2.21 (340)
दर्शनाच्च
darśanācca

darśanāt—due to seeing or philosophical understanding; ca—as well.

TRANSLATION

(Equanimity in the face of happiness and distress) can also be obtained by seeing the world through the lens of correct philosophical understanding.

COMMENTARY

Philosophical understanding is the beginning of spiritual realization, because it brings detachment—one can see that the happiness and suffering is caused by one's own actions in the past, and one must tolerate these perceptions because they are temporary. Eternal happiness lies beyond this material world when we transcend the material desires, and the fruits of past actions have been consumed. Unless one is detached, even the practice of devotion doesn't work, because one maintains materialistic goals, and devotion is used for fulfilling the materialistic desires. Thus, we see that many so-called religious people are extremely materialistic; they talk about God, but what they really want is material prosperity. This kind of devotion—which exists without a philosophical understanding—is useless. It is a pretentious religion, that doesn't lead one to any spiritual realization. The first step is a philosophical understanding of this material world—i.e., how and why we are entangled. With this understanding, one becomes detached from the suffering and enjoyment of this world. This equanimity then stops the further production of material desires and karma. Once this detachment to the material world is acquired, then devotional practices produce the real joy, as one performs devotion for the Lord's pleasure because the materialistic goals have ended, so every activity must be performed for a transcendent purpose. This is also called 'pure' devotional service. Without detachment, devotional practices are impure and imperfect. And without correct knowledge, the beginner doesn't acquire detachment or equanimity. Of course, one who has true devotion doesn't need the philosophical understanding; they are already situated in perfect bliss and the pleasure and suffering of the material world has become irrelevant to them. So, they don't need philosophy to become detached from the world. Thus, at some point, the philosophical understanding ceases to be important. However, for the beginner, it is the essential bedrock on which the practice of devotion itself must be erected.

Topic 6

QUESTION

You earlier said that everything can be used in the service of the Lord. Now you are saying that a person must be detached from this material world. How can we reconcile these two contradictory statements? Should we accept everything or reject everything? What is the correct path to transcendence?

3.2.22 (341)

प्रकृतैतावत्त्वं हि प्रतिषिधति ततो बरवीति च भूयः

prakṛtaitāvattvaṃ hi pratiṣedhati tato bravīti ca bhūyaḥ

prakṛta-etāvattvam—all that has been created until now; pratiṣed-hati—rejects; tato—then that; bravīti—says; ca—and; bhūyaḥ—that I exist.

TRANSLATION

When a person rejects all that has been created until now only then he says that "I exist" (i.e., that I am different from all that has been rejected).

COMMENTARY

The term *prakṛta* means something created. It also means one's nature. When these two meanings are combined, then we can see that what we consider our nature is both created and something that we consider to be ourselves. This *prakṛta* is comprised of three aspects—our roles in the world, our cognitions and experiences, and our desires or personality of likes and dislikes. This has been described to be 'external' to the soul, and yet the soul identifies with these things and considers them his true nature. Thus, we identify with the roles in society and say that "I'm a father", "I'm a mother", etc. We identify with our cognitions and abilities, and say that "I'm strong", "I'm intelligent", "I'm creative", etc. Then we identify with our emotions and say that "I'm loving", "I'm angry", "I'm happy", etc. There is an "I" or the self, and relations, cognitions, and emotions, are the properties of this self. The soul also has innate properties, which manifest from within as its internal energy, just like a cow manifests from a mammal. However, until these external creations and identifications have been discarded, the internal things remain unmanifest and invisible. Examples of such identifications are citizenship, gender, race, language, etc. People may talk about spiritual life, but they remain attached to these identifications. The sūtra states that unless we keep identifying with these external attributes, we will never realize who we are distinct from these material attributes. And if these attributes always keep changing, identifying with them will lead us to believe that we are also changing; in short, that an eternal "I" doesn't exist.

There is, however, no contradiction between renunciation and association, if the material energy is identified as the Lord's property, rather than our property. In short, just because we are currently situated in a nation, gender, race, or linguistic identity doesn't mean that's who we are. The devotee sees these as coverings of the soul and identifies them as the Lord's properties rather than his property or, worse still, himself. Thus, a rich devotee doesn't think "I'm rich". He rather says: this richness belongs to the Lord, I'm also the Lord's property, and hence one property (myself) is engaging another property (the riches) into the Lord's service. In short, both the soul and the riches are instruments. One instrument engages the other instrument in the Lord's service. However, we must also understand that this is an advanced stage of self-realization. The preliminary stage of realization is that I'm not this body and its associated attributes. Once we strip out all these attributes, then we come to ask: Who am I?

The answer to that question is: "I'm a servant of the Lord". Once this question is answered, then we can ask: "What are these things currently associated with me?" and the answer to that is also: "These are servants of the Lord". Then one servant engages another servant into the service of the Lord. If the first question—i.e., "Who am I?"—is not answered correctly, then the subsequent answers also remain incorrect. The answer to the first question also involves many components. The first component is that "I'm not this body". Following this answer, we can say that "I exist even if all the bodily attributes are changed". If our eternal existence is established, then we ask a further question: "What is the purpose of my existence?". Note that existence and purpose are quite different questions. I can exist eternally purposelessly. Or I can exist eternally with an eternal purpose. If the first question of my eternal existence is not answered properly, then the answer of eternal purpose is also wrong.

Hence, this sūtra states that first we must realize that we are not this body. And this is possible if we reject all the attributes associated with the body. The impersonalist states that our questions end with this one answer. But the devotees disagree. They say that after we have established our eternal existence, we must also ask about our eternal purpose. If I exist eternally, and a lot of other souls exist eternally, should we be involved in our self-interest? Or, is there a common interest that goes beyond the interests of the individual souls? So, the answer that "I exist" is incomplete. The further realization is "others exist too". And then a further realization is that there is a shared purpose. But, to progress in these successive realizations, one must first reject the bodily identity.

QUESTION

But if one rejects the body and the mind, then how can one think of the Lord? The soul, as you have clarified, is only the potentiality for relation, cognition, and emotion. How can this potentiality be converted into a reality without the body? How will the soul in the disembodied state think and perceive?

3.2.23 (342)
तदव्यक्तम् आह हि
tadavyaktam āha hi

tat—that; avyaktam—is not manifest; āha—says; hi—certainly.

TRANSLATION

That (body and mind by which the soul perceives and conceives the Lord) is certainly unmanifest (at the present) thus it is said (by the scriptures).

COMMENTARY

The impersonalist thinks that the body that covers the soul is always an external envelope of the soul, and when this envelope is discarded, there is no other body. This is, however, a false understanding. There is another kind of body that is unmanifest right now and will be manifest from *within* the soul. Just like a seed manifests into a tree, similarly, the soul can also manifest a body. This body is hidden inside the soul in an *avyakta* or unmanifest form, just like the tree exists inside the seed, and yet unless the seed is watered, the tree remains unmanifest. The water is external to the seed, but the tree is internal to the seed. When the material body is used to serve the Lord, that is like watering the seed. Under these conditions, the tree comes out of the seed automatically. The purpose of the material body is the developing of the spiritual body.

If we identify with this body, then we engage in materialistic activities and the seed is not watered. If we reject the body prematurely, then, we can see how the soul is separate from the material body, but the seed is not watered. Thus, both conditions of materialism (identifying with the body) and impersonalism (rejecting the body) culminate in the same result—the seed is not watered. And unless this seed is watered, the tree of the spiritual body is unmanifest.

QUESTION

Does this mean that the body manifest from the soul is just like this present body in the sense that it can also be used for perception and conception?

3.2.24 (343)
अपि च संराधने प्रत्यक्षानुमानाभ्याम्
api ca saṃrādhane pratyakṣānumānābhyām

api ca—and moreover; saṃrādhane—in perfect meditation (it is experienced); pratyakṣa-anumānābhyām—for direct perception and inference.

TRANSLATION

And moreover, in perfect meditation (on the Lord) (the body) can be used for direct perception and inference (about the Lord, just like this body).

COMMENTARY

A person might simultaneously exist in many roles such as father, employee, citizen, husband, etc. but they are not simultaneously manifest. In the same way, the spiritual body of the soul exists inside the soul in an unmanifest form. It is said that necessity is the mother of invention. That necessity is desire in the soul. When this desire is created, then a body suitable to fulfill that desire is produced. And once this body is produced, then it enters a relation to the Lord. If the soul's desires change, then it can manifest a different body, and using that body, the soul can enter a different relation to the Lord. Even in the material world, as we have discussed earlier, the chit-śakti or the body is manifest after the māyā-śakti. The Lord injects the soul into the māyā-śakti, and based on the desires, a suitable type of body for enjoyment is acquired.

An example of the desire in the soul is that it wants to eat tasty food. Then, māyā-śakti creates varieties of cuisines—e.g., Indian food, Mexican food, Chinese food, Mediterranean food, etc.—and the soul chooses one such flavor at one time. Once the soul accepts one such taste, then it develops into the desire for the place where this food is available. Once the soul reaches that place, then he develops a desire for a menu of dishes within a type of flavor. And then the soul picks up some dishes within that menu. Finally, the soul enjoys a certain type of food. The basic desire about "I want tasty food" thus successively manifests into the desire for a cuisine, a place that serves the cuisine, a menu about that cuisine, and a dish within that cuisine. The soul doesn't create all this variety, however, that doesn't mean that it doesn't have a desire for eating.

The impersonalist claims that if the māyā-śakti did not create varieties of cuisines, then the soul will not have a desire for taste. This is a false idea. If nothing is available, then the soul can remain content for some time, and this contentment is called Brahman. But when the desire for tasting develops, then the soul falls again into māyā-śakti, gets a desire, and then gets a body.

In the same way, when the soul develops a desire for the Lord, then he wants to see, hear, smell, touch, and taste the Lord. Again, māyā-śakti produces many kinds of desires, and the soul accepts them and acquires a body. Both spiritual and material bodies are produced from māyā-śakti, but they are described to be two different kinds of māyā: yoga-māyā and mahā-māyā. Under mahā-māyā, all the desires are devoid of the Lord; thus, the soul wants to see, taste, smell, hear, and touch, but those things must not be the Lord. Under yoga-māyā, the soul only wants to see, taste, touch, hear, and smell the Lord.

This sūtra says that with a spiritual body one acquires direct perception of the five senses. In this direct perception, we can hear sounds, but we must infer the meaning. We can see bodily expressions, but we must infer the emotions. We can see the actions, but we must infer the roles. This inference is performed by the mind. Therefore, the spiritual body also has mind and senses, and it can directly perceive taste, smell, sound, touch, and sight, and it can infer moods, roles, and meanings. The spiritual body is hence just like the material body. The difference is simply that the spiritual body can see, taste, touch, smell, and hear the Lord, but the material body cannot. Therefore, everything about the Lord is inaccessible through the material body, and the Lord hence appears in the form of a deity so we can see and touch, in the form of a scripture so we can hear, and as the remnants of His food that we can taste and smell. We can perceive and understand these things through the material body, and as we engage our senses and the mind in this activity, the soul develops attraction for the Lord. When that attraction is developed, then a spiritual body is acquired. Through the spiritual body, the soul can directly perceive and understand the Lord.

QUESTION

I can understand that the body is unmanifest presently, and is manifest from within the soul, but isn't there still a difference between the body and the soul? If so, how can the body be considered the nature of the soul itself?

3.2.25 (344)

प्रकाशादविच्चावैशेष्यं प्रकाशश्च कर्मण्यभ्यासात्

prakāśādivaccāvaiśeṣyaṃ prakāśaśca karmaṇi abhyāsāt

prakāśādivat—like light etc.; ca—and; avaiśeṣyaṃ—no difference; prakāśaḥ—the light; ca—and; karmaṇi—in the actions (or the effects of the light); abhyāsāt—on account of the work, practices, or the habits (of the soul).

TRANSLATION

And just like there is no difference between the light and the actions or the effects of the light (e.g., heat and illumination) (similarly, there is no difference between the soul and) the work, practices, or the habits (of the soul).

COMMENTARY

The body and the soul are different and non-different. They are different because the soul can accept different bodies; this acceptance comes in the form of having different moods, perceptions, and relations. They are also non-different because the part is inside the whole and the whole is inside the part. Thus, our body is a part of the soul because bodily awareness is one of the types of awareness of the soul, and the soul is present in each part through its consciousness. This mutual permeation is indicated by two factors— (1) the soul controls the body, and (2) the body serves the soul. The body springs from the desire for enjoyment, and this desire leads to control of the body. However, when the body is created, then the body parts serve the other body parts because they are serving the soul. This cow is different from the mammal, because even if the cow ceased to exist, then mammal would still exist. And yet, the mammal is present in the cow. Similarly, if the body ceased to exist, then the soul will still exist. And yet, while the body exists, the soul is present within the body.

This sūtra makes a profound point about the mutual presence of cause and effect within each other. The claim is that the cause and effect are different and non-different. Why? The effect existed inside the cause and was manifest from the cause. Similarly, once the effect is manifest, we can know the cause of that effect from the effect. If the effect wasn't in the cause, then the effect would appear from nothing— ex-nihilo creation. Likewise, if the cause wasn't in the effect, then we could not say which of the many causes created the effect.

Suppose you see a moving billiard ball. You know that its motion was caused by something that was moving, and hence, the effect of motion was produced by a cause in which the energy of motion previously existed. But the billiard ball could be moving because it was struck by another billiard ball or by a billiards cue. Which of these two are the real cause? In modern physics we say that we have no way of knowing whether the billiard ball or the cue caused the motion, unless we go back in time and see what caused it. But in this sūtra, it is indicated that we can know the cause simply by observing the effect. That means that the cause is immanent in the effect—as the cause of the effect.

As an example, the theists say that God created the world, which means that the world must have existed in some form in God prior to the creation. This is the effect existing inside the cause. However, once the effect is created, the theists draw a separation between matter and God, and the materialist now latches on to this separation and says: How do you know that God created the world? This creation is also consistent with a big bang! Since we cannot go back in time to know what caused the universe, we have no empirical way of knowing the universe's origin. Thus, both theists and atheists accept that effects are in the cause, but they don't accept that the cause is inside the effect. In monotheistic religions of the West, even the effect is not accepted to be in the cause; they, for instance, claim that God created the universe *ex nihilo*, which means an infinite amount of energy was created from nothing. If we don't take that position, then by the law of conservation of energy, God would be diminished upon creation. Thus, monotheism removes the effect from the cause, which materialism does not. But materialism removes the cause from the effect. Hence, monotheism and materialism posit different kinds of cause-effect notions.

By removing the effect from the cause, an unscientific doctrine is produced—because energy conservation is rejected. And by removing the cause from the effect, an incomplete science is produced—because the same effect can be explained by innumerable causes, so you cannot know the cause from the effect. The result of the first claim is that the cause is not necessary for an effect—because the effect comes out of nothing. The result of the second claim is that no cause is necessary as other causes can explain the effect, and therefore, no explanation can be considered a sufficient explanation of the effect. Once we take out necessity and sufficiency, then science itself becomes meaningless.

Therefore, we must understand that causes within the effect, and effects within the causes are required for necessity and sufficiency, which are in turn necessary for science. However, necessity and sufficiency come at the cost of conventional logic—namely, that the cause and effect are within each other. The problems of logical violations must now be addressed by modalities. There are two such modalities—possibility and will—which must now be accepted. The effect exists inside the cause as a possibility, and the cause exists inside the effect as a will. This means when we see an effect, we can say two things. First, this effect is manifested from the cause by a will, and the will is within the effect as the purpose of why the effect was manifest. If we know the purpose of things, then we know the cause that produced them. If we reject will and possibility, then our explanation is incomplete (or there is no explanation). If we accept both possibility and will, but we don't describe them as different modes of existence, then we have a self-contradictory explanation. Modal explanations are therefore necessary for any cause-effect explanation and the cornerstone of this modality is simply that the cause exists within the effect as its purpose.

The soul similarly exists in the body as the purpose of the body, and God exists in the world as the purpose of the world. That doesn't mean that the soul is the body, or that God is the world. They are different and non-different. Likewise, the body was previously within the soul, and the world was within God.

In modern science, when a photon is absorbed, we cannot say whether this photon came from the sun or the lamp. Likewise, from the perspective of the sun or the lamp, we cannot say whether the photon will illuminate the table or the chair. This is incompleteness of the theory, because we cannot tell the effect from the cause (i.e., whether the table or the chair will be illuminated) and we cannot tell the cause from the effect (if the illumination was due to the sun or the lamp). In classical physics we could say that if the source of light existed, then the destination will be illuminated, but in atomic physics we cannot even say that—because the emission of the photon is indeterministic. To solve these problems, we must say that the photon is a possibility in the source of light, and it is emitted by a will, and this will is immanent within the illumination.

In atomic theory we also say that light is emitted only when it can be absorbed. Therefore, the sun doesn't emit the light unless there is an atomic object whose present and subsequent state differences exactly match the energy in the photon. And in Vedic philosophy, we further say that the light is received at a destination due to karma—i.e., it is not merely purpose but also the receiver must be deserving of the light. Hence, the effect of illumination is not just the sun or the lamp; it is also the receiver being capable of receiving and deserving of the light. Thus, the explanation of light is extremely complicated, but all this complexity is necessary and sufficient for a complete theory of vision.

The impersonalist doesn't know how the cause and the effect mutually permeate each other. He simply says—the body is the effect, and the soul is the cause, but they are different as māyā and Brahman. He cannot explain how the soul falls into māyā, because the will of fall is within the soul, and that will is possible only when the soul is an individual person. The māyā serves this will but while māyā serves the will, the will is immanent in māyā. Therefore, the world is not moving automatically due to māyā. It is moving because there is a will, and that will is moving the māyā from within—due to immanence. Therefore, in one sense, we can say that māyā is itself moving because there is no external cause, and it would be true because the cause is within māyā. In another sense, we can say that the will emanated from the soul or God, so there is a transcendent cause of this will, which subsequently became immanent.

The position of the soul is described nicely in the Bhagavad-Gita by differentiating the passenger from the chariot. The passenger says: I want to go to place X. The chariot then drives the passenger to X. The causality in the passenger is simply about the intention, but the mechanism of the chariot is not controlled by the passenger. In short, *how* the chariot is moving is due to māyā, but *why* it is moving is due to the soul. Finally, *when* and *whether* the chariot moves—despite our will—is decided by the Lord. Thus, the soul, māyā, and God are collectively moving the chariot, and we cannot separate them, because if either one of them was absent, then the chariot would not move. But that doesn't mean that the questions of why, how, and when are identical. The questions are different, but the answers to these questions are combined in the effect.

QUESTION

If the spiritual body of the soul is non-different from the soul, then, does it mean that even the spiritual body of the Lord is non-different from the Lord?

3.2.26 (345)
अतोऽनन्तेन तथा हि लिङ्गम्
ato'nantena tathā hi liṅgam

atah—therefore; anantena—with the infinite; tathā—in the same way; hi—certainly; liṅgam—the form.

TRANSLATION

(Since the soul and its spiritual body are non-different), therefore, in the same way, a form (is associated) with the infinite (namely, the Lord).

COMMENTARY

This sūtra clearly refutes the impersonalist doctrine by stating that the infinite is also a form. This infinite has two components—will and power to fulfill that will. The form of the Supreme Lord is due to will; it is not a material form; the shape of the Lord's body is the form of will or desire for pleasure. The form of the Lord's Śakti is the form of the power that fulfills this desire for pleasure. Will and power are not formless, although if the will is unmanifest or the power is not being used, these forms remain invisible. The invisible state also has a form, although the form is only visible when it creates an effect. Just like if we don't see an apple, the apple remains a possibility of being seen. In this state, there is a form, although the form is unmanifest. When we observe the apple, the form becomes visible. The visible form is just like the invisible form, although, the invisible form is the cause, and the visible form is the effect.

The previous sūtra noted the example of light producing the effects of heat and illumination. If light is not manifest, then it exists in an invisible form. When it is manifest, then it becomes an effect of heat and illumination. So, when we see the light, we don't call it an illusion of our vision. We rather say that there was an objective reality which was previously in an unmanifest state.

Similarly, the Supreme Soul is the potential for all experiences. And when these potentials are realized, then the body of the Supreme Soul is the experiences. In different situations or contexts, different potentials are realized. As a result, the same Supreme Soul can manifest many kinds of bodies. It's not that the other bodies have disappeared; it is just that they are unmanifest. They continue to exist in the Supreme Soul as potentials or possibilities. Based on this manifestation, the Supreme Soul is identified by different names and forms. All these forms are the same Supreme Soul, but depending on the extent of manifestation, some of these forms are called 'superior' to the other forms.

QUESTION

You keep talking about manifest and unmanifest states. Why do these two states are being distinguished? Why can't we just have only one state? Also, if the unmanifest state is not observable, why do we recognize its reality?

3.2.27 (346)

उभयव्यपदेशात्त्वहिकुण्डलवत्

ubhayavyapadeśāttvahikuṇḍalavat

ubhayavyapadeśāt—due to both being stated; tu—but; ahi-kuṇḍalavat—just like a serpent that is coiled, or in straight and coiled serpent states.

TRANSLATION

Just like a serpent can exist in a coiled or straight state (similarly), (the manifest and unmanifest states are) both declared to be real or true.

COMMENTARY

David Bohm—a British physicist—used the evocative terms 'enfolded' and 'unfolded' to describe the two states of reality (it is rumored that he got this idea of unmanifest and manifest from discussions with Jiddu Krishnamurti). The analogy is pervasive in yoga philosophy where kundalini is said to be a form of 'coiled' material energy and is compared to a coiled snake. When this snake uncoils, then the energy is manifest. Yoga practitioners are therefore trying to uncoil this unmanifest form of energy present in every individual. The coiled snake analogy is also depicted in many ancient traditions where the coiling of the snake is replaced by the snake swallowing its head, and the snake is supposed to merge back into itself because it swallows itself completely.

The question is—since this energy is not visible in most people, how can we say that it even exists? Why even postulate the existence of this unmanifest energy? Shouldn't we not accept the reality of anything that we cannot observe? The answer to this question is that if we reject the unmanifest state, then we would be hard-pressed to explain its appearance. We would have to say that the manifestation must be because something existed somewhere else, and this preexisting thing is conserved, so when energy appears in one place, it must disappear in another place. This idea of conservation—when taken to its logical extreme in the origin of the universe—entails that an infinite amount of energy must be concentrated in a very small region of space. This enormous concentration of energy is then supposed to create a 'black hole' which sucks itself inward, and there is no reason for this 'black hole' to become the 'big bang'. So, the origin of the universe itself becomes a huge problem due to a singularity.

The contrary thesis is that everything preexists as a possibility. And these possibilities are 'enfolded' like a coiled snake. They are manifest when the snake 'unfolds'. Thus, the effect exists within the cause, and nothing that we see is newly created. It is simply becoming visible from a previous invisible state.

This brings us to the question of whether energy is conserved. The answer is yes and no. What do we mean by conservation? We mean that if some energy disappears here, then it must appear elsewhere. In short, energy conservation entails that energy is always manifest. But this is not true. Energy can become unmanifest or 'enfolded' and exist in the source in a 'coiled' form. When the energy becomes coiled, it is not observable, and yet it exists. There is infinite amount of energy in our bodies, but it exists in an enfolded state. The yogi tries to unfold this energy through a mystical process. But the Lord is the supreme mystic. He keeps the entire creation enfolded within, and then unfolds it by His will. Then, when He is bored of this creation, He enfolds it again within.

Therefore, the energy is conserved, but that conservation of energy is not according to classical physics—where energy is always manifest in one place or another, in one form or another. The conservation is rather quantum mechanical, where the energy becomes a possibility. In this state of possibility, infinite energy is present within the Lord, and this packing of energy doesn't create a 'black hole' or 'singularity'. The black hole conundrum arises in modern physics because we think that nature is without will. Therefore, if energy exists, then it must be emitted, and if it is not being emitted, then it must be because the gravitational pull must be preventing its escape. These ideas about black holes are false, and they arise because basic problems in quantum physics remain unresolved. For instance, we are unable to explain how a possibility is converted into a reality. In the case of these black holes regions of space that don't interact with us—i.e., they don't emit light to us, so we cannot see them, we just think that the reason they are not emitting light is because light is being sucked inward. But that is not true. The light is being selectively emitted to certain destinations, just not to us. This selection is due to choices and entitlements.

According to Vedic cosmology, the light of the sun is not received in the upper four planetary systems, the lower seven planetary systems, and the hellish planets. Therefore, the sun is also a black hole according to living entities in all these places, because they can never see the sun. But is the sun a black hole? No. It selectively emits the light to the three planetary systems. The other planets where the light of the sun doesn't reach have other sources of light, which will seem to be black holes to us. Since the parts where the sun's light doesn't reach are much bigger than the parts that we can see, therefore, the number of black holes are far more numerous than all the stars that we can see. All these objects in space keep the energy coiled and uncoil them upon will.

QUESTION

You have used many analogies to describe the unmanifest state— the seed from which the tree springs, the lake that gives rise to rivulets, the source of light that emanates the particles of light, the meanings that are expressed as words of speech through a speaker's mouth, or the snake that remains coiled and becomes uncoiled. Each analogy seems to capture the idea in a limited way, but they are also quite different in other ways. Which is the best analogy?

3.2.28 (347)

पूरकाशाश्ररयवद्वा तेजसत्त्वात्

prakāśāśrayavadvā tejastvāt

prakāśa-āśrayavat—like the shelter or the substrate of light; vā— moving from (the substrate); tejastvāt—from the light.

TRANSLATION

The analogy of the light separating from the substrate of light.

COMMENTARY

For nearly a century now, scientists have suspected that atomic theory has something to do with the nature of consciousness. This suspicion is confirmed here. Light is not itself consciousness, but it has many properties like that of consciousness. This also means that we should stop thinking of light in terms of material particles. One such idea is that light travels. According to this idea, since light travels, by the time it reaches us, it has become 'detached' from its source. Therefore, we cannot distinguish between sunlight, moonlight, or bulb light. We just know it as light, and the source of light is no longer knowable. But we also know from atomic theory that light is simply a state, not a particle. The particle is the sun, the moon, or the bulb. So, we cannot detach the state from the particle, and claim that light is traveling; we should say that the sun, the moon, or the bulb has a state that modifies the states of other particles. And the laws of this change must be based on the particle, rather than the state. Since all of matter is a state, the particle must be non-material, and to understand light as a state, we must understand how a non-material particle causes change. As we have discussed, the particle is the soul, and the cause is the desire and consequences of actions. So, unless we model the particle as something with desire and responsibility for its actions, we cannot understand the nature of light.

The analogies of the tree, the ocean, and the snake can also be interpreted physically, but the analogy of light cannot be interpreted in this way. For example, one can say that if the tree comes out of the seed, then the seed comes out of the tree. Therefore, everything created by the Lord must be equally capable of creation, which is false. Similarly, one can argue that the ocean is created only when the rivers flow into the ocean, but we can see that the rivers never come out of the ocean; therefore, the ocean is not the source; it is only the sink. Finally, we can say that the snake—even when coiled—always remains visible, and it occupies the same amount of space in the coiled and uncoiled states; hence, we cannot say that the uncoiled state is the manifestation of energy. Therefore, we must understand that many examples are given in the Vedic scriptures only as analogies. These analogies are useful to some extent, and not useful in other ways. In contrast, the example of light is not an analogy. If we study the nature of light, along with the source and sink of light, then it is not an analogy. It is rather the general template by which many other things can be understood. Hence, the sun is called Sūrya Nārāyana, and the sun-god has been worshipped in many religions. His creation is just like that of the Lord's creation.

QUESTION

What happens if someone wants to study light, without the source of light?

3.2.29 (348)
पूर्ववद्वा
pūrvavadvā

pūrvavat—as before; vā—alternatively.

TRANSLATION

Alternatively, as already discussed earlier.

COMMENTARY

The study of light alone is incomplete because light cannot be perceived unless there is an object that it illuminates, and the cause of that illumination cannot be explained unless there is a source. Therefore, impersonal doctrines that describe reality as merely a field of energy are incomplete. The complete theory of light requires a source and a destination. Since these destinations can be manifest from the source, and the light is itself manifest from the source, therefore, the source is by itself complete. Therefore, if we only study the source, then our theory is complete. But if we only study the objects manifest from the source or only the light that moves between the objects, then the theory is incomplete. All impersonalist claims that there is only light, and no source of light, or that light is itself its source, will forever remain incomplete.

In earlier discussions, we have seen that we can repeat the same question and if the context demands, a new or nuanced answer is generally given. However, if the answer is not new, it is not repeated. We just reference the earlier answer. This is often seen in mathematical proofs, when we reduce a new question to an older question, and then substitute the older question with the older answer. This substitution is not novelty. The novelty is that sometimes the same question can be answered differently based on the context. We have seen that novelty previously, and we are seeing the traditional approach here. Since sometimes questions can be answered in different ways, some of these questions may also be repeated—in anticipation of a new answer. That doesn't mean that the answer must be new; this sūtra refers to the older answer. The conclusion is that we must not speak unless we have something new to say.

This injunction also applies to the glorification of the Lord. While it seems that we are advised to chant the names of the Lord repeatedly, we are not repeating the same thing again and again. Every utterance of the name clears up some clutter from the past and therefore even for the neophyte, the repeated chanting is not the repetition of the same thing. As a devotee advances in spiritual life, every name has a unique meaning since different aspects of the Lord are realized through every utterance of the name. Therefore, Lord Chaitanya says: ānandām-budhi-vardhanaṁ prati-padaṁ, which means that the ocean of bliss is expanding at every step. The impersonalist says that the soul is a drop and Brahman is the ocean, and that ocean is static. But according to Lord Chaitanya, the ocean is infinite, and it is constantly expanding. As a devotee advances in glorifying the Lord, every new glorification describes the Lord in a novel way. Therefore, the devotee doesn't become silent just because the whole truth has already been stated. He speaks because the same truth is constantly expanding, and his speaking is the expansion of an already infinite ocean. The impersonalist says that once you know the whole truth, there is nothing more to be said, and he advocates silence. But the devotee turns around this injunction and says: yes, it is already full, but it can be expanded even more.

QUESTION

If the study of light without the source of light is impossible, then why are so many people still wanting to obtain an understanding in this way?

3.2.30 (349)

परतषिधाच्च

pratiṣedhācca

pratiṣedhāt—due to forbidding; ca—as well.

TRANSLATION

Due to forbidding as well (we develop the desire for it).

COMMENTARY

Impersonalism is the forbidden fruit. But precisely because it is forbidden, we start desiring it. This is the rebellious nature of the soul: when something is forbidden, it becomes more attractive. The rebellious soul asks: Why has it been forbidden? Obviously, there must be something great about it, which is why we have been excluded from enjoying it. Thus, forbidding makes the fruit attractive. If the scriptures did not forbid something, then they would be accused of not giving the correct path. But if the scriptures forbid something, then they make it more attractive to the rebellious soul. Thus, we find atheists who love to interpret scientific theories as indicating a denial of God, without checking what the theory's limitations are. Impersonalist philosophers similarly like to interpret everything according to their goggles of impersonalism, whether it is true or not. In short, we seek the forbidden fruit, not because it has been proven to be true or right or good. We seek it simply because it has been forbidden.

Topic 7

QUESTION

If the soul is incomplete without the Lord, then doesn't this soul feel incomplete even as part of Brahman where the Lord is not fully understood?

3.2.31 (350)

परमतःसेतून्मानसंबन्धभेदव्यपदेशेभ्यः

paramataḥ setūnmānasambandhabhedavyapadeśebhyaḥ

param—the Supreme Reality; ataḥ—therefore; setu-unmā-na-sambandha-bheda-vyapadeśebhyaḥ—is described as the bridge between the standard (of measurement) and the different (individuals) through a relationship.

TRANSLATION

The Supreme Reality is therefore described as the bridge between the standard (of measurement) and the differences through a relationship.

COMMENTARY

Another example is given here to illustrate the incompleteness of the soul without the Lord. Suppose we say that an object is '5' without specifying the standard of measurement, then '5' is meaningless. This '5' becomes meaningful when the standard is specified—e.g., 5 kilograms, 5 meters, 5 minutes, etc. The number '5' is a quantity, but without the quality—i.e., kilogram, meter, or minute—it is meaningless. Furthermore, even to call something '5' we must know what '1' is. This one is the standard of measurement, the primary unit. And by this standard of measurement, we define both the quality and the quantity.

The Lord is the standard of measurement, which defines both the quality and the quantity. A meter for example is the definition of length as well as the measure of length. In relation to a meter, we can measure the different objects and order them. The standard of measurement—e.g., the meter—is the reference for everything else. So, based on this standard, if we say that something is half-meter, then the meter is implicit in this description. So, the meter is outside the individual thing being measured, but it is also inside the thing after the measurement, because the measurement embedded the meter in the thing. And this embedding of the meter in each thing is the relation to the meter. If we don't perform the measurement, both the quality and the quantity are unknown.

The individualist thinks that each person can become their own standard. That is, we are both the quality and the measure of everything. But this leads to a problem—Why should you be the standard?

Why can't I be the standard? With the known problem of jealousy, we reject that anyone is the standard. But if there are many things, then we cannot live without a standard; we have to say something is bigger or smaller, higher or lower, etc. Therefore, it is not enough to say that nobody is a standard; we must also say that even these different things do not exist, because that removes the need for a standard.

Thus, after saying that nobody is a standard, we also reject the idea of a standard, collapse all the differences, and merge everything into a single undifferentiated identity since it removes the need for measurement. If we reject the differences between the individuals, then we get the 'infinite'. But infinite of what? Is it infinite meters, or infinite seconds, or infinite kilograms? The impersonalist has no answer to this problem, because to say that something is infinite kilograms, there must be something which is 1 kilogram, and that would be finite. To speak of this infinity, we must remove all qualities. So, we can say that Brahman is 'infinite', but it is not infinite kilograms, meters, or minutes. It is just a quantity and has no associated quality. And this makes it meaningless.

QUESTION

The example of measurement that you are giving here involves distinct objects—such as a kilogram and an apple. A materialist will say that these standards are arbitrary. For instance, it could also be a pound instead of a kilogram. And that would entail that anything can be a standard. Then, how does the Lord being called the standard of measurement address this issue?

3.2.32 (351)

सामान्यात्तु

sāmānyāttu

tu—but; sāmānyāt—on account of the merger (of the part in the whole).

TRANSLATION

But on account of the merger (of the part within the whole).

COMMENTARY

When we measure against a standard such as a kilogram, the kilogram is separate from the object being measured. This makes it possible to use arbitrary standards. However, this sūtra states that the standard of measurement is the whole, and the parts are measured against it. Of course, since the whole is successively divided into parts, there can be many standards that are bigger relative to the part. However, the Absolute Truth is the limit because it is only the whole and not the part of anything. So, even if we employ larger wholes to understand the parts, there is the whole truth which is itself Absolute.

This problem can further be understood if the whole is defined as 1, and everything else is a fraction of 1. The whole object is the first object. Then there are parts of this whole object, which are second, third, fourth, fifth, etc. We can divide the whole into parts, forming a tree structure, where the smallest part is a part of a larger part, which is part of an even larger part, which is part of the whole, etc. Since there are infinite such parts, in principle, the whole is 'infinite'. And because this whole is the first object, the whole is also '1'. In mathematical language, we can say that the Absolute Truth is cardinally infinite, and ordinally first. Since everything is inside the whole, therefore, we can also talk about the 'oneness' among the varied diversities. And yet this oneness doesn't take away the diversities, and the diversities never 'merge' into the oneness.

The diversities are always defined in relation to the whole. Since there is nothing other than the whole, the whole is the standard, but because the whole is 1, therefore, the standard is 1—not infinite. Since it is 1, we can conceive and perceive it. If this standard was infinite, then we could never know it. The standard is not without qualities; in fact, the standard is the fullness of knowledge, beauty, power, wealth, fame, and renunciation. And everything else has these qualities partially. So, when we divide the whole into parts, we are not cutting the whole *quantitatively*. We are rather saying: given that the whole knowledge is everything that can be known, what are the different departments of knowledge, that are parts of everything that can be known? The method of cutting the whole into parts is based on qualities, not quantities. Thus, for example, we don't say that physics is 1% of the whole knowledge. We rather say: physics is that part of knowledge that deals with the objectification of sense perception. The characterization of knowledge as 1% is meaningless, because another subject—e.g., economics—could also be 1%. If everything is divided into the smallest parts, then we can also count, and based on this counting we can derive quantities. Therefore, quantities are derivative of qualities. The qualities are primary and should be the basis of counting and numbering.

The impersonalist has the reverse viewpoint—drop all qualities, merge all quantities, and come up with infinity of nothing. If we multiply infinity with nothing, is it infinity or nothing? Nobody knows the answer, and the impersonalist rides on this confusion. The Buddhists say that infinity of nothing is nothing. And the impersonalist says that infinity of nothing is infinity. Thus, it is sometimes said that Advaita is Buddhism in a hidden form. It works off the same premises as Buddhism but arrives at a different conclusion. But the fact is that neither conclusion explains the world, although it is a grandiose philosophy. Such pretentious philosophies should be rejected by true seekers.

QUESTION

The measurement of the part against the whole seems quite strange. We measure a part against another part, but you are talking about a new type of measurement. How do we understand this type of measurement?

3.2.33 (352)
बुद्ध्यर्थः पादवत्
buddhyarthaḥ pādavat

buddhi—comprehension; arthaḥ—the meaning; pādavat—like parts.

TRANSLATION

It is possible to comprehend (if we see these) like parts of meaning.

COMMENTARY

We have noted this idea about the whole-part relation being between concepts many times earlier in the purports. This is the first sūtra that states this understanding explicitly. The reason is that we just noted that the soul is incomplete without the Lord, and this incompleteness was described as the standard. Now, if we think of wholes and parts physically, then we can have the whole as the standard, but we can also have the parts as the standards. A classic example of parts that become standards is that we define a standard of length as 'meter'— which is a part of the universe—and then we measure the expanse of the universe in terms of the meter. In the physical view of wholes and parts, either of these can be considered the standards. Greek philosopher Protagoras, in fact, came with up with the dictum that "man is the measure of all things". This claim by Protagoras counters the claim in the Bible: "God created man in His own image". Which of these two claims must be regarded as true? Is God a larger-than-life image of ourselves, or are we the smaller image of God?

These questions remain unanswerable due to the relativity of standards. But they become answerable when we consider the hierarchy of concepts. When you see a cow, there is no reason to postulate that it is also a mammal, unless you have seen horses, tigers, and dogs. Thus, our knowledge is limited by what we have seen. Conversely, if we haven't seen horses, tigers, and dogs, then the deeper level reality of a cow being a mammal will elude us. If instead we begin in the most abstract idea, then knowing that there is a cow entails that it is also a mammal. When you see a shade of red, you say it is part of the class of redness, it is part of a general class of colors, and it is a part of the general class of things that can be seen. In fact, it is impossible to understand a shade of red without understanding red, colors, and seeing. Therefore, in a physical conception of reality, anything can be a standard. However, in the semantic conception of reality, only the whole truth is the standard. Therefore, "God created man in His own image" can only be justified with a semantic viewpoint.

QUESTION

If the whole and the part are considered meanings, then, how do we understand the different locations that are part of the whole? Does it seem that the whole will become the origin, and the parts will be the individual locations? This seems like a strange notion of space in which everything is the origin, and the parts of this everything are different locations within this everything.

3.2.34 (353)
स्थानवशिेषात् प्रकाशादिवत्
sthānaviśeṣāt prakāśādivat

sthānaviśeṣāt—from the differences of places; prakāśādivat—like light etc.

TRANSLATION

The different locations are like light (originating from the candle).

COMMENTARY

This sūtra again invokes the example of a candle and its light to explain the nature of space. This example has been quoted several times before but always in a new context. The latest context is that the whole and the part are described as meanings, and therefore, the light is like the partial meaning emanating out of the source, which is the original and complete meaning. Apart from the spiritual implications that we will discuss shortly, it also means that the source of light and the light emanating from that source are not physical things; they are symbols of ideas. Each light particle therefore is a symbol of a partial meaning. The light source is the symbol of the complete meaning. And the light particle is related to the other light particles through the differences in meaning.

Like a cow is defined by the idea 'cow', by the idea of 'mammal', and by distinction to tigers, similarly, each light particle—when understood as a symbol, is not an isolated or independent object. It is connected to the whole because the idea 'mammal' is immanent within the cow. It is also connected to the whole because it is defined by a distinction to tigers. Finally, every time we see other cows, they are connected to each other by a mutual distinction. This means that the connection comes to us in three ways— (1) by universals such as a mammal, (2) by individuals such as other cows, and (3) by contexts such as tigers.

Thus, we know the cow through two assertions (namely that it is a cow and a mammal), and two negations (that it is not a tiger, and not other cows). In modern science, we only know things through assertions and not negations. Furthermore, we only know things through one type of concept—e.g., a cow, and the hierarchy of concepts is discarded. Finally, even the concept of cow is discarded and only properties such as height, weight, color, etc. are employed. This is the current state of atomic theory, which tries to describe light in terms of physical properties, and neglects all kinds of concepts—cows, mammals, not tigers, and not other cows. This theory is well-known to be incomplete.

Once we understand the nature of light, then we can speak about its application to the nature of space. When light is identified as symbols of meaning, then the directions and locations in space are also meanings. We can call this a 'semantic space'. This space has a hierarchical structure, like a tree. As a result, the distinction between direction and location in this space is collapsed. Everything is also a unique *type* of thing. Thus, there are unique types of individuals, identified by their personality. There are unique types of bodies, identified by concepts. And there are unique types of roles, identified by their duties.

We sometimes distinguish between a dimension and a location due to the hierarchy—the higher node is the dimension, and the lower node is a value on that dimension. However, since the lower node is also a dimension relative to an even lower node, therefore, everything is both a value and dimension. Hence, we can say that a cow is a type of mammal, and Gir is a type of cow. As we have discussed earlier, the dimension becomes a space, and the value becomes an object. Therefore, everything is both a space and an object. Things are objects relative to the 'larger' space, and they are spaces relative to smaller objects. 'Big' and 'small' are more abstract and more detailed concepts.

The origin of this light is abstract relative to all the symbols of light, and it contains all the symbols prior to their manifestation as a possibility. The origin is therefore just one point in the expanded space. The origin is also the entire space in an unmanifest form. Therefore, when the world expands from the Lord, the Lord seems to be one of the many individuals. But He is also the whole existence. When we think of the world physically, then the Lord cannot be a part of existence. But when the we think of the world semantically, then the whole truth can seem to be only one part of the existence. Similarly, the whole truth is also present in each of the parts. Thus, the light particles are in the candle, the candle is one of the light particles, and the candle is in all the light particles. Likewise, all the souls are in the Lord, the Lord is a soul, and the Lord is in all the souls. The materialists and the impersonalist philosophers cannot understand how the Lord is a soul, contains all souls, and exists in all souls. Therefore, they try to collapse all these things into a single undifferentiated 'field'.

QUESTION

Since the parts are emanating from the whole, how does this division of the whole into the parts occur? What is the cause of the division into parts?

3.2.35 (354)
उपपत्तेश्च
upapatteśca

upapatteḥ—due to reasoning or logical conclusion; ca—and.

TRANSLATION

And (the whole divides into parts) due to reasoning or logical conclusion.

COMMENTARY

The term *upapatti* is constituted of two roots—*upa* or secondary, and *pat* or falling. If we understand an inverted tree, then we can see that logical reasoning is the emergence of a branch (secondary) from the root, which is lower (fallen) than the root. In computing theory, reasoning is often identified as tree traversals. We represent knowledge in an inverted tree structure, and we traverse this tree—from root to leaves—to check the answer. Many theorem proving algorithms work in this way—they try to construct statements following a tree structure, and if the statement can be constructed, then it is proved.

The term *utapatti* is also constituted of two roots—*uta* or emergent, and *pat* or falling. Thus, *utapatti* refers to the creation or production, and *upapatti* refers to reasoning. The method of production is the method of reasoning. That is, in both cases, the emergent thing is lower than the source of the thing. Again, if we understand the inverted tree, then production means reasoning. Therefore, everything is created from the Absolute Truth by the process of reasoning, and this process operates by dividing the whole into parts, and then combining the various parts. During the annihilation of the material universe, these combinations are first destroyed, and the universe is reduced to the parts. Then these parts collapse back into the whole. While the universe exists, the parts exist as atoms (which are symbols) and these atoms combine in many ways. Thus, by the process of reasoning, the world is created, changed, and destroyed.

QUESTION

Our normal understanding of reasoning goes from premises to conclusions. But you refer to a model of reasoning in which the conclusion is the part and the premise is the whole, and reasoning goes from whole to part. How do we understand this model of reasoning, contrary to the other models?

3.2.36 (355)
तथान्यप्रतषिधात्
tathānyapratiṣedhāt

tathā—similarly; anya-pratiṣedhāt—due to denial of other things.

TRANSLATION

(Just as the whole divides into parts) similarly, (the parts are created) by the denial of other things (i.e., the denial of certain parts of the whole).

COMMENTARY

In modern thinking, we start with some simple premises and use logic and reasoning to construct complexity. Thus, the axioms are simple, and the theorems are complex. But what are these simple axioms? The modern definition of 'simplest' is the smallest. It is an extension of physical thinking where big things are made from small things. In Vedic philosophy, the 'simplest' is the largest. For example, the simplest idea we can carry is that of *knowledge*. And yet, this idea contains everything that can ever be known. By this shift in the definition of 'simple', the model of reasoning changes. In modern thinking, we take the smallest axioms and construct larger propositions. In Vedic philosophy, we take the largest axioms, and divide them into smaller parts. This is not a physical division—we are not trying to break down the word 'knowledge' into individual letters. We are rather dividing the meaning knowledge into various types of knowledge. Thus, every branch of knowledge is produced by rejecting or negating some other part or aspect of the root of knowledge itself.

We have discussed this rejection before—a cow is not a tiger, it is not other cows, and the cow is never in two places at the same time. These negations are within the cow, and by these negations, the cow is connected to the tigers, to other cows, and to all the other locations where the cow is not present. All these are absent in a specific cow because the cow is *not* those things. And yet, because they are negated in a cow, they are present in the cow as negations.

These negations are called *abhāva* or non-existence in Nyāya. When we know that something is a cow, we know that it is not a tiger. Therefore, the non-existence is within the existence, but they are separate modes of existence. In modern science, we only consider the *bhāva* or existence and hence we think that everything exists independent of other things. But we cannot explain how by knowing something is X, we also know that it is not-not-X. This double negation is simply taken for granted in logic, but never explained in terms of the real world. Thus, logic remains separated from the material reality. If we try to reconcile logic with the real world, then the negation of tiger is in the cow. And the reason for that negation is that the cow is created from a mammal by obfuscating some aspects of mammals which are seen in other mammals.

The basic mechanism of reasoning in modern thinking is combining, joining, or mingling the atomic parts to create complex wholes. But the basic mechanism of reasoning in Vedic philosophy is dividing, splitting, and obfuscating the whole into atomic parts. Thus, the Vedic system of reasoning or logic—which is called *upapatti*—is completely different from the modern system.

QUESTION

When knowledge is created by the combination of atomic axioms, then knowledge becomes infinite, because there is no limit to how much these axioms can be combined. Therefore, many people argue that there is nothing called 'knowledge' because it is the set of all the provable theorems. And since this set is infinite, we cannot call any individual claim as 'knowledge'. How does that change if knowledge is defined as the division of the whole?

3.2.37 (356)
अनेन सर्वगतत्वमायामशब्दादिभ्यः
anena sarvagatatvamāyāmaśabdādibhyaḥ

anena—by this; sarvagatatvam—the all-pervasiveness; āyāma—the extent or measure; śabdādibhyaḥ—known from scriptural statements, etc.

TRANSLATION

By this (method of dividing the whole into parts), (knowledge) is both all-pervading (i.e., everything is knowledge) as well as measurable (because it was produced by subdivision); this is the understanding of the scriptures.

COMMENTARY

If we define the idea of 'color' as the set that contains all the individual shades, then unless all the shades have been collected, the set is incomplete and hence the definition of 'color' is incomplete. If the number of shades is infinite, then the set called 'color' can never be completed. And unless it has been completed, nothing in the set can be called 'color'. Since the shades are infinite, there can never be a definition of color, and unless we obtain that definition, we won't be able to identify the shades as types of colors and include them in a set. This recursive dependence on the set and the member is solved only when we begin with meanings—i.e., we don't start with shades; we start with color. And we divide this color into parts—which can be as nuanced as we like. Even if the nuancing of the shades is left incomplete, the definition of color is still complete, and therefore even the coarse-grained shades can be considered colors.

Similarly, if we begin with knowledge, then everything produced by its subdivision is also knowledge. We may or may not know the smallest possible particles, but that isn't considered incomplete knowledge, because the method of constructing the knowledge is top-down rather than bottom-up. Thus, for example, the knowledge that there is an apple—although we don't see the atoms of the apple—can't be called an illusion. It is still knowledge, although more details about the apple can be known. The absence of these details doesn't make the knowledge of an apple an illusion. Similarly, even though we can divide the apple into smaller and smaller parts, thereby constructing an infinite number of knowledge propositions, the knowledge of 'apple' remains finite. Thus, the infinite division of the apple doesn't make the knowledge of the whole impossible. Rather, both the apple, and its atomic constituents, can be known, and by this knowing they form separate kinds of knowledge.

Topic 8

QUESTION

If knowledge is created by reasoning, then what about the results of our actions? The creation of knowledge is an effect, and the creation of the results of actions are the consequences. Are consequences also created by logical inference? If not, we would have two processes for effects and consequences.

3.2.38 (357)

फलमतःउपपत्तेः

phalamataḥ upapatteḥ

phalam—fruits (of actions); ataḥ—thus; upapatteḥ—due to reasoning.

TRANSLATION

Therefore, the fruits (of actions) are created due to reasoning.

COMMENTARY

Modern science recognizes the existence of a reaction that is equal and opposite to the action; the reaction always acts upon the cause. However, this reaction is identical to the transfer of energy—if you push a cart, the cart appears to push back; but this backward pressure is equal to the energy transferred. Modern science calls this a 'reaction' rather than an 'effect' because the term 'effect' is reserved for the changes caused to other objects. Thus, for example, if you get tired after working, then, science will call that a 'reaction' rather than an 'effect'. But these distinctions are based on the premise that the external action is the reason for an action, while the 'reaction' is simply a side effect. This is often a false premise; for example, if someone lifts weight to build their body, the goal of lifting weights is to build the body, not to lift the weights themselves. Therefore, to call the outcome of a stronger body a 'reaction' to weightlifting is somewhat counterintuitive. The stronger body should rather be called an effect, and the changes to the lifted weights should be considered a 'reaction'. In fact, it might be better to just call both these 'effects' produced by a transfer of energy, rather than calling one an 'effect' and the other a 'reaction'. Factually, both 'effect' and 'reaction' are created simultaneously and on different objects.

Once we set aside these 'reactions' as effects, then we can speak about consequences, which come in three varieties. First, every action leaves an imprint or memory in the actor; the collection of all these imprints is called *chitta*. Second, every action forms a new habit or destroys an existing habit; so, if you have done something once, it is more likely that you will perform that action again, and if that action was against your previously formed habits, then, it might alter the earlier habits; the collection of all the habits is called 'nature' or *guna* as it conditions us to behave in different ways. Third, all actions produce a moral consequence based on a person's role, duty, or responsibility. Note how each of these consequences hinges upon the fact that the actor is a conscious person. There would be no need for a memory imprint if the person wasn't conscious. Similarly, habits can be associated only with conscious persons. Finally, moral consequences are possible only when the actor has a choice and free will.

The habits, imprints, and consequences are different from the 'effect' and 'reaction', which can be described physically. These are described as meanings. The imprints are cognitive meanings or what we consider true and false, the habits are what we find good or bad, and the moral consequences are based on the judgments of right and wrong. Thus, the consequences must be distinguished from the physical 'effects' and 'reactions' as they are a causality based on meanings. When reasoning follows physical causality, then there are only effects from causes. But in semantic causality, there are consequences too. So, the creation of consequences is an intrinsic part of semantic reasoning.

Scientists have thought about perpetual motion machines—those which produce an endless cycle of cause and effect. However, if the causation only involves causes and effects, then such perpetual motion is impossible A self-perpetuating cycle of causation is produced due to consequences. Every consequence of an action becomes the seed for a new cause. The evolution of a soul through various bodies is one such self-perpetuating cycle and ending this self-perpetuating cycle of causation is the primary goal of liberation. The cycle can come to an end when consequences are not created. Thus, karma-yoga for instance focuses in the cessation of karma, dhyāna-yoga focuses on the cessation of all imprints on the chitta, and jñāna-yoga aims at the cessation of all habits. Each of these three forms of yoga take a soul to liberation. The process of bhakti-yoga, however, encourages the formation of divine impressions and habits, and when actions are performed due to love of God, there are no consequences. Thus, bhakti-yoga doesn't aim for liberation from activity, perception, and the body. It rather encourages this cycle arising out of the recollection of the Lord in the chitta, and the desires emanating from one's spiritual guna or qualities. This cycle is still considered liberation because there is no effect of karma.

QUESTION

If knowledge is created by reasoning, and the scriptures are considered knowledge, then does it follow that the scriptures are created logically?

3.2.39 (358)

श्रुतत्वाच्च

śrutatvācca

śrutatvāt—that which emerges from scriptures; ca—also.

TRANSLATION

That which emerges from scriptures too (utilizes logical reasoning).

COMMENTARY

One of the contentions of Mīmāṃsā philosophy is that the Vedic scriptures are logically necessary—like mathematical theorems derived from axioms. Many Mīmāṃsā philosophers believed that it wasn't God who spoke the scriptures; rather, just as the world is created logically, similarly, the scriptures are also created logically. The sages who codified these scriptures weren't, therefore, following the word of God (and some of them claimed that there is no God). It is rather that the scriptures are 'generated' by a logical process, and their meaning would be uncovered by the linguistic analysis of these texts. A parallel to this idea in modern times is the study of generative grammars which, given some alphabets and grammatical rules, can be used to produce sentences. The essence of knowledge was to obtain the generative rules. Since the world is symbolic meaning, therefore, it too can be generated using the same rules. And applying such generative rules would obtaining a result by our actions.

Thus, rituals were seen as generative actions, and the rules of these generations were obtained from the study of how the scriptures were generated. The theoretical study of scriptures led to the discovery of rules, and the practical use of rules in rituals and linguistic performances led to desired results.

This sūtra echoes the Mīmāṃsā contention that the Vedic scriptures are produced through a generative process. As we have discussed before, the world exists as a tree, which is generated from the root by the embedding of the three modes within each other. Knowledge is similarly also a tree, and it has been generated from the same root. In the previous sūtras, this generative process was described as logic, although not the logic of modern thinking because this logic has effects and consequences. This means that if we knew the generative process, then all the Vedic texts that were lost over time could be recreated. Any books that potentially have been modified can be corrected. And the truth of these books follows necessarily from the universality of the generative process. This is a purely linguistic method of confirming the truth of scriptures.

QUESTION

You said that knowledge is created logically, and then you said the Vedic scriptures are also generated logically. But these scriptures also prescribe the duties for the different classes of people. If the scriptures are logically necessary, does it mean that the social duties are also necessary in this way? Moral codes are generally considered normative rules—i.e., created as norms by society—rather than logically and rationally provable descriptive rules. But you seem to be saying that even the moral codes are logically necessary.

3.2.40 (359)

धर्मं जैमनिःअत एव

dharmaṃ jaiminiḥ ata eva

dharmaṃ—the duties; jaiminiḥ—(sage) Jaimini; ata eva—in the same way.

TRANSLATION

The sage Jaimini opines that the duties (are necessary) in the same way.

COMMENTARY

This and the previous sūtras are connected as the explanation of scriptures, and the explanation of duties described in the scriptures. Jaimini, as we have seen, was the preeminent Mīmāṃsā philosopher. His opinion is cited in this regard as a follow-up to the previous sūtra by stating that the *dharma* is not a societal construct. The organization of society, the roles and duties of people in it, and the economic and political mechanisms are all logically necessary. In other words, there is no difference between natural laws and social laws. The laws of moral consequences and duties are therefore also natural laws.

The government in a country, for instance, has a head of state, a judiciary, a military etc. But these functions can be separated into different roles or combined into a single role. The duties of a role depend on whether these functions have been combined or separated. Hence, right and wrong is contextual, but not arbitrary. It can change with time, but it exists objectively at present. Each institutional structure brings an objective right and wrong, although we may not understand that objective duty, and misdemeanors lead to karma.

QUESTION

Earlier it was said that Bādarāyana is the author of Vedas. Now you are stating that these scriptures are produced through a process

100

of logical derivation. How can we reconcile these two apparently contradictory contentions?

3.2.41 (360)
पूर्वं तु बादरायणःहेतुव्यपदेशात्
pūrvaṃ tu bādarāyaṇaḥ hetuvyapadeśāt

pūrvam—earlier; tu—but; bādarāyaṇaḥ—Bādarāyana; hetu-vyapadeśāt—on account of being declared to be the cause (of the scriptures).

TRANSLATION

Earlier it was said that Bādarāyana is declared the cause of Vedas, but (we also recognize the logically necessary status of the Vedic scriptures).

COMMENTARY

This sūtra states that there is no conflict in stating that the scriptures are logically necessary and that Bādarāyana is their author. Just like a human can prove mathematical theorems, similarly, Bādarāyana can be called the author of scriptures. However, the fact that a human proves a mathematical theorem doesn't make the truth of the theorem subject to that person's opinions. Thus, we speak about Pythagoras' theorem, because Pythagoras proved it. However, there is no contradiction in saying that Pythagoras is the author of the theorem and that the theorem is logically necessary. The fact is that someone else could have proved the same theorem, and it would be considered equally true.

This claim seems to contradict the Mīmāṃsā claim in which the scriptures are treated as a natural phenomenon and are hence considered authorless. But any such claim by Mīmāṃsā is rejected here. The knowledge is indeed necessary and independent of authors. However, knowledge can be codified into texts by an enlightened author. Therefore, Bādarāyana is said to be the Lord's empowered incarnation who codified the Vedas about 5000 years ago. However, the Vedas are also said to be spoken by Brahma, and the knowledge is said to be imparted by the Lord to Brahma. Thus, three contradictory doctrines of the origination of the scriptures—namely, divine origination, logical necessity, and historical authorship—are simultaneously accepted as being true.

This flies in the face of modern contentions that if scriptures are of divine origin, then no human could have written them. Or, that the truths of science are logically necessary and hence their existence contradicts divine authorship. The Lord is the source of the scriptures, but His process of creation is logical. The same logical process can also be used by humans. If the same process is followed, then humans can author scriptures on par with the Lord. Their historical appearance doesn't make them human creations, just like the historical appearance of Pythagoras doesn't make his theorem a human creation.

There is a lesson here for religions that claim divine origination, such as the revelation by an angel to an apostle, followed by a historical human authorship of revelations or conversations. The lesson is that the logical necessity associated with the claims in revelation or authorship cannot be rejected. When historical accuracies and divine revelations are challenged, it is not necessary to prove them. It is also possible to prove the logical necessity of the claims.

SECTION 3

Topic 1

QUESTION

Since Vedānta Sūtra is the conclusion of all Vedic knowledge, are the statements of Vedānta Sūtra also produced by the process of logical reasoning?

3.3.1 (361)

सर्ववेदान्तप्रत्ययम् चोदनाद्यवशेषात्

sarvavedāntapratyayam codanādyaviśeṣāt

sarva-vedānta-pratyayam—all Vedānta conclusions; codanādi—are rules etc.; aviśeṣāt—from the undifferentiated (or one without distinctions).

TRANSLATION

All Vedānta conclusions (subsidiary claims—*pratyaya*) are rules etc. produced from the undifferentiated (axiom—that which is without distinctions).

COMMENTARY

When reasoning combines axioms to produce a conclusion, then it requires more than one axiom. If these axioms were considered the primitive reality that precedes the manifested world, then this reality will have to be multiple axioms. However, when reasoning divides the axiom into parts, then it requires only one axiom, and this primitive reality is the Absolute Truth. This sūtra confirms that the primitive reality is the undifferentiated existence from which many kinds of differentiations are produced by a logical process. Earlier it has been said that Vedic texts, the duties and roles, and the cycle of self-propelled change are all produced by rules. This sūtra now extends this conclusion to the Vedānta Sūtra itself, noting that this text is *nyāya-prasthāna* or a logical treatise.

QUESTION

If all the texts are produced due to logical progression, then why are all the texts different? Shouldn't all these texts be uniform in their progression?

3.3.2 (362)
भेदान्नेति चेत् न एकस्यामपि
bhedānneti cet na ekasyāmapi

bhedāt—due to difference na—not; iti cet—if it be said; na—not so; ekasyāmapi—even in the same (text).

TRANSLATION

If it is said that (the texts) should not be different (due to logical progression) (then we say) not so (because) the one is also (the source of many).

COMMENTARY

A confusion arises due to the previous sūtra, where all texts—i.e., śrutī, smriti, and nyāya—are designated as logical treatises. These texts obviously follow different patterns, often have different descriptions, and don't seem to follow the same pattern in the Vedānta Sūtra. Then how can we call all of them logical progressions, when there are obvious differences between them?

The short answer is that there are many meanings of 'logical progression'. For instance, the Bhagavad-Gita describes a progression from jñāna-yoga to aṣṭānga-yoga, to karma-yoga to bhakti-yoga. A student approached a teacher and obtained knowledge—the method of jñāna-yoga. Then the student tried to realize this knowledge by meditation—the method of dhyāna-yoga. As portions of this truth were realized in meditation, one's life was transformed, and the realization had effects on all day-to-day activities—the method of karma-yoga. Finally, the nature of the self and its purpose of existence was realized—the method of bhakti-yoga. Therefore, there was a progression in the process, and the description in the Bhagavad-Gita reflects it; it is logical, although this 'logic' is based on ever-deepening nature of the soul's conditioning and the methods prescribed for the purification or removal of this conditioning.

Similarly, a pattern in the Purāṇa is the discussion of material nature, followed by the problem of birth, death, and suffering, the process by which liberation is attained, and the nature of the liberated state. The Tantra, similarly, discuss the nature of reality, followed by processes of practice that lead to liberation, and finally the result of these processes. The four Vedas follow a template in which reality is described in the Rig Veda, the rituals for attaining this reality are noted in the Yajur Veda, the deities to be worshipped through this ritual are described in the Sama Veda, and the methods of performing the rituals are present in the Atharva Veda. The Itihāsa follow a different template in which a hero is born among greatness, falls from grace, struggles during this fall, and then reclaims the position of greatness due to this struggle. The greatness at the beginning and the end might be different in many cases. In all these cases, an overview of the text may be provided in the beginning, along with the processes and the nature of reality in a summarized form, like an author captures the overview of the text in a preface or an introduction. However, this summary is succinct and is followed by a detailed recapitulation later.

The template for Vedānta Sūtra is quite different. It is a logical treatise because it follows the question-and-answer dialectical pattern of a debate, learning, and arriving at the complete knowledge. This template also exists in the Purāṇa, Tantra, and the Upaniṣad as teacher-student conversations, but it is always a subsidiary pattern within the overall pattern of heroic transformation or the ordinary person who is not born a hero although takes the heroic path of spiritual practice anyway. The Vedānta Sūtra is unique in solely adhering to the dialectical pattern of logical process. However, every other scripture is also considered a logical treatise even though it follows different kinds of logical patterns. The point is that all Vedic scriptures follow a logical template, although the nature of these templates is different across different scriptures.

The simplest meaning of logical progression is a heroic storyline; another meaning is the journey of a non-hero who becomes a hero by undertaking the process of spiritual life, undergoes the tribulations of the process, and finally attains the perfection of life. Yet another meaning is the dialectical method of question and answer. And then there is a logical progression from the description of truth, followed by the righteous practices that result in the attainment of this reality, and the good that comes from its attainment. Sometimes, the righteous practices or dharma can be divided into an abstract description, followed by the details of the deities to be worshipped and their various qualities, followed by the detailed methods of performing the ritual. Thus, by 'logical treatise' we mean these templates of logical progression. There are many such templates, and all these templates can be considered 'logical progression'.

When the dialectics is emphasized, then the text is called nyāya-prasthāna. When the progression through a heroic cycle is emphasized, then the texts are called smriti. When the ordinary person becomes the hero through the practice of spiritual life, then the process is called śrutī. Thus, the Vedic texts are classified into three categories as śrutī, smriti, and nyāya. They all follow a logical progression, although, the patterns of this progression are quite different. Sometimes these templates are combined, although one template remains dominant. Therefore, 'logic' here is a general description of textual templates.

Once we note the existence of such varied templates, then we can also note that all these templates exemplify the question-and-answer template. The heroic character, for instance, is the premise; his fall from grace is the question; and the recovery into a state of greatness is the new conclusion. Similarly, the non-hero entangled in the material world can be the premise; following this, the process of becoming a hero is the question; and finally, the attainment of greatness is the new conclusion. Likewise, the description of reality is the premise; the method of attaining this reality is the question; and the results obtained by this attainment are the new conclusion. The elucidation of reality, though a succession of questions and answers, is yet another illustration of this pattern.

The previous sūtra said that the Vedānta Sūtra follows a logical pattern, and we have described this as the premise-problem-answer pattern. This sūtra now states that all other scriptures are only variations of this single pattern. In this pattern, we begin with a premise, we are then led to a question, problem, or contradiction, and the solution of this question, problem, or contradiction is a new premise. The sequence of premise-problem-answer forms a tripartite cycle. This cycle can be seen in the story of a hero. For example, their heroic status is the premise, the heroism being tested by difficulties is the question, and the reestablishment of the heroic status is the new conclusion. The journey of a non-hero can be a longer cycle, because accepting the premise that someone is a non-hero—e.g., entangled in the material world—can be long-drawn; similarly, the discovery of the processes by which the non-hero can become a hero can be even longer; finally, the implementation of these processes through practices can also be a long-drawn endeavor. Within this cycle, one might often go back to the question of whether he or she is a non-hero, what must be done to solve the problem, and how expediently must that method be implemented.

Some cycles—that involve short-term results, such as the results produced through a ritual—can be shorter. And the cycle of question-and-answer to attain knowledge is the shortest. Since this sūtra states that all these are variations of the same basic method of logical progression, we must understand that variety is produced by nesting of the shorter cycles inside the longer cycle. Thus, when a hero falls from grace, he might start learning the method of restoration of this greatness, and this process of learning can itself form a smaller cycle. Likewise, the implementation of this process to restore greatness can be another cycle. This sūtra claims that even the śrutī and smriti are outcomes of applying the same type of premise-question-answer cycle, although the pattern is not as obvious as in the case of Vedānta Sūtra. Therefore, the various scriptures are all produced logically, employing a common pattern of logical progression.

QUESTION

Even if we say that all these scriptures are logically necessary, and produced by the same method of logical progression, what is the need for so many scriptures? I can understand the necessity for Vedānta as the conclusion of all knowledge. But what about the many other scriptures which prescribe practices for the material world? Isn't the presence of so many scriptures a source of confusion, as they provide different instructions that seem conflicting?

3.3.3 (363)

सूवाध्यायसुय तथात्वेन हि सिमाचारेऽधिकीराच्च सववच्च तन्नयिमः

**svādhyāyasya tathātvena hi samācāre'dhikārācca savavacca
tanniyamaḥ**

svādhyāya—practice or the regular study; asya—of this (the scriptures); tathātvena—in accurate form, or just as they are, without concoction; iti—because; samācāre—in the action according to instruction; adhikārāt—due to qualification; ca—and; savavat—like liberated; ca—and; tanniyamaḥ—those rules.

TRANSLATION

The practice or regular study of these (scriptures) which is provided in accurate form (i.e., the scriptures are precise) (is suggested) because in the action according to the instruction (given in the scripture), due to the proper qualification, one becomes liberated (from material existence) and (from) those rules (of duty which have to be followed by everyone non-liberated).

COMMENTARY

When we say that scriptures are logically necessary, we create a problem—it seems that logical necessity implies that all scriptural injunctions are universally true. This universal truth would imply that the scriptural injunctions would apply even when one is liberated or transcendent to material nature. This notion of logical necessity is derived from the belief that whatever is logically true is true in all possible worlds. This sūtra, however, distinguishes between the injunctions of this world, and those that are transcendent to the world by saying that by following many injunctions one becomes free of these injunctions. There are certain scriptural injunctions whose purpose is to take a person to liberation whereupon the rules and regulations cease to be applicable. There are, however, other statements which apply even beyond the material world, which were noted in the previous sūtra where Vedānta was described as transcendental knowledge. The contention is that we must not equate the statements applicable to the material world with those that are transcendent. Instructions about the material world are like a ladder used to attain liberation. The ladder is useless after that. However, the statements about the transcendent reality are not a ladder, because they remain true and important forever.

QUESTION

If these diverse scriptures are not eternally relevant, then how can they be considered to lead one to eternal truth? Isn't there a fundamental contradiction between saying that some instructions are only contextually applicable, and yet following them leads one to the understanding of the universal truth?

3.3.4 (364)
दर्शयति च
darśayati ca

darśayati—sees (the eternal truth through all scriptures); ca—also.

TRANSLATION

(One can) also see (the eternal truth through the contextual statements).

COMMENTARY

All relative truths are produced by dividing the Absolute Truth. When they are so divided, the Absolute Truth also enters the relative truths in three ways. First, the Absolute Truth is present in the relative truth as the idea from which the relative truths are produced. For example, when you see a cow, you also see a mammal, an animal, and a living entity. Second, the Absolute Truth is present in each relative truth as the purpose of the relative truths' existence. The existence of diversity is not due to chance and it is not purposeless. Third, the Absolute Truth controls the working of the relative truths. The interaction of one relative truth with another is caused by the will of the Absolute Truth.

In modern science, we see one out of the three types of presences. For example, the laws of physics are applicable to diverse phenomena. We still cannot say that these phenomena manifested from a common source and that each phenomenon has a shared purpose—the other two kinds of innate presences. Nevertheless, by the applicability of natural laws to a wide range of phenomena, we say that the contextual truths also reveal the universal truth.

This is truer of the Absolute Truth where apart from control, the Absolute Truth is also present in everything as their purpose and the original concept. However, to the extent that everyone may not see how the Absolute Truth controls everything, is the source of everything, and is the purpose of everything, one might not see this innate presence. Then, it seems that the Absolute Truth must be different from all the relative truths. Such a claim is rejected here. The relative truths are not equated to the Absolute Truth, but the Absolute Truth can be known from the relative truths. Thus, for instance, a bicycle is not Newton's laws of motion, but Newton's laws of motion are innate in the bicycle. This sūtra similarly says that the Absolute Truth is present in everything, however, a deeper investigation may be needed to understand this presence.

Topic 2

QUESTION

So, you are saying that all these contextual methods of religious practice are also valid means for attaining the transcendental state beyond matter?

3.3.5 (365)
उपसंहारोऽर्थाभेदाद्वविधिशेषवत्समाने च

upasaṃhāro'rthābhedādvidhiśeṣavatsamāne ca

upasaṃhāraḥ—the destruction of that which is secondary; arthābhedāt—due to the difference in the meaning; vidhiśeṣavat—like the subsidiary rites of a main sacrifice; samāne ca—are also merged (into the main sacrifice).

TRANSLATION

When all that is secondary (in a religion) is destroyed due to the differences of meaning or purpose (across these religions being destroyed), just like the subsidiary rites (of a main sacrifice) are also merged into the main sacrifice.

COMMENTARY

The basic paradigm for material life is selfishness, and the basic paradigm for spirituality is sacrifice. The sacrifice is also called a *yajñá*, and it has three components—*agni, soma,* and *vāyu*. The soma represents our pleasure, the agni is the purpose for which this pleasure is sacrificed, and vāyu is the process of sacrifice. Thus, yajñá means sacrifice of our pleasure (soma) for a higher purpose (agni) through a legitimate process (vāyu). In human life, we make many kinds of sacrifices—for our parents, children, community, society, and nation. These are also called yajñá, but they are not the supreme yajñá. The ultimate yajñá is when our happiness is sacrificed for the Lord. Everything has emanated from the Lord, and in a yajñá, those same things are put back into the Lord and used for His pleasure. A person worshipping a river, for example, takes the water of river and pours it back into the river, while chanting a mantra.

This idea is compared to the performance of elaborate yajñá in the Vedic system. There is a main yajñá which is performed at the beginning and at the end. Then there are also subsidiary yajñá which are performed in parallel to the main yajñá. When the subsidiary yajñá end, then the main yajñá is completed. In the same way, there are many duties and regulations which are subsidiary processes of the main process—i.e., the attainment of the Absolute Truth. If this main process is misunderstood, then the subsidiary processes seem contradictory. But if the main sacrifice is understood, then the other sacrifices are only seen as the subsidiary processes used in the service of the main sacrifice. This sūtra indicates that one must keep the main sacrifice—devotion to the Lord—as the primary sacrifice even while performing the subsidiary sacrifices.

Topic 3

QUESTION

However, if we say that there are many spiritual paths, then people

believe that the practice of each path is itself the goal, and they get tied to the rules and regulations of that path and may sometimes fail to see the goal beyond the rules and regulations. How should one avoid incurring this kind of mistake?

3.3.6 (366)

अन्यथात्वं शब्दादिति चेत् न अवशेषात्

anyathātvaṁ śabdāditi cet na aviśeṣāt

anyathātvaṁ—there are other injunctions; śabdāt—from the scriptures; iti cet—if it be said; na—not so; aviśeṣāt—due to non-difference (of purpose).

TRANSLATION

If it is said that there are other injunctions from the scriptures, (then we say) not so, because of the non-difference (of the purpose in these injunctions).

COMMENTARY

The use of the term *aviśeṣāt* or non-difference is indicative of the whole-part relationship. The part is not separable from the whole, and yet, the part is not equal to the whole. Furthermore, the whole is always present in the part. Since the whole is present in the part, the parts cannot be whimsically rejected. Since the parts are not equal to the whole, the parts cannot be whimsically accepted. Thus, both blind acceptance and blind rejection are frowned upon.

If you want to travel to a destination, you might first walk to your car, then drive the car, then take a flight, then take a taxi, and finally walk to the destination. For each method of fulfilling the purpose—i.e., reaching the destination—you might follow different rules. For example, you must drive according to the rules of the road; you must pay for the flight and follow the regulations of sitting in an airplane; you pay the person who drives your taxi; etc. So, it seems like we are following different rules and regulations in each case. However, the ultimate regulation is that you must reach your destination. If you missed a flight, you could catch a bus or a train. A different set of rules may then apply, but those differences are immaterial because the main regulation of reaching the destination must be fulfilled. In the same way, the injunctions of scriptures are not false, but they are like the rules of driving on the road, flying in a commercial flight, or catching a taxi. The rules are not optional, but the method is itself optional. For instance, you might not use a flight; you can as well catch a train or a bus. However, if you use a flight (or a train or a bus) then you must follow the rules. Therefore, it is said that rules of day-to-day activity are necessary. But those day-to-day activities are themselves not necessary if the purpose of performing those activities is achieved in an alternative manner.

Each of the rules exists to achieve a purpose. The purpose of the rules of the road is that people must be safe. The purpose of paying a taxi driver is that the driver can continue driving. The trains must run on time so that people can reach their destination on time. But what is achieved by everyone being safe, the taxis running, or reaching the destination on time? All such rules are partially justifiable, however, the Absolute Truth justifies them completely. If the complete justification did not exist, then the partial justification would also not exist. The ultimate justification manifests into partial justifications, which then become the causes of the rules, which then seem diversified prescriptions. However, if we seek the justification underlying a justification, we will find that they are not self-justified—i.e., they are not self-evident principles. The Absolute Truth as the source of all happiness is hence the self-justified principle.

In the same way, the processes of karma-yoga, dhyāna-yoga, jñāna-yoga, and bhakti-yoga have different rules. The various types of yajñá also have different rules. These rules are not optional—if you are following that process. However, it is not necessary to follow any of these processes. These processes have a common purpose—namely, attaining devotion to the Lord. When the processes are followed, then their rules are justified by the goal to be attained—namely, devotion to the Lord. When the processes are not followed—because another process is more suitable for the goal—then the neglect of a process is also justified by the same principle, namely, devotion to the Lord. Therefore, the purpose justifies the rules when a process is followed, it justifies the selection of a process, and it justifies why any process even exists. As the innate justification of processes and rules, the purpose is non-different from the processes and rules—i.e., it is not identical, and yet not totally separable.

QUESTION

If we say that all the paths and injunctions have the same purpose, then doesn't it mean that all the paths will lead to the same destination and therefore no path can be considered superior or inferior to any of the other paths?

3.3.7 (367)

न वा प्रकरणभेदात् परोवरीयस्त्वादवित्

na vā prakaraṇabhedāt parovarīyastvādivat

na vā—rather not; prakaraṇa-bhedāt—on account of the difference in the context; parovarīyas—the greatest good; tvādivat—that which is like the source of everything (that has been manifest).

TRANSLATION

(We) rather not (claim that all the paths are equivalent) because of the difference in the activities and the context (of application). However, they are all manifest as diversities from the (purpose of delivering the) greatest good.

COMMENTARY

After rejecting the blind acceptance and blind rejection of all the paths, this sūtra clarifies that everything is not always good. They are all manifest from the purpose of delivering the greatest good, but they deliver that goodness depending on the context. This can be understood by comparing 'good' to 'health'. We say that health is good, but since everyone is diseased in a different way, health must be achieved in different ways. One suffering from cold must eat hot things to nullify the effects of cold. And one suffering from heat, must eat cool things to nullify the effects of heat. They are both aiming for health, but the methods of achieving this health depend on the illness that prevents health. A blind acceptance of these injunctions would mean that even a person suffering from heat would be given hot things, or one suffering from cold would be given cold things. Likewise, a blind rejection of the injunctions would mean that a person suffering from cold would not be given hot things, and a person suffering from heat would not be allowed cold things. Due to the contextuality, both blind acceptance and blind rejection are frowned upon. Furthermore, one must understand the purpose—e.g., the goal of health—to apply the contextual injunctions. Different injunctions apply to achieve the same goal in varied contexts.

Thus, the rituals, duties, roles, responsibilities, and practices are not the ends in themselves. They are methods to attain a goal, and while the goal remains unchanged, the methods can change, depending on the type of hurdle to be crossed before attaining the goal. Thus, marriage laws, the laws of property inheritance, the job duties of employment, etc. are highly contextual. For certain places, times, roles, and people, these injunctions are useful. But they are not universal truths. Hence, we can distinguish between the contextuality of ordinary religions and the final goal—i.e., the love of God—which they are expected to deliver. If the rules of social behavior are universalized, then contradictions between the different religions are created. But if we see their purpose—to elevate a different kind of person to the point of devotion to the Lord—then their unity is perceived. So, unity exists within the diversity as its purpose.

If you live next to a destination, then you can just walk to the destination. If you are little farther away, then you might take a taxi. If you are even farther away, you might use a train, followed by a taxi, followed by walking. And if you are very far, then you might use a flight before the other means of transport. Therefore, we cannot say that everyone must use a flight, let alone the same flight. Everyone need not use a train, let alone the same train. We might use different flights or no flights at all. We might use different trains, or no train at all. Thus, all these methods are optional. They are all created so that we can reach a destination, but the method may or may not be used by everyone.

QUESTION

The contextual application of injunctions makes the problem very hard, because we don't know which context requires which injunction. How can one know what is the right injunction to be applied in which specific context?

3.3.8 (368)

संज्ञातश्चेत् तदुक्तम् अस्ति तु तदपि

saṃjñātaścet taduktam asti tu tadapi

saṃjñātaḥ—by a complete and balanced knowledge; cet—if; tat—that; uktam—is said; asti—it is; tu—but; tat—that; api—even.

TRANSLATION

By a complete and balanced knowledge (of the context and the paths) if one says that (this path is the best), then it is (the path); but, even that (path) (must achieve the goal, and should not be accepted based on blind faith).

COMMENTARY

As the contextual application of injunctions is difficult, this sūtra advises two things. First, we must have a full understanding of the context, and the various possible paths. Without this understanding, one would be limited by their own knowledge, and prescribe only what they are familiar with, even though that path is not suitable for the present context. Second, even as one chooses this path, one must not abandon the sight of the goal. If the path is not achieving the goal, then one must reevaluate the path, and pick the path that will reach the goal. Therefore, even if one makes a mistake in selecting a path, continuous evaluation of the progress made because of following some injunctions cannot be abandoned. The paths can be changed provided some contextual injunction is not working appropriately to attain the goal. By employing these two methods—i.e., a full understanding of the context and the paths, and continually revising the path if it is not helping achieve the goal—one can find the contextually appropriate path that will attain the desired purpose.

Topic 4

QUESTION

But the problem of progress is itself very nebulous. How can one know that they are progressing in spiritual life if things keep changing all the time? Sometimes we think we have progressed, and at other times we think we haven't. So, how can a person know that there is indeed progress in life?

3.3.9 (369)

वयाप्तेश्च समञ्जसम्

vyāpteśca samañjasam

vyāpteḥ—the pervasiveness; ca—and; samañjasam—without conflict.

TRANSLATION

(By) the pervasiveness and overcoming the conflicts (in experience).

COMMENTARY

The problem of progress often comes up in science—how do we know that the newest theories of reality are advancing our understanding of nature? How do we know that science is progressing? The answer to that question is two-fold: consistency and completeness. Completeness means that the same theory can be applied to ever-increasing number of phenomena. Consistency means that as we try to explain a greater number of phenomena, our explanations are not mutually contradictory. Ultimately, both criteria point toward the unification of science. Consistency forces us to reconcile contradictory theories. And the result of this reconciliation is that a single theory explains everything. This means that we cannot blindly reconcile contradictory theories if the combined theory explains less than what the diversified theories explained earlier.

The same criteria are listed here for spiritual progress. In the beginning, we apply different injunctions for different problems, and these injunctions temporarily solve those different problems. But as one progresses, one uses the same injunction for every problem, and that injunction must solve all the problems. Therefore, if one is applying different injunctions in different situations, one must know that they haven't progressed. Only when the same injunction is being applied in all the contexts, can we say that we have indeed advanced.

A neophyte devotee, for instance, relies on many different injunctions for controlling the body, the mind, the intellect, the ego, and morality. They might practice regulations for a healthy living, exercise, and diet control. They might practice meditation to control the mind. They may read many books to train the intellect. They may practice methods of humility to control the ego. And they may follow the societal rules to remain moral. But as one progresses in devotion, there is only one injunction necessary—always remember the Lord, and never forget Him. To attain this goal, one engages in activities that increase the remembrance of the Lord and avoids those things that lead to forgetfulness of the Lord. Both sides of the requirement must be met because if one only tries to avoid those things that lead to forgetfulness, then by the rejection of all these activities one would be left with nothing. On the other hand, if one focuses on the engagement in the activities that lead to increased remembrance but doesn't give up the activities that lead to forgetfulness, then the effort of increasing the remembrance doesn't yield the desired results due to continual forgetfulness.

Every other rule pertaining to the body, the mind, the intellect, the ego, and morality is replaced by a single rule—always remember the Lord, and never forget Him. This rule is the universal theory that produces the benefits of the separate rules of body, mind, intellect, ego, and moral control. Thus, unification in our rules and theories is considered scientific progress as it delivers a greater amount of consistency and completeness: (1) consistency because the rules of the body aren't conflicting with the rules of the mind, etc. and (2) completeness because the same rule results in control of both the mind and the body.

In our day-to-day life we encounter many difficult situations. These difficulties hinder the practice of our chosen process. However, if one path is impossible, or very hard, we can choose another path—provided it leads to the same goal. Thus, every crisis can be converted into an opportunity—by changing the path. The scriptures state that devotion to the Lord can never be hindered in any situation. This means that every crisis also presents an opportunity, and difficulties are impetuses for us to choose a different path, but the devotion to the Lord is a goal that cannot be hindered by any problem.

Topic 5

QUESTION

Does this mean that one who is advanced in spiritual life has no need for the contextual rules and injunctions? That they can follow only the injunction that works in all these diverse contexts, and ignore the contextual rules?

3.3.10 (370)
सर्वाभेदादन्यत्रेमे
sarvābhedādanyatreme

sarvābhedāt—due to non-difference in all things; anyatra—in all the other places; ime—these (same rules and injunctions become applicable).

TRANSLATION

Due to the non-difference of all things (i.e., everything having the same purpose), in all the other places (situations) these (same rules and injunctions can be applied, and hence they are now treated as the universal truths).

COMMENTARY

Today we accept that laws of nature apply to all phenomena, but we do not accept that nature has a common purpose. Therefore, there is no guiding principle for choices. Everyone chooses based on their own interests. If choice is self-interested, then society cannot exist unless self-interest is subordinated to some laws that maximize collective interest. Since the laws that subordinate self-interest to collective interest are mostly man-made, therefore, we don't see the consequences of manipulating the laws. The rich and powerful can change the laws for their benefit, and their connivance would not affect them. In short, choices have consequences for the poor and destitute, but not for the rich and powerful. By replacing a divine purpose with self-interest, and then replacing morality with man-made laws, society becomes a slave to the rich and powerful. People could recognize God, and their choices would then be subordinated to this purpose and they would then be servants of God. But the rebellion in the soul against the service of God makes him the servant of ordinary people.

However, there is an alternative—the choices are free, and yet God is the universal governing principle for all 'good' choices. When this principle is discarded, only 'bad' choices are made. The universal governing principle for choices is also a universal law—i.e., it can be applied to all situations. This sūtra states that the satisfaction of the universal purpose is the governing law for all choices; this law replaces all contextually right laws. The universal truth is that essence which is visible in all phenomena. And the universal good is the person to be satisfied through all the phenomena. However, there is also contextuality of the right—the duties, or what needs to be done in a context (i.e., the specific actions or duties)—as they are not universally determined. Therefore, there is universal truth, universal good, and contextual right. The solution to this contextual right is obtained when we subordinate it to the universal good.

The previous sūtras stated that contextual injunctions should neither be accepted nor rejected blindly, which raises the question about how contextual choices must be made. The answer to that question was that the decision of right and wrong is dependent upon whether the goodness of purpose is achieved. Goodness was then defined as the universal guiding principle for choices. However, once this universality is obtained, then contextuality can be ignored.

Thus, the conversation has moved from universal truth, to contextual rightness, to universal good (rejecting contextual rightness). The arguments underlying this progress are complex, but the conclusion is quite simple—the Lord is the Supreme Truth and the Supreme Good. If we keep these two in mind, then the Supreme Right is automatically achieved, and we don't have to worry about what is right or wrong separately in each context. That eliminates the problem of diverse scriptures giving us diverse instructions for different contexts. The rejection of these contextual instructions is not absolute—they are useful because they take us to the point where the Supreme Truth is equated to the Supreme Good—i.e., the Absolute Truth is recognized as a *person*. If this goal is achieved, then it supersedes the contextual rightness. If this goal is not being achieved, then the purpose of contextual injunctions is unsatisfied. Therefore, the contextual injunctions are to take a person to the point of accepting the Supreme Lord as the Supreme Good; after that, they are unnecessary.

Topic 6

QUESTION

People follow contextual rules of right and wrong, as it does them good—i.e., right action brings happiness, and wrong action brings unhappiness. You are saying that these right and wrong actions can be subordinated to the satisfaction of the Supreme Person. But that doesn't address the fundamental question about how each person becomes individually happy by their choices. Unless the question of individual happiness is addressed, isn't the doctrine of universal truth and universal good ultimately pointless for an individual?

3.3.11 (371)
आनन्दादयःप्रधानस्य
ānandādayaḥ pradhānasya

ānandādayaḥ—happiness etc.; pradhānasya—is the main goal.

TRANSLATION

The happiness (of each person) is the main goal.

COMMENTARY

In previous sūtras, we discussed the questions of universal truth, contextual right, and individual good. Since the contextual rightness presented grave problems—How do we decide what to do and when? —a guiding principle of universal goodness as proposed as the replacement for contextual right. However, now the principle of universal goodness conflicts with individual goodness: If we are always trying to satisfy the Supreme Person, then what about our happiness? Remember that the earlier criterion for deciding 'good' and 'bad' choices was their outcomes for the self—good is that which makes *us* happy, and bad is that which makes *us* unhappy. The new principle—of making God happy—may address the problem of contextual rightness, but does it address the question of individual happiness? This sūtra says that it does. The replacement of contextual right by universal goodness is not to take away individual goodness. In short, universal good produces both contextual rightness and individual goodness. Therefore, the individual good—i.e., our self-interest—is in the satisfaction of the Supreme Person. Serving the Supreme Person is not contrary to the idea of individual good, as it is also satisfied in the process. Thus, we can continue upholding the ideas of universal truth, contextual right, and individual good, and the principle of universal good can be used to determine what is contextual right, which then also achieves individual good. The pursuit of universal good doesn't contradict individual good, so everyone can employ this principle to decide what is right action to obtain happiness.

Happiness is obtained by the fulfillment of a purpose. The soul has an innate purpose, but it can also create alternative purposes. When those alternatives are created, the purpose is not always fulfilled because the soul doesn't have the power to always fulfill the purpose, and that creates unhappiness. However, when the innate purpose is accepted, then the power for its fulfillment comes from the Lord, and by fulfilling the purpose the soul becomes happy. The difference is simply that the soul can always use the Lord's power to satisfy the Lord, but he cannot always use the Lord's power to satisfy himself.

QUESTION

If individual good is indirectly achieved through the universal good, then why do we reject the notion of individual good—i.e., selfish happiness?

3.3.12 (372)

पुरयिशरिस्तवाद्यपुराप्तःःउपचयापचयौ हि भेदे

priyaśirastvādyaprāptiḥ upacayāpacayau hi bhede

priyaśirastvādi—ultimate happiness etc. aprāptiḥ—is not obtained; upacaya—increase; apacaya—decrease; hi—because; bhede—due to difference.

TRANSLATION

Ultimate happiness (of each person) is not achieved (if we pursue individual happiness) because of the difference between increase and decrease (i.e., increasing one's happiness means decreasing someone else's happiness).

COMMENTARY

After subordinating individual good to the universal good, and then stating that individual good is achieved by the universal good, one can ask: If the individual good is anyway the guiding principle, then why not uphold it as a fundamental principle in itself? This sūtra answers: because if we pursue individual good, then increase in the happiness of one person entails the decrease in the happiness of another person. And if each person's happiness is alternately increasing and decreasing, then ultimate happiness is not achieved.

Thus, even though each person's happiness is the goal, this goal must be subordinated to the Supreme Person's happiness because only by subordinating individual happiness to the Supreme Person's happiness is everyone's happiness naturally achieved. Hence, individual and collective happiness are not contradictory, if individual happiness is subordinated to the happiness of the Lord. They are contradictory when individual happiness is placed above the Lord's happiness. The happiness of the Supreme Person is therefore the best self-interest of each person; the pursuit of individualistic and selfish happiness is contrary to the self-interest, as happiness and distress come alternately.

QUESTION

You are therefore saying that the happiness of the Supreme Person entails the happiness of all living entities? And, that by satisfying the Supreme Person, every other individual (including the self) is also satisfied in the process?

3.3.13 (373)
इतरे त्वर्थसामान्यात्
itare tvarthasāmānyāt

itare—other; tu—but; arthasāmānyāt—due to identity of purpose.

TRANSLATION

(The happiness of) others is but identical to the purpose (of the self).

COMMENTARY

Some atheists argue that the practice of religion is also selfish because it only aims at one's own happiness. In fact, since in this pursuit of selfish happiness one may reject some social duties, therefore, others may be forced to suffer. Thus, individual happiness remains contrary to the happiness of others. And since this contradiction in seen in the spiritual pursuits, therefore, there is no difference with the other selfish activities where self-interest is supreme.

This sūtra dissolves the contradiction between self-interest, other-interest, and supreme-interest. When service to the Supreme Person is adopted as the fundamental principle, then whoever serves the Lord makes everyone else happy because the Lord is the complete truth, and His happiness is the complete happiness. When the complete is satisfied, then all the parts are satisfied. Therefore, service to the Lord is the source of service and happiness of everyone else. Even if the person serving the Lord is satisfied by his actions, this pleasure is not contrary to the pleasure of others. The self- and other-interests are contradictory when the supreme-interest is ignored. When a common purpose is established—i.e., the Lord is the supreme purpose—then harmony between the purposes of all living entities is established and contradictions between the diverse purposes of the different living entities are naturally dissolved.

The service to the Lord is, therefore, also the universal service principle. Of course, the selfish living entities may not agree; they may claim that while the Lord is being served, I'm not being served. But even as they pursue their own happiness, it comes at the cost of the happiness of others. And this cost entails that they too must pay the price for pursuing their happiness. But when the principle of selfishness is discarded, and the satisfaction of the Supreme Person is adopted as the fundamental principle, then everyone is automatically satisfied. The service to the other living entities is not necessarily service to the Lord, and since this service will always exclude some living entities, therefore, it becomes a selective service in which some individuals are benefitted while others are hurt. Universal happiness is achieved only when a common purpose is restored, and each person's activities fulfill this common purpose. If my self-interest is fulfilled by others' activities, then I'm pleased by the result just as the other person is pleased. Thus, service to the Supreme Person is happiness for everyone. Conversely, service to humanity, nature, animals, etc. is not ultimate happiness because each such service excludes some other living entities.

Topic 7

QUESTION

There are many people who may worship the Supreme Lord, not with the intention of pleasing Him, but with the goal of obtaining something from Him. Since this type of worship is selfish, and yet it is focused on the Lord, does such selfish meditation on the Lord also entail the happiness of everyone?

3.3.14 (374)
आध्यानाय प्ररयोजनाभावात्
ādhyānāya prayojanābhāvāt

ādhyānāya—pensive and sorrowful meditation, or recollection with regret, hesitation, or dissatisfaction; prayojana-abhāvāt—due to missing the purpose.

TRANSLATION

Unhappy meditation (is rejected) due to missing the purpose.

COMMENTARY

In earlier chapters, the worship of demigods was rejected in favor of the Lord's worship—even if one is desirous of material enjoyments. Under such desire, a person begins meditation on the Lord in an unhappy state—" Lord, I don't have this or that, and I want you to give me what I want". This pensive, unhappy, dissatisfied, hesitant, and sorrowful mental state for meditation is rejected in this sūtra as being devoid of the main purpose. Since meditation is a means, and not the end, it doesn't constitute the happiness of the Lord. It is preferred over the worship of the demigods because one is asking the Supreme Person. However, since the meditator is asking for their happiness, rather than the happiness of the Supreme Person, this meditation is only a more advanced form of selfishness and not the principle of a shared purpose for everyone. This sūtra rejects such meditation as being the ultimate purpose of meditation.

QUESTION

But one might argue that such meditation is at least satisfying them, and since self-interest is ultimately their goal, their goals are being fulfilled. How can we convince someone that this self-interest is not the real purpose?

3.3.15 (375)
आत्मशब्दाच्च
ātmaśabdācca

ātmaśabdāt—on account of statements about the self; ca—also (rejected).

TRANSLATION

On account of statement about self (being the purpose) are also (rejected).

COMMENTARY

The previous sūtra stated that the Lord is not satisfied by selfish meditation. So, one might say: "At least, I will be satisfied by this meditation". And the response to that claim is: "Not necessarily". The Lord doesn't fulfill the material desires which the demigods cannot. He only grants what is within one's karma, just like the demigods. The worship of the Lord is still better because He can fulfill our desires in many departments—health, wealth, love, knowledge, etc. whereas each demigod can fulfill the desires in only one department.

Therefore, meditation on the Lord is better than the meditation on demigods because by this meditation one only needs to ask one source for everything. However, the results delivered by this meditation are also within one's karma. This karma is like money—it can be spent on whatever goods we want. If we have the money, but we are not getting the opportunity to buy the goods we want, then the worship of the demigods or the Lord can create the opportunity where we can spend our good karma in obtaining the desired goods. But this worship cannot deliver the goods beyond the deserved karma. Thus, it is incorrect to assume that by worshipping the Lord we can obtain whatever we want, and all our unhappiness would be overcome through such worship.

Since the previous sūtra spoke about unhappy meditation, and this sūtra talks about the self, it can also be translated as 'meditation on the self'. Since the previous sūtra rejected such meditation as delivering ultimate happiness, the 'meditation on the self' would also be considered rejected due to the use of the word *ca* or 'also'. While such a translation is possible, it breaks the logical continuity of the discussion, and hence we have preferred the alternative that 'statements about the self being happy by selfish meditation are rejected'.

Topic 8

QUESTION

In many places in the Vedic texts, self-interest is emphasized as the goal of life. For example, it is said that each person is suffering in this world, and they should aim for permanent happiness, which entails that the pursuit of one's happiness is the goal. How do we reconcile these statements with those you have made now—that the Supreme Person's happiness is the main goal?

3.3.16 (376)

आत्मगृहीतिरितिरवत् उत्तरात्

ātmagṛhītiritaravat uttarāt

ātmagṛhīti—the self-interest; itaravat—as in other texts or in other places; uttarāt—on account of the subsequent qualification or clarification.

TRANSLATION

The statements about self-interest in other texts are modified or clarified in subsequent texts (by saying that the Supreme Person is the main interest).

COMMENTARY

A person absorbed in selfish pursuits is only motivated by self-interest. To motivate them, the problem of suffering is often brought up in all religions: that material existence brings the problem of repeated birth, death, old age, and disease. So, if we want to be free of these problems, then it is in our selfish interest to pursue a transcendental life which is eternal and free of suffering. Once the person is convinced that they must reject the pleasures of material existence, because they are always accompanied with suffering, then the preliminary background for subsequent discussion is set. Subsequently, however, the pursuit of individual happiness is modified or clarified: it is said that to obtain eternal happiness, one must satisfy the Supreme Person. This modification then shifts the focus from a selfish pursuit of happiness to a selfless devotion to the Lord. Of course, the devotion to the Lord could be prescribed upfront. But most people are not interested; they tend to question the existence of the soul and God, ask for many kinds of proofs, and wonder how this concerns them.

Some religious doctrines, such as Buddhism and Advaita, begin and end in the problem of suffering and how to overcome it. They remain selfish throughout: The spiritual aspirant only aims for their happiness, and not the happiness of the Lord. But they fail to realize that all happiness comes from the fulfilment of desires, and desires necessitate individuality. If individuality is lost, then desires are lost, and there is no happiness. Therefore, these are not spiritual doctrines because, although they lead to cessation of suffering, they do not lead to the creation of eternal pleasure. The pursuit of the cessation of suffering is selfish, and the pursuit of Lord's happiness is unselfish. If a person is in pain, then relief from suffering itself seems like happiness. But the cessation of suffering is not happiness. It just seems like happiness from a material viewpoint.

In so far as cessation of suffering is important, self-interest is emphasized. But in so far as genuine happiness is concerned, unselfish love is emphasized. Those engrossed in materialism can hardly see beyond the body; it is very hard for them to understand the existence of a transcendental body of the soul and the Lord, and loving relationships between them, a world where these loving pastimes are carried out, and how that world is also eternal and ever-expanding. For them, cessation from material miseries is prescribed as the starting point.

However, as one progresses in this understanding, and can see the soul is different from the body, then he can also understand the form of the soul and the Lord, their non-difference, their loving relationships, and a transcendental world that exists beyond this world. Therefore, this sūtra states that after prescribing selfish cessation from suffering, the doctrine is revised later to speak about unselfish love of the Lord. This revision should not be viewed as a contradiction between doctrines, but as incremental progress in realization.

QUESTION

So, are you suggesting that the claims of impersonalism and personalism, or selfish spiritual liberation and the unselfish love of God, are not contradictory (although they are progressive) because both are stated in the scriptures?

3.3.17 (377)
अन्वयादतिचेत् स्यात् अवधारणात्
anvayāditi cet syāt avadhāraṇāt

anvayāt—due to contradiction; iti cet—if it be said; syāt—it is possible; avadhāraṇāt—on account of the differing conceptions (in scriptures).

TRANSLATION

If it is said that (confusion is imminent) due to contradictions (between earlier and later claims) (we say) it is possible due to different conceptions.

COMMENTARY

This sūtra acknowledges that confusion can result from the preliminary claims that one must aspire for freedom from material suffering, and the subsequent claims that one must aspire for eternal happiness by serving the Lord. There is also implicit acknowledgement that such confusions are common.

The Vedic system is a progressive path for self-realization. At the basic level, the rules of moral living are prescribed as the Varṇāśrama system of social organization—i.e., the right type of sociology, economics, and politics. At a more advanced level, the worship of the demigods is prescribed for fulfillment of desires. At an even more advanced level, the demigod worship is rejected, and the worship of the Supreme Lord is preferred even for those desirous of material happiness. Beyond such selfish and materialistic love of the Lord, there is the aspiration to be liberated from material existence and its imminent suffering. Beyond the state of liberation is the pursuit of eternal happiness by acquiring the qualities of the Lord, and living in the same place as the Lord, which is devoid of all suffering. And even beyond this desire to be happy is the pure unselfish love of God in which even the suffering is considered a pleasure if that pleases the Lord. The rules of social organization, the worship of demigods, or the worship of the Lord for material happiness are paths within the material world. The desire for liberation from suffering is the aspiration for Brahman. The aspiration for living in the proximity of the Lord, having the same type of form and qualities, and never entering the material world, is the life of Vaikuṇṭha. And the unselfish love of the Lord, in which the devotee is satisfied even in the material world if the Lord is pleased, is the life of Goloka.

These different descriptions can seem contradictory as they are described in different texts, and the resulting confusion is imminent. However, they can be understood as progressive stages of spiritual realization. Once this progression is grasped, then the apparent contradictions naturally disappear.

It was earlier stated that the nature of the Absolute Truth is only grasped by the study of diverse scriptures and reconciling their apparent contradictions. Those who take these contradictions on face value and reject one doctrine in preference for another—without understanding the progression—cannot be considered to have a full understanding. There are indeed contradictions between different levels of understanding, but these contradictions can be resolved if one understands that these are progressive levels of realization.

Topic 9

QUESTION

Does this entail that the scriptures should be understood in order

of their progression, and see how later claims modify the previously made claims?

3.3.18 (378)

कार्याख्यानादपूर्वम्

kāryākhyānādapūrvam

kāryākhyānāt—from the descriptions of work; apūrvam—unprecedented.

TRANSLATION

From the unprecedented (i.e., not present in the previous texts) descriptions of actions (the successive processes of spiritual realizations are judged).

COMMENTARY

After acknowledging that scriptures can make conflicting claims, this sūtra says that the successive texts make novel claims, i.e., those not made earlier. In 3.3.16 (376) the term *uttarāt* or 'subsequently' was used about the modification of previous claims. In this sūtra, the term *apūrvam* or 'not previously' is used to refer to the novelty of the new claims. It might seem that these two are saying the same thing, but they are not. There is a subtle difference between 'successor' and 'not the predecessor'. Suppose you are tasked to sequence objects based on their colors—let's say from red to purple. This ordering produces a unique sequence only if there is one object for each color. If there are many objects with the same color, then there is no way to decide which of the many red objects should be ahead in a sequence. The same problem exists in the case of sentences. If we are ordering them by their meaning, then there is no way to decide which of the many sentences with identical meaning should be ahead of the others. With this understanding, we can now speak about the ordering of scriptures. The 'successor' indicates the next object or sentence. The term 'not the predecessor' means all the objects with the same color, or sentences with the same meaning, are not included. So, using 'successor' we get new objects or statements, and using 'not the predecessor' we exclude the same type of object or the statement with the same meaning. The 'successor' is the physical ordering of things and 'not the predecessor' is the semantic ordering of things.

In this case, we are speaking about the scriptures, which can be distinguished physically as different books and semantically as different doctrines. The term 'successor' indicates the order in which the texts have appeared, and it constitutes physical ordering. The term 'not the predecessor' indicates the progression in their meaning, and it constitutes semantic ordering. Thus, self-realization is emphasized in the four Vedas but in the Purāṇa, Tantra, and Itihāsa the devotion to the Lord is emphasized. But this sequence of texts is not the regression of meaning from greater to lesser perfection. It is rather the progression of meaning from lesser to greater perfection. Many people claim that the four Vedas are the superior original texts, and the later texts are the inferior modified texts. According to these claims, perfect knowledge came before it was diluted: the idea of the soul or the pursuit of self-realization was primordial perfect truth, and the idea of God or the pursuit of God-realization was added subsequently. This change was engendered by the problem that most people could not think of the self; they were used to thinking about something other than the self. Therefore, a Supreme Self was added to help them think of the self. The Supreme Self had the same properties as the self. However, it was more convenient to think about the self in this way, instead of self-realization.

If this doctrine of progression from superior to inferior is accepted, then the later texts would not be called *apūrvam*. The term *apūrvam* is never used derogatorily. It means novelty, newness, freshness, originality, etc. The order in the Vedic texts is therefore about progressive understanding rather than regression from perfection to imperfection. When the terms *uttarāt* and *apūrvam* are used in combination, there is a clear indication of a strict order—the previous is inferior and the subsequent is superior. It is not the other way around.

Topic 10

QUESTION

But you have earlier explained that manifestation progresses from the full truth to the partial truth. How can we now say that a more

complete truth follows a partial truth? Your above statement implies that a preliminary truth about liberation is described initially followed by a more complete devotional truth. How do we reconcile the full to partial manifestation with the above idea that the partial truth is manifest before the full truth is later described?

3.3.19 (379)
समान एवञ्च अभेदात्
samāna evañca abhedāt

samāna—reconciliation; evam—like this; ca—also; abhedāt—on account of non-difference.

TRANSLATION

Reconciliation (among the diversities) like this (i.e., from preliminary to advanced) is also (possible) due to non-difference (between doctrines).

COMMENTARY

The Absolute Truth is described in three ways—as Brahman, Paramātma, and Bhagavān. As we have discussed, Bhagavān is the source of light, Brahman is the light, and the Paramātma is the representation of the source within each particle of light (identifying that this particle emerged from a source). Brahman is individual existence, Paramātma is the purpose of individual existence, and Bhagavān is the reference of that purpose. The purpose and reference are noted separately, because the purpose is in everyone, but the reference is common. In a different sense, Brahman is the diversity, Paramātma is the unity within the diversity, and Bhagavān is the diversity within the unity. Likewise, in a mathematical language, we can call these the set, the class, and the instance. Bhagavān is knowledge and the knower; the knower is a set, and knowledge is within that set. That set contains many knowers, which are called Brahman, or the many individuals. And when knowledge enters these partial knowers, the representation of knowledge is called Paramātma, or the class called knowledge.

Existence is preliminary understanding, the purpose of existence is more advanced, and the source of existence is the most advanced. If we complete the triad of understanding, it doesn't matter whether we begin in existence, proceed to purpose, and then identify the source, or we begin in the source, proceed to existence, and then identify the purpose of existence. The source also exists as the whole, and has a purpose, due to which the whole divides into parts. Likewise, we exist, we have a purpose, and as parts we have a source. So, the path that progresses from existence to purpose to source is not problematic just as the path from source to purpose to existence is the complete path.

The use of the term *ca* or 'also' indicates that the path from existence to purpose to source is also a legitimate path, after it was said that the path from the source to purpose to existence is the more perfect understanding. The reason is that in the pursuit of knowledge, we start from what is certain, and then proceed to what is uncertain. When we are pursuing knowledge, then our existence is certain, and the Lord's existence is uncertain. Therefore, we go from our existence to the existence of the Lord. However, when the Lord is creating knowledge, then His existence is certain, and the existence of other things is a possibility. Therefore, the Lord goes from His existence to the diversities manifested from His existence. Hence, there are two ways to look at the Veda—is this the pursuit of our knowledge, or the expression of Lord's knowledge?

The expression of the Lord's knowledge is given to Brahma, who then expresses this knowledge—primarily dividing it into four Vedas. The Veda is originally succinct, but it is then elaborated and expanded by Brahma. This knowledge is further expanded beyond the four Vedas by Bādarāyana, an empowered incarnation of Lord Viṣṇu. These expansions present the human quest. In short, it is assumed that the student is like a child, who needs to be taught the preliminary knowledge first, and advanced knowledge later. Therefore, the existence is followed by purpose, followed by the source. Therefore, even though the knowledge is divine—i.e., spoken by the Lord—its expression is meant for humanity, and therefore the order of expression is reversed.

This sūtra states that all these stages of knowledge are non-different. Just like the purpose is within the existence, and this internal purpose points to the external source, therefore, any detachment of the existence from the purpose and the source will always remain incomplete. Just like when we say, 'the sky is blue', there is a purpose—i.e., to describe the nature of the sky, and the word 'sky' refers to an object outside the sentence itself—similarly, the soul is also a sentence that has a meaning which refers to something other than the sentence. The purpose and the reference become important only when the sentence is understood semantically. If we look at the sentence physically, then we can see that the sentence exists, but we don't know its meaning—i.e., what it is stating, and the external object that is being referred to by the sentence. Brahman realization is the study of the soul as an existent. Paramātma realization is the study of the same soul as a sentence with meaning. And Bhagavān realization is the study of the same soul as the reference to the object being described.

Since each of them pertains to the study of the soul, therefore, they are non-different—the same reality is described in three successively more advanced ways. Hence, the Brahman understanding is not *wrong*—it is the existence of the soul. But it is incomplete because the sentence is treated like an object without a meaning. When the meaning and the reference of the meaning are realized, then the sentence is understood in a more complete manner. If we study the world as physical things, then the conclusion is that all this diversity springs from a single existent—Brahman. However, if we study the same diversity as distinct sentences, then the diversity leads us to meaning and reference. Unless a person is convinced that "I exist eternally", it is impossible to talk about the eternal meaning of their existence, and what this meaning refers to. So, even though the existence comes out of the source, the initial step for a spiritual aspirant is to understand that he is the soul before they understand God.

Topic 11

QUESTION

We have many times spoken about how everything expands from the whole, which then leads to the inverted tree model of reality in which the complete source must be understood before the parts are known. Now you are saying that knowledge can also be acquired from incomplete to complete—i.e., from minute details to the full truth. Can this be called a general method? Or is this method restricted only to the understanding of the Absolute Truth?

3.3.20 (380)
संबन्धादेवमन्यत्रापि
saṃbandhādevamanyatrāpi

saṃbandhāt—due to relation; evam—like this; anyatra—in other cases; api—also.

TRANSLATION

Since (the full-to-partial and partial-to-full) are like this (non-different) due to their relation (to the object of study), they can be used in other cases too.

COMMENTARY

Under a physical conception of the world, we think that the bigger truth is necessarily outside the partial truth—like a city is beyond the house, a country is beyond the city, etc. However, if the same reality is understood semantically, then even as the country is beyond the city, the nationality is embedded in each city, and the quality of that city is embedded in each house. Hence, people might say: "this looks like any American city", or "this looks just like a European town", or "this looks like an Indian village". The American, European, or Indian nature of something is a broader level reality, but it is also embedded in each part of that broader reality. Therefore, the study of a *broader* reality is also the study of a *deeper* reality. To know the broader reality, we don't necessarily have to go outward; we can also go deeper inward. Scientists today think that to know the full reality we must always look outward—through microscopes and telescopes. In the Vedic system, however, to know the full reality, we must withdraw the consciousness inward and look deeper within—beyond the bodily, mental, intellectual, egotistic, and moralistic coverings of the soul.

This process of spiritual realization is applicable to material study as well. For example, when you meet a person, you only see their skin color, body size, dress, and appearance. But you don't know anything about them—e.g., their family, occupation, friends, values, morals, etc. If you engage with them, then you can also know them 'deeply'—i.e., their family, upbringing, occupation, friends, values, and morals. All these are within the person, and yet not easily visible. To understand these deeper realities, we must ask different types of questions; if our quest is limited to their bodily appearance, then we will not discover the deeper nature of a person. Different realities are revealed only when different types of questions are asked. In the case of material study, the simplest question is: Does it exist? A more advanced question is: What is it? And an even more advanced question is: What can it be used to achieve? Thus, the method of knowing the self applies to the knowing of the world.

QUESTION

The impersonalist will say that the idea of 'deeper reality' is drawn from the study of matter, where there are many deeper levels of reality, beginning with the body. The soul is supposed to be the deepest level of reality. But you are insisting that there are deeper levels of understanding even in the soul. Why can't we say that there is just the soul, rather than levels in the soul?

3.3.21 (381)
न वा वशिेषात्
na vā viśeṣāt

na vā—rather not; viśeṣāt—on account of difference.

TRANSLATION

(We shall) rather not say (that the soul is one thing) due to the differences (between the many aspects of the understanding about the soul).

COMMENTARY

The impersonalist conception of the soul is that it exists, but is devoid of qualities; qualities, rather, are imputed upon the soul by matter. If these material qualities are removed, then the soul is itself without any qualities, and if there are no qualities, then there is no differentiation between souls. This conception of the soul is based on the physical view of things. When the same thing is understood as a symbol, then the symbol exists, the symbol has a meaning, and the symbol's meaning refers to something other than the symbol. We cannot equate the existence to the meaning or to the reference. So, the claim that the soul is without modes of understanding, and these modes are only added due to matter, is a flawed idea. The soul's understanding is also modal; existence, meaning, and reference are the three modes of the soul's understanding.

The term viśeṣāt can have many meanings: (1) differences, (2) qualities, (3) modalities, (4) individualities, etc. All these meanings when applied to the soul or God refute impersonalism. They are certainly observed in the case of matter. The difference between matter, soul, and God is that God is the reference to Himself, the soul can be reference to itself or to God, and matter is always a reference to something other than itself—either soul or God. The principle of symbolism is upheld in all three cases; they only differ in their references. There is hence a similarity between matter, soul, and God, and there is a difference. The similarity is that they are all symbols of meaning. The difference is that they have different references. The soul also has different references in the material world, in Brahman, and in the spiritual world (directed toward matter, directed toward self, and directed toward God). The impersonalist claims that Brahman is undivided, and matter is divided. But when the soul is undivided, then it has no individuality. Without individuality, there is no desire. And without the fulfillment of desire there is no happiness. The soul merely exists, but it doesn't know why it exists. This incomplete knowledge of the soul is not perfection.

QUESTION

When we have an ordinary experience, the existence, meaning, and reference are all equally present. In fact, it seems that we cannot even distinguish between these three things in experience because every experience has the notion of self-existence, the meaning of existence, and the thing being seen. So, is this tripartite distinction a theoretical one, or can it be observed as well?

3.3.22 (382)

दर्शयति च

darśayati ca

darśayati—experienced; ca—also.

TRANSLATION

(The distinction between existence, meaning, and reference) is also experienced (so, it is not merely a theoretical distinction between aspects).

COMMENTARY

Ordinary experiences generally come with existence (or self-experience), the meaning (or the purpose of one's existence), as well as the reference of this purpose (the external object by which our purpose is to be fulfilled). This might lead us to think that these are inseparable aspects of experience, and if they are inseparable, they cannot be considered as deeper realities; we must rather consider them as a single reality because they are experienced simultaneously. This sūtra states that each of the three can be separately experienced. Therefore, there is an experience in which we know "I exist" but we don't know the meaning of existence and the object that fulfills this existential meaning. Then there is an experience in which we experience both our existence and the meaning; this is when we decide that we are going to dedicate our life to some ideals, although we may not know how these ideals will be fulfilled. Then, we map this existential meaning to external objects or individuals that fulfill it. This is when we experience our existence, the existential ideal, and the object that fulfills this ideal. The successive experiences include the previous experiences, so there is an order or hierarchy between them. But since the experience progresses from existence to meaning to reference, we can see them separately. Therefore, the experience of Bhagavān is not contrary to the experience of Paramātma or Brahman; it includes it. Likewise, the Paramātma experience includes Brahman experience, but goes beyond it. Finally, the Brahman experience stands by itself, and may not include Paramātma or Bhagavān experiences. The possibility of this self-experience, however, doesn't preclude the other experiences; it is only a less inclusive experience of the self-existence alone.

Topic 12

QUESTION

If you accept that the existence of the self can be experienced even

in material observations, then why do you say that separation from matter is required to know who we truly are? Aren't we seeing ourselves in every experience?

3.3.23 (383)
संभृतदियुव्याप्त्यपि चातः
saṃbhṛtidyuvyāptyapi cātaḥ

saṃbhṛtiḥ—possessed of; dyuvyāptiḥ—pervading the space; api—also; cātaḥ—and hence (we cannot consider this as the true nature of self).

TRANSLATION

Possessed of (this body and its connections) (we think of ourselves) as also pervading the space, and hence (this identity isn't the real identity of the soul).

COMMENTARY

Emotion, relation, and cognition exist in this world and use these to define our identity in relation to other people and things, the attributes of our body and its achievements, and the enjoyment of materialistic pleasures. Thus, we might consider ourselves rich because we own property, beautiful if we have an attractive body, famous if we are known by many people, powerful if this body controls the others, etc. Since all these are temporary, therefore, our identity is also temporary. But in the pursuit of this identity, we are distracted toward the external world. Spiritual life begins when the material connections are severed and only the relation to the self exists. Now, we are neither masters nor servants; we are neither enjoyers nor the enjoyed; we neither own anything nor are we owned. The self is defined not in relation to the world, but in relation to the self. Further progress involves the realization that the self is a part of the whole, that its purpose is defined by the whole, and its experiences must be directed toward the whole. Since this identity is permanent, therefore, it cannot be called an illusion. This sūtra states that the material notion of owning a body and its properties and by externalizing our consciousness into these objects we lose the real self of identity and self-existence. In fact, most us would consider ourselves diminished, and our identity lost, if these things were destroyed.

Topic 13

QUESTION

But as long as we are in the material world, we have to relate to this world through this body and so how can we give up these material identities?

3.3.24 (384)

पुरुषविद्यायामिव चेतरेषामनाम्नानात्

puruṣavidyāyāmiva cetareṣāmanāmnānāt

puruṣavidyāyām—the knowledge to become the master; iva—as if; ca—and; itareṣām—of the others; anām—the non-names; nānāt—from numerous.

TRANSLATION

From the numerous non-names (i.e., false designations of master etc.), the imaginary (as if) knowledge to become a master of the others (arises).

COMMENTARY

The previous sūtra stated that the real self-identity is unknown unless the association with the material world is discarded. So, a naïve interpretation of this claim can be that we must reject the material world, discard our roles and duties, and live in isolation. This sūtra, however, states that the real problem isn't those associations but the idea that we are the master of this body and everything associated with it. The term *eva* means 'certainly', and the term *iva* means 'as if' or 'just like'. The indication is that we are not truly masters, but we behave as if we are the masters. When this false sense of being the master is destroyed, then all the non-names (i.e., the false designations in relation to the world) are also destroyed. Therefore, we don't have to give up the roles and duties but must give up the idea that we are the masters of the world. Once this idea is given up, then we can use the roles and duties to serve the Lord.

Topic 14

QUESTION

Is this rejection of being a pretentious master like selflessness? Some people compare this idea to that of a hollow inside a coconut, stating that the self is viewed as nothing, although the body and its associations can continue?

3.3.25 (385)
वेधाद्यर्थभेदात्
vedhādyarthabhedāt

vedhādi—making a hole etc.; arthabhedāt—due to different meaning.

TRANSLATION

Making a hole etc. (is not accepted) due to a different meaning.

COMMENTARY

The cessation of false mastery doesn't entail the cessation of existence. A disease can be cured by killing the patient, but we don't consider that killing as a legitimate method of cure. In the same way, if we ceased to exist, then we will cease to be a master. But that is like killing the patient to cure the disease.

The real cure is not the cessation of existence, but the cessation of false mastery. It is achieved by the soul becoming a servant of the Lord. The advocates of voidism claim that if these material associations are given up, then the person ceases to be a father, mother, citizen, employee, etc. and if all such designations are removed, then we would not be left with any 'self'. Since all these designations are temporarily created due to association with material objects, therefore, the voidist claims that they are all false (which is correct). However, he also goes on to claim that there is really no self if all these designations are removed (which is incorrect). The notion of being a master is a false covering of the soul, but the existence of the soul is not itself false. This is borne by practical experience that even when a person gives up material identities, he doesn't cease to exist. Therefore, the meaning of giving up material identities is not to leave a 'hole' within, which would entail that there is no self. The idea is rather to remove the false attachments borne out of the idea of being a master.

Topic 15

QUESTION

But if all kinds of material attachments have been given up, and the associated identities are lost, then what type of identity can one claim to have?

3.3.26 (386)

हानौ तु उपायनशब्दशेषत्वात् कुशाच्छन्दस्तुत्युपगानवत् तदुक्तम्

hānau tu upāyanaśabdaśeṣatvāt kuśācchandaḥstutyupagānavat taduktam

hānau—a loss; tu—but; upāyana—engagement; śabdaśeṣatvāt—from being called the remainder; kuśā—a rope; cchandaḥ—verses; stuti—the prayers; upagānavat—just like singing as a subordinate; tat—that; uktam—is said.

TRANSLATION

There is a loss (of the material identity) but due to engagements (which cannot be destroyed), (the soul) is still said to remain; it is said that he is bound by the rope of verses like a servant singing the prayers to that (the Lord).

COMMENTARY

We can see a progression in these sūtras— (1) the soul carries false identities, (2) these false identities are destroyed when one gives up the idea of being a master, (3) however, the destruction of these identities doesn't leave a void, (4) because the soul is still bound to the Lord through devotional prayers.

The term *guna* or material modes are sometimes called a 'rope'. Similarly, the term *kuśā* also denotes a rope. The soul is never liberated from these bondages, and the idea of 'liberation' as being completely free is false. Only the nature of the rope is changed. If we say that the destruction of material identity destroys the soul (as the Buddhists claim) then this claim is rejected here. The soul is permanently bound to the Lord by prayer, and temporarily bound to the material body and its associations. When this temporary binding is removed, then the permanent binding remains. This permanent binding is the soul's identity. The soul is neither a standalone reality nor does it become non-existent by the destruction of the material identity. It rather regains its spiritual identity, that is defined as a 'rope' which binds the soul to the Lord devotionally.

Topic 16

QUESTION

When the material identities are destroyed, and the soul is situated only in relation to the Lord, what does he desire through that identity and relation?

3.3.27 (387)

सांपराये तर्तव्याभावात् तथा ह्यन्ये

sāṃparāye tartavyābhāvāt tathā hyanye

sāṃparāye—on the attainment of transcendence; tartavya-abhāvāt—from absence of desires; tathā—in the same way; hi—for; anye—others.

TRANSLATION

From the absence of (material) desires on the attainment of transcendence, in the way that (there are mundane achievements) for the others.

COMMENTARY

We desire achievements because we feel incomplete; achievements help us temporarily relieve the sense of incompleteness. We associate with the body, its relationships, and the material objects because they temporarily make us feel complete. And we pursue such objects, and become attached to them, because we seek to overcome the inner incompleteness by filling it with temporary distractions. When the soul has attained the devotion to the Lord, then his material aspirations—like those of the materially conditioned souls—are destroyed. Such a person has no material aspirations because he has no incompleteness.

QUESTION

Since such a person can still exist in the material world, what does he do? Does he reject the material relationships, or does he continue to accept them?

3.3.28 (388)

छन्दतःउभयावरिोधात्

chandataḥ ubhayāvirodhāt

chandataḥ—according to his liking; ubhaya-avirodhāt—due to there being no contradiction between the two (acceptance and rejection of the world).

TRANSLATION

(Such a person lives) according to his liking because there is no contradiction between the two (the acceptance and the rejection of the world).

COMMENTARY

The Vedic texts describe two contradictory paths; these are called *pravritti* or engagement, and *nivritti* or detachment. Transcendence can be obtained by either of these paths. The path of engagement requires a person to keep performing their prescribed duties but becoming detached from their results. The path of detachment requires a person to voluntarily severe the attachments by cutting of the activities themselves. As the saying goes: "out of sight, out of mind". The path of detachment pursues this ideology, and advocates cutting off the worldly attachments to take our mind off the world. The path of engagement, however, says that just because you live in a jungle doesn't mean you are not thinking about the city. Out of sight doesn't necessarily mean out of mind. The real goal is not to put things out of sight, but to take them out of our minds. In fact, a test of detachment is that these things exist in your sight, but you are not tempted by them. Engaging in the activities, but progressively developing the detachment is, therefore, a better path. Of course, one might suit a person better than others. But they have the same goal—detachment from the material desires, but they are attained in two different ways: renounce the actions or renounce the desire for the results of these actions. However, for one who has attained devotion to the Lord, the results of both paths are already achieved. So, he has no need to renounce the material world, because he has renounced the materialistic goals. And he has no need to engage with the world because he has no materialistic goals. Thus, even as engagement and renunciation are contradictory paths for ordinary people, for the devotee they are not contradictory. Therefore, he can renounce, or he can engage, according to his liking.

Topic 17

QUESTION

But he still must make some decisions—i.e., to accept or reject. Even if both acceptance and rejection are identical for him, he still must make some decisions. Without a purpose, how can decide what course of action to take?

3.3.29 (389)

गतेररथवत्तत्वमुभयथा अन्यथा हि विरोधः

gaterarthavattvamubhayathā anyathā hi virodhaḥ

gateḥ—the actions; arthavattvam—by their utility; ubhayathā—in two ways; anyathā—otherwise; hi—certainly; virodhaḥ—a contradiction.

TRANSLATION

His actions (are determined) by their utility in two ways (i.e., useful and useless); otherwise, certainly (everything is) a contradiction (to his purpose).

COMMENTARY

The term *artha* denotes meaning or purpose. We normally measure the purpose in relation to our materialistic goals. But for the devotee, such goals are gone. However, the devotee still has goals—the pleasure of the Lord. Therefore, he decides whether something is useful or useless to the service of the Lord. Even if he has no selfish goals, he has the desire to please the Lord. So, the utility of the world is not lost; the utility is just measured in relation to the Lord. Everything else, which seems not useful to the service of the Lord, is considered a contradiction to the goal of pleasing the Lord and is therefore rejected.

QUESTION

But the purpose (of the Lord) may not always be satisfied in this world; there are so many hurdles to devotional service due to atheistic people. How can a devotee deal with such hurdles and difficulties in making choices?

3.3.30 (390)
उपपन्नःतल्लक्षणार्थोपलब्धेःलोकवत्
upapannaḥ tallakṣaṇārthopalabdheḥ lokavat

upapannaḥ—obtained; tat-lakṣaṇārtha-upalabdheḥ—as the symptoms of the achievement (of the purposes of the Lord); lokavat—just as in this world.

TRANSLATION

(Whatever is) obtained that has the symptoms of fulfilling (the purpose of the Lord) (is accepted) just as in this world (people take things good for them).

COMMENTARY

When a devotee is detached from materialistic goals and has developed devotional goals, he may decide to serve the Lord by engaging the material things into His service. But there are many practical difficulties—there is often resistance to such service by atheistic people and there are hardships in obtaining the resources for such service. When such difficulties arise, a devotee is inclined to ask: Is this hardship worth the effort, since results are hard to come by? Based on this hardship, should I continue to engage with the world, or renounce it? This sūtra answers this question. The devotee continues to serve the Lord in whatever way possible. Even if great results are not obtained, he accepts whatever results are obtained (or not obtained) with graciousness. He doesn't feel unhappy or bitter about the world being opposed to his devotional service. In short, effort continues to matter; the results thus obtained are immaterial.

Topic 18

QUESTION

Since you say that the devotee can accept or reject the prescribed duties, it seems that the rules of performing the duties in the scripture don't apply to him? Does this mean that he is contradicting the scriptural injunctions?

3.3.31 (391)

अनियमःसर्वासाम् अविरोधःशब्दानुमानाभ्याम्

aniyamaḥ sarvāsām avirodhaḥ śabdānumānābhyām

aniyamaḥ—there are no rules; sarvāsām—(applicable) to all; avirodhaḥ—non-contradiction; śabda-anumānābhyām—due to scripture or reasoning.

TRANSLATION

The rules that are applicable to everyone are not applicable to him; (by rejecting these rules) there is no contradiction to scripture or reasoning.

COMMENTARY

Rules are impersonal, and the Lord is a person. The person gives the rules for those who cannot see or understand the person, and by following those rules, we indirectly follow the person. However, if we can directly follow the person, then we would also fulfill the purpose for which those rules were given.

In the material world, however, the soul forgets the purpose of these rules as the satisfaction of the Lord. He just sees these impersonal rules and considers them to be meant for the satisfaction of the only person he knows—himself. As a result, he thinks that whenever he follows the rules, then he must also get something in return. For example, we pay our taxes so that the government will protect us from miscreants, or from unforeseen difficulties, in return. In short, there is a covenant between the lawgiver and the law-follower. In a primitive form, religion is such contracts between the Lord and His followers, and it is primitive because there is hardly any love; it is merely a contract between two parties. Thus, the devotion between the soul and God is deemphasized and the rules of the contract are emphasized; the followers of the religion also believe that by accepting these rules and regulations they are *entitled* to liberation. After all, that is the nature of the covenant—both parties are bound by it.

The advanced devotee of the Lord is, however, beyond such contractual obligations. He serves the Lord out of love. He doesn't need rules as contracts because he is not expecting anything in return. Thus, he is not bound by the contracts because a contract involves an entitlement, but the devotee has no entitlement. The devotee loves the Lord causelessly, not due to contractual reasons, and he becomes free from all such contractual laws. Instead, he binds the Lord by his causeless devotion: The Lord becomes dependent on the love of His devotee, but the devotee is not asking for anything in return from the Lord.

The religion of rules and regulations is primitive; it can make a person indirectly follow the Lord by making him follow the rules given by the Lord. Obedience to rules raises a person to the understanding of the Lord, provided one follows these rules as a matter of natural duty, and not because there is something expected in return. If rules are followed to get something in return, then the rules remain impersonal contracts, and the Lord is not understood. If the understanding of the Lord is obtained, then the rules cease to be meaningful. The devotee, upon a full understanding of the Lord, becomes the lawgiver and the Lord becomes the law-follower. Bound by the love of the devotee, the Lord becomes the devotee's servant, and their mutual affection grows incessantly.

Topic 19

QUESTION

Does this mean that the rules and regulations of the material world continue to apply to the person who hasn't developed the devotion to the Lord?

3.3.32 (392)
यावदधिकारमवस्थितिरिाधिकारिकाणाम्
yāvadadhikāramavasthitirādhikārikāṇām

yāvat-adhikāram—as long as one has the sense of rights; avasthi-tiḥ—(there is material) existence; ādhikārikāṇām—for those who feel righteous.

TRANSLATION

As long as one has the sense of rights, (there is material) existence for those who feel righteous (i.e., expect results in return for their religious duties).

COMMENTARY

All rules are meant to define the sense of right and wrong. But underlying all these rules is an expectation—if I do this correctly, then I will get this reward. Morality is based on this sense of right and wrong, and the laws of religion constitute morality. Morality is, however, not real religion. It is merely obedience to laws in return for something else. The followers of moral injunctions remain attached to the results, and they expect that the Lord must reciprocate with material benedictions, liberation, or protection, in return for the obedience to the laws. In short, the righteousness that we accept by obeying the moral injunctions is also applied back to the lawgiver, and one doesn't follow the laws because it pleases the Lord; one follows them because there is something in return. This contract constitutes the sense of righteousness. This sūtra states that as long as one has this sense of righteousness and expects reciprocation for following the laws, he remains bound by the laws. Righteousness is impersonal, and devotion is personal. We cannot love laws; we can follow them in return for something else. We can however love the Lord, who gives these laws.

Many people who follow religious practices become disenchanted quickly if they find that following the rules and regulations is not producing the expected results—i.e., material benedictions, liberation, or protection from suffering. They can't see the effects of karma, and how their suffering, entanglement, and vulnerability is caused by their own past actions. They may even blame the Lord for not reciprocating in accordance with their perceived covenants. This perceived breach of trust with the Lord then dissolves their obedience to the laws they were previously following. A new set of problems are now created, and the cycle of breaking the laws and bearing its consequences repeats.

Modern society is afflicted with the idea of rights. These began with the contracts between man and God, as Abrahamic religions taught covenants with God; they were extended to contracts between a citizen and their government; and slowly, all relationships—including marriages—became contracts. In every contract, there are rights and duties: You give something to get something in return. All relationships become business dealings, as everyone is calculating the profit and loss in a relationship, rather than loving each other. A slight reduction in a profit, or a slight increase in the loss, immediately leads to the disruption of the relationship. Thus, people have no patience and tolerance. The idea of contracts, covenants, and rights creates a society devoid of love. The other person is not a person; they are only the portals for giving and taking. The problem begins in a faulty conception of religion: If we cannot love God selflessly, then how can we love anyone else selflessly? If God is only following a contract, then how can every other relationship not also be contractual?

A religion of covenants is like a marriage bound by a prenuptial agreement. There is some love, but it is not irrevocable. Hence, this type of religion is considered imperfect. It is meant for those who find it hard to love God. If we maintain a sense of rights, then we must also be bound by duties. When we give up rights, then we also become free of duties. A perfect society can only exist if the living entities serve each other not because they are expecting something in return as determined by a covenant; rather, because they are bound by love.

Topic 20

QUESTION

If the soul is bound to the material world by his sense of righteousness and entitlement for actions, then how is the soul liberated from this existence?

3.3.33 (393)

अक्षरधियां त्ववरोधःसामान्यतदभावाभ्यामौपसदवत् तदुक्तम्

akṣaradhiyāṃ tvavarodhaḥ sāmānyatadbhāvābhyāmaupasadavat taduktam

akṣaradhiyāṃ—surrendering to the infallible; tu—but; avarodhaḥ—without hurdles; sāmānya—due to similarity; tadbhāvābhyām—by being imbued with His nature; upasadavat—just like worship; tat—it; uktam—has been said.

TRANSLATION

Surrendering to the infallible but without the hurdles (of rules and regulations), due to the similarity (between the soul and the Lord) by being imbued with His nature (by constantly remembering Him), just like worshipping Him, (the transcendental existence is obtained); thus, it has been said.

COMMENTARY

The previous sūtra stated that one may follow the laws of God, but if he treats them as contractual laws, his material existence continues. Thus, a religion that teaches one to obey a contract with God doesn't lead to transcendence. It merely repeats the cycle of birth and death because we expect a return on our investment. If one desires to transcend, then one must give up the transactional mindset and surrender to the Lord. The rejection of rules and regulations is part of that surrender—we are not becoming immoral; we are rather rejecting the expectation of getting favorable returns for being moral. The Lord is not bound by laws of morality, because He doesn't act with return of expectations. When the soul acts in the same way, he also acquires the qualities of the Lord—i.e., freedom from the laws. This doesn't mean defiance to the Lord; it rather means serving the Lord without expecting anything in return. So, the transcendental state is beyond morality, not averse to morality. Under morality, we expect good things to come to us if we follow the rules and regulations. Giving up morality simply means discarding this expectation of returns. Rules and regulations may or may not be followed; since the desire of the soul has changed to please the Lord alone, such action has no consequences. Therefore, the sense of right and wrong ceases to exist, and consequently the laws of karma.

Topic 21

QUESTION

Isn't there anything else required for the attainment of transcendence?

3.3.34 (394)
इयदामननात्
iyadāmananāt

iyat—only so much; āmananāt—due to acceptance.

TRANSLATION

The acceptance of (surrender to the Lord) is enough (for transcendence).

COMMENTARY

The previous sūtra stated that by surrender to the Lord one can attain transcendence. The sūtra before that said that if the surrender is not accepted, then transcendence is not attained. Therefore, the previous two sūtras said that the surrender to the Lord is *necessary*. This sūtra states that surrender the Lord is *sufficient*. Generally, if there are many causes responsible for an effect, and each cause is necessary, then the absence of those causes will preempt the effect. By that calculation, the surrender to the Lord is necessary—so we can say that it is at least one of the causes of transcendence. But there is still a possibility that there are other causes because of which the surrender to the Lord may not be sufficient. This sūtra rejects the existence of any additional causes; it states that 'only so much'—i.e., the surrender to the Lord—is enough for transcendence. It follows that no other cause is required; however, this cause is necessary.

Topic 22

QUESTION

Why do you consider the surrender to the Lord as necessary and sufficient, when there are so many other legitimate paths described in the Vedic texts?

3.3.35 (395)

अन्तरा भूतग्रामवत्स्वात्मनः

antarā bhūtagrāmavatsvātmanaḥ

antarā—the innermost; bhūtagrāmavat—just like the first of the existents; svātmanaḥ—the meaning (or the mind) of the self (if the self is the body).

TRANSLATION

(The surrender to the Lord is necessary and sufficient because He) is the innermost reality, the first among all the other existents, and the meaning (or the mind) of the self (if the self is identified as the body of that mind).

COMMENTARY

As already discussed, the existence of the soul is an incomplete understanding. A more complete understanding is that this existence has a meaning or purpose. Just like the body exists, but the meaning of the existence is given by the mind, similarly, the soul is here compared to the body, whose meaning (i.e., the mind) is the Lord. The paths of spiritual realization—e.g., karma-yoga, jñāna-yoga, and dhyāna-yoga—are sometimes incompletely understood when they are expected only to deliver the liberation from material existence. Using these paths, the soul can become detached from the laws of material nature, but because it doesn't yet know the purpose of its existence, it likely falls again into the material world. Only when a transcendent purpose of existence is realized, then the soul doesn't fall (assuming it doesn't forget its innate purpose).

The existence of the soul is therefore like a symbol. Deeper than this existence is the meaning of existence. The existence and the meaning are inseparable in one sense—because the meaning is within the soul. And yet, the existence is not identical to the meaning—because we can know the existence and yet not know the meaning (although when we know the meaning, we also know the existence). Therefore, the meaning of existence goes beyond existence, and is considered more complete. We should not therefore think that self-realization is the end, if by this end, we simply know that the soul is different from the body. The greater self-realization is knowing the purpose of existence.

The comparison of the Lord to the mind is significant here because we are generally prepared to accept that the mind is different from the body. By calling the Lord the mind, the soul is now accepted as the body. Therefore, like a materially entangled person is considered inferior to one who is self-realized, similarly, the self-realized person is considered inferior to the Lord's devotee. This idea about the relation between the soul and the Lord is the basis of the Viśiṣṭādvaita doctrine in which the soul is the body of the Supreme Soul.

QUESTION

The distinction between the soul and the Lord was predicated upon the Lord being separate from the soul. Now you are saying that the Lord is like the mind of the body (of the soul) which means that since the mind is inside the body therefore there is no distinction between the soul and the Lord. So, rather than saying that the Lord is different from the soul, you are saying that these two are identical. Doesn't it contradict the previous statements on this?

3.3.36 (396)

अन्यथा भेदानुपपत्तिरिति चेत् न उपदेशान्तरवत्

anyathā bhedānupapattiriti cet na upadeśāntaravat

anyathā—erroneously; bheda-anupapattiḥ—the distinction is not clearly understood; iti cet—if it be said; na—not so; upadeśānta—the final teaching; ravat—roaring or yelling (declaration with the greatest emphasis).

TRANSLATION

If it is said that (the Lord being the purpose of the soul) erroneously makes the distinction (between the soul and the Lord) unclear, (we say) not so; (the Lord being the purpose of the soul) is roaringly said to be the final teaching.

COMMENTARY

The distinction between the Lord and the soul has already been established as whole and part, and that distinction—or Dvaita—is not to be denied. However, if we keep this separation, then it is hard to explain why the soul must be devoted to the Lord. Of course, we can say that the soul is part of the Lord, but that begs the question: How can the soul go against the Lord if it were part of the Lord? Then again, if the Lord and the soul are truly separate, then how can the soul know the Lord, given the separation between the knower and the known? In Advaita philosophy, all illusions arise due to the knower-known distinction and certainty is established only regarding self-existence. This idea is also well-known in Western philosophy where Descartes noted that he can doubt everything but could not doubt his own existence, because the existence of that doubt necessitated the existence of the doubter. Therefore, the separation of the soul and Lord brings new problems of knowledge. This problem, however, disappears if we say that the Lord exists inside the soul as the purpose of his existence. In so far as we cannot doubt our existence, we can also perceive the purpose as a deeper reality. In this perception, we are not looking 'outside' to know the Lord. We are rather looking deeper inside. This internal looking doesn't mean that the Lord is not outside; it just means that the source from which everything emanates is also embedded in each thing as its purpose.

The Lord is both outside and inside the soul, and this creates contradictions only when we think of 'outside' and 'inside' physically. When the world is looked at semantically, these problems disappear. Just like mammal is the source of the idea of cow, and yet mammal is also present inside the cow, similarly, the Lord can be outside every-thing as their source, and inside everything as their purpose. If the Lord is only outside, then God-realization is necessarily different from self-realization. If the Lord is only inside, then self-realization is iden-tical to God-realization. But if the Lord is both inside and outside, then self-realization is complete only with God-realization, and this self-realization doesn't make us God. This is the founding principle of non-difference.

The sūtra further states that this understanding of the Lord existing within the soul—after it has been said that He is outside the soul—is 'roaringly' asserted to be the final teaching. In short, this understand-ing is Vedānta. This sūtra is the basis of the Bhedābheda doctrine in which the Lord is both outside and inside the soul. This understanding proceeds through several stages. First, it is said that soul is different from God. Second, it is said that the soul is a property of God, like the body is a property of the soul. Third, it is said that God is captured in the soul and is hence bound by love within the soul. These successive viewpoints are not contradictory; they are rather the progression of the loving relation between the soul and the Lord. When the soul is averse to the Lord, then the two are separate. When the soul becomes devoted to the Lord, then he is a property of the Lord. But when this devotion toward the Lord gradually intensifies, then the Lord is bound and captured inside the soul. Finally, when the soul is overwhelmed by this love, then he acts just like the Lord, and the distinction between the soul and the Lord is dissolved for all practical purposes. Hence, the soul and the Lord are different, related as object and property, non-dif-ferent from each other, and finally, they become identical.

Thus, all positions of Vedānta are true, but they are not simultane-ously true. They are rather progressive statements about the devotion to the Lord. The identity between the soul and the Lord is the highest understanding, but this is not the impersonal unity devoid of individ-uality, love, and devotion.

Topic 23

QUESTION

If you call this the final understanding of Vedānta, does it apply

only to the soul, or is it applicable even to the others—such as the relation between the Lord and the material nature, or between the soul and the material nature?

3.3.37 (397)

वृयतिहारःवशिषिन्ता हीतरवत्

vyatihāraḥ viśiṃṣanti hītaravat

vyatihāraḥ—reciprocity (of existence—whole in the part, part in the whole); viśiṃṣanti—distinct existence; hi—certainly; itaravat—just like the others.

TRANSLATION

The reciprocal distinct existence (of the whole within the part, and the part within the whole) is certainly (applicable) just like the other (doctrines).

COMMENTARY

The term *vyatihāraḥ* indicates alternation, reciprocity, or interchange. The term *viśiṃṣanti* indicates distinct or separated existence. This understanding is then applied to everything (not just the relation between the soul and the Lord). Just as the Lord and the soul are distinct existents, and yet, the Lord is inside the soul and the soul is inside the Lord, similarly, matter and the Lord are also distinct, and yet, matter is a part of the Lord and the Lord is within matter. When the soul exists in the material world, similarly, we can say that the soul is inside a material body (i.e., the soul is entangled within the material body), and the material body is inside the soul (as the soul's experience). If the body was merely a soul's experience—a position called Idealism in Western philosophy—then we could not say that the soul is entangled in matter; after all, the soul has full control over the material experience as it is within the soul. Conversely, if the soul was within the body, but the body wasn't within the soul—a position called Realism in Western philosophy—then we could not say that the soul is suffering due to its entanglement; after all, the body would only be a covering of the soul, and the soul and matter would be separate things.

To say that the soul is entangled in matter, we must accept that matter is distinct from the soul. And to say that the soul is suffering due to this entanglement, we must accept that the matter produces effects within the soul. Matter must enter the soul in order to create an experience. And yet, matter must be outside the soul for an objective external reality to exist and the material bondage—e.g., the laws of nature that force the soul—to be considered real.

We have discussed this problem earlier. When we have an experience, there is an objective external reality, and yet, there is a picture of that reality within the observer. The reality and its picture are physically distinct, but they are semantically identical. For instance, the external apple has taste, smell, color, shape, etc. and the internal apple also has those same properties. Due to this similarity, the external and the internal apples are identical (or can be identical if everything in the external apple becomes our conscious experience). And yet, the external apple will never be identical to the internal picture. The distinction between the external reality and the internal picture indicates that the soul and matter are physically distinct entities. And yet, during an experience, the apple enters the soul, and the soul enters the apple, and by this interchange or reciprocity, they become semantically identical. Therefore, even though the soul and the apple are physically distinct, they also become identical during an experience. If the experience ends, then they are individually separate.

Most people can accept the idea that the apple enters our mind, but they have a hard time accepting that the mind enters the apple. In short, they believe that we experience the world, but we are not bound by the world. So, the world is within us, but we are not within the world. Factually, there is no such experience. When you see an apple, you are not seeing the stars in the sky, hearing the people talking in the background, or aware of the pressure of the chair on your back. The exclusion of everything else means that we are in the apple, not anywhere else. But since we can focus on other things, therefore, we are outside everything. Therefore, the soul is different from the world because it can choose to experience different parts of the world or withdraw from all experiences. However, during an experience, the soul enters the perceived object. Hence, despite being separate from the world, the soul is bound by the world.

If the soul was always separate, then it could not experience anything, and duality of soul and matter leads to the mind-body problem in Western philosophy. If the soul is identical to the world, then we must at once experience everything in the world, which is again false. Therefore, we cannot assert duality, and we cannot assert identity. Now we say that the soul enters an object and becomes its part. The part is not identical to the whole, so identity is rejected. And the part is not separate from the whole, so duality is rejected. Our ability to focus on one thing means we are in that thing. Our ability to experience other things means they are all within us. And our ability to withdraw from all things implies that we are different from all things. Thus, various contradictory claims are made. They are all true, but not simultaneously true. They become true one after another as we (1) remain without experience, (2) get absorbed into one experience, and (3) change our experience from one thing to another.

The paradigm of reciprocity and interchange is applicable to all kinds of distinct realities—i.e., God, the soul, and matter—and their interrelations. The previous sūtra stated this idea in the context of the soul-God relation. And this sūtra advocates this reciprocal and interchange viewpoint along with others.

Topic 24

QUESTION

You have earlier described the Absolute Truth as comprised of masculine and feminine aspects. Now you are saying that each aspect is within the other aspect. How does this change the understanding of the Absolute Truth?

3.3.38 (398)
सैव हि सत्यादयः
saiva hi satyādayaḥ

sa eva—the same; hi—certainly; satyādayaḥ—the original truth.

TRANSLATION

The same (whole-part doctrine) certainly applies to the original truth.

COMMENTARY

In our earlier discussion, we noted how the Absolute Truth has masculine and feminine aspects—the masculine is the potential for desire, and the feminine is the potential to fulfill that desire. As potentials, the masculine and feminine are separate. However, this sūtra states that the masculine and feminine also enter each other and become inseparable from the other. As a result, two different entities—masculine and feminine—are both separate and inseparable. The same philosophy of mutual existence within each other is applicable.

The will is separate from power because the power may not be utilized by the will. When the power is used, the resulting effect is a combination of will and power, therefore, we say that they are inseparable. But this combination is also experienced, due to which the will enters power, and power enters will. In short, the combination of will and power is not a physical mixture of sugar and milk in which they remain separable. Conscious experience is the will entering power, and the power entering the will. For example, a powerful person may feel insecure and to reassure himself, he may look at the things that make him powerful. By absorbing himself in those things, he feels powerful. Then, when he feels this power, he is also tempted to use that power. Under this temptation, the will and power are separate. However, the power may be subordinated to the will—i.e., I will do what I want. Or, the will may be subordinated by the power—I will do what my power lets me do. When this dominant-subordinate relation is defined, then the will and the power combine to produce an effect. Finally, after the power is used to achieve the intended goals, then a sense of power enters the will as contentment and fulfillment. Thus, will and power are different, inseparable, will is within power, and power is within the will.

All these claims are true, but not simultaneously true. They become true one after another. When the Lord doesn't enjoy with His Śakti, the two are separate. When the Lord glances at His Śakti, He enters the Śakti, and feels powerful. This sense of power creates the temptation to enjoy, and the Lord combines with His Śakti to produce an effect. In this combination, however, the Lord may be dominant, or the Śakti may be dominant. Once that effect is achieved, the Śakti enters the Lord, and the Lord feels the contentment and fulfilment within.

Depending on which aspect of this process we focus upon, we can say that the Lord and His Śakti are separate, inseparable, the Lord is within the Śakti, the Śakti is within the Lord, the Lord is superior, or the Śakti is superior. All such claims are potentially true always, but they are not simultaneously true.

Topic 25

QUESTION

You earlier said that in the material world, the Lord and His Śakti enter an unmanifest state during annihilation, and the world is again created when the desire springs in the Lord. This desire also separates the Śakti from the Lord. But if they are merged in an unmanifest state, then what causes the desire?

3.3.39 (399)
कामादीतरत्र तत्र च आयतनादभ्यिः
kāmādītaratra tatra ca āyatanādibhyaḥ

kāmādi—the cause of desire; itaratra—in the other; tatra—thereafter; ca—also (the other into the cause); āyatana—the abode or resting place; ādibhyaḥ—the two causes (being the mutual resting places for the other cause).

TRANSLATION

The cause of desire (causes the desire) in the other; thereafter, also (the reverse happens). The two causes become the resting place for the other.

COMMENTARY

In the previous sūtra, we discussed how the feminine rests within the masculine as power, and He feels powerful. This is the unmanifest state of the material creation. However, it is also a contented and self-satisfied state. But sometimes, the self-satisfied state leads to a desire. What causes the desire?

The answer is that either the will or the power can produce the desire. Sometimes the feeling of being powerful creates a desire in the masculine. This is a common experience in all of us—when our body is strong, then desire is automatically produced in us. When the body becomes weak, then all desire vanishes. Thus, a healthy and strong person will develop many kinds of desires; and the same person, when sick will feel listless and devoid of all desires. Conversely, sometimes the desire is created first. This desire then agitates the power, and the person who was feeling rested earlier now feels powerful. Once this feeling of power is created in us, the will is also strengthened. Thus, through a mutual causation either will or power can be the other's cause.

The cause of desire is the *kāmādi*. The Lord is predominantly cause of desire in the material world, and His Sakti is predominantly the cause of desire in the spiritual world. This sūtra doesn't draw this distinction between the material and the spiritual worlds. It just says that the cause of desire evokes the desire in the other by entering the other. In this regard, we can note that there are different kinds of desires in the masculine and the feminine. The feminine desire is to be desired; the Lord's Śakti wants the Lord to be attracted toward Her. The masculine desire is not the desire to be desired, and so, the Lord is self-satisfied. However, He is still attracted to the Śakti not to feel attractive, but to fulfill the desire in His Śakti. Since the Lord is self-satisfied, therefore, He is said to be superior. But since the Śakti can cause Him to develop a desire, so She is said to be superior. The feminine is superior because She has the power to agitate the Lord. And the Lord is superior because She craves for His attention.

Even in this world, we see that women are attracted to confident and contented men. Women want to be desired and pursued by such confident men. But they don't like the men who come off as being needy or dependent. So, there is a contradiction in a woman's desire— she wants to be pursued, but the pursuer should not be needy. In fact, the woman would like to think that the man is totally self-satisfied when it comes to other women, but she has the power to agitate even this self-satisfied man, so she must be very special. Therefore, women try to be attractive to agitate and tempt the confident and contented men, but they get angry if some needy man is attracted thereby.

In the same way, the Lord's Śakti is attracted to the Lord precisely because He is not attracted to anything—He is totally self-satisfied and contented. The Śakti wants the self-satisfied Lord to be agitated by the desire for Her. The Lord is not needy or dependent. But He enjoys being attractive to the devotee.

The feminine desire arises in a need, and the masculine desire arises in a want. In the material world, this need is perverted, and some women pursue men because they need the man's riches, power, influence, etc. But this is not the real need. The real need is to be wanted. Therefore, women who have material riches, power, and influence, still need a man to want them. This need to be wanted exists even in the spiritual world and characterizes the feminine. Similarly, even though the Lord is self-contented, He is also chivalrous. When He sees that a devotee needs Him, His chivalry creates a desire in Him. The impersonalist thinks that if the Lord has desire, then He must be needy. But the Lord is not needy, although He is chivalrous. If the devotee expresses neediness, then the Lord's chivalry creates a want in Him. But if the devotee turns away from the Lord, then the Lord remains self-satisfied. The Lord doesn't initiate the loving relationship with the devotee. He has no desire to dominate or control anybody else because He is self-satisfied. But if the devotee demonstrates a neediness and dependence on the Lord, then the Lord responds.

The difference between the feminine and the masculine is neediness and chivalry. The feminine need is to be wanted, and the masculine want is to be needed. This is seen in this world too, so, by the knowing of the nature of love between men and women, we can understand the Lord and His Śakti.

Topic 26

QUESTION

Your descriptions of the masculine and feminine aspects of the Absolute Truth are dangerously close to the materialistic ideas of sexuality. Isn't it risky to describe the Absolute Truth in this way because it can seem to justify the male-female attachment in this world, which then repeats the cycle of birth and death? How can we say that this understanding leads to transcendence?

3.3.40 (400)
आदरादलोपः
ādarādalopaḥ

ādarāt—due to respect; alopaḥ—there is no (need for) cessation.

TRANSLATION

Due to respect, there is no (need for) the cessation (of sexual desires).

COMMENTARY

There is a famous saying—Everything in this world is about sex, except sex itself; sex itself is about power. The foundation of material sex life is control, domination, and authority. All manifestations of this controlling mentality—such as those seen in politics, management, etc.—are modifications of the material sex desire. The controlling mindset is not the expression of confidence and self-satisfaction. It is rather the expression of neediness and dependency. The dominant person needs to be loved, but they express their need as domination, because they don't want to show that they are factually needy of others.

The sexual interaction between the Divine Couple is not based on domination; the feminine is self-sufficient, and yet She wants the masculine to desire Her. The masculine is self-satisfied, but due to that self-satisfaction He is also compassionate and loving. There is a subtle but important difference between the self-satisfied nature of the masculine, and the self-sufficient nature of the feminine. The self-satisfied person has the capacity for making everyone happy, and the self-sufficient person has the capacity for fulfilling their desires. The feminine cannot dominate the masculine because He is self-satisfied. And the masculine cannot dominate the feminine because She is self-sufficient. The central theme of materialistic sex life—i.e., domination—is, hence absent.

This separation between desire and power is crucial to the process of divine love. She is powerful, and He is desire. The feminine doesn't dominate the masculine because She wants the masculine to desire Her. The masculine is love, but He doesn't need to dominate anyone because He is self-satisfied. In fact, the self-satisfied nature of the masculine produces love in Him. Thus, there are two archetypes—the wanting to love, and the needing to be loved. Their interaction is based on love, rather than the desire to dominate or exert control.

In the material world, when men are dominant, they already have the power and riches to attract the women; the women are attracted to them because they are weak and seek a man to give them power. In short, men have both desire and power, while the women have desire, but no power. This results in the exploitation of women by the men. Conversely, when women are dominant, they already have the power and riches to attract the men; the men are attracted to them because they are weak, and they need the women to provide them power. In this case, women have both desire and power, and the men only have desire. This results in the exploitation of the men by the women.

The situation in the spiritual world is different. The feminine is already powerful; She doesn't need power from the masculine. But She wants to be desired and loved by the masculine. When She needs the masculine, She doesn't become powerless; but She wants the masculine's love. Likewise, the masculine is self-satisfied, and doesn't need anything from anyone else, including the power from the feminine. But when the feminine needs, He loves Her.

The comparisons between the loving affairs of the Divine Couple and mundane sex life are misplaced. In fact, if one understands the nature of their love, all materialistic sex desires are naturally destroyed. This sūtra states that there is ādara or 'respect' between the Divine Couple. This can be seen in contrast to the material sex life of domination where this mutual respect is missing. The feminine knows that the masculine is self-satisfied and doesn't need anyone; there is hence gratitude when the masculine desires Her. The masculine also knows that the feminine is self-sufficient and doesn't need anything from Him other than His love. He is honored to be desiring a self-sufficient person. This mutual respect and gratitude between the Divine Couple differentiates their loving dealings from those of the materialistic sex life of ordinary couples.

QUESTION

Even if we say that the loving affair between the Divine Couple is different from material sexuality, doesn't it still entail a sexual union between Them?

3.3.41 (401)
उपस्थितेऽतःतद्वचनात्
upasthite'taḥ tadvacanāt

upasthite—secondary presence; ataḥ—therefore; tat-vacanāt—from their words.

TRANSLATION

From their words (spoken by the source and comprehended by the other), therefore, a secondary presence (within each other).

COMMENTARY

Material ideas of sexuality involve physical intercourse between the masculine and the feminine. But such ideas of intercourse are rejected here. Earlier it was stated that the Lord impregnates the material energy simply by glancing at Her. When our senses perceive the object, there is an impression of the object in our senses, and an impression of the senses in the object. We normally understand that by seeing an object we get an impression of the object. But why should the observer be present in the observed reality? The reason is that before the knowledge from the object is transferred into the observer, the object must know which observer the knowledge must be sent to. This mutual identification of the source and destination of the knowledge is called 'entanglement' in atomic theory: Energy is transferred only when the destination is identified at the source. This identification is fixed by the senses entering the object to perceive them. Similarly, in this sūtra it is said that the sexual intercourse between the masculine and the feminine is just like the words being spoken. When the words are spoken, there is an impression of the meaning in the receiver, and an impression of the listener—to whom the meaning is intended—in the receiver. Therefore, words are not spoken without knowing the listener. We speak always keeping in mind the intended listener. Sometimes when we talk to ourselves, we may be the intended listener. Or, we may have the imaginary presence of someone else two whom we imagine to be talking. In either case, there is an intended listener. So, the listener is within the speaker before speaking, and the speaker is within the listener after speaking. The listener and speaker enter each other, but this doesn't constitute physical sexual intercourse.

The sexual intercourse between the Divine Couple is looking at each other, talking to each other, understanding each other, desiring each other, and giving something pleasing to each other. They enter each other because they are the source and destination of meaning, and this source and destination must be present within each other for any communication to occur between them.

Topic 27

QUESTION

But isn't it possible that the cause of desire isn't external; that the desire can also arise internally? Why do we say that the cause of desire injects a desire in the other, whereupon the result of the desire is fulfilled? Could we not also say that the desire arises automatically whereupon it is being fulfilled?

3.3.42 (402)

तन्नरि्धारणानयिमः:तद्दृष्टे:पृथग्ध्यपरतबिन्ध:फलम्

tannirdhāraṇāniyamaḥ taddṛṣṭeḥ pṛthagdhyapratibandhaḥ phalam

tat-nirdhāraṇa-aniyamaḥ—no rule in deciding that (i.e., what comes first); tat-dṛṣṭeḥ—upon seeing that; pṛthak—separate (person); hi—certainly; apratibandhaḥ—no restriction; phalam—the effect (being the cause).

TRANSLATION

There is no rule in deciding that (which comes first); upon seeing that separate (person), certainly there is no restriction of the effect (being the cause).

COMMENTARY

When we look at the world, then the world can sometimes create a desire in us. Alternately, the desire can arise without an external provocation, and it can then be fulfilled by the world. Since both alternatives are possible, it is hard to say whether the world creates a desire in us and then fulfills it, or whether the desire arises first is then is fulfilled by it. The world can be the cause of the desire, and the desire can be the effect. Likewise, the desire can be the cause, and changes to the world can be the effect. Such alternatives cannot be fixed universally, but they are always fixed in a context. In the same way, the feminine can be the cause of instigating the masculine into a desire; in this case, She is the cause and the desire in Him is the effect. Conversely, the desire can arise automatically in the masculine, and She can be the effect that follows the cause—i.e., fulfills the desire. Due to this reciprocal model of causality, it is hard to say which comes first—the desire in the masculine or the power in the feminine. In between these two, there is no 'original cause'; they are hence said to be collectively understood as the Original Truth, not prior to one another.

Topic 28

QUESTION

But if the desire can arise in either masculine or feminine, why don't we say that these desires are selfish? That each side wants to satisfy themselves, and therefore, this interaction is just like the mundane worldly sexual activity?

3.3.43 (403)
पुरदानवदेव तदुक्तम्
pradānavadeva taduktam uktam

pradānavat—just like an offering; eva—certainly; tat–those; uktam—words (which are spoken, and then enter the listener).

TRANSLATION

(Because) those words (which are spoken and then enter the listener) are certainly like an offering (of a devout into the fire as in the case of a yajñá).

COMMENTARY

The process of yajñá is divided into three components—Soma or the offering, Agni or the fire, and Vayu or the process of offering. Soma indicates desire, pleasure, what we like, etc. Agni indicates the cause, reason, or purpose for which we sacrifice our desire, pleasure, or what we like. All of us make sacrifices to achieve something—e.g., you may work hard to earn some money, sacrificing your energy and personal time. To get something, we give away something. This is the principle of material exchange: The desire arises before the sacrifice is made. But in the process of love, which is also a yajñá, the sacrifice is made not to get anything, but simply to satisfy the receiver. The receiver also gives back, not to receive anything, but just to satisfy the giver. Thus, there are two kinds of sacrifices—in which one gives to receive, and the other in which one simply gives, without expectation of receiving anything. There is pleasure obtained in both cases, but the pleasure of selfish desire is generally unfulfilling because one provides only after calculating what they are going to receive.

Accordingly, there are two ways in which conversation can move. First, someone has a question, and they ask a question to get an answer. So, the questioner speaks first and demands an answer. The responder then provides an answer. Second, the questioner has a question but never asks. And yet, the responder simply answers the question by understanding that the questioner has a question that needs answering. Therefore, when desires are fulfilled after we ask, the process resembles a material transaction. However, when the desires are fulfilled even without asking, then the process is considered spiritual.

Thus, a first-class devotee is one who fulfills the Lord's desire without the Lord asking for it. The second-class devotee is one who fulfills the desire after it has been asked. And third-class devotee is one who counter questions, challenges, and demands an explanation—why should you desire this, and not that? How will I benefit from fulfilling your desire? Why should we not do this another way? Etc. If one asks submissively—e.g., Lord, I know you want something from me, but I'm not clear about it; can you please explain what I should be doing?—then he can be considered as good as a first-class devotee. Ultimately, such first-class devotees acquire a full understanding of the Lord, whereupon they don't even need to ask what the Lord wants. They automatically understand the desires in the Lord and fulfill them before He asks.

The Lord is also like that. He doesn't like asking anyone. Love is based on shyness—How can I demand? I'm already indebted by so many things I have received; how can I ask for more? Due to this shyness in the Lord, the conclusion of the scriptures—i.e., devotion to the Supreme Lord—is hidden from the non-devotees, because the Lord doesn't like to demand love from others. This conclusion is revealed only when someone asks: What is the greatest form of perfection? Such a seeker is a first-class devotee, although he may not know how to satisfy the Lord. The Lord then explains how He can be satisfied.

Topic 29

QUESTION

But we are talking about the Absolute Truth. If there is only shyness, then what about boldness? Is that considered to be absent in the Absolute Truth?

3.3.44 (404)

लङि्गभूयसत्वात् तद्धि बलीयःतदपि

liṅgabhūyastvāt taddhi balīyaḥ tadapi

liṅga-bhūyastvāt—because of presence of indicatory marks; tat—that (the Absolute Truth); hi—certainly; balīyaḥ—having boldness; tat—that; api—also.

TRANSLATION

That also; because of the presence of indicatory marks, that (the Absolute Truth) certainly (can be said to) possess boldness (not merely shyness).

COMMENTARY

Materialistic people are bold in asking for things but shy in giving back. The devotees are their opposite: There is shyness in asking, but boldness in giving. Due to this, the devotees give the Lord what He wants, even if He says: "Oh, it's not necessary". So, the combination of shyness in asking, and boldness in giving, constitutes a loving relation. The Lord is also shy in asking, but bold in giving. For a devotee, He gives without being asked, or even if the devotee says: "no I don't want". Thus, the devotee says to the Lord: "I don't want anything—not material prosperities, not respect and honor, not even liberation; I only want your loving devotion." And yet, the Lord gives to such a devotee everything—material prosperity, respect and honor, and liberation from the cycle of birth and death. The devotee out of shyness says: "I'm unqualified". This is not a fact, but it is also not pretentiousness. It is the genuine feeling in a devotee's heart, by which the devotee feels unqualified to serve the Lord, and yet, also feels gratitude at having obtained an opportunity to serve the Lord.

In the material world, boldness and humility are considered opposites. For example, most people think that talking politely is humility, and talking aggressively is boldness. But real boldness is giving up attachment to every material identity. And real humility is being ready to accept any kind of difficulty arising in the Lord's service. A devotee is both bold and humble—bold because he can leave this world even if there is happiness, and humble because he can stay in this world even if there are difficulties. The mundane visions of politeness and aggression are not the correct understandings of humility and boldness.

QUESTION

Several methods of spiritual advancement were mentioned earlier such as karma-yoga, jñāna-yoga, dhyāna-yoga, and bhakti-yoga (the performance of regulated devotional activities). The aim seems to be the combination of boldness in giving and shyness in asking. With this mood, can the other activities also be considered just like the loving relation within the Absolute Truth?

3.3.45 (405)

पूर्ववकिल्पःपरकरणात्स्यात्क्रिया मानसवत्

pūrvavikalpaḥ prakaraṇātsyātkriyā mānasavat

pūrva-vikalpaḥ—the earlier alternatives; prakaraṇāt—due to the context; syāt—may be; kriyā—a sacrifice; mānasavat—if they are the nature of the mind.

TRANSLATION

The earlier alternatives (which were prescribed) depending on the context (of a person), may be (considered) sacrifices if they are the nature of the mind.

COMMENTARY

The mind is responsible for understanding the meaning. This meaning comes in three forms— (1) universal, (2) contextual, and (3) individual. In different contexts, we might do different things, with different short-term goals. But there is a long-term goal or an overarching purpose. For example, we might get dressed, drive to work, attend meetings, do our assignments, etc. and each such activity involves a short-term goal, which are contextual goals. But there is also an overarching goal, namely, that we might want to earn money. We can call this the universal. But we can also ask: What do we do with this money? The answer is: We want to satisfy ourselves—the individual. Hence, there are contextual goals, universal goals, and individual goals. The context serves the universal, and the universal is pursued for the purposes of an individual.

In the same way, several contextual activities are prescribed for spiritual advancement—e.g., study scriptures, perform austerities, meditate on the Lord, and live a regulated life. The aim for all these contextual activities is a universal, which pervades throughout the activities—the idea of getting liberated from suffering and obtaining eternal happiness. But whose suffering and whose happiness? Generally, the answer is the individual self. Thus, contextual goals lead to the universal goal for happiness, but that universal is subordinate to an individual. The problem is simply in defining that individual person whose happiness is attained. We consider happiness as a universal goal, but we don't consider the person who embodies the universal happiness as the goal.

The true nature of the mind is that the universal is the knowledge of the Lord, the individual to be satisfied is the Lord, although the Lord can be satisfied differently in many contexts. If this mind is hidden, then a partial understanding of the universal is obtained. It is no longer the perfection of happiness but what I consider to be happiness. This partial understanding of happiness is then applied to the self—i.e., my happiness. And then all the contextual activities are tailored to selfish happiness. This is not the true nature of the mind. By the mind we can understand that happiness is a universal goal. But what is that type of happiness that exists in everyone must also be understood. If this happiness is understood, then the goal of happiness is the person who embodies this primordial notion of happiness, which pervades in everyone. If the mind is restricted in this understanding, then the universal is applied to the self.

There is hence a difference between *mānas* and *manas*—the former means 'mental', and the latter means 'mind'. The former represents the pure, primordial, and expansive mind, whereas the latter is the small and restricted mind. The great mind aims for the highest goal, the highest truth, and the highest relation. The limited mind seeks smaller goals, smaller truths, and smaller relationships. The minds of people in this world are mostly very small; they are not even interested in their spiritual well-being. They only care about the body. Somewhat more expansive is the mind that seeks liberation from the material suffering. And even more expansive is that mind which seeks to relate, to know, and to serve the Lord. This most expansive mind is the original mind, identified by *mānas*. The materialistic mind is produced by restricting the *mānas*.

QUESTION

You seem to be indicating that there are many kinds of minds. What do you mean by the great mind? How does it differ from the ordinary mind?

3.3.46 (406)
अतदिशाच्च
atideśācca

atideśāt—due to the reach to end of space; ca—also.

TRANSLATION

Due to the ability to reach to the end of space also (the mind is great).

COMMENTARY

The term *deśa* or space refers to the space of concepts or ideas. This space is very expansive, because it comprises all the concepts or ideas that can ever be understood. The soul has a position in this space which determines what we can understand. Things that are 'near' our mental state are cognized by us. Things are 'far' from our mental state cannot be understood by us. When a person has a small mind, there are things that he can and cannot understand. The person who has a great mind can reach to the limits of the space, which means that he can understand everything. Thus, there is nothing alien to him.

When one acquires devotion to the Lord, by understanding His nature, he also develops a very broad mind, that can comprehend any subject. People with a narrow mind can comprehend one subject—e.g., mathematics, physics, biology, economics, sociology, psychology, art, music, literature, etc. But the person with a broad mind can understand everything. People with a narrow mind can relate only to a specific culture, racial identification, social order, etc. But the person with a broad mind can relate to people in any culture, society, or racial denomination. Their ability to understand the expanses of space allows them to see the good and bad in everything. Hence, they can accept the goodness in any culture, just as they can reject the follies of any society. If they reject or criticize something in another culture, it is not because of malice toward others. However, those who have such attachments cannot appreciate their broadmindedness. They think that anyone offering criticism must be alien. For such people, whatever belongs to their culture is considered good, and whatever is alien to their culture is regarded as bad. They might blindly accept the follies in their culture as goodness, and think the goodness in the other cultures to be bad.

This sūtra says that a spiritually advanced person can go to the far ends of space. And by that reach, he doesn't consider himself to be restricted to a specific nation, society, or culture. This is the definition of broadmindedness.

QUESTION

Does this ability to know everything mean that they accept everything as the truth? Or, there is a difference between the meaning and the truth?

3.3.47 (407)
वदियैव तु नरिधारणात्
vidyaiva tu nirdhāraṇāt

vidyā—knowing; eva—indeed; tu—but; nirdhāraṇāt—due to being fixed.

TRANSLATION

(They can) certainly know (everything) but (the perfect knowledge) is fixed (i.e., they don't accept everything known as the perfect knowledge).

COMMENTARY

Understanding everything doesn't mean accepting everything as true. The previous sūtra stated that the devotee of the Lord can understand everything. That doesn't mean he appreciates, likes, desires, or considers it true. He can distinguish between the diversities which are partially true, and the Absolute Truth, which is completely true. Even these partial truths have their purpose in the Lord. Therefore, the devotee can engage everything in the Lord's service. But in this engagement, he doesn't become attracted, attached, or bound to those partially true things, and doesn't become influenced by them. For example, a devotee can use wealth in the Lord's service, but he doesn't become attached to the wealth. Even though he may seem engaged in dealing with wealth, he is not like the ordinary person who is counting pennies. Likewise, a devotee can study many subject matters of the world and engage them in the Lord's service. But by this engagement he is not influenced by those ideas. He understands their place and role in knowledge, always accepting the Lord to be the Absolute Truth. Various fields of knowledge are contextually true, and hence they can be employed in different situations. This engagement with the world is said to be devotion if the mind is expanded in a way that even as everything is understood, only the Lord is accepted as the complete truth.

Ordinary people cannot distinguish between the engagement of the contextual knowledge in the Lord's service and the engagement with that knowledge. They think that everyone engaged with the worldly things, such as wealth and knowledge, must be just like the mundane people engaging with it. They urge others to reject these worldly diversities as they cannot see how the Absolute Truth exists within the diverse things. Their viewpoint amounts to the philosophy of māyāvāda in which the world is false, and transcendence is true.

QUESTION

The problem with diverse fields of knowledge is that they present different pictures of the world. Accordingly, those who think about these things with their minds also adopt these different viewpoints, which conflict with other views. Thus, it is said that philosophy cannot capture the whole truth. But you are saying that a broadminded person can understand things fully.

3.3.48 (408)
दर्शनाच्च
darśanācca

darśanāt—because the philosophy; ca—also (can be complete).

TRANSLATION

Because the philosophy can also (be complete) (therefore, we reject the idea that anything known by the mind must necessarily be incomplete).

COMMENTARY

The senses, the mind, and the intellect of this world are limited, and the sign of that limitation is that the whole truth cannot be understood. The impersonalist now attributes the problem to the existence of the senses, mind, intellect, itself, and claims that only when these are rejected is everything correctly known. This means that to attain transcendence, one must be devoid of perception, thought, judgment, etc. The devotees reject this conclusion. The material senses, mind, and intellect are certainly limited. But there are also pure senses, mind, and intellect which can see the whole truth. The material world can be characterized as the partial knowledge of parts. For example, we might look at a table—which is a part—and then know it partially (e.g., we may not know how the carpenter created it, where the wood for the table was sourced, etc.). The spiritual world is characterized either as the partial or the full knowledge of the whole. Even if a devotee knows the Lord incompletely, since the Lord is the whole truth, the devotee's knowledge is considered transcendence. Of course, the devotees who know the Lord well, also come close to knowing Him completely. There is no limit to our understanding of the Lord, and anyone can obtain a full understanding. Therefore, philosophy is also not limited. Our minds can, however, be limited if we remain unprepared to know the full truth. The shortfall in our mind and intellect cannot be imputed back to philosophy, i.e., just because our mind and intellect cannot grasp the whole truth, we cannot say that the problem lies with philosophy. That is a sour-grapes mentality in which when we fail to do something, we claim that it must be impossible. By pushing the problem elsewhere, we avoid the effort necessary for understanding. So, calling something unknowable is just a symptom of laziness and ineptitude, compounded with the arrogance that it could never be my shortcoming.

QUESTION

But many people cite scriptures (or the statements of those who are considered equivalent to the scriptures) that the full truth cannot be known through philosophy, although they accept that can be known by experience. What would you say in regard to such claims that are based on scriptures?

3.3.49 (409)
श्रुत्यादबिलीयस्त्वाच्च न बाधः
śrutyādibalīyastvācca na bādhaḥ

śrutyādi-balīyastvāt—on the strength of the scriptures etc. and others just like it; ca—also; na bādhaḥ—cannot be refuted, or there is no restriction.

TRANSLATION

On the strength of scriptures or others just like it also (the claim about philosophical knowledge being complete) cannot be refuted or isn't restricted.

COMMENTARY

In previous sūtras it was stated that those with the purified mind can know the full truth. This purification is achieved by devotion to the Lord because the basic impurity in the soul is self-centeredness and from that narrowing of the purpose of life from the Lord to the self. Further narrowness is subsequently produced—e.g., preoccupation with the body and its well-being. When the mind is narrowed in many ways, it is impossible to comprehend the full truth. And philosophizing then becomes useless because we are unable to think beyond our limited existence. But if the soul gives up the self-centered approach to life and becomes the Lord's devotee, then it is fully purified. Thereafter, there is no restriction to the philosophical understanding. Nevertheless, because many people engage in philosophy with a self-centered and restricted mind, the scriptures often state that one should give up philosophizing and become the Lord's devotee. It is true that an unpurified mind cannot grasp the whole truth, and without devotion the Lord cannot be known. However, it is incorrect to say that even a purified devotee also cannot explain the Absolute Truth. Those who cannot see the difference between the pure and the impure mind take such scriptural statements—that urge a person to only focus on devotion—as a universal rejection of the philosophical understanding. They claim that it is in principle impossible to state the nature of the Absolute Truth. They draw a false equivalence between a limited mind, which cannot understand the full truth to the mind of the devotee who can perceive and explain this truth.

This sūtra rejects the idea that the Absolute Truth cannot be explained philosophically. Even if there are statements in the scriptures, or by others whose words are considered equivalent to the scriptures, they are only meant to push a person toward purification of the mind before they attempt philosophy. Philosophizing without devotion can never be complete. But the converse is also true: Devotion without a philosophical understanding is incomplete. Therefore, those who claim to be devotees but cannot explain the nature of the Absolute Truth—citing the inability of philosophical expression to capture the nature of this truth—cannot be considered perfected devotees. The contradiction between devotion and philosophy exists only for the imperfect devotees. This contradiction is dissolved for the advanced devotee because for him everything that can be directly experienced can also be explained philosophically.

The supposed contradiction between faith in the Lord through devotion and the philosophical explanation through reason is at the root of many faults in religious practices today. Those who have no understanding of the Absolute Truth often feign devotion to the Lord. And because they claim that the Absolute Truth cannot be known by reason, there is no way to check their understanding. They pass on as perfect devotees while carrying numerous imperfections. They remain narrow-minded while talking about the Absolute Truth. Their followers also remain devoted to them fanatically because there is no way to know if the person is truly advanced as they keep appealing to their private experience without being able to explain this experience to anyone else. The genuine seekers should not be cheated by such pretentious spiritualists.

QUESTION

But there is a fundamental contention between devotion and knowledge. Those pursuing knowledge say that the devotees are unintelligent and emotional. And the devotees then cite scriptures and say that the Lord is known only through devotion. How do we reconcile this basic contradiction?

3.3.50 (410)

अनुबन्धादिभ्यःप्रज्ञान्तरपृथक्त्ववत् दृष्टश्च तदुक्तम्

anubandhādibhyaḥ prajñāntaraprthaktvavat drṣṭaśca taduktam

anubandhādibhyaḥ—beginning with the subordinate binding (to the Lord); prajñāntara—knowledge appears within; prthaktvavat—as if they were different from each other; drṣṭaḥ—are seen; ca—and; tat-uktam—that (the understanding obtained by devotion) is then spoken (through philosophy).

TRANSLATION

Beginning with the subordinate binding (to the Lord), knowledge of the many seeming diversities (which are not truly separated) appears within as they are perceived (by direct experience). That (the understanding obtained by direct experience) is then spoken of (as the philosophical presentations).

COMMENTARY

After the previous sūtra rejected the claims of not being able to explain the Absolute Truth philosophically, this sūtra says that devotion to the Lord comes first. When someone becomes a devotee of the Lord, knowledge appears within as revelation. In this revelation, the diversity is only superficial because there is also a unity. The diverse views of the philosophers become incomplete parts of the whole truth. If this direct experience is obtained, the same understanding is then presented as philosophical conclusions to those who aren't yet devotees, who may not have obtained the inner revelation, or who may be baffled by the varieties of mutually contradictory philosophical positions. Therefore, the discovery of knowledge is through revelation. But that knowledge can be verified philosophically. Thus, one who knows the truth can use philosophy to explain the Absolute Truth, and others can learn the Absolute Truth from this expression of revelation. Since it is presented philosophically, the revelation can also be verified rationally. But if someone doesn't know, and doesn't obtain the knowledge through such revealed sources, and only searches for the truth by philosophical speculation, then knowledge can never be obtained. This is the difference between discovery and verification: Devotion is needed for discovery; philosophy for verification. However, since everything revealed can also be stated clearly and verified by reason, therefore, one must not blindly accept the claims about revelation unless they can also be verified rationally.

Scientists too have revelations: They get answers in dreams, or in spurts of insights that weren't preceded by a step-by-step process of reasoning. But such revelation isn't considered science unless it is explained through a logical argument. That logical argument may not be how they saw it initially. But it is necessary that all revelations must be formulated logically for it to be called science. A dream or hallucination is no less clear than the waking experience, and private revelations stand on par with such dreams and hallucinations. Just like we are convinced that we have a dream, but upon waking up we reason about it, and conclude that it was merely a dream. Similarly, if we want to be sure that a revelation is truth, rather than a dream or hallucination, it must be verifiable. This verification is not just important for others; it is equally important for each person who has this revelation to know that it wasn't a hallucination.

QUESTION

Many people claim that if they join a religious practice, and they follow the behaviors of devotees, then there is no need for philosophical understanding because a devotee automatically attains the Lord's abode. Then there are others who emphasize philosophy too much and are constantly engaged in debates with others, which may distract them from devotion. There are hence extremes of devotion without knowledge and knowledge without devotion.

3.3.51 (411)

न सामान्यादपि उपलब्धेःमृत्युवत् नहि लोकापत्तिः

na sāmānyādapi upalabdheḥ mṛtyuvat nahi lokāpattiḥ

na—not; sāmānyāt-api—despite the similarity; upalabdheḥ—is obtained; mṛtyuvat—upon death; na hi lokāpattiḥ—nor by worldly objections.

TRANSLATION

(Perfection) is not obtained, despite the similarity (of one's actions to those of the perfected souls) upon death (if they lack a perfect understanding). (Conversely, this understanding is) also not limited by the worldly objections.

COMMENTARY

Two extreme situations are discussed here. First, one may pursue some religious practices but not develop an understanding of the Absolute Truth. This sūtra states that although such people look like the pure devotees, the Lord's abode is not attained by them. Second, one may present this knowledge to others, but people may reject it. This sūtra states that such objections do not restrict a devotee's entry into the Lord's abode. These two extreme situations arise due to contradictory requirements. First, we say that something is not true if one claims to have divine experiences, but these cannot be explained rationally. Second, we say that even if we explain something rationally, many people may not accept it, either because they cannot understand it or because despite understanding it, they don't want to accept its truth. In the first case, a lot of people believe that a person is a devotee, but he is not. In the second case, a lot of people think that a person is not a devotee, but he is. Therefore, the criterion for entry into the Lord's abode is neither the superficial appearance of devotion (and the acceptance by many people), nor a superficial rejection of a devotee (by those who are not well-accepted by many—especially if they accept superficial devotees). Thus, popular consensus by many people is rejected as the qualification and popular rejection is not a disqualification. Not knowing and being popular is not qualifying and knowing but being unpopular is not disqualifying. On both sides, the sūtra rejects the opinion of the common ignorant people.

QUESTION

If popular opinion is rejected, then how does one know themselves to be advanced? Both direct experience and philosophical quests are being rejected as incomplete—direct experience because it could be a hallucination, and philosophical quest because it doesn't alone lead one to the complete truth.

3.3.52 (412)

परेण च शब्दस्य ताद्वधियम् भूयस्त्वात्त्वनुबन्धः

parena ca śabdasya tādvidhyam bhūyastvāttvanubandhaḥ

parena—the transcendental experience; ca—and; śabdasya—of the scriptures; tādvidhyam—the knowledge of that (can be obtained); bhūyastvāt—from their existence; tu—only if; anubandhaḥ—there is a connection.

TRANSLATION

The transcendental experience and the knowledge of those scriptures (is obtained) only if a connection exists (between them).

COMMENTARY

Many people say that they have seen God. But if we ask them how God looks like, they tend to give descriptions that don't conform to the scriptures. Likewise, many people study the scriptures, but they cannot see God, reject God's existence, or don't understand them. This sūtra states that only when both are present—i.e., direct experience according to the tenets of the scriptures, and the profound understanding of the scripture due to direct experience—can we say that the person is a devotee. The scriptures are the descriptions of direct experience, but we cannot understand the scriptures unless we have the experience ourselves—how can you know the meaning of ginger, unless you have tasted ginger? Likewise, if we have an experience that doesn't conform to the descriptions in the scriptures, then it is not divine. Thus, experience is needed to understand scripture, and scriptures are needed to confirm the experience.

The process of spiritual advancement is progressive and iterative. One begins by studying scriptures, and if initial conviction is obtained through a rational understanding, then one molds their life according to their tenets. But since the scriptures are incompletely understood in the beginning, one follows them incompletely or incorrectly. Even with a limited understanding, however, one progresses and acquires experiences by which the scripture becomes clearer. With that clarity, one molds their life again—this time with a slightly better understanding of the scripture. And that remolding leads to a better experience, which leads to a deeper understanding, and the process repeats until one obtains the full understanding along with experiential confirmation.

Topic 30

QUESTION

Are such devotees—who have both divine experience as well as complete understanding of the scriptures—found in the material world? Most of the so-called religious people seem to lack either of the two, and often both.

3.3.53 (413)
एक आत्मनःशरीरे भावात्
eka ātmanaḥ śarīre bhāvāt

eka—some; ātmanaḥ—of the soul; śarīre—bodily; bhāvāt—from existence.

TRANSLATION

From the bodily existence of some souls (we can say it is possible).

COMMENTARY

The use of the term *eke* indicates that the perfected souls are rare. While many people practice religion, they either don't have any spiritual experience, or those who have some spiritual experience lack a perfect understanding of the scriptures. In fact, many who have had some religious or mystical experience consider that to be the ultimate truth; they distort the understanding of the scriptures to fit that experience, denying themselves the chance to obtain greater perfection, and misleading others into believing that their experience is the ultimate truth. A follower is limited by the guidance of a teacher. If the teacher is imperfect, then the student necessarily is limited by the teacher's perfection. Since the perfect teachers are very rare, finding such a teacher, and then learning from them, becomes the difficult prerogative of the student.

This is, however, not a denial of the existence of perfected souls. Perfect knowledge always exists, and perfected souls are always present. Such souls, however, may not always be popular. As noted in the earlier sūtra, many such souls with perfect realization are often rejected by society, because the society is not seeking such perfect knowledge. When this happens, then the Lord advents to make the perfect truth popular again. But even if the Lord hasn't appeared, and the truth is not popular, the truth always exists. If a seeker is sincere, then he can find such knowers of truth. Popularity of the truth is an extra facility provided by the Lord's appearance, and many people accept the truth simply because it is popular. However, if the truth is unpopular, then the seeker must make additional effort to find the teacher of the unpopular truth.

QUESTION

Why do you say that such devotees are rare? Isn't religion and transcendence meant for everyone? Why should it be hard if it is meant for everyone?

3.3.54 (414)

व्यतरिकःतद्भावाभावति्वात् न तु उपलब्धवित्

vyatirekaḥ tadbhāvābhāvitvāt na tu upalabdhivat

vyatirekaḥ—different; tadbhāva-abhāvitvāt—feeling the absence of that nature (the Absolute Truth); na—not; tu—but; upalabdhivat—as if obtained.

TRANSLATION

Understanding that the Lord is different from them, feeling His absence, but not (feeling His absence) as if (the Lord is) already obtained.

COMMENTARY

This sūtra describes why true devotees are rare. Generally, we suppose that if we are seeing something, then we cannot be separated from it. Conversely, if we are separated then we cannot see that thing. But the pure devotee lives in a paradoxical state—he constantly feels separated from the Lord, and due to that separation constantly thinks of the Lord. The example of an Indian bride is sometimes given to illustrate this point. She goes to her husband's house, but everyone seems strange. Meanwhile, the husband has left the house and gone to a far-off land on business. The wife behaves politely with her husband's family members, but in her heart, she constantly remembers her husband. The husband is at once present and absent. The material union is based on the body, and the spiritual union is based on the senses and the mind. In a dream, our senses and the mind can see things, even though the body cannot touch them. The devotee relies on this fact, and even when the body is separated, his senses and the mind are united with the Lord—just like a vision in a dream.

Now, the materialists like to say: If you are seeing God just like we see dreams, then God must be your hallucination. To this, the simple answer is that there is nothing wrong in having a hallucination if it lasts permanently and is always pleasing. What is so great about your impermanent and painful reality anyway? In fact, the definition of hallucination is that it appears and disappears, that it may sometimes be pleasing and sometimes be painful. By that definition of hallucination, the materialistic reality is a hallucination because it appears and disappears, and it is sometimes pleasing and sometimes painful. So, the materialist argument about hallucination works against the materialist.

Factually, the devotees don't consider the material world a hallucination. The waking experience involves the body, along with the senses and the mind. The dreaming experience only involves the senses and the mind. If we can see things that the body is not in contact with, then this reinforces the idea that the seer is different from the body. The materialist likes to think that there is no seer apart from the body, but he cannot explain the origin of dreams, where you can see things that have never been seen previously in this life. Since they were never seen before, therefore, they cannot be the resurrection of memory stored in the brain. It follows that our seeing is not limited to the body. Therefore, the dreaming experience is considered superior to the waking experience in Vedic philosophy because it leads to the view that there is more to our existence than the body. Now, the materialist says that these dreams are simply chemical activity in the brain, and you are not factually seeing anything. But if that is the case, then even the waking experience must only be chemical activity in the brain, and whatever you call reality is only your brain hallucination.

Since materialists like to claim that God's vision is a hallucination, as a counterargument, it is sometimes said that whatever mechanism makes God's experience a hallucination, also makes everything else you consider a reality a hallucination. Therefore, you cannot call God's experience a hallucination and claim a reality for everything else. What you call science, or measurement and observation, must also be hallucinations created by your brain chemicals.

Now, we must remember that this is not a factual acceptance of the world as a hallucination. It is simply a reductio ad absurdum demonstration of the fact that if you say that God's experience is a hallucination, then by extension every other experience also becomes a hallucination. If God doesn't exist due to hallucination, then matter also doesn't exist due to hallucination. If matter doesn't exist, then hallucination cannot be created out of thin air. Therefore, by claiming hallucination, the argument undercuts the existence of hallucination. The materialist argument can thus be silenced by this counterargument.

But the clever impersonalist exploits this line of argumentation. He says: We accept your suggestion that both the vision of God and the vision of the world are hallucinations. Since these are all hallucinations, therefore, only the observer is real, and the diversity of observers simply arises due to the difference of bodies, therefore, even this diversity must be unreal. This argument cannot be refuted based on evidence, because whatever evidence you provide against it would be termed a hallucination. Therefore, the correct response to such an argument is: What is wrong with hallucination if it is permanent and always pleasing? Isn't it true that by your doctrine of impersonal oneness you are trying to attain eternal happiness? From what you say, it seems that you must die to obtain that oneness, but the devotee can attain it right now.

Topic 31

QUESTION

Do such devotees ultimately give up the different branches of knowledge and practices for spiritual attainment, and focus only upon the Lord?

3.3.55 (415)
अङ्गावबद्धास्तु न शाखासु हि प्रतिवेदम्
aṅgāvabaddhāstu na śākhāsu hi prativedam

aṅgāvabaddhāḥ—as a part is tightly bound (to the next bigger part); tu—but; na—not; śākhāsu—in the branches; hi—because; prativedam—everything known must be known in relation or connection to the Absolute Truth.

TRANSLATION

Just as a part (e.g., a leaf) is tightly bound (to the next bigger part—e.g., a branch) but still not (bound) in the branches because ultimately everything must be known only in relation or connection to the Absolute Truth.

COMMENTARY

The devotion to the Supreme Lord is the root, while the various other processes of spiritual advancement are like branches of the tree.

One begins with the branches, and slowly proceeds to the roots. However, this sūtra states that the devotee is connected to the branches and yet not connected. The connection to the branch is that the devotee doesn't give up the prescribed duties which are like contextual services to the Lord. And yet, He is not bound to these services, because the devotee's goal is ultimately to please the Lord. Thus, for instance, a scientist can keep doing science as their prescribed duty; but they are no longer bound by science, as their goal is to serve the Supreme Lord. Hence, the devotee doesn't renounce the activities that he is capable of through the body and mind, and yet, he doesn't remain attached to those activities.

The use of the term *prativedam* is illustrative; *prati* means 'mutual' or 'toward', and *vedam* means 'knowledge'. By knowing the Lord, we know ourselves, and by knowing ourselves fully, we know the Lord, because the Lord as the cause is present in the effect (the soul), and the soul as the effect emerges from the cause (the Lord). From the perspective of the soul, the term *prati* can indicate understanding the Lord as the soul is directed toward the Lord. Or, it can also mean mutual understanding—i.e., understanding the self along with the source of the self. The terms *anga* or 'parts' and *śākhā* or 'branches' further clarify this idea: the parts have emanated from the whole, so the whole is the cause and the parts are the effect. However, the whole is present in the part as the cause is present in the effect. Thus, by knowing the cause, we can know the effect. And by knowing the effect, we can know the cause. This is mutual knowledge. Nothing is completely known unless the complete is known.

QUESTION

But the different spiritual paths also required different kinds of practices. For example, the different branches of the Vedic system prescribe the chanting of different mantras. How can we say that in the practice of all these different paths, only the Absolute Truth is worshipped by these types of practices?

3.3.56 (416)

मन्त्रादविद्दवाऽविरोध:

mantrādivadvā'virodhaḥ

mantrādivat—like mantra etc.; vā—even; avirodhaḥ—is no contradiction.

TRANSLATION

Even if the (different) mantra (are chanted) there is no contradiction.

COMMENTARY

Every attribute can be applied to the Lord, but not to every other object. For example, if we say that the Lord is honest, then the claim is true. But even if we say that the Lord is a thief, the claim is true. If we say that the Lord is monogamous, it is true. But even if we say that the Lord is polygamous, it is true. If we say that the Lord is kind, then it is true. But even if we say that the Lord is cruel, it is considered true (the Vraja residents accuse the Lord of being cruel).

All these qualities—honest vs. dishonest, monogamous vs. polygamous, kind vs. cruel—are meanings. The object to which these properties are applied can be ordinary people, or the Supreme Lord. When most people chant mantras described in the different branches of the scriptures, they think that the mantras refer to different personalities, such as the Sun, Moon, stars, demigods, etc. This is not entirely false, because the meanings being attributed to such personalities are indeed their qualities. But this doesn't mean that the Lord is devoid of these qualities and the mantra cannot be applied to Him. For example, the Gayatri mantra states—"I worship that personality which illuminates the three worlds (*bhū, bhuvar* and *svarga*), one whose energy is seen in morning light, one who makes the demigods shine with splendor, and who is the cause, origin, and instigator of everything." The sun-god Sūrya is not mentioned, but because of the mention of 'morning light', most people tend to associate this mantra with Sūrya. However, one can even chant this mantra, pronouncing the same words and meanings, but with a different *reference*—the Supreme Lord, because He is indeed illuminating the entire world, is the cause of the entire world, and He is the powerful behind all the powerful. This is the fundamental property of the tree—the leaves are properties of the branches, the branches are properties of the trunk, and the trunk is a property of the root. Therefore, even the leaf can be called a property of the root, although there are branches in between.

In previous sūtras we saw how the Lord was said to be the origin of space, and since the entire space exists within Him, therefore, every point in space is a property of the origin and is defined in relation to that origin. This is the nature of the whole-part reality that the diverse locations in space are not separated from the origin, and yet, they are not identical to the origin. Like a property is different from an object, and yet the property is not separate from the object (you cannot separate the mass of a particle from the particle, and yet, the particle is not the mass), similarly, everything is a property of the Lord.

The difference is simply in the reference of meanings. The non-devotees think that they are praising different personalities by describing different qualities. And the devotee thinks that he is praising the Supreme Lord by describing the same qualities. The meanings are identical, but the reference is different. The impersonalist thinks that by using the term nirguna he is describing Brahman, which is devoid of qualities. But the devotee says that nirguna means one who is not bound by material nature, and that is the Supreme Lord. So, the impersonalist feels detachment by calling the Brahman nirguna. But the devotee feels ecstasy by praising the Lord as nirguna. For the impersonalist, if something is nirguna, then it cannot be saguna. But for the devotee, the Lord is also bound by the love of His devotees. So, He is free if someone tries to force Him. But He is bound if someone tries to love Him. These terms nirguna and saguna are not contradictory for the devotee. Therefore, the devotee can chant the mantra which uses the word nirguna just as He can chant the mantra that uses the word saguna. There is no fault in any mantra, if the reference is the Supreme Lord, rather than demigods, etc. This too is pure devotion to the Lord.

Topic 32

QUESTION

But even if many mantras can be attributed to the Lord, there are also many mantras which directly name the respective deities. How can we say that even such mantras don't need to be abandoned since you have previously said that the demigod worship must be abandoned for devotion to the Lord?

3.3.57 (417)

भूम्नःक्रतुवज्ज्यायस्त्वं तथा हि दर्शयति

bhūmnaḥ kratuvajjyāyastvaṃ tathā hi darśayati

bhūmnaḥ—generally; kratuvat—as in the case of sacrifice; jyāyast-
vam—the most excellent; tathā—so; hi—certainly; darśayati—sees.

TRANSLATION

Generally, even in the case of sacrifices, the most excellent (is
worshipped), so, certainly (the most excellent) is always seen (to be
worshipped).

COMMENTARY

The demigod worship was previously rejected. But now a caveat
is being added, namely, that when the Supreme Lord is worshipped,
the worship of the demigods is like worshipping the root of the tree
along with the branches and leaves. By implication, we can understand
that the previous rejection was that of demigod worship alone. The
key point is that no activity needs to be rejected (unless it is explicitly
forbidden) if the Lord is added to that activity. It is a general practice
that the demigods are never worshipped without the Lord. This general trend is called *bhūmnaḥ* or 'mostly' here. Thus, for instance, the
Lord is offered flowers first, following which even the demigods are
offered flowers. When the demigods are thus worshipped along with
the Lord, it is understood that the main person being worshipped is
the Lord, and the others are secondary to Him. Because the Lord is
present, it is understood that unless otherwise specified, everything
said is about Him. Even if some things are not said about Him, by calling out others, they are only said after the Lord is worshipped.

Topic 33

QUESTION

**The impersonalist also echoes a similar idea. Many of them say
that whenever any demigod is worshipped, the Supreme Lord is
worshipped. Therefore, these names of demigods are many ways to
reference the same personality, and one can choose whatever name**

or mantra one wants to worship the Lord. Are you indicating a similar approach, or do you disagree with such a claim?

3.3.58 (418)
नाना शब्दादिभेदात्
nānā śabdādibhedāt

nānā—different; śabdādi-bhedāt—owing to difference of words etc.

TRANSLATION

(The demigods are) different, owing to the difference of words etc.

COMMENTARY

In the previous sūtra, the worship of demigods was endorsed provided they are always the secondary personalities being worshipped.
This endorsement, however, doesn't equate to the claim that all these
demigods are as good as the Supreme Lord, and there is no difference between their worships. This sūtra clearly states that the demigods are different from the Supreme Lord, otherwise, the names used
to call them would be different. The names or words used to describe
the demigods can denote three things—the role of a person, the qualities of a person, and the individual person. The qualities of the demigods can be applied to the Supreme Lord, and the Lord can also take
the many positions occupied by the demigods. But the Supreme Lord
doesn't become the same person as the demigods. The demigods are in
a certain role, and have certain qualities, temporarily. The same qualities in the Lord are eternal, and if He wants, He can also accept the
role eternally. Therefore, unless one claims that the Supreme Lord also
has temporary qualities, any equivalence between the demigods and
the Supreme Lord is false. An impersonalist, however, claims that the
qualities in the Supreme Lord are products of material covering, which
means that the Lord falls into matter and His qualities are not eternal. If one makes such a claim, then this sūtra states a clear difference
between the two.

Topic 34

QUESTION

You have earlier said that the Lord can also be worshipped in the place of demigods, even for material gains. Now that you are saying that the demigods can be worshipped along with the Supreme Lord, were you indicating the worship of Supreme Lord alone, or the Supreme Lord with the demigods?

3.3.59 (419)

वकिलृपःअवशिष्टि-फलत्वात्

vikalpaḥ aviśiṣṭa-phalatvāt

vikalpaḥ—alternative; aviśiṣṭa-phalatvāt—due to non-specific results.

TRANSLATION

(The Supreme Lord is) an alternative, due to non-specific results.

COMMENTARY

All our material results are given to us due to karma. However, since karma is like money, which can be spent in many ways, by performing the rites for demigods, one can find an alternative way of spending karma—different from what is currently being delivered or expected to be delivered. However, the Supreme Lord doesn't even entertain such requests, unlike the demigods. When a devotee asks the Lord for material benedictions, the Lord simply ignores it, and the results are delivered according to the direction of the demigods. Since the demigods are working according to the principles laid out by the Supreme Lord, the Lord doesn't interfere with their free will. After all, they too have the good karma to enjoy their freedom as they wish. If the Lord started interfering with every demigod's work, then those demigods won't be able to utilize their freedom. Therefore, the previous recommendations about worshipping the Supreme Lord for material gains were the worship of the demigods in the presence of the Supreme Lord. Such worship ensures that a person recognizes that even when the demigods are delivering the results, they are still subordinate to the

Supreme Lord. Furthermore, this sūtra states that the Lord should be worshipped for "non-specific results". The indication is that the demigods give results in specific areas—e.g., wealth, health, family life, power, fame, beauty, etc. The Lord doesn't interfere with this working, but if one wanted something non-specific—i.e., which transcends the divisions of this material world—then only the Supreme Lord can deliver such results. Thus, the previous understanding of the demigod worship is nuanced by this sūtra, and the role of the Supreme Lord as the source of "non-specific results" is stated.

Topic 35

QUESTION

If the demigods are only delivering our karma, and the Supreme Lord doesn't interfere in this activity, then what is the use of worshipping the demigods? How can the demigods produce an outcome other than the destiny?

3.3.60 (420)

कामयासतु यथाकामं समुच्चीयेरन्न वा पूर्वहेत्वभावात्

kāmyāstu yathākāmaṃ samuccīyeranna vā pūrvahetvabhāvāt

kāmyāḥ—desires; tu—but; yathākāmam—according to one's desire; samuccīyeran—one may (repurpose) the accumulated (karma) for oneself; na vā—or not; pūrva-hetu-abhāvāt—due to absence of previous reason.

TRANSLATION

(Karma is meant for fulfilling material) desires; but, (according to one's desire), one may (repurpose) the accumulated (karma) for oneself, or not; there is no predetermined result (i.e., the delivery of karma is not fixed).

COMMENTARY

Deserving is always relative to desiring. If we have performed good deeds, then the results of those deeds will be available to us as good results. However, the definition of that 'good' is up to us. For instance, if we enjoy a simple life, the good karma will be delivered as a life close to nature. If, on the other hand, we like an opulent life, then the result of the same karma can be delivered as material opulence. Karma simply means enjoyment or suffering but based on our nature—i.e., what we enjoy or suffer—karma can produce different outcomes. Thus, the total amount of good or bad things we encounter is fixed; they can, however, be delivered in different forms based on our proclivities.

This sūtra states according to one's desires, a person can repurpose their karma. For example, suppose you were born with the proclivity toward music, but over time, your nature has changed, and you are more interested in sport. Based on the proclivity at the time of birth, the delivery of karma was fixed—i.e., it will deliver the results in relation to music rather than sport. So, if one's proclivities have changed, the worship of demigods is meant to alter the delivery of good or bad results in relation to the new proclivity. If one has good karma, it can be revectored toward sport rather than music. Likewise, if one has bad karma, then the results will also be delivered in relation to the new proclivity. This is the extent of the demigod interference in our lives; they cannot increase or decrease the good and bad outcomes; however, they can revector the good and bad from one type of desire to another. Thus, it is appropriate to think of karma as money; based on the nature of birth, there is a pre-established destiny; however, this destiny can be altered if our desires change. Just like money can be spent for buying good food or good clothes, likewise, karma can also be spent in different ways. However, such changes need demigod intervention. Unlike money, which we can choose to spend whichever way we like, as regards karma, we need to seek the permission of the demigods prior.

Topic 36

QUESTION

You have indicated numerous paths so far. You earlier rejected demigod worship, but you have now allowed demigod worship, or the regular performance of ordinary duties as legitimates practices for spiritual enlightenment. Since there are many paths to develop devotion to the Lord, how does one decide the path? Are these paths to be considered mutually equivalent?

3.3.61 (421)

अङ्गेषु यथाश्रयभावः

aṅgeṣu yathāśrayabhāvaḥ

aṅgeṣu—regarding the many paths; yathā-śraya-bhāvaḥ—as one wants to take the shelter of a specific type (of path, one can do so).

TRANSLATION

Regarding the many paths, as one wants to take the shelter of a specific type (of path, one can do so).

COMMENTARY

There is a false conception among many people that each path leads to a different destination. This conception is based on the misunderstanding that the activities of these paths are themselves the goals. Factually, every path is meant to develop devotion to the Lord. For example, the path of jñāna-yoga is to develop knowledge of the Supreme Lord. The path of karma-yoga is meant to worship the Lord through one's prescribed duties. The purpose of aṣṭāṅga-yoga is to meditate upon the Lord's form in our heart. And the purpose of bhakti-yoga is to develop the devotion to the Lord through singing, dancing, offering, and worshiping the deity. In jñāna-yoga, we dovetail our intellect to the Lord. In karma-yoga, we serve the Lord through our senses. In aṣṭāṅga-yoga we devote our mind to the Lord. And in bhakti-yoga we dedicate our ego to the Lord. Each of these is a part of our material existence, and these parts can be offered to the Lord—by serving the Lord through our senses, mind, intellect, and the ego. Since the soul is associated with all these parts, therefore, the engagement of any part eventually leads to the engagement of the soul.

This sūtra states that one can choose the path one likes—according to their preference, proclivity, or desire. If the soul is being devoted to the Lord through the senses, mind, intellect, or the ego, the main purpose is being served. Thus, from the standpoint of purpose, all the paths are identical. And yet, since different parts of our existence are being devoted to the Lord, these paths are not equivalent. If the mind is controlled, then the senses are automatically controlled; therefore, devoting our mind to the Lord through aṣṭānga-yoga achieves the purpose of karma-yoga. Similarly, if the intellect is devoted to the Lord, then the mind is automatically devoted; therefore, the practice of jñāna-yoga achieves the results of both karma-yoga and aṣṭānga-yoga. Finally, if the ego is devoted to the Lord, then the results of all other yoga systems are achieved. Therefore, due to the hierarchy in these elements, some yoga systems are superior to others. But this 'superiority' is a material perspective. Ultimately, the soul is superior to all these elements, and the purpose of such engagements is the attainment of the soul's devotion to the Lord. Thus, there is no contradiction between different paths, some paths being superior to others, and all the paths having the same purpose. All such statements are true in different ways.

QUESTION

It is sometimes said that different methods should be applied based on one's progress. Is this approach of selecting a path also considered valid?

3.3.62 (422)
शषि्टेश्च
śiṣṭeśca

śiṣṭeḥ—from the remainder; ca—also.

TRANSLATION

From the remainder (i.e., after some progress is achieved, and other progress is remaining) also (we can decide the path useful for the remainder).

COMMENTARY

While each path can be employed to develop devotion to the Lord, each path is also specialized for different aspects of this devotion. For example, the first step in developing devotion to the Lord is detachment from the material world. If one is attached to the material world, then even spiritual activities are performed for materialistic purposes. Detachment is attained by karma-yoga; however, this detachment isn't positive knowledge about the self. Detachment simply indicates that I'm not this body, and the soul is separate from the body. This detachment from the body, and the eternity of the soul is an incomplete understanding. A more complete understanding is that my life also has a divine purpose. This purpose is understood by meditation on the Paramātma in the heart, through the process of aṣṭānga-yoga. With this meditation we understand that we are the parts and there is a whole, and the part must be devoted to the whole. However, the nature of the whole is still not understood. The process of jñāna-yoga is meant to bring a complete understanding of the whole, the different types of parts, and their interrelations. However, this only gives us a theoretical knowledge of the whole, not its direct experience. Therefore, the process of bhakti-yoga is recommended so that a spiritual aspirant can advance their experience from the self (in aṣṭānga-yoga) to the Absolute Truth.

Thus, different branches or spiritual practices can also be selected based on the current state of advancement in the spiritual aspirant, and what is remaining. If a person is not detached from material desires, he cannot meditate; even if he sits down to mediate, the mind wanders everywhere, and the meditation remains poor. But a person who has become detached from material desires can meditate on the Supreme Lord in the heart because the mind now becomes steady. By this meditation, he becomes convinced that perfection is not self-realization but dedicating the self to the Absolute Truth. Then he is qualified to pursue the knowledge of the Absolute Truth. If one is not convinced that the Absolute Truth is different from the self, and the self is part of that Absolute Truth, the pursuit of knowledge doesn't produce the desired result. It merely produces deviant, selfish, or voidistic philosophies. So, the appropriate time to pursue knowledge is when one knows that one is incomplete, and completeness is obtained by surrendering to the complete. Once knowledge of the complete is acquired, then one can pursue devotion. Unless one acquires a theoretical understanding of the Absolute Truth, the pursuit of devotion is trivialized as fanatic following rather than the experience of a scientifically known reality. Thus, acquisition of knowledge is the precursor to the practice of bhakti-yoga. In this way, there is also a progressive path toward spiritual attainment.

QUESTION

Some people say that all these paths can also be practiced in parallel. For example, as detachment progresses, one can meditate better. As meditation progresses, one can acquire better knowledge. And as knowledge is acquired, devotion in the Lord is reposed with conviction rather than fanatic belief. Do you think these paths can also be pursued in tandem and combination?

3.3.63 (423)
समाहारात्
samāhārāt

samāhārāt—due to the combined practice (perfection is attained).

TRANSLATION

Due to the combined practice (of many paths, perfection is attained).

COMMENTARY

Even though devotion to the Lord is the goal, the practice of this devotion remains incomplete unless the progress obtained by the other paths is also incorporated in the devotional practice. For instance, those who haven't acquired the detachment by the practice of karma-yoga assume that their service to the Lord must always produce the intended results. They don't realize that devotion is performing the activities for the Lord's pleasure, without expectation of a favorable outcome. Thus, sometimes a devotee may be appreciated for his work, and sometimes he may be criticized. The true devotee, who has developed detachment, remains equanimous in both cases. Those who haven't developed the detachment, on the other hand, are carried away by appreciation and become proud, and are easily demotivated or angry upon criticism. As their mind is overtaken by pride and frustration, the devotion to the Lord takes a backseat and pursuing fame and punishing critics becomes the main goal.

Similarly, those who haven't perfected their meditation, fail to understand that devotion is a mystical process by which the Lord becomes visible in the heart. They may be detached from materialistic engagements, but without the understanding of the mystical process, they remain focused upon the activities of their body. They may follow rules and regulations strictly, but they cannot experience the bliss in the heart. Since nobody can continue a process unless this bliss is experienced, most people attached to strict rules and regulations, but without a mystical experience, either fall back to enjoying mundane pleasures or sometimes even become angry opponents of the process itself.

Likewise, those who haven't developed a theoretical understanding of the Absolute Truth cannot understand how the name, form, and pastimes of the Lord are different from those in this world. They think that the body of the Lord is just like our body, rather than the form of knowledge. They cannot see that this form of knowledge contains the soul and is also contained in the soul. Even though they might do regulated practices, they remain influenced by many conflicting ideas—e.g., if the Lord is transcendent, then He cannot be immanent; if the Lord is kind, then He must not be cruel; if the Lord is masculine, then He cannot be feminine; if the Lord is omnipotent, then He cannot become subordinate to the devotee; if the Lord is different from the devotee, then He cannot act like the devotee; etc. Conditioned by all these contradictions, the person justifies his actions by one-sided arguments—i.e., those that consider one aspect of the contradictory feature of reality. This leads to needless arguments, in which a person is trapped in a false understanding and keeps doing misdeeds thinking that their one-sided understanding is indeed justified by the scriptures.

The process of devotion includes detachment, mysticism, and knowledge. Anyone who pursues devotion without bringing in these three components is likely to remain stuck in the stage from which progress is possible only by adding the missing ingredient. Therefore, devotion is not contradictory to detachment, mysticism, or knowledge. Those who claim such a contradiction haven't truly understood the nature of devotion. This sūtra states that these different processes can and should be combined. Whether we practice them alternately or include the benefits of the paths in the practice of devotion—i.e., cultivating detachment, mysticism, and knowledge—along with the devotion to the Lord is left to the individual person's judgment. But all of them are necessary.

QUESTION

But wasn't it said earlier that other than the devotion to the Lord, all other processes are conditioned by the modes of material nature? So, if one follows these other processes, then one also remains conditioned by the modes?

3.3.64 (424)

गुणसाधारण्यश्रुतेश्च

guṇasādhāraṇyaśruteśca

guṇa-sādhāraṇya-śruteḥ—the scriptural statements (about many paths) being conditioned by material modes, is an ordinary statement; ca—also.

TRANSLATION

The scriptural statements (about the many paths described in scriptures) being conditioned by material modes, is also an ordinary statement.

COMMENTARY

When scriptures advise a person to become detached, and act without desire for results, the likely outcome is that the renunciation of desires also leads to the dereliction of duties. The absence of desire for results makes a person ask: If I'm not expecting anything in return, then why should I do anything? This outcome is like that of a sad or frustrated person who can't get the results of their actions and rejects their duties under *tamo-guna*. Similarly, when scriptures advise a person to practice meditation and seek mystical experience beyond the waking and dreaming experiences, the likely outcome is that the person starts pursuing material power—bodily strength, mental or intellectual acuity, and mystic powers. The practice of meditation naturally makes a person inclined toward material enjoyment, much like a person who performs severe austerities under the mode of *rajo-guna* only to acquire greater power. Finally, when the scriptures say that one should acquire knowledge, the likely outcome is that a person gives up all consideration of mystical experience and a day-to-day confirmation of knowledge through bodily activity. Under the influence of *sattva-guna* the person gives up real and verifiable answers and becomes engrossed with theoretical speculation that cannot be practically realized.

We have also noted above that if someone practices devotion without detachment, mysticism, and knowledge, he is bewildered by success and failure, cannot find real happiness within, and remains confused by contradictions.

Thus, every spiritual pursuit can get riddled with negative outcomes, and therefore the ordinary statement is that all these processes are potentially imbued with the effect of the three modes of nature. However, we can also see that when these methods are combined, then they preserve the benefits of the other processes, and cancel out their negative effects. For instance, mystical experience cancels out the negative effects of detachment—one is not only detached from the day-to-day events but also attached to something beyond. The pursuit of knowledge cancels the materialistic tendencies of mystical pursuits, as one realizes that each individual person only knows the full truth partially, so mystical experience is always a partial understanding of the whole truth. Likewise, mystical experience also cancels out the negative effects of knowledge because one ensures that even if the full truth cannot be verified in a single experience, experience remains important to verify parts of those truth contextually. Finally, detachment cancels out the negative effects of knowledge because this knowledge should be universally applicable to all circumstances; we cannot call something knowledge if it applies only to a few contextual scenarios.

Since knowledge, mysticism, and detachment have this tendency to cancel each other's negative effects, they can also be mutually contradictory. For example, if someone wants to pursue theoretical knowledge, without concern for the mystical or everyday confirmation of the knowledge, then the needs for practical and everyday confirmation will always distract them from the theoretical concerns of completeness, consistency, coherence, etc. Those pursuing mystical experiences will not be concerned about universal truth—if it gives them immense power to manipulate nature according to their will. And if someone acquired such power, their inclination toward detachment—which generally arises when one is frustrated by their efforts—would dramatically reduce. Therefore, we can see that there are natural conflicts between all these paths. And the conflicts between them entail that it is hard to combine them.

However, the devotion to the Lord reconciles these conflicts. Detachment arises because the goal is the pleasure of the Supreme Lord, not the outcomes in the material world. Detachment is not contrary to mystical experiences, as the devotee is ecstatic by this service. And the conflict between the universality of the Absolute Truth, and the contextuality of individual experience doesn't exist. Devotion selects the positives from each path and removes the conflicts by rejecting the negatives from each path, and thus combines them. Thus, detachment, mystical experience, complete knowledge, and devotion to the complete truth are simultaneously reconciled by the presence of devotion.

If the paths are kept separate, then they are individually incomplete and collectively contradictory. Thus, the general case is that of faults in each path (i.e., they are individually incomplete) and they are collectively flawed (because of contradictions between them). However, the special case is that if they are combined under devotion to the Lord, then both the incompleteness of the individual paths and the inconsistency between the paths is at once resolved. Therefore, in separated form, they seem conditioned by faults or the modes of material nature. But in combined form, they are free from all such faults.

QUESTION

The coexistence or combination of all the paths you are mentioning here doesn't seem to be mentioned by the scriptures, which only talk about the paths separately. How can we justify their combination based on scriptures?

3.3.65 (425)

न वा तत्सहभावाश्रुतेः

na vā tatsahabhāvāśruteḥ

na vā—rather not; tatsahabhāva-aśruteḥ—their coexistence not being mentioned by the scriptures (or not previously heard).

TRANSLATION

It is incorrect to say that the coexistence of that (the many paths) is not mentioned in the scriptures (as they are implicitly implied by the scripture).

COMMENTARY

A classic example of this coexistence is found in the Bhagavad-Gita, where Lord Kṛṣṇa describes karma-yoga, jñāna-yoga, dhyāna-yoga, and bhakti-yoga. Even as Arjuna rejects these paths due to their flaws and difficulties, since they are spoken by the Lord, they must be considered the perfect truth. It has been previously noted that scriptures are correctly understood only when the many seemingly contradictory statements are reconciled. This becomes even more important when such contradictions seem to exist within a single scripture, and the correct understanding of the scripture is that these are not contradictory. However, to the extent that spiritual life begins with detachment, then progresses into mystical experience of the self, then proceeds into a theoretical understanding of the Absolute Truth, and finally culminates into the devotion to the Absolute Truth, there is a progression from detachment to devotion. At each step in this progression, the pursuits of the past may seem incomplete or contradictory to the present pursuits. However, when the final goal of devotion to the Lord is achieved, then all these seeming contradictions are resolved. Since the final goal reconciles these contradictions, an avid practitioner must keep in mind that the rejection of a path is necessarily temporary and incomplete. Furthermore, progress means the simultaneous coexistence of all the paths.

QUESTION

If these paths must be reconciled because they are mentioned in the scriptures, doesn't it entail that the philosophical contradictions between the different paths—e.g., of engagement vs. renunciation—must be corrected?

3.3.65 (425)

दर्शनाच्च

darśanācca

darśanāt—from the philosophical systems; ca—also.

TRANSLATION

(The contradictions between paths must be reconciled) from philosophical systems as well (e.g., the systems of Yoga, Sāñkhya, Nyāya, Vaiśeṣika, Mīmāṃsā, and Vedānta, which are considered the six systems of philosophy).

COMMENTARY

In this sūtra, compared to the previous one, a distinction between scripture and philosophy is emphasized. After stating that there is no contradiction in the scripture, this sūtra states that any such contradiction in the philosophies must also not exist. Notably, these philosophical systems are based on Vedic texts, but the proponents of these systems have historically conflicted with each other. For example, many commentators in Vedānta reject the validity of other systems such as Sāñkhya, Yoga, and Vaiśeṣika. They might say that because Sāñkhya deals with the material categories, therefore, it has no reality, and only Brahman is real. Likewise, since Vaiśeṣika deals with the existence of atoms, and Brahman is undivided, therefore, any atomic division must be unreal. Finally, even the idea that there are separate ātmā and Paramātma, which then need to be united by Yoga, is flawed if these are factually not separated entities. Thus, in trying to establish the validity of a system of philosophy, the other systems are rejected, and this rejection of the other systems is forbidden here. Even as these systems can seem contradictory to many people, they are not contradictory. Their seeming contradiction is only a puzzle or paradox to be solved by the reader, by finding the understanding the reconciles all of them. The implication is that any understanding of Vedānta that rejects the truth of the other systems of philosophy can be immediately discarded. This is not to deny the presence of seeming contradictions, or even to gloss over these contradictions irrationally. It is only to assert that contradictions indicate the presence of a deeper truth that reconciles them. Unless they are reconciled, this deeper truth has not been described, and therefore their rejection or acceptance is superficial.

SECTION 4

Topic 1

QUESTION

It is sometimes said that of the four endeavors of man, only one (liberation) is transcendental. Therefore, it follows that many of the practices—such as the performance of duties—are not related to transcendence. If you say that all such practices can be spiritually elevating, doesn't it contradict this statement?

3.4.1 (426)

पुरुषार्थोऽतःशब्दादिति बादरायणः

puruṣārtho'taḥ śabdāditi bādarāyaṇaḥ

puruṣārthaḥ—the goal of life; ataḥ—therefore; śabdāt—from scriptures; iti—in this way; bādarāyaṇaḥ— Bādarāyana (who authored scriptures).

TRANSLATION

All the goals of life (dharma, artha, kāma, and moksha) are therefore (attained) from the scriptures, authored by Bādarāyana (i.e., the Vedic system).

COMMENTARY

The Vedic system describes four *puruṣārtha* or the purposes of life. These are called dharma or the performance of actions, artha or the obtainment of results, kāma or the fulfillment of desires, and moksha or liberation. All dharma involves a person's role, and these roles are relational. For example, you cannot be a father unless someone is a child; you cannot be a wife unless someone is a husband. This relational reality is called *sat* or awareness. It defines us by connecting us to something else. Similarly, while artha is sometimes translated as 'money', it includes every material object—house, car, land, cattle, jewelry, etc. Artha denotes 'meaning', and everything we find meaningful is artha. Artha springs from the *chit* of the soul; it includes both the things we find meaningful and the activities that give meaning to our life. Finally, *kāma* or the desire for pleasure springs from the ānanda of the soul. It includes selfish desires as well as selfless love; when a desire is fulfilled, we become happy. The simple sequence is that one performs the duties of one's role, obtains meaningful things, and enjoys with these things. While the roles, objects, and desires can seem mundane, there is a spiritual basis of these three aspects within the soul.

Unless one understands this spiritual basis of dharma, artha, and kāma, it is believed that these three are only for this world, and after these are renounced, then one attains moksha or liberation. Thus, moksha is incorrectly understood as freedom from roles or dharma, from cognition and activity, and from desires. But this is a wrong understanding. The *sat*, *chit*, and ānanda of the soul are eternal potentialities. They can remain in a dormant stage, but they can never be lost. Therefore, moksha or liberation means getting out of temporary roles, cognitions, activities, and desires, and being situated in eternal roles, cognitions, activities, and desires. This eternal dharma, artha, and kāma are obtained in relation to the Lord, when the soul is situated in a relationship to the Lord, sees the Lord and serves Him, and desires to make the Lord delighted. Liberation means the soul doesn't keep changing its dharma, artha, and kāma.

So, if we look at the puruṣārtha from a mundane perspective, then dharma, artha, and kāma must end with the material world, while moksha is a one-time achievement. But if we look at the same situation transcendentally, then moksha is a one-time achievement, but dharma, artha, and kāma are eternal.

The mundane view of puruṣārtha applies to all the spiritual paths, beginning with the pursuit of detachment through karma-yoga. Once we become detached from results, then we just keep performing our duties, but we are not interested in the pursuit of artha or results or selfish pleasure or kāma. But this is a limited understanding of puruṣārtha. The purpose of the soul doesn't end with liberation. Therefore, a more nuanced understanding of puruṣārtha is that everything continues beyond liberation, and this is possible only when we say that the pursuit of transcendental knowledge, love of the Lord, the vision of the Lord in the heart, and services to the Lord are not mundane puruṣārtha. When devotion is a legitimate kāma, then relation to the Lord is legitimate dharma, and the cognition and activities in that relation are legitimate artha. This transcendent relation, cognition, and emotion is itself the nature of mukti.

The combination of the multiple paths described earlier is meant for the attainment of this puruṣārtha even beyond the material world. If the broader view of paths is rejected, then many puruṣārtha (e.g., the pursuit of knowledge or the satisfaction of the Lord in this material world) would also be rejected.

This sūtra indicates that the combined practice of many paths is unique to the Vedic system because detachment, mystical experience, transcendental knowledge, and devotion are simultaneously pursued (or at least one after another). In other systems of religion, one or more of these are found missing. Thus, for instance, there are many mystical traditions that don't emphasize knowledge, devotion, or detachment; they only talk about mysticism. There are philosophical approaches which only speak about knowledge, but not about devotion or mystical experiences. Then there are methods of austerity which emphasize renunciation and may encourage devotion to the Lord, but there is little focus on philosophical understanding and mystical experiences. Therefore, the system propounded by Bādarāyana is unique in this respect.

QUESTION

You have mentioned that when the Lord is worshipped in any process, that process—even though demigods may be worshipped alongside—is considered spiritual. What if the goal of the worshipper is not liberation, but simply material enjoyment? Will that still be considered the ultimate puruṣārtha?

3.4.2 (427)
शेषत्वात्पुरुषार्थवादो यथाऽन्येष्वतिि जैमनिि
śeṣatvātpuruṣārthavādo yathā'nyeṣviti jaiminiḥ

śeṣatvāt—from remainder; puruṣa-arthavādaḥ—are called selfish purposes of the enjoyers; yathā—just as; anyeṣu—in other cases; iti—thus; jaiminiḥ—(the individual worship of demigods as defined by) Jaimini (are not spiritual).

TRANSLATION

The remainder (of processes—which don't have transcendence as the goal) are called selfish purposes of the enjoyers, just as in other cases such as those described by Jaimini (e.g., the worship of demigods is not spiritual).

COMMENTARY

During the previous discussion on Jaimini's philosophy, the worship of demigods was decried. Subsequently, demigod worship was accepted if the Supreme Lord is worshipped as the superior personality. Now it is said that even the worship of the Lord along with the demigods is considered not the final goal (puruṣārtha) if the purpose of that worship is material enjoyment. If only the demigods are worshipped, then it is obvious that the person is interested only in material enjoyment, hence, it is easy to reject such worship. If only the Lord is worshipped, then there are several nuances. First, the Lord may be worshipped for obtaining material enjoyment, and not transcendence. Second, there may be some devotion for the Lord, mixed with the desire for enjoyment to be obtained through the demigods. Third, either the Lord alone or together with the demigods, may be worshipped to obtain liberation. It is understood that when the Lord is worshipped, then the soul is gradually purified of material desires. It is also understood that the demigods can assist the soul in the pursuit of liberation so that worship is not completely rejected. Ultimately, the main criterion is the intention of the worshipper. There are many methods for fulfilling each goal, but puruṣārtha is the goal, not the method of achieving it.

Thus, after clarifying many positions about who should and should not be worshipped, it is said that if the goal is not transcendence, then everything is considered material. This includes the worship of demigods in isolation (as given by Jaimini). However, the use of 'just as' indicates that even other methods where the Lord is worshipped for material gains are considered selfish endeavors. Since one can interpret the previously endorsed worship of demigods along with the Lord as a blanket acceptance of using worship for material ends, therefore, this sūtra rejects that conclusion by noting the importance of intention as the final determinant of whether something is considered a puruṣārtha.

QUESTION

But you previously also said that truth is obtained only by reconciling the diverse philosophical positions, and Mīmāṃsā is such a philosophical position. Doesn't the rejection of Jaimini contradict the previously stated position?

3.4.3 (428)

आचारदर्शनात्

ācāradarśanāt

ācāra—the established precedents (aiding dharma, artha, and kāma); darśanāt—from the six systems of philosophy (and may be incongruent).

TRANSLATION

The established precedents (aiding dharma, artha, and kāma) are from the six systems of philosophy or the visions of reality (and may be incongruent).

COMMENTARY

There is a fundamental difference between how philosophy is treated in the Western world, and how it was treated in the Vedic system. Everything in philosophy begins with some 'given'. The 'given' in Western philosophy is generally our experience, and the goal of philosophy is to explain this given. The 'given' in the Vedic system is the Vedic texts, and the goal of Vedic philosophy is to explain the Vedic texts. When we start explaining the 'given' we often limit ourselves to limited parts of the 'given'. For example, in science, we might explain the body, but not the mind. Or, we might explain physical motion but not how this motion is controlled by choices, why choices can be right and wrong, and how the morality of choice determines consequences. Due to the focus on limited parts of the 'given', a philosophical system can be incomplete. This is true for the Vedic philosophical systems as well. For instance, Sāñkhya focuses on the nature of matter, but has a limited focus on choices and their consequences. A more complete theory would have to add karma, which must then be followed by a doctrine of liberation, which then requires a description of the spiritual world, and finally the description of God who produced everything. At each successive step, new contradictions may be found in the philosophy.

The Vedic philosophical systems have divided these elements of a complete philosophy into several distinct aspects. For example, Sāñkhya describes matter as universals. Vaiśeṣika describes the individuals created from these universals. Yoga describes the nature of consciousness. Mīmāṃsā discusses the relation between choice and consequence. Nyāya identifies the principles of logical reasoning. There is always some overlap between these varied doctrines. But the differences of focus in them means that all possible details—which arise when we try to formulate a complete understanding—may not be present in them.

Thus, philosophies are often accused of incompleteness—some aspect of experience hasn't been explained. We might also find difficulties in reconciling different doctrines. When faced with these twin problems, philosophers often come up with new ideas or ways to reconcile these problems. But on what grounds can we accept one answer over another? The debate now moves away from the real problem, into the methods by which something is accepted true. The realist says—my solution solves a problem that you are unable to solve. The instrumentalist says—but we might be able to solve it in the future, and when I solve it, I will also provide the evidence for my chosen solution.

The real problem is that the realist should be able to explain and justify any claims of reality based on reason and experience, but they may not have the wherewithal for it. But instead of acknowledging the shortcoming, the argument is reversed, and the instrumentalist is accused of being biased toward observation and reason. That accusation leads to the counter-accusation of accepting the reality of things even when they cannot be observed or reasoned. The acrimonious debate then leads to both sides rejecting each other's views.

In one sense, the rejections are completely false. In another sense, the reasons for rejecting them are true, but these may not be the only reasons. There may exist reasons due to which the rejection can be rejected but the reason for the rejection can be accepted. The goal of philosophy is to identify the missing reasons, and their discovery improves our understanding because what wasn't known previously is now known. Until such additional reasons are found, the conflict between claims keeps simmering. Thus, this sūtra says that philosophies are the visions of the established knowledge. This is an indirect indication that reality is bigger than the vision, and the vision can be enhanced to completely describe the reality—whereupon these rejections will disappear.

QUESTION

If the philosophical systems are merely interpretations of the Vedic texts, then why can't we completely reject these interpretations, and just rely on the texts? What is the benefit of these interpretations if they are sometimes inconsistent with the texts? Doesn't this lead to many confusions for the aspirants?

3.4.4 (429)
तच्छ्रुतेः
tacchruteḥ

tat-sruteḥ—that the scriptures directly declare.

TRANSLATION

Those (philosophical systems of interpretation) are directly declared in the scriptures (so they are not arbitrary or whimsical creations).

COMMENTARY

Sāñkhya and Yoga are examples of philosophical systems directly mentioned in scriptures. Vedānta is seldom mentioned because it the conclusion of the Vedas. Mīmāṃsā, Nyāya, and Vaiśeṣika are not part of the Vedic texts, but they are mandatory additions because they deal with fundamental questions such as: What are the means to knowledge? How should a text be interpreted? What is language? How is it produced and how does it encode meanings? After we understand the meaning, how do we verify its truth? Even as the Vedic texts take epistemology, hermeneutics, and linguistics for granted, the questions are not less important, and they are examined by other philosophical systems.

For example, Vedic texts do not define the methods of knowledge such as pratyakśa (experience), anumāna (inference), śabda (revelation), upamāna (comparison), etc. But because these methods are used in the Vedic texts, questions naturally arise: How many methods must exist? Which method should be used when? Do these methods exhaust everything that can be known?

The key point is that the philosophical systems should not be whimsically rejected, because: (1) they are directly mentioned in the scriptures, (2) they are summaries of the scriptures, and (3) they explain the process of interpreting, verifying, reasoning, learning, judging, understanding, etc. The Vedic texts present knowledge, but the processes of understanding the texts are supplementary information. Just because linguistics, grammar, and logic are not explicitly discussed in the Vedic texts, doesn't mean they are human creations. They too are divine, but their nature is assumed without explanation in the texts.

Language and logic cannot be taught unless language and logic pre-exist within us in some primordial form. To learn a language, we must use a language; so, if there wasn't a language in us, then no other language can be learned. Likewise, to learn logic, we must use logic. If there were no logic within us, then we cannot be taught logic. So, language and logic are innate in all of us. Their presence is indicated using the term śabda-brahman, but the understanding of language and logic is as complex and involved as the collection of all the systems of philosophy. Every system of philosophy is nothing other than language and logic, and it is taught using the language and logic within us. This process is called 'purification'. The thing to be purified already exists, but it is imperfect, unclean, and contaminated. The external knowledge is not giving us anything new; it is cleaning up the thing that already exists within us.

QUESTION

But there are already so many Vedic texts, which are hard to reconcile. How does adding more philosophical systems to this not make the process of reconciliation worse? We are now expected to reconcile even more topics!

3.4.5 (430)
समन्वारम्भणात्
samanvārambhaṇāt

samanva—reconciliation; arambhanāt—for the reason for beginning.

TRANSLATION

(Philosophies exist) for the purpose of beginning the reconciliation.

COMMENTARY

The six philosophical systems extract all the fundamental ideas from the Vedic texts. Vedānta, for example, summarizes the relation between the whole and the part and describes matter and soul as the parts. The Yoga system discusses how the soul is entangled in matter and how it can be liberated from this entanglement. The Sāñkhya system describes the nature of matter, and how it creates both knowledge and illusion. The Mīmāṃsā system discusses the nature of knowledge, how it is embodied in texts, and how meaning must be extracted from the texts. And Nyāya discusses what types of proofs may be employed to know. Since words can represent God, soul, and matter, therefore, the entire system of whole-part relationships, how they are separate and inseparable, exists in language as well. Knowledge involves universals, but their expression creates the individuals. Vaiśeṣika is the study of how the universals become individuals; the individuals are not things but embodiments of meaning. How these individuals (matter and soul) evolve in a rational manner—e.g., that premises lead to questions, which then lead to answers, which then become the new premises; or that this succession of premises, questions, and answers forms an iterative, linear, and hierarchical structure—is the Nyāya system.

The collection of all these systems constitutes a 'science' that spans matter, soul, and God, as it covers all the fundamental topics of epistemology, ontology, hermeneutics, ethics, linguistics, logic, happiness, and transcendence. The comprehension of these topics, and their reconciliation, can be aided by the philosophical systems. This sūtra says that if one wants to understand the Vedic texts, then one can begin by understanding the philosophical systems. These systems are not added complexity; they are the means to understand it.

QUESTION

Does this philosophical understanding alone constitute the ultimate purpose of life? Or is this understand a preliminary step toward a practice?

3.4.6 (431)
तद्वतो विधानात्
tadvato vidhānāt

tadvataḥ—accordingly; vidhānāt—from the performances (or activities).

TRANSLATION

Accordingly (i.e., based upon the philosophical conclusions) from the performances (or activities) (i.e., knowledge must lead to changed behaviors).

COMMENTARY

Philosophy is of limited value if it doesn't translate into a change in our lives. Armchair speculation loses touch with reality, and the day-to-day concerns. One such disconnection is that philosophy may not tell us what to do in everyday life. This sūtra states that correct knowledge must lead to correct actions. If knowledge doesn't change our behavior, then it cannot lead to happiness, because happiness depends on the changes in our actions. Most modern pursuits of knowledge don't tell us what is right and wrong. Science can tell us how to make different things, but how do we use those things? When and where must they be used? Whether they should be used? And by whom? If knowledge is silent on behavior, then the advancement of the under-standing of material nature can be very dangerous; it gives us powers but doesn't tell us how to use that power. Without guidance on the use of power, power is prone to be misused. And that misuse entangles the soul in suffering. Knowledge must make us happier. But if knowledge leads to increased suffering, then it doesn't fulfill the purpose for which we do everything—i.e., happiness.

QUESTION

But what if someone doesn't have the time, inclination, or the intelligence to pursue a philosophical understanding? How do they achieve the goal of life?

3.4.7 (432)
नयिमाच्च
niyamācca

niyamāt—due to the prescribed rules; ca—also.

TRANSLATION

(Those who cannot follow philosophy can attain perfection) also by following the rules and regulations (of behavior that follow the philosophy).

COMMENTARY

Every religion prescribes rules on how to live life, although they may not explain why these rules are important. Without true knowledge, people are prone to invent new rules whimsically. And with such manufactured rules, whatever could have been achieved by following the rules borne out of a real philosophical understanding is also lost. In fact, religions start differentiating themselves based on these rules and regulations as 'divine revelation' without the ability to explain and justify why any such rules must be followed.

This sūtra states that those who cannot understand philosophy can also reap the benefits of philosophy by following the rules and regulations borne out of the philosophy. This doesn't mean that nobody needs to understand the rules. It just means some people can rely on the rules given by others—but those who give the rules must understand the reason why such rules are prescribed. In the Vedic system, only the Brahmana—i.e., the most intelligent and educated class of people—were involved in philosophical understanding. Everyone else simply followed the rules prescribed by the Brahmanas. The rules, however, were based on the understanding of matter, soul, and God. As the philosophical understanding declines—with the disappearance of the Brahmana—the rest of the population is simply left with rules and regulations. They cannot explain or justify why certain rules must be followed. And, over time, they discard the rules or invent new ones. Whatever benefits could have been achieved simply by following the previously devised rules (even without a philosophical understanding) now also disappears rapidly. Therefore, it is essential to establish the philosophical understanding before we formulate the rules. Although most people might simply follow the rules, if someone is intelligent enough to question why these rules are to be followed, there will be an explanation.

QUESTION

What if someone restricts themselves to philosophical understanding? Many philosophers are fond of hairsplitting irrelevant differences, arguing about nuances, which might sometimes create confusion rather than clarity.

3.4.8 (433)

अधिकोपदेशात्तु बादरायणस्यैवम् तद्दर्शनात्

adhikopadeśāttu bādarāyaṇasyaivam taddarśanāt

adhika-upadeśāt—from excessive teaching; tu—but; bādarāyaṇasya—of Badarayana's (view); evam—in this way; tat-darśanāt—from that vision.

TRANSLATION

But (the result) from excessive teaching of Bādarāyana's philosophy in this way (the result is same as that obtained) from that philosophy.

COMMENTARY

The study of scriptures is not considered different from the meditation on the Lord, the performance of mystical practices, or other such methods of spiritual advancement, because if properly performed, they deliver the same result. Thus, some people may focus more on deity worship, others may perform more meditation, while some others may study the scriptures more often. The key point is to devote our senses, mind, intellect, and consciousness to the Lord. Whichever that concentration is attained—through deity worship, by meditation, or by scriptural study—if the result is attained, then the processes by which they are attained are not considered superior or inferior. When our consciousness is focused on the Lord, then all perfection is already attained.

QUESTION

On the other hand, there can be people who aren't inclined to philosophy but may be interested in detachment, mystical experience, and devotion. If they attain these experiences and personality change, is philosophy still necessary for them? Or they also attain the results of philosophical understanding?

3.4.9 (434)
तुल्यं तु दर्शनम्
tulyaṃ tu darśanam

tulyam—equivalent; tu—but; darśanam—the philosophical conclusions.

TRANSLATION

(Those who obtain detachment, mystical experience, and devotion) are but equivalent to (those with the perfected) philosophical conclusions.

COMMENTARY

If you can see the sky, then you don't need a description of the sky. The description of the sky is needed to motivate one to see the sky—if they haven't seen it. Or, to tell them that once they see, they must know what demarcates the sky from a forest. If people don't know about the sky, then they will not be motivated to see the sky. Or, they might see a forest, and think that they are seeing the sky. But, for one who has seen the Absolute Truth, the preliminary steps of motivation and confirmation are already achieved. Therefore, theoretical knowledge is neither necessary nor sufficient. Not necessary because the vision of the Absolute Truth can be obtained through detachment, mystical experience, and devotion. And not sufficient because even those with theoretical knowledge may not obtain such vision. Nevertheless, to the extent that most people are not motivated without a theoretical description, and they may not know what to look for without such a description, these are important.

QUESTION

Then, can we say that knowledge is not universally required? That everyone doesn't need to know if they only follow the rules and regulations?

3.4.10 (435)
असार्वत्रिकी
asārvatrikī

asārvatrikī—not universally necessary.

TRANSLATION

(Knowledge is) not universally necessary.

COMMENTARY

The Vedic social system comprises four classes—Brahmana, Kshatriya, Vaisya, and Sudra. Out of these four classes, only the Brahmana are expected to be knowledgeable as they devise the rules and regulations for the other classes. The other three classes merely follow these regulations, without a profound philosophical understanding. Their relative ignorance about the philosophy, however, is not a hindrance to spiritual advancement, because all the four classes are treated as souls, equally qualified for spiritual pursuits. In fact, it is quite possible that those with philosophical knowledge don't put this knowledge into practice, while those without this philosophical knowledge are extremely diligent about the practice. Therefore, philosophical knowledge doesn't guarantee spiritual advancement, and philosophical ignorance doesn't deter one from spiritual advancement. This sūtra states that the acquisition of knowledge is not universally necessary. However, before one jumps to the conclusion that Brahmanas are not needed in society, we can note that if knowledge disappears in society, then rules and regulations become meaningless, over time they are altered whimsically, and the other three classes become incapable of spiritual pursuits. Therefore, the fact that a few Brahmanas pursue knowledge, while the rest of the population follows the rules enacted by them, doesn't undermine the importance of knowledge. The denial of universal necessity doesn't equate to universal non-necessity. It means some people must pursue knowledge.

There are two ways in which negations are employed, in relation to the term 'all'. When we say, 'not all', sometimes we mean 'none', and sometimes, the same 'not all' means 'some'. For example, one can claim that 'all men are handsome', and if this claim is denied, then there are two possible interpretations: (a) none of the men are handsome, and (b) some men are handsome. Factually, these are two different kinds of negations, but in current logic, we don't have the ability to make such distinctions. Therefore, the denial of 'all' is taken to be the acceptance of 'some'. Hence, if 'all men are handsome' is rejected, then it is accepted that 'some men are handsome'. But there is a problem. You could say 'energy is never conserved', and its rejection would mean 'energy is sometimes conserved'. By this rejection you will come to a partial truth. Conversely, if the claim that 'energy is always conserved' is denied, and we conclude that 'energy is sometimes conserved', then there is no difference between the denial of 'energy is never conserved' and 'energy is always conserved'. In both cases, 'all' and 'none' are replaced by 'some'. Therefore, these principles of reasoning cannot be applied universally and only context delineates what we mean.

QUESTION

Can someone even hope to know everything that is potentially knowable? The pursuit of complete knowledge seems very difficult due to numerous departments of knowing because one can only pursue few areas sufficiently.

3.4.11 (436)
वभिागःशतवत्
vibhāgaḥ śatavat

vibhāgaḥ—the divisions; śatavat—in the hundreds.

TRANSLATION
The divisions (of knowledge) are in the hundreds.

COMMENTARY
Knowing the whole truth isn't the same as knowing all the parts. This conception of knowledge arises when the whole is treated as the sum of the parts and the whole has no separate existence. But when we treat the whole semantically, this problem doesn't arise. Just like one can understand the meaning of 'mammal' by just understanding a few types of mammals—e.g., cows, dogs, cats, etc.—and doesn't need to know every type of mammal, similarly, it is not necessary to know every division of knowledge before the whole truth is understood. This is not a rejection of the other types of mammals, nor is it a claim that the meaning of 'mammal' could not be understood through other types (i.e., not cows, dogs, and cats). This sūtra says that it is impossible for anyone to know everything, without rejecting the existence of the complete knowledge.

Every division of knowledge involves different phenomena, which can be explained in many ways. If we use the phenomena to discover, compare, and then eliminate the explanations, then a very large number of divisions and a much larger number of phenomena will ensure that the perfect explanation—that applies to every division of knowledge—can never be found. However, if one accepts the explanation in the Vedic texts, then any division of knowledge can be used to verify the explanation. Since the whole truth can be verified through any division of knowledge, therefore, each such division serves as a perfect method for verification, and the result of that verification is perfect knowledge. But this perfect knowledge is not the complete verification of the truth across every possible domain of knowledge. In that sense, the knowledge can be complete, but the verification of that knowledge can be incomplete.

Verification of knowledge is an infinite process if we take the verification cognitively. However, if the application of knowledge leads to happiness, then that infinite process is shortened—we are convinced of its truth not because we verified it everywhere, but because it leads to perfect happiness right now. Thus, the classical method of epistemology—i.e., the discover by observation and experiment—is rejected in the Vedic system because you can never get perfect knowledge in a finite time. The verification of revealed knowledge is accepted as a valid method of convincing ourselves about its truth. However, for a persistent doubter, even this verification is infinite. Therefore, the ultimate solution is to obtain the happiness by the application of the knowledge.

This change in epistemology is wrought by the question: Why do we doubt? What gives rise to suspicion, that something may be wrong? And the answer is unhappiness. If we are unhappy, we are also suspicious. Suspicion can be partially overcome by verification. But it is completely rooted out only by happiness. Thus, it is said that all doubts are destroyed from the heart of a devotee when the happiness produced by the Lord's love is established. This means that the devotee hasn't verified the knowledge in every situation. But he is not suffering from the doubt to seek such verification. Simply by the perfection of happiness, he is convinced that the knowledge will always be true.

QUESTION

If you acknowledge that the divisions of knowledge are in the hundreds, and therefore it is practically impossible for anyone to know everything, then what is the purpose of producing these diverse forms of knowledge? Wouldn't it be better to just have the conclusion without its diverse manifestations?

3.4.12 (437)

अध्ययनमात्रवतः

adhyayanamātravataḥ

adhyayana—the detailed study; mātravataḥ—as if only for that.

TRANSLATION

(The divisions of knowledge are) as if only for detailed study.

COMMENTARY

Knowing the truth is not the same as verifying the truth. For example, many people believe that atomic theory is true, but they have never seen atoms, and have never verified atomic theory. They rely on someone else's verification. And yet, the theory is available for everyone to verify—whether they choose to verify it is up to them. Now, if we eliminated the possibility of verification, then the theory's truth could still be upheld by a few people, but most people will reject the theory because it cannot be verified. In the same way, the Absolute Truth can be accepted on faith, without verification. Just like atomic theory is accepted by many on faith because they trust others who have verified it. This trust can, for instance, be reposed in a teacher. However, if everything simply depended on trust and faith, and the claims could not be verified, then most people would reject this knowledge. Therefore, the necessities of both faith and verification are rejected. The truth can be known by faith, so verification is not necessary. But that doesn't make faith necessary; the truth can also be verified, and faith is not necessary, provided someone wants the verification.

The meaning of this sūtra is that the many diverse branches of knowledge exist if one wants to verify. But since verification is not necessary, therefore, all these divisions are unnecessary. That, however, doesn't make faith in the Absolute Truth necessary, because verification of this truth is also possible. Those who are intelligent and inquisitive will want to verify the truth, and the many divisions of knowledge are open to them for verification. Those who are not intelligent or inquisitive, can accept the conclusion based on faith in the scripture, or based on the numerous verifications by the inquisitive people.

QUESTION

There is a view that says that all the diverse fields of knowledge are illusory because the ultimate truth is their unity. Therefore, we must reject these diversities as illusory forms of confusion, and only focus on the unity. You have also emphasized the unity earlier, as opposed to the diversity. So, the proponents of the unity take this emphasis further and reject the diversity.

3.4.13 (438)
न अवशीषात्
na aviśeṣāt

na—not; aviśeṣāt—the claim of unity (alone).

TRANSLATION

We reject the claim of unity alone (denying the reality of diversities).

COMMENTARY

The rejection of diversity, based on the supposed opposition to the unity, is based on a physical conception of reality. For example, a chair is the whole, and if you break it apart into legs, backrest, seat, etc. then none of them is the chair. Therefore, if we look at these individual parts, then we can never know the whole chair. To know the chair, we must stop looking at the parts—i.e., backrest, seat, and legs—and only by that rejection of the parts we will know the whole truth. The problem, however, is that if you reject all these parts, then you cannot verify if there is really a chair. You will just have the idea of a chair, with no verification if that idea is indeed real, true, or existent. Now, if we change our conception of reality from physical to semantic, then chair is present in every part of the chair, and yet the chair is beyond all these parts. The physical conception of whole and part says that the whole is transcendent to the parts. But the semantic conception of the whole and part allows the whole to both be transcendent and immanent. This semantic conception of reality is easily understood if we say that the Absolute Truth is not just a thing, but also a *theory*. For example, the laws of Newton's mechanics can be verified through a bicycle, hammer, billiard ball, steam engines, etc. So, these laws are governing all these diverse objects, and hence they are immanent in those objects. And yet, even if the bicycle is destroyed, the truth of Newton's mechanics is not; therefore, the laws are also transcendent. Furthermore, because Newton's laws can be verified through a bicycle, bicycles are *sufficient* for knowledge. And yet, since the laws can also be verified through locomotives, therefore, bicycles are not *necessary*. The whole exists in each part and is outside of the parts.

So, these claims about the rejection of the parts and acceptance of the whole are flawed; they are based on a physical conception of reality in which the whole is transcendent to the parts, so none of the parts can lead to the whole truth. There are many pseudo-spiritualists who decry the importance of diverse fields of knowledge, claiming that these don't lead one to the Absolute Truth. These people also suffer from the materialist and impersonalist ideas. They think that the Absolute Truth is like a table or chair, different from other things in this world. If we keep looking at the material things, then we can never know that transcendent object. They don't know that the Absolute Truth is like a theory—i.e., a semantic object—which is inside and outside of everything. Impersonalism and materialism are similar ideas, and people who reject materialism simply take to impersonalism without deepening their understanding.

QUESTION

Contrary to the view that diversity is an illusion, there is also a view that the unity of knowledge is impossible. Thus, many divisions of academia operate independently, and so great is their focus on the individual study, that they may sometimes even reject the possibility of Absolute Truth. They claim only the existence of piecemeal and fragmented knowledge. What would you say to such claims that oppose the unity by exemplifying the diversification?

3.4.14 (439)

स्तुतयेऽनुमतिर्वा

stutaye'numatirvā

stutaye—for the praising; anumatiḥ—permission; vā—alternatively.

TRANSLATION

Alternatively, for the praising (of diverse fields of knowledge), permission (to people who are interested in expanding the diverse fields of knowledge).

COMMENTARY

For many practical concerns, diverse fields of knowledge, such as economics, physics, mathematics, psychology, medicine, cosmology, etc. are often required. The rejection of these fields of knowledge as 'illusion' is not going to end their existence. Rather, most people will find alternative ideologies by which to practice these areas, if a consistent and coherent alternative understanding in the Absolute Truth isn't found. The search for such alternatives, in fact, is likely to yield a description of the world contrary to the Absolute Truth. This, as we can see, is the norm at the present in modern science, which professes itself as the main opponent of Western religions. On the other hand, if the Absolute Truth is seen as being manifest in all the diverse fields of knowledge, then not only can one advance in the understanding of the Absolute Truth through such diverse studies, but contradictions between the diverse fields, and the seeming contradictions between diversity and the unity, can also be dissolved. Moreover, not everybody is interested in the Absolute Truth alone. Many are simply curious about the workings of nature, the human mind, the material body, and so on. They can develop an interest in the Absolute Truth through the study of the diversities that leads to the unity. Thus, for (1) practical reasons of day-to-day living, (2) to prevent the emergence of conflicting alternative ideas that try to solve focused areas of problems in different ways, and (3) to get people interested in the Absolute Truth who are may not otherwise be so interested in religion, the diverse fields of knowledge are encouraged.

The Vedic system of medicine, called Ayurveda, for example, describes the body not as chemicals, but as three conflicting tendencies called kapha, pitta, and vāta. Health is defined as their 'balance' and sickness as their 'imbalance'. This sets the precedence for a broader understanding of nature as the three modes called sattva, rajas, and tamas, which are constantly conflicting and become dominant or subordinate. These dominant and subordinate structures entail that no position in the world is permanent. Therefore, we must balance these alternatives through choices, and every situation needs a different choice. The world cannot exist without such choices, and hence the soul is necessary. Since the soul can make mistakes in its choices, therefore, there must be laws of morality. But these moral laws themselves are contextual, so there must be an absolute principle by which we can make the correct choices. This absolute principle is devotion to the Lord. Therefore, we can see how the study of the body leads to the gradual understanding of conflict, choices, morality, and eventually God. In so far as health and medicine are common concerns for everyone, people will invent theories about health and the body. We can reject medicine as being irrelevant to transcendence, but we can also understand medicine compatible with the nature of transcendence. This doesn't make medicine the most important subject, but it remains another way for the doctors and the patients to develop the knowledge of Absolute Truth through medicine.

QUESTION

But isn't this diversity prone to some misuse for mundane purposes? For example, many people today use Yoga merely as bodily exercises. The purposes of controlling the mind and focusing it on the Paramātma doesn't exist. In the same way, medicine can be used simply for materialistic purposes. So, don't you consider these things as being prone to misuse by materialists?

3.4.15 (440)

कामकारेण चैके

kāmakāreṇa caike

kāmakāreṇa—for fulfilling the desires; ca—also; eke—sometimes.

TRANSLATION

(The diverse fields of knowledge) may also be sometimes used for fulfilling the (material) desires (and not merely for spiritual emancipation).

COMMENTARY

A hungry or a sick man cannot practice spirituality. A person who is constantly unhappy cannot understand philosophy or practice it. Even if people are well-fed and healthy, have peaceful lives and can practice devotion to the Lord, they are not yet advanced enough to do it all the time. The senses and the mind are very strong, and they drag a person toward their respective objects of enjoyment. If the senses and the mind are completely cut off from their objects, the result is not spiritual progress. Rather, one develops a sick body and mind, becomes unhappy, and eventually loses all interest in spiritual pursuits. There-fore, an intelligent person practices alternating enjoyment and renun-ciation. If this enjoyment doesn't result in sinful reactions, the practice of incremental enjoyment and renunciation isn't antithetical to the ulti-mate spiritual goals.

This sūtra uses *eke* or sometimes to affirm that knowledge cannot be used for limitless enjoyment. All enjoyment must be regulated. The two initial steps in the aṣṭāṅga-yoga system are *yama* and *niyama*. Yama is the end of sinful activities. Niyama is the regulated practice of various types of activities, including material enjoyments. Yama is things that should never be done, and niyama is those things which should be done regularly. Examples of niyama are eating on time and a fixed amount every day, sleeping for a few hours every day, restric-tions on sex life, as well as practicing spiritual life for a fixed duration every day. If the life is regulated in this way, then this occasional enjoy-ment is not considered contrary to the spiritual goals. The problems arise when enjoyment violates yama (the sinful activities) and niyama (limitless enjoyment).

QUESTION

It is sometimes said that occasional enjoyments lead to the destruction of desires. But others also say that suppression of desire enhances these desires. Aren't these contradictory outcomes? How can both be considered true?

3.4.16 (441)

उपमर्दं च

upamardaṃ ca

upamardaṃ—destruction; ca—and.

TRANSLATION

(The occasional fulfillment of desires) also leads to destruction (of desires).

COMMENTARY

A common argument against restrictions on enjoyment is that when desires are regulated in this way, then the 'suppression' of desires enhances the desires, and the person is subsequently unable to control the desires. This argument confuses the 'regulation' of desires with their 'suppression'. Indeed, the senses and the mind are very strong, and given their previously formed habits of enjoyment, sudden cessation of all enjoyment will certainly lead to sudden indulgence. However, if one practices alternating indulgence and cessation, then the mind and the senses can be trained to form new habits. We must note that the senses and the mind are material. They don't 'need' enjoyment. The force of the senses and the mind exists only due to habit formation. Over numerous lifetimes, the soul has become accustomed to various types of enjoyments, and these habits and desires are therefore called our guna or 'nature'. It is not spiritual nature, but it exists as preformed habits. We cannot change our habits overnight. If we try to do so, the process will certainly be 'suppression', and since nature operates through alternating phases of dominance-subordination, a phase of suppression will certainly be followed by reckless indulgence. The correct process of changing the habits is forming new habits—gradually.

In fact, reckless indulgence doesn't lead to desire cessation. It rather forms new habits. The senses and the mind are not permanently satisfied if we do something excessively. Yes, we may get temporarily tired of a certain type of enjoyment, but in the process, we have formed a new habit of enjoyment. It will certainly return after a while, and the next indulgence will be bigger than the previous one, because new kinds of habits are being formed. Therefore, indulgence never leads to cessation of desires; it rather forms new habits. The process of change involves the formation of new habits, and that is possible only through gradual change. During this change, we should not suddenly stop all enjoyment. We should rather endeavor to reduce it gradually over time.

Of course, even if one stops all enjoyment suddenly, one is still forming a new habit. Yes, one may fall back into enjoyment after a while, but the old habit of renunciation will come back, and the next time one will be better equipped with renunciation. However, since the next indulgence also reinforces the old habits, the person—through alternating extreme renunciation and extreme indulgence—is now developing conflicting habits that move between the excesses. This is a painful path because sudden renunciation leads to a difficult time controlling the mind and the senses, and if one indulges again, he feels guilty about the enjoyment. Therefore, stopping indulgence suddenly is still progress, but it is not a recommended path due to resulting oscillations.

QUESTION

But you have said the desiring and enjoyment are fundamental properties of the soul, and hence they are eternal. It means the cessation of material enjoyment doesn't mean the end of the desires of enjoyment in the soul. So, there seems to be revectoring of desires from sense perception toward spiritual goals. How should we understand the gradual change in a person's desires?

3.4.17 (442)
ऊर्ध्वरेतस्सु च शब्दे हि
ūrdhvaretaḥsu ca śabde hi

ūrdhvaretaḥ su—the semen rises upward in them; ca—also; śabde—this is stated (by those practicing sense control and in yoga philosophy); hi—certainly.

TRANSLATION

Certainly, the semen also rises upward in them; such is the statement (of those who have practiced sense control and is noted in yoga philosophy).

COMMENTARY

The Ayurveda system of medicine describes the body as comprised of seven layers; the outermost layer is called the 'skin', and the innermost layer is called 'semen'. The 'skin' here doesn't mean the sense of touch; the sense of touch is a subtle material element that is beyond the gross body. By 'skin' we mean the gross material covering of the body. Within this skin is flesh, blood, bones, and within the bones lies the 'semen'. This 'semen' exists in both male and female bodies, and it should not be confused with the male procreative fluid. A more accurate understanding of this 'semen' is the potentiality from which the body is manifest. Modern science, for instance, speaks about the stem cells that exist within the bones, which can transform into any other type of cell, including skin, blood, flesh, and even the bones. The stem cells are the most primordial type of cells, and from these cells every other type of cell is formed. Therefore, the body in its more primitive form is these stem cells or 'semen'. The Ayurveda understanding of the body is that as one indulges in sense enjoyment, the 'semen' is gradually depleted. Thus, the body becomes tired, the bones feel weak, and the skin becomes shriveled, etc. On the other hand, if one refrains from sense pleasures, then the 'semen' gradually grows, and the result is stronger bones, better blood circulation, stronger body, shinier skin, etc.

Now, as the body is rejuvenated, there is greater tendency toward sense enjoyment. As we have discussed earlier, desire is stimulated by power, and power is used by desire. A stronger body naturally leads to more desires. And controlling these desires becomes harder. Thus, it is often seen that when someone renounces pleasure suddenly and prematurely, very soon the level of desires in the body increase significantly. One might then commit hedonistic acts which would have been unthinkable earlier. Under the influence of increasing power in the body, one might even display the adverse symptoms of power—e.g., cruelty, egotism, anger, etc. However, if one gets past such impulses through continued restraint, then the 'semen' in the body continues to grow, and makes the body, bones, blood, and the skin stronger and healthier.

In Freudian psychoanalysis there is a well-known process called 'sublimation' in which if our enjoying tendencies are suppressed in one avenue, then they automatically manifest in another avenue. Thus, for instance, Freud believed that sports, politics, and other passionate endeavors are simply sublimations of the sex desire. Freud, however, could not recognize how sublimation can also take one toward higher goals in life. He always thought that suppression of desire leads to sublimation, and this sublimation of the original desire in a convoluted form is the root cause of all the psychological illnesses.

The yogic understanding of sublimation, however, states that when the bodily strength is conserved by restraining from sense pleasure, then it initially seeks the previously dominant channels of enjoyment. So, the yogi is taught to be careful about these avenues of enjoyment. The goal is to keep shutting off the varied outlets of pleasure so that the energy can be continually sublimated. When all the mundane outlets of the energy have been shut off, then the same energy is sublimated toward spiritual goals. This sublimation of the energy toward higher purposes is called the 'rising of the semen'. We must not think of this process in physical terms—i.e., 'semen' is not rising like a liquid in a body. It is rising in the sense that the energy in the body changes form and different forms of energy are useful for different purposes. Modern science recognizes many forms of energy—kinetic, potential, thermal, etc. But in the Vedic system, this energy is typed—it can take innumerable forms. Thus, in one form, the energy is the passion and ability for music; in another form, the energy is the passion and ability for sports. The highest form of the energy ('height' indicating hierarchy of purposes) is spiritual activities. Thus, the 'rising' of the 'semen' is the change in the form of the material energy toward higher purposes.

The Śrīmad Bhāgavatam narrates the story of Hiraṇyakaśipu to illustrate this fact. He performed such severe austerities sitting in one place, that the ants had eaten away all the skin and flesh. And yet, he was alive because the 'semen' exists inside the bones, and the ants could not eat away the bones. The living force or the prāṇa exists in all the seven layers of the body, but even if the other layers are destroyed, the prāṇa continues to exist inside the bones. Thus, a person can continue living even if the only thing left in the body is bones. Śrīmad Bhāgavatam also gives the example of Maharshi Dadhīchi whose bones had become so strong due to austerities that they were the only material out of which the strongest weapon could be built for killing the demon Vṛtrāsura. Despite his immense power, he was compassionate and agreed to leave his body (actually, just the bones) for the preparation of the said weapon. This weapon came to be known as Vajra—the strongest owned by the demigod Indra.

The point is that the body is not just the skin, flesh, and bones; the deepest level of the body is the 'semen', and the body can remain alive even if the other layers are destroyed. The rising of the 'semen' is the transformation of this material reality into new forms suitable for the highest kinds of pursuits.

In an earlier sūtra it was said that material enjoyment is a necessity for most people. In a subsequent sūtra it was said that material enjoyment can be gradually reduced by regulated living. And this sūtra states that when this enjoyment is reduced, the energy is sublimated for higher purposes. Thus, a progressive path from the necessity of enjoyment, to occasional enjoyment, to the sublimation of one form of enjoyment into higher forms is understood.

Topic 2

QUESTION

But many people say that the reduction of material desires is only for those in the renounced order of life—also known as *sannyāsa*. For those in the family life there is no need for renunciation, and they can continue enjoying unlimitedly. What would be your response to this type of claim and argument?

3.4.18 (443)

परामर्शं जैमिनिरिचोदना च अपवदति हि

parāmarśaṃ jaiminiracodanā ca apavadati hi

parāmarśam—conclusion; jaiminiḥ—by. Jaimini; acodana—there are no restrictions; ca—and; apavadati hi—because it is certainly a bogus argument.

TRANSLATION

Such a conclusion is drawn by Jaimini; there are no restrictions (for practicing renunciation) and this is certainly a bogus argument.

COMMENTARY

Jaimini, and the Mīmāṃsā system, considered the performance of rituals as the essence of religion. Renunciation of material desires was possible, but it was only for those who had entered the sannyāsa stage of life. For the householders or grihastha, such renunciation was not accepted or recommended. Since people generally enter the sannyāsa stage very late in life, and by that time the body is already weakened, such renunciation by disability is not true renunciation. Even when the body is weakened, the desire to enjoy persists in the subconscious mind. Unless one has practiced renunciation throughout their life, the renunciation by disability doesn't help in spiritual advancement. Thus, we can see many old people being bedridden and unable to enjoy life. This bedridden state devoid of enjoyment cannot be considered renunciation. Therefore, the claim that renunciation is only for the old is called a bogus argument.

QUESTION

So, you are recommending the practice of desire control and renunciation throughout one's life, and all four stages of life must practice renunciation?

3.4.19 (444)

अनुष्ठेयं बादरायणःसाम्यश्रुतेःहि

anuṣṭheyaṃ bādarāyaṇaḥ sāmyaśruteḥ

anuṣṭheyam—should be practiced; bādarāyaṇaḥ—(so says) Bādarāyana; sāmya—uniformly (throughout life); śruteḥ—as the scripture enjoins.

TRANSLATION

(Renunciation and desire control) should be practiced, according to Bādarāyana, uniformly (throughout one's life) just as the scripture enjoins.

COMMENTARY

The practice of the āsrama system, comprising of four stages—called Brahmacharya, Grihastha, Vānaprastha, and Sannyāsa—is meant for inculcating gradual renunciation. In the Brahmacharya stage (that goes from 1-25 years) a student lives in a place offered by his teacher, begs for alms from householders, and eats after offering food to the teacher. In the Grihastha stage of life (from 25-50 years), one lives in their own house, but they donate a large fraction of their earning to the weaker sections of society, and whatever is left is enjoyed in a very regulated manner. In the Vānaprastha stage, men give up family life, and make a shelter in the forest, subsisting only on what nature provides, while women live with their children giving up the pleasures they enjoyed previously with their husbands. Finally, in the Sannyāsa stage, one gives up even the house in the forest, and simply travels from place to place—never staying in one place for more than 3 days—and subsisting on whatever they can get. Thus, out of the four stages, three stages—Brahmacharya, Vānaprastha, and Sannyāsa—explicitly forbid enjoyment, and the Grihastha stage is restricted enjoyment.

This sūtra states that one must uniformly practice sense control throughout their life. It is not possible to suddenly renounce everything in old age if one hasn't practiced renunciation throughout their life. The habits formed during childhood and early age, followed by continued practice of regulations, is the main practical recipe for a person to finally give up material desires.

QUESTION

But when a person is young, the senses and the body are strong, and the drive toward enjoyment is strong. This makes the sense control during youth very difficult. How can one practice renunciation if it is so difficult?

3.4.20 (445)
वधिर्वा धारणवत्
vidhirvā dhāraṇavat

vidhiḥ—injunctions (of regulated living that result in renunciation); vā—rather; dhāraṇavat—according to one's capacity to hold.

TRANSLATION

The injunctions (of regulated living that result in renunciation) must rather be applied according to one's capacity to hold (the difficulties of renunciation).

COMMENTARY

In earlier sūtras it was said that one should practice renunciation gradually. However, since every person may have achieved different levels of spiritual advancement in their previous lives, the recommendation is not for everyone to emulate the most renounced. Rather, one must understand their own capacity to renounce material pleasures, and then act accordingly. This is not a license for unlimited enjoyment. It is rather a statement about making progress from where one is presently situated—if one is deeply addicted to material pleasures, then the level of renunciation will naturally be lesser than one who has practiced such renunciation in the past and has progressed significantly. In short, the tendency to universalize rules and regulations must be avoided. These rules have a purpose—to elevate a person from their current state to a future better state. Habits are changed slowly, and one must consider the present habits and desires before undertaking ambitious steps in renunciation. Ambition and renunciation don't work together well. Some ambitious people take to harsh forms of renunciation hoping to emulate the most advanced personalities. However, that ambitious renunciation generally fails because ambition is used to suppress the desires for some time, but the desire is sublimated in other ways. Those sublimations of material desire then destroy the renunciation.

Topic 3

QUESTION

Since so many people have failed in renunciation, many people argue that those trying to renounce are simply doing it for obtaining praise. Sometimes it is also said those who have failed in life make a show of renunciation. And conversely, the renounced are also viewed as failures in life. What can we say to those arguments that renunciation is for show, or a sign of one's failure?

3.4.21 (446)

सुतिमात्रमुपादानादिति चेत् न अपूर्वत्वात्

stutimātramupādānāditi cet na apūrvatvāt

stutimātram—mere praise; upādānāt—due to appropriation; iti cet—it be said; na—not so; apūrvatvāt—on account of its incomparable nature.

TRANSLATION

If it is said that (renunciation is) merely for appropriating praise (from the gullible) (we say) not so because it is incomparable to (the enjoyment).

COMMENTARY

It is a common misconception that renunciation is another type of enjoyment. If someone has failed materially in life, then they take up renunciation to prove that they haven't truly failed. And because renounced people get a lot of respect from others, their actions are merely for appropriating praise. The flaw in this argument is that renunciation is progressive; one doesn't begin by renouncing some pleasures, and then fall back into those same pleasures. Those who do so, are certainly to be considered appropriating (false) praise. The intelligent people can see when someone pretends to be renounced only for getting more followers, wealth, power, fame, worship, etc. This is not renunciation; it is factually cheating and therefore worse than honest gratification. Real renunciation is described here as being incomparable to material enjoyment. In short, we cannot claim that renunciation is another type of enjoyment. This incomparable nature is seen due to progression. Just as a materialist becomes more and more attached to the enjoyment, similarly, the true renouncer becomes more and more detached from material enjoyment. The false renouncers remain attached to enjoyment, and sometimes, tend to enjoy—even pretending to be renounced—far more than those who claim not to be renounced.

The term *apūrva* has many other meanings, such as novelty, a new beginning, unprecedented, not done in the past, etc. All these meanings can be applied in this case if we understand that renunciation is progressive. It is not a temporary flash in the pan; it is rather a new beginning that progresses continually. It is not repetition of what one has done in the past; it is unprecedented. This doesn't mean that no renouncer appropriates praise. It only means that the definition of a renouncer is one who has arrived at an irrevocable point in their life; they are not renouncing as another way of extending enjoyment. They are renouncing because they have rejected the previous ways of their life.

QUESTION

From your answer it seems that you are implicitly accepting the possibility of false renunciation. If so, how can we know when it is false or true?

3.4.22 (447)

भावशब्दाच्च

bhāvaśabdācca

bhāva—the mood or intention; śabdāt—from the words; ca—also.

TRANSLATION

(Renunciation can be known) from the intention of the words as well.

COMMENTARY

Meanings are grasped in three stages—universal, contextual, and individual. By universal, we mean the dictionary meanings which are known to the speakers and listeners of a language. Typically, the same word has many meanings, and the context of speaking reduces the number of possibilities. For example, if someone says "no" to a proposal, then "no" has a universal meaning—i.e., the rejection of the proposal—but it also has a contextual meaning based on what was previously said (as it is the denial of what was previously said). However, even the context doesn't completely fix the meaning. After all, the word "no" may be uttered sarcastically, jokingly, or as a factual denial. Thus, to know the true meaning, one must delve into a person's intentions. The discovery of intentions requires us to broaden the context even further—we must know what a person believes in, their current and past goals, their habits (e.g., of lying or being sarcastic), etc.—which require knowing a person's true nature.

Linguists in the West have problems with the last two stages. They easily accept the stage of universal mapping of words to dictionary meanings. But they have difficulties in accepting how meanings are subject to context. Although many linguists now accept that context plays a huge role in deciphering meaning, the universalist nature of logic and mathematics ensures that this method is less understood and can never be automated into machines. Finally, practically everyone claims that a person's intentions can never be known. So, the conclusion is that the intended meanings can never be truly known.

But consider the case where a detective is trying to solve a serial murder. The first step is generally to find the murder weapon or methodology, because many things about the crime can be known from the way the murder was committed. But this is often not enough because the same methodology can be used on different victims. So, the detective also looks for patterns in the victims. This pattern then leads them to some understanding of the nature of the criminal, and why they might be committing these crimes. Then they use this pattern to look for potential persons who might commit such crimes, thereby widening their search through past events, crimes, even across locations and times. Thus, we can see that we go from physical evidence to the types of victims, to find the potential motives, and then use these motives to identify the criminal. So, the claim that motives can never be truly known is a false premise. Likewise, when it is hard to find the physical evidence, and the context cannot be broadened, many individuals are indicted simply if they are known to have motives, and there is a lot of circumstantial although inconclusive physical evidence.

So, the claim that we can never know the intentions underlying speech is false. Yes, it is possible that if we don't know enough about a person, we cannot understand the intended meaning. But this just means that we must broaden our understanding of the person by looking into their past behaviors. Sometimes, we might observe a person's body language, facial expressions, voice tones, and other things that indicate an emotional state. The point is that we always try to decipher a person's mental state as the explanation of their bodily actions. And we seek that explanation which spans their entire life holistically. The simplest explanation based on universal meanings, or even actions in a particular context, may conflict with those in other contexts. And this conflict is resolved by finding alternative explanations for events in other contexts.

This process of discovering the intentions is universal, and it applies to the detection of renunciation as well. A person may seem renounced in some cases but isn't renounced in other cases. The correct explanation is that which covers both scenarios, rather than one of them, and the context must be widened.

This method of deciphering the intention from empirical evidence is, however, not the only way. Those who have a developed mind, can directly perceive a person's mental state. This point was also made in an earlier sūtra in response to questions about how to know who a true devotee is. A preliminary response what that a devotee exhibits symptoms of bliss on their body. A deeper explanation, however, is that one must know their mental state. The difficulty in this mental perception is that it takes one to know one. You cannot identify a devotee by the mental perception process unless you are a devotee. Likewise, you cannot identify an evil person unless you are also evil. When something is alien to our nature, it doesn't fit into the 'molds' of our mind, and it goes unperceived. Our senses and the mind are like sockets of different shapes, into which objects of different shape fit. If the object and the mold are incompatible, then either the object is modified to fit the mold, or the mold is modified to fit the object, or they remain disconnected. Therefore, if we don't have the mold, we will either change the description of reality to fit what we understand, or we will change our molds of thinking to fit our mind to the external world, or we will simply say that the world cannot be understood using the present mind.

The advanced devotee—called an *uttama adhikārī*—sees everyone as a devotee because they have no other mental mold, and they cannot see evil. Likewise, a neophyte devotee—called a *kanistha adhikārī*—sees everyone else as a neophyte, because they have no other mental mold. In between these two, there is a class of people—called *madhyama adhikārī*—who are pure, but they also carry the mental molds to perceive evil. Sometimes, the pure devotee learns these evil mental modes to discriminate between the good and the evil.

Given this problem of perception, in which you change your mind to understand the mental reality, other methods such as trying to find the best explanation of a broad set of action is employed. They are essential for those without mental perception, but unnecessary for those with mental perception. The same can be said of the renounced people as well. If one is truly renounced, he can see who is or is not renounced. But if one is not renounced, he might accept non-renounced as renounced, only to find later that perception was false. Such mistakes are detected over time as a person's nature is better understood.

Topic 4

QUESTION

But sometimes people say that a person is progressing in spiritual

life, and since they haven't perfected it, they are sometimes renounced and sometimes indulgent. Such an argument begs for leniency against the practitioner by stating that they are not perfect, but they are much better than the others who seem much more indulgent. Should this claim be accepted as true or false?

3.4.23 (448)
पारप्लिवार्था इत चेत् न वशिेषतित्वात्
pāriplavārthā iti cet na viśeṣitatvāt

pāriplavārthāḥ—the intention being unstable; iti cet—if it be said; na—not so; viśeṣita—their uniqueness; tvāt—from that (which is their worst state).

TRANSLATION

If it is said that the intention in a person is unstable (i.e., a person is sometimes good and sometimes bad, and hence we should average the two results), (we say) not so; their uniqueness is from that (which is their worst state).

COMMENTARY

If someone commits a murder, we don't say that this person only commits murder occasionally; most of the time he is not killing other people. Likewise, for a thief, we don't say that he only steals occasionally; the rest of the time he is an honest person. The same holds true for every other case. The true nature of a person is the worst thing he can do. The worst and best exists in us in a potential form. When the circumstances are ripe, some situations bring out the best in us, while others bring out the worst in us. Most of us will behave quite well if the circumstances are favorable to our desires. We are only tested by the unfavorable circumstances, which bring out the worst in us. Therefore, when the situation is good, a person's true nature remains unknown. It is known only when the situation worsens, that we see the bad qualities in a person, and that is their true nature. As a person advances in spiritual life, the cleaning of the mind happens from the grossest to the subtlest. This means that certain types of gross crimes—such a murder, violence, cheating etc.—will disappear first. Over time, other subtle maladies such as anger, egotism, and sadness will also go away. The process of purification is not only that we stop performing certain actions, but we also wipe out the potentiality of that action ever in the future. If, for whatever reason, the actions are invisible, but the potentiality exists, then the lowest such type of potentiality defines the true nature of the person.

It is said that a chain is only as strong as its weakest link. The same is true of a person. He or she is only as good as their worst quality. The fact that these qualities may not always be visible to others doesn't make such people saints. Therefore, the argument that a person sometimes exhibits good qualities and sometimes exhibits bad qualities, and we should view the situation compassionately by erring on the side of the good rather than the bad is rejected.

Vedic texts are replete with narrations of demons like Hiranya-kaśipu and Rāvana, who perform severe penances, obtain great mystical powers, and possess immense knowledge. But all these good qualities are immediately nullified by a single bad activity—namely the abduction of Mother Sita by Rāvana, or the torturing of Prahalad by Hiranyakaśipu. We do not praise the numerous good qualities in Hiranyakaśipu and Rāvana, even though their good qualities may be better than many others. A person's nature is judged by their worst quality because under appropriate circumstances that's all that we will see. The purport is that the renunciation must be judged by the worst indulgence. If one is capable of murder, although in a saint's dress, then he is a murderer.

QUESTION

Many people may not commit crimes but may incite others into the crimes. Should we consider them better than those who commit the crimes?

3.4.24 (449)

तथा चैकवाक्यतोपबन्धात्

tathā caikavākyatopabandhāt

tathā—similarly; ca—also; eka—occasionally; vākyataḥ—from the speaking; pabandhāt—(we know) being bound due to (their qualities).

TRANSLATION

(Just as those committing crimes are criminals), in the same way, also those who occasionally speak (incite others into crimes) are bound (by their qualities).

COMMENTARY

Those who incite, encourage, or demand others to commit sinful activities are not any better than those who follow these instructions. Thus, it is said that those who kill animals, transport the dead body, sell the meat, or cook it, are equally liable for the killing as the person who eats the meat. This is because if one of these steps did not occur, then the subsequent chain would collapse. Thus, for instance, if there is no demand for meat in a market, then the killing, transporting, selling, and cooking of meat will also end. Likewise, if the killing stops, then transportation, selling, cooking, and eating will also end. Therefore, everyone involved in the succession of such actions is equally implicated.

Topic 5

QUESTION

If everyone is equally implicated in a sequence of actions, doesn't it imply that they should be equally responsible and punishable for their actions?

3.4.25 (450)

अत एव चाग्नीन्धनाद्यनपेक्षा

ata eva cāgnīndhanādyanapekṣā

ata eva—therefore; ca—also; agni-indhanādi—fire and that which is lighted into fire, etc.; anapekṣā—should not be distinguished or compared.

TRANSLATION

Therefore, also there is no need to draw a distinction between whether the fire was caused by the initial spark of fire or by the wood that was ignited.

COMMENTARY

One can say that he only offered the initial spark of fire, and if the wood was not combustible then there would be no fire—thus trying to shift the blame to the combustible wood. This argument is rejected because the choice of the combustible wood was also made by the person who was offering the spark of fire. However, the responsibility is not taken away from the wood. Therefore, both the initial spark of fire and the combustible wood are equally responsible for the fire. Any attempt to move the responsibility from the spark to the wood, or from the wood to the spark, is rejected here. The purport is that since both parties are equally responsible, the resulting consequences are also equal.

Topic 6

QUESTION

If everyone is responsible for an action, doesn't it mean that even with good deeds, the good results of the deed must be received by all involved?

3.4.26 (451)

सर्वापेक्षा च यज्ञादिश्रुतेःअश्ववत्

sarvāpekṣā ca yajñādiśruteḥ, aśvavat

sarvāpekṣā—everyone's expectations; ca—also; yajñādi-śruteḥ—the scriptures state that the (benefit of) yajñá; aśvavat—just like the horse.

TRANSLATION

The scriptures state that a yajñá (or sacrifice) also fulfills everyone's expectations—even that of the horse (who may be sacrificed as part of the yajñá).

COMMENTARY

Just like the responsibility for a bad deed is shared by all those involved, similarly, the consequences of a good deed are also enjoyed by everyone involved. The example of the Ashvamedha yajñá is cited here, in which a horse is let loose by a king and wherever the horse goes, the king becomes the ruler of that land, unless the current ruler of that land holds the horse, fights with the king, and wins. At the end of the yajñá, the horse is sacrificed, but due to the participation in the yajñá, the horse ascends to heaven, while the king enjoys the kingdom. Thus, if the yajñá is performed according to prescribed rules and regulations, then, everyone benefits: the horse gets a better life, and the king rules over a much bigger kingdom. If, however, the yajñá is not performed according to the rules and regulations, then the king loses the battles, the horse is slaughtered for no good reason, and everybody loses in the process. This example is given to illustrate the fact that it is not just humans who share the consequences of good deeds, but even the animals are benefitted from it. The purport is that just as suffering is shared by the participants in a bad deed, similarly, the benefits are distributed among the those participating in a good deed.

QUESTION

We were speaking about renunciation, or detachment from the results of one's actions. But now we are saying that these actions bring good and bad results, and therefore one may be motivated by these results, which is then counterproductive to the goal of detachment. So, how can one perform the activities in a way that is renunciation of results, but not of the activities?

3.4.27 (452)

शमदमाद्युपेतःस्यात्तथा'पि तु
तद्वधिस्तदङ्गतया तेषामवश्यानुष्ठेयत्वात्

**śamadamādyupetaḥ syāttathā'pi tu
tadvidhestadaṅgatayā teṣāmavaśyānuṣṭheyatvāt**

śama—tranquility; damādi—self-control, etc.; upetaḥ—possessing; syāt—if; tathā api—even then; tu—but; tadvidheḥ—knowing that (the Absolute Truth); tadaṅgatayā—being a part (of the Absolute Truth);

teṣām—those; avaśya—necessarily; anuṣṭheyatvāt—from being just like the performance.

TRANSLATION

Even if one possesses tranquility and self-control, one must submissively and necessarily become the performance (of the activity), knowing that (the Absolute Truth) and behaving just like the part (of that Absolute Truth).

COMMENTARY

There is a difference between doing an activity and becoming that activity. The term *anuṣṭheyatvāt* means that a person has become just like the activity. The use of 'just like' means that the person and the action are not identical. And yet, the person is so completely absorbed in the action, that the two have become non-different. But what does such a kind of non-difference mean?

When a materialistic person performs a yajñá, he offers something to the deity and expects something in return. But if a person becomes that activity, then the distinction between the person and the activity is dissolved. Then, the person offers himself to the worshipped deity. The deity is the agni, the worshipper is the soma, and the activity is the vāyu. There is a difference between the worshipper and the activity, but during the sacrifice, if the person offers himself, then the activity of offering and the object being offered are identical.

The earlier sūtras spoke about detachment and renunciation. But this sūtra states that this detachment is only the first step. The next step is that one offers himself because he is not expecting anything in return. When there is a desire from a yajñá, then there is a difference between the offering and the person making the offering. But if these desires are destroyed, then one surrenders oneself to the person being worshipped, and offers himself in the sacrifice.

Thus, the previous discussion about renunciation is now connected to the process of yajñá and is therefore equivalent to the process of yoga. In a yajñá, an offering is made. But in yoga, the self is offered. In a yajñá, there can be selfish expectations—I'm giving you this, so that you will give me that. But in yoga, there is no such expectation—I'm giving you myself, and since I have given myself to you, I have become your property; you can use me ask you like. If one is not detached from material enjoyment, then every offering is made with the expectation of a return, and even as one performs yajñá, one doesn't become that yajñá. When there is accompanying detachment, one offers oneself.

The results of good and bad actions are shared by the participants, if there is a difference between the activity and the person—i.e., when there is a desire to obtain something other than the performance of the activity itself. However, when this distinction is lost, then the results of good and bad actions disappear because one is no longer asking for results; one is offering oneself in the process, and the good and bad results are now owned by the person being worshipped.

The example of the whole and the part illustrates this idea. Suppose you hit someone using your hand. Then, you don't say: I did not hit you; it was only my hand. You own the responsibility of hitting, not the hand. In the same way, when the devotee offers himself to the Lord, and acts on the Lord's behalf, then the responsibility of the actions is not on the part; it rests with the whole. The Lord being absolute is not implicated by the actions—good or bad. Unlike the previous sūtras, which said that one will get good or bad results according to their actions, this sūtra says that if one offers oneself in the process, then the responsibility of the actions is no longer applicable to the actor. These actions are the responsibility of the Lord, and He is not implicated by the actions. Therefore, by offering oneself to the Lord, the soul is liberated from karma.

Topic 7

QUESTION

But if the killing of a horse is justified as part of the performance of yajñá, then many people extend this to say that we can kill the animals for our food, if this food is offered to the Lord. In fact, it is said that these animals have been given to us for our consumption by the Lord, and the Lord is therefore responsible for giving these animals for us, and He owns the result of the killing.

3.4.28 (453)

सर्वान्नानुमतिश्च प्राणात्यये तद्दर्शनात्

sarvānnānumatiśca prāṇātyaye taddarśanāt

sarva-anna-anumatiḥ—permission to take all sorts of food; prāṇātyaye—when life is jeopardized; tat-darśanāt—from that philosophy.

TRANSLATION

The permission to take all sorts of food (is granted) only when one's life is jeopardized; that is the philosophical conclusion (of the scriptures).

COMMENTARY

The basic principle of a yajñá or sacrifice is that something lower is sacrificed for something higher. Thus, a soldier may die defending a country, and that death is called a 'sacrifice'. But if the country could be defended by other peaceful means, then wars should not be waged, and soldiers should not be sacrificed unnecessarily. In short, when a sacrifice is to be performed, then we should also make endeavors to identify the lowest thing to be sacrificed.

When a horse was sacrificed in the Aśwamedha yajñá, the sacrifice was not merely for the satisfaction of the king's pride. Rather, a higher moral principle was be served by this yajñá, and only those kings who aimed to create a moral society by their rule would undertake such a sacrifice. The Brahmanas would perform this yajñá for the great kings, as a method to bring immoral rulers under the control of the moral ruler. The horse sacrifice was acceptable because the loss of the horse was smaller relative to the gains by this sacrifice. This wasn't indiscriminate killing of animals. It was a carefully considered bargain of identifying the least amount of loss for the greatest amount of gain. Thus, for example, a king would not indiscriminately kill the defeated rulers, if they accepted the rule of the superior king. The defeated king was only expected to present a token gift to the winning ruler, as a mark of acceptance of their superiority and authority. They did not lose their kingdom, or their position as the rulers. They, however, accepted the superiority of a more powerful ruler.

This general principle of sacrifices applies to our eating habits too. While eating, we sacrifice some life to sustain our life. However, this sacrifice is acceptable under two conditions—(a) our life must factually be superior to the lives of those whom we sacrifice, and (b) the least amount of sacrifice must be performed in the process. It is generally accepted that human life is superior to animal life, so animals can be sacrificed for human benefit. However, animal life is also superior to plant life. Therefore, by the principle of the least amount of sacrifice to obtain a gain, humans are allowed plant-based food, rather than meat. An exception is cow's milk, after the calf has had the mother's milk, and the cow still has surplus milk. In short, humans are not allowed to sacrifice a calf's hunger to satisfy their hunger. Even in the case of plants, the sacrifice must be minimized. For instance, trees cannot be cut indiscriminately, and firewood must come from the dried, fallen branches. Fruits can be plucked from trees because they are of no use to the tree. Grains can be used, after the harvest is ripe. It is said that jīvā jīvasya jīvanam, or life depends on other life. Therefore, some sacrifice is necessary. But this sacrifice must always be minimized.

This principle is enunciated in this sūtra by saying that animal food is allowed only when our life is in danger. If we cannot obtain plant-based food, and our life is in danger, then we can sacrifice animals (assuming our life is producing a greater good than the animal's life, which is implicitly presumed here). The principle of sacrificing something lower for something higher still holds true. This principle is only extended to meat-eating in rare cases.

QUESTION

You are saying that violence is not contrary to religious principles, and non-violence is not a universal principle. Rather, both violence and non-violence can be applied depending upon what is being gained and sacrificed?

3.4.29 (454)
अबाधाच्च
abādhācca

abādhāt—because of a non-contradiction or non-forbidding; ca—and.

TRANSLATION

Because of a non-contradiction or non-forbidding (both non-violence and killing can be employed, as they are a person's dharma in different cases).

COMMENTARY

The principle of dharma is identifying the best possible action under given circumstances. Sometimes violence is necessary, and at other times non-violence is required. If the greater good is served by violence, then violence is accepted. But if the greater good is served by non-violence, then non-violence is dharma. The soldier sacrifices his life for a greater good, and the soldier kills others for a greater good. The ruler must sometimes punish the criminals because that serves the greater good—the correct example is set for everyone. And the ruler must sometimes demonstrate kindness—because it teaches others to be kind. Cruelty and kindness are not universal principles; yajñá, which involves sacrificing something inferior for something superior, is the universal principle.

QUESTION

But we don't find such descriptions of violating moral principles in the śrutī. How can we justify such claims when they are absent in the śrutī?

3.4.30 (455)
अपि च स्मर्यते
api ca smaryate

api ca—moreover; smaryate—in the smritis.

TRANSLATION

Moreover, the smritis say (that a sacrifice for a higher gain is acceptable).

COMMENTARY

In this regard, there is a pertinent story from Rāmayana, where Lord Rāma asks his brother Lakshman to take Mother Sīta to the forest on a sightseeing trip, and then leaves Her in Sage Valmiki's aśrama. At the time of abandonment, Mother Sīta is pregnant with twins—Lava and Kuśa—who are then born in Sage Valmiki's aśrama. As the twins grow up, Sage Valmiki becomes their teacher, and under his tutelage, they become formidable warriors. One day while playing, they find a majestic horse running through the forest, and not knowing that the horse was sent by Lord Rāma to conquer other lands as part of an Aśvamedha yajñá, they capture the horse. The soldiers following the horse request the children to return the horse, but the twins refuse to do so. Eventually a battle starts, and Lava and Kuśa defeat every forthcoming warrior. Everyone is stunned that two five-year old boys have defeated an entire army. The word reaches Lord Rāma and He arrives on the battlefield to fight with the twins. But Sage Valmiki intervenes to stop the battle, informing the children that they are the sons of Lord Rāma, and the twins return to their father.

The story of their separation and union is tearful. But within it is a lesson about why Lord Rāma had abandoned Mother Sīta. The Rāmayana narrates the story that Lord Rāma abandoned Mother Sīta because He heard a washerman saying to his wife, that he is not like Lord Rāma to accept a woman after she was abducted by another man—a snide reference to Mother Sīta's abduction by Rāvana. Some people claim that Lord Rāma abandoned Mother Sīta because He was attached to His prestige and honor. The belief underlying such a claim is that since Mother Sīta was innocent, She should not have been abandoned. And by the principle of not punishing the innocent, Lord Rama must have turned a deaf ear to such false allegations. But the reasoning in the Rāmayana is different—Lord Rama sacrificed His and Mother Sīta's happiness for a greater cause of setting the right example through Their behaviors that promiscuity was unacceptable, even though in their specific case promiscuity did not exist.

There are examples in the smriti where the Lord Himself lies or urges others to lie for a greater good. For example, during the Mahabharata battle, Lord Kṛṣṇa asked Yudhishthira to tell Dronāchārya that Aśvatthāmā had died (when Dronāchārya's son Aśvatthāmā hadn't died, although an elephant named Aśvatthāmā had been killed), so that he would drop his weapons out of grief for his son. Lord Kṛṣṇa also asked Arjuna to shoot arrows at Bhīṣma while standing behind Shikhandī—who was a woman in his previous birth—because He knew that Bhīṣma would not retaliate, and Arjuna will be able to shoot Bhīṣma down. These things may sound unethical from our mundane perspective, but they are not. Dronāchārya and Bhīṣma were such great warriors that they could never be defeated. Bhīṣma had the boon of voluntary death, so he could never be killed unless he chose to leave his body voluntarily. And yet, defeating the side on which they were fighting on was the greater good.

We have earlier discussed how dharma is truthfulness, but these sūtras now reject that conclusion by stating that even lying is good when it serves the greater good. Thus, the understanding of dharma is gradually nuanced.

QUESTION

But isn't it likely that when the greater good is preferred as a higher principle, then everyone can claim some greater good and do whatever they want? Wouldn't the application of this principle lead to greater bad than good?

3.4.31 (456)
शब्दश्चातोऽकामकारे
śabdaścāto'kāmakāre

śabdaḥ—the scriptures; ca—and; a tu—but forbid; kāmakāre—acting according to one's wishful or whimsical desires.

TRANSLATION

And hence the scriptures forbid (applying the principles of greater good to sacrifice lesser good) by acting based on one's wishful or whimsical desires.

COMMENTARY

Even when the principles are described clearly, their application is not easily understood by everyone. For example, we discussed earlier how religions have been killing other people in the name of God's love. The same point is now made for the greater good—we cannot invent notions of good whimsically. Wars waged to spread democracy or capitalism are examples of such whims. Here is an indication that reading scriptures is not a substitute for intelligence on how to apply the scripture's injunctions. If that intelligence is missing, then scriptures are misinterpreted whimsically and used for selfish purposes.

Bad people misuse any good system to produce bad results. And a good person can use a bad system to produce the best results. The system is not always the cause of the good or the bad. Often, the people who use these systems are responsible for the good or bad results. When a system is put in the hands of an intelligent, well-meaning, and moral person, then the results are mostly good. When the same system is put in the hands of foolish, ill-meaning, or immoral people, then the results are mostly bad. Any system of principles, rules, and regulations is impersonal. We cannot encode principles, rules, and regulations in a machine and expect it to make the best decisions. An intelligent, moral, and well-meaning person is essential to use the system correctly.

Therefore, people who are foolish, ill-meaning, and immoral are forbidden from reading scriptures, because they misapply the scriptural principles. As these principles are misused, people blame the system, rather than the foolish, ill-willed, and immoral people employing it; the system is rejected, and all potential for goodness is destroyed. There is a real danger in the foolish, ill-willed, and immoral people ascending to any position of power and influence in a society—even when the society is structured according to a good system.

Modern democratic societies can already see such outcomes. The founding fathers of a nation may have been moral, intelligent, and well-meaning, and they might have created a system that can produce good outcomes. But when that system falls in the hands of foolish, ill-meaning, and immoral people, the results are always bad. Then people talk about changing the system—e.g., by creating new laws, structures, or regulations in society. But these new creations again fall into the hands of the foolish, ill-willed, and immoral people, and the changes to such laws, structure, and regulations don't create the desired outcomes. Hence, every society keeps trying to create the best system, rather than create the best people. They have imbibed the false idea that if the system was perfected, then the outcomes would naturally be good. In short, they think that a system of rules and regulations constitutes a machine that will coerce people to create good outcomes. They don't realize that the machine is controlled by immoral, foolish, and ill-willed people, who keep misusing the system.

Therefore, no amount of knowledge, education, or clarity in rules, and regulations can replace the judgments of a moral, well-meaning, and intelligent person. A system can be used to create more such moral, well-meaning, and intelligent people, only if the system is presently under such good people. If the system is under foolish, ill-meaning, and immoral people, we cannot expect the system to automatically produce a better future. Goodness doesn't begin in building a better system. It always begins in empowering better people.

The Vedic scriptures are eternal, and the knowledge in them is eternally true. But this eternal truth is visible, beneficial, and practically demonstrated only by the pure devotees of the Lord, who have the highest level of intelligence, the greatest understanding of the ultimate good, and the best ideas about when to apply which principle, for how long, and upon which people. Unfortunately, in the present age, every fool considers himself qualified to read the scriptures, understand their true meanings, and apply their principles. But the reality is that such fools drag themselves down, hurt other people by misapplying the scriptural principles, and bring a bad name to the system itself.

Topic 8

QUESTION

But since most people are prone to misinterpretation of the principles of greater goodness, and are likely to misuse such principles toward selfish ends, what do we do? Obviously, we cannot stop reading the scriptures or trying to understand them. And we cannot just wait for the perfect people to arrive.

3.4.32 (457)

वहितित्वाच्चाश्रमकर्मापि

vihitatvāccāśramakarmāpi

vihitatvāt—since they are prescribed by the scriptures; ca—and; āśrama-karma—the duties of the āśrama (the four order of life—Brahmacharya, Grihastha, Vanaprastha, and Sannyasa); api—also.

TRANSLATION

And because the duties of the āśrama are prescribed in the scriptures (we can fall back upon them) also (in case of doubts about the greatest good).

COMMENTARY

We can now see how religion—which originates in the love of God, is then reduced to the moral values of excellence and virtue, which is again reduced to a sensible choice of sacrifice—eventually reduces to a system of rules and regulations. The reason is that people don't know how to love God. They are unable to grasp the nature of virtue. And they cannot even decide what should be sacrificed in order to enhance and preserve virtue. Given the free will to love God, pursue the moral virtues, or choose the sacrifice, most people simply misuse these higher principles of love, virtue, and sacrifice for selfish purposes. Then, the recommendation is to forget about the love of God, the pursuit of moral virtues, or even choosing the sacrifices. Simply follow some rules.

Once these higher principles are taken out of religion because their practitioners are foolish, ill-willed, and immoral, then nobody can understand why such rules and regulations were given anyway. With the loss of the underlying motivations—namely, that they were meant to produce a population that is loving, virtuous, and sacrificing—people start thinking that these rules and regulations are only the means for oppressing the common and innocent people. Now, even these rules are disregarded, and society descends into chaos.

This, by and large, is the fate of the Vedic system today. There are remnants of traditional Varṇāśrama system of social organization—i.e., the rules and regulations of classes—which is at present called the 'caste system'. Nobody understands that this system was rigidly enforced after people lost the ability to make good choices about what should be sacrificed and what should be preserved. This loss in judgment was preceded by the loss of virtue, and the loss of virtue was preceded by the loss of the love of God. Through such progressive decline, we are now left with a meaningless caste system, which is exploited by politicians as vote banks, and this system is now being slowly dismantled.

The people who criticize this system, however, aren't sacrificing, virtuous, or devotees of God. They can't even tolerate a regulated life. They like to have indiscriminate sexual partners, eat whatever can be digested, and fill their empty and meaningless lives with the fleeting pleasure of shiny things. And they consider this inconsequential existence better than one where one had the opportunity for gradual upliftment to the highest perfection of life. The wise man pays no heed to their criticism. The wise man tries to understand, revive, and practice those regulations that can lead one to the perfection of life.

QUESTION

But given that modern society is indeed declining and unable to follow the rules and regulations of the Varṇāśrama system, what can be done?

3.4.33 (458)

सहकारित्वेन च

sahakāritvena ca

sahakāritvena—by practicing mutual cooperation; ca—also.

TRANSLATION

By practicing mutual cooperation also (the society can be uplifted).

COMMENTARY

The Varṇāśrama system is hierarchical, with the Brahmanas, Kshatriyas, Vaisyas, and Sudra as the four classes. In the present age, there are hardly any Brahmanas—the well-intentioned, moral, and knowledgeable sages have been replaced by pseudo-intellectuals struggling to survive the academic system by publishing pretentious, unimaginative, and repetitious papers. There are hardly any Kshatriyas—the fearless leaders who make virtuous and bold decisions have been replaced by cowards who prefer self-preservation over change for good. There are hardly any Vaisyas—those who know that society's main wealth is land, forests, rivers, mountains, and domestic animals, have been replaced by bankers who create schemes of converting debts into assets for fleecing innocent investors. Society is now dominantly Sudras—the laborers toiling in factories and sweatshops to mass-produce goods without the artistry that was previously the hallmark of carpenters, weavers, potters, and jewelers.

The bankers and the politicians are the cheaters, and the academics and the workers are the cheated. When a bank fails, the politicians bail it out by levying extra taxes on the workers. Then, when the banks are doing well, the politicians allow the banks to charge high interest rates on the wealth that the toiling workers previously paid as taxes to bail out the banks. Meanwhile, the banks lend money to the politician's cronies, which are cycled back to the politicians to help them continue in power. Thus, the endless cycle of cheating continues.

When the Varṇāśrama system declines because the top three classes in the society are gone, and society is reduced to the battle between the cheaters and the cheated, then, there is no point in speaking about a class system. There is simply no morality, courage, or commonsense to understand the value of such a system, and there are also no people that belong to the higher classes. How can the Varṇāśrama system exist when the upper three classes are missing? The best action is to first put an end to the dishonesty and corruption in society. This is possible if everyone acts cooperatively as a single class of people. Such a cooperative system is sometimes called 'socialist democracy' at present.

In a socialist democracy, the moneyed class is accountable to the courts of laws and investigative agencies that bring transparency; the courts of law and the investigative agencies are accountable to the politicians; and the politicians are accountable to the people. Any break in the chain of accountability destroys the socialist democracy. For example, if politicians manipulate people's opinion through propaganda about the false ideals of race, caste, creed, and nationality, then they are able to wrest control over the entire system of courts of laws, investigative agencies, banks, businesses, and the workers. The result is a totalitarian state which looks like hierarchical Varṇāśrama, because there is indeed a powerful ruler at the top, the military and courts below him, the banks below these, the moneyed class below these banks, and the workers below this moneyed class. But it is not righteous, truthful, and progressive. People may often love such a ruler because they hate everyone else more. And the rulers justify their authoritarian rule by appealing to the false ideals that brought them into power and use intimidation to silence those who question their actions.

Due to the structural similarity between authoritarian power structures and the traditional hierarchical societies based on morality and virtue, people often confuse one with the other. When faced with the problem of chaos in society, they support a dictator thinking that it is a replacement for Varṇāśrama.

This conclusion of substituting Varṇāśrama by an authoritarian rule is rejected in this sūtra. If a society cannot follow the rules and regulations of Varṇāśrama because there are no qualified Brahmanas, Kshatriyas, and Vaisyas, then the solution is cooperation, rather than authoritarian control.

What is the difference between cooperation and authoritarianism? In an authoritarian structure, the ruler is above the laws, and in a cooperative structure, the laws are above the ruler. But how you can put laws above the ruler, unless there is another ruler who enforces the laws? Therefore, cooperation simply means a system in which power is distributed over many ruling positions. Each such ruler in a distributed system is controlled by the other rulers in the system. The hierarchy of power is then replaced by the distribution of power.

In previous sūtras, we discussed how intelligent people can choose the sacrifice; in short, laws are not sacrosanct; the ultimate arbiter is the person. When this system fails, because everyone is not capable of making good choices, then the next system is Varṇāśrama, where some people are qualified to make good choices, and the choices of others are subordinated to their direction. Thus, the Brahmanas have the greatest freedom in the choice of what must be sacrificed; the Kshatriyas below them have a reduced choice, the Vaisyas have even lesser choices, and the Sudras have the least choice. When even this system fails, because there are no qualified Brahmana, Kshatriya, and Vaisya, then no ruler is above the rules, and the ruler has no choice for which rules to follow or disregard. In short, nobody is above the law, and nobody has the choice of which laws to apply in which situation. Whatever freedom of choice exists, only exists within the restrictions imposed by the law. But what happens if someone doesn't follow the law? That's when the system of checks and balances kicks in, and different divisions in a cooperative structure have the power to remove those not following the law. An authoritarian ruler is above all laws; he can define the laws for others, and choose which laws apply to him, and nobody has the power to remove him, although he can remove everybody. A ruler in a cooperative system is never above the law, all laws are defined through mutual approvals, the laws must always be applied (even if it doesn't make sense), and every ruler can be appointed and removed from their position of power.

Quite simply, a cooperative structure is the subordination of persons to an impersonal system of rules and regulations. The novelty is that the rules of governance are created by the rulers—not given by an external authority. In common language, this is called the rule of people, by the people, for the people. In every action, there are three causes—what, why, and how. The system of rules fixes how things must be done; every decision or action must follow a predefined procedure, so there is no choice of how things must be done. Similarly, the system of rules fixes why things should be done—no ruler has power to create the big-picture vision, although all the rulers can collectively create smaller and shorter-term goals permissible within the charter. Once the how and the why are fixed, the ruler is given the freedom to decide what must happen. However, this decision can be reversed by the other rulers. The meaning of cooperation is that they would not reverse each other whimsically and thereby paralyze the entire system of governance by undoing each other. But the power of undoing each other always exists in case it is ever needed.

Cooperation doesn't mean offering free advice to each other, which the receiver can ignore. That is called consulting. Cooperation is also not the joint ownership of the process and decision. That is called collaboration. Cooperation is specifically a distributed system of power in which everyone holds some power over the other, and this power is used to restrict and restrain them.

A system of cooperation is built on the premise that everyone is prone to mistakes, if not outright evil, but collectively they can counteract each other's errors. The Varṇāśrama system is built on the premise that a few people—i.e., the Brahmana—are never evil, and above almost all mistakes. The system in which everyone can choose the type of sacrifice can be made is built on the premise that nobody is evil, and nobody is likely to make many mistakes. Therefore, one can have an egalitarian society, a hierarchical society, or a society bound by rules. Everyone is free in an egalitarian society; some are freer than others in a hierarchical society; and nobody is free in a cooperative system. The progression in the discussion indicates the successive decline of freedom from an egalitarian system to a hierarchical system to now a cooperative system. This decline is necessary when most people are wicked, or prone to mistakes.

We might note that authoritarianism is not bad per se. It works perfectly if the leader is intelligent, well-intentioned, and moral because then he knows which scriptural injunctions to apply in which cases, to what extents, and to which people, in which places, and at what times. When the leaders lack these qualities, then they either universalize injunctions, or apply the wrong principle to a problem, or chose a principle based on their convenience at that time. Their intentions may not always be bad; but the road to hell is paved with good intentions. Good intentions are only one of the three ingredients of good decision making; the other two are a superior intellect and moral courage. When leaders don't have these qualities, good intentions can produce bad results. Without these traits, power corrupts, and absolute power corrupts absolutely. The prescription is to replace a centralized power by a distributed system of power.

This is not an ideal system, by the way. The ideal system is being led by a perfect devotee of the Lord. If such a leader is absent, then the next best system is being guided by intelligent people who know how to apply scriptural injunctions in different situations—i.e., what to sacrifice and what to preserve under different circumstances—while preserving the goal. If intelligent people are not available, then one must adhere to the regulations of Varṇāśrama—e.g., people in the Sannyasa order must not handle money, manage property, or interact with women; their prerogative is traveling and teaching alone. If people are unable to even follow the principles of Varṇāśrama strictly, then the next best system is one based on the rule of law with many checks and balances. If these principles are disregarded, then we must know that the leaders have whimsically created their own system, which is not expected to work correctly.

QUESTION

Your prescriptions about the social order are fine, but how does living in a society relate to the attainment of spiritual enlightenment? How is one going to attain the divine love of God through such social rules and regulations?

3.4.34 (459)
सर्वथापि त एव उभयलिङ्गात्
sarvathāpi ta eva ubhayaliṅgāt

sarvathā api—in all the cases (described above); te eva—they must certainly; ubhaya-liṅgāt—(remain devoted) owing to the two-fold deities (i.e., the masculine and the feminine aspects of the Absolute Truth).

TRANSLATION

In all cases (described above—i.e., the distribution of power, the rules of Varṇāśrama, or an enlightened and judicious application of the principle of sacrifice), they must certainly (remain devoted) to the two-fold deities (i.e., the masculine and feminine aspects that together represent the Absolute Truth).

COMMENTARY

Religion is a private issue, but morality is a public issue. Religion is a private issue because the love of God cannot be forced on anybody. However, morality is a public issue because we can only live in a system governed by morals. We cannot live in a society if everyone lies. We cannot live in a society if everyone is selfish—e.g., nobody pays taxes. We cannot live in a society if everyone is inconsiderate of the others—e.g., people running off to courts for resolving minor disputes. And we cannot live in a society if nobody follows procedures—e.g., the rules of the road, garbage segregation, or the drawing of contracts. Therefore, morality is reduced to four publicly enforceable principles—truthfulness, austerity, compassion, and cleanliness. These are non-negotiable principles; their specific detailed implementation may change from one society to another, but no society can exist unless these principles are implemented and enforced. However, even as one follows these rules, one may choose to devote oneself to the Lord or may simply live by the moral code. Of course, the goal of life is not achieved if one only follows the moral codes of conduct. One must develop devotion to the Lord as well. However, these two are separate issues. Therefore, after dwelling on the moral conduct, this sūtra reiterates that morality is not enough; one must also become devoted to the two-fold deities.

This stance, however, leads to a big question. The humanists argue that society can be organized morally, without accepting soul and God. Does this mean that religion is so private, that it is totally unnecessary in defining the public conduct? The modern secular system of morality takes this stance.

But this stance is false because no social system can ever be perfected unless the people are perfect. And people cannot be perfected unless they have a higher purpose in life. The people will accept a higher purpose only when life doesn't end with death. Rather, whatever good or bad has been committed in this life must necessarily be enjoyed or suffered in another life. Since this oscillatory process of enjoying and suffering is dissatisfying, therefore, one must seek transcendence from this material existence, and that transcendence is the higher purpose. But that higher purpose necessitates devotion to God.

The humanist idea about an ideal society without God is a pipe dream because such idealism is possible only when people want to become ideal. Why would they want to be ideal unless there is an incentive attached to that perfection and a disincentive attached to the imperfection? Under a humanist conception, there is no life after death. Therefore, the rich and powerful are entitled to exploit, subjugate, and manipulate others—to maximize their happiness within this life. If they have very low risks of being punished for their actions, then why should they be truthful, compassionate, sacrificing, or agreeable?

Now the humanist invokes an evolutionary argument and says that every species wants to ensure its long-term collective survival, and altruistic behavior helps that collective survival, therefore, by the principle of evolution, altruism is nothing but the need for long-term collective survival. The problem with this argument is that it presupposes altruism to explain altruism. The claim about a species wanting its long-term collective survival is itself altruistic. So, that desire in us cannot be used to explain the emergence of altruism. We must rather ask: How did this altruism arise? For example, why should I care that the whole world will be dead after I'm dead—to act unselfishly in the first place?

The fact is that there can never be a moral society without a higher purpose in life and that higher purpose cannot exist without the realization of the soul and God. As a result, even if someone doesn't actively pursue devotion to God, they must have a conception of the soul and God to even behave morally. When the notions of the soul and God are lost, then the sense of higher purpose in life is lost. Then everyone acts with their short-term goals of pleasure in mind, and disregard everyone else's interests. Society then descends into an immoral abyss. The result of rejecting the soul and God is the destruction of the social order. No atheistic society can survive for very long. All atheist, communist, humanist, and materialist societies shall die due to inner moral decline.

Communists know this, and the earlier communist regimes were predominantly authoritarian—altruism did not come naturally to people, and nobody wanted to think about the collective benefit of the society, which is why everyone who did not agree with the collective good over the individual good had to be slaughtered. After the collapse of inhumane communism, a new wave of 'humane' communists arose. This new version of communism says that social unity must be propped up by ideas like nationalism and racial identity. After all, for us to be altruistic, we must believe in a larger-than-life identity, and that identity can be a person's race and country. But even these 'humane' communists know that nationalism and social identity cannot produce cohesion. Therefore, this 'humane' communism is married to economic prosperity. Thus, in this new version of communism, social cohesion exists due to three reasons: (1) material prosperity, (2) racial identity, and (3) historical nationalism.

But here is the problem. The unity doesn't exist because of racial identity and historical nationalism. Those are simply tools of propaganda, which even the communists don't believe in; if they believed in this idea, then they would not marry individual prosperity with national and racial identity; they would have simply proceeded with the communist rule of a race with nationalistic ideals. The society under this type of communism is cohesive only because of economic prosperity. People believe that if they have lived in poverty for centuries, then any system that gives them a better life is acceptable. It has nothing to do with racial or nationalistic identity. In short, cohesion exists because there is collective prosperity, not because people are fundamentally altruistic.

Humanism is totally contradictory to the Vedic system. All unity comes when we serve the Lord. And we can live together even in difficult times because we have a higher purpose. Whether in happiness or distress, the devotees always pray to the Lord. They don't blame each other for their suffering. They blame themselves for their misdeeds which brought them to the current situation. When a spiritualist owns up the responsibility for his life and actions, then he asks: If I am responsible for my life, then why am I in this situation? Everyone else is shifting the blame to someone else, but they can't shift it forever. Someday, the blame will be shifted back to those shifting it to others.

QUESTION

But we find it very hard to combine social duties and spiritual pursuits. If we have spiritual pursuits, then we neglect our social duties. And if we follow the social duties, then the spiritual pursuits are almost always neglected. How can someone do both—i.e., social duties and spiritual pursuits in parallel?

3.4.35 (460)

अनभभिवं च दर्शयति

anabhibhavaṃ ca darśayati

anabhibhavaṃ—not overwhelmed; ca—and; darśayati—sees.

TRANSLATION

One who is not overwhelmed (by social duties) also sees (the Lord).

COMMENTARY

The previous sūtra said that one must be devoted to the two-fold deities even while performing their social duties. And this sūtra acknowledges the fact that either of these paths can be overwhelming. If one follows the spiritual path but neglects the social duties, then one might be ostracized from society, and lose their spiritual pursuits as well. On the other hand, one might perform their social duties diligently, but may largely neglect the spiritual goals. The result would be that one lives in a society but fails to achieve the goal of living. The recommendation is thus to not become overwhelmed with social duties.

Our social endeavors are overwhelming when we fear that not doing them will lead to a catastrophe. So, we keep devoting our time to social duties and neglect spiritual pursuits. But if we try to reduce our engagement in social duties then we will find that nothing catastrophic happens. Life just goes on as before, and people who were relying on us, learn to rely a little less. As they reduce their reliance on us, they also become less reliable, and then we are compelled to reduce our reliance on them. The trouble is that our distancing from others leads to others distancing from us, and we cannot tolerate that others are disengaging from us. Due to fear of abandonment, most people get sucked back into the engagement. But if we accept that something higher requires the sacrifice of something lower, then we gradually increase disengagement, which then creates the time for spiritual pursuits. I can say this from experience: I have devoted a lot of time to writing, which would have been impossible if I truly believed that my worldly disengagement would produce a catastrophe.

Topic 9

QUESTION

But what if someone is not able to reduce their social engagements, due to their specific circumstances, or due to the specific phase of life they are in? For example, students might have to spend a lot of time with their studies, and a mother may have to devote her entire day to taking care of children, or a man may have numerous responsibilities which he is unable to truly forego. How can they not be overwhelmed by their duties even as they keep doing them?

3.4.36 (461)
अन्तरा चापि तु तद्दृष्टेः
antarā cāpi tu taddṛṣṭeḥ

antarā—by the difference; ca—also; api tu—even though; tad-dṛṣṭeḥ—that can be realized or seen.

TRANSLATION

Even though (someone may not be able to disengage from social duties), simply by seeing the difference (between life and death) also that is seen.

COMMENTARY

One of the main causes of becoming overwhelmed is the (false) belief that the present situation will never end. A student feels that their education will never finish; there is always one subject after another and then the original subject comes back. A mother feels that her duties never seem to end; it is one chore after another, one duty after another, and then it starts all over again. A man overworked by numerous duties feels that life never seems to end; that he is running from one pillar to another, and then back to the same pillar again.

But all these things do end. Whatever seems overwhelming right now will fade away one day. Eventually, our parents will die, friends will abandon us, children will grow up to lead their own lives, and our colleagues will disappear. Ultimately, we will be left all alone, totally underwhelmed by the receding waves of the life's ocean, as the sun sets into the distant horizon. When one comes face to face with their loneliness, then all the overwhelming disappears. Everything seems meaningless and pointless, as it all just fades into oblivion.

This meditation is valuable since it forces us to think about death. Death is the final stop for everyone as far as this life is concerned. And at the point of death, we will be totally alone. Nobody is coming with you or for you. Every medal, award, or prize you have gotten in this life stops being yours. Since others only see the body, they won't even know that you got these medals once you enter the new body. Nobody would know you, or where you are going to go. You must walk alone into the next stage of your life. If life seems overwhelming right now, just imagine how underwhelming death would be.

We feel overwhelmed by our mundane duties because we cannot see the underwhelming nature of death. Therefore, anyone who feels that they cannot give up their duties to pursue spiritual life, must meditate upon death. Spiritual life may be imaginary for some people, but death is real for everyone.

QUESTION

You have previously asked me to meditate on the Paramātma in the heart, the Universal Form of the Lord, and the sound of the names of the Lord. Now you are asking me to meditate on death. How does that even make sense?

3.4.37 (462)
अपि च स्मर्यते
api ca smaryate

api ca—furthermore; smaryate—the smriti makes such recommendations.

TRANSLATION

The smriti also recommends (that we can meditate upon death).

COMMENTARY

This is the fourth and final occurrence of the sūtra—*api ca smaryate*. The previous three times, the same sūtra was used in 1.3.23 (86), 2.2.45 (216), and 3.4.30 (455). The repetitive use of sūtras is indicative of the fact that they are like the words 'yes' and 'no'. They don't have a context-independent meaning. Rather, only the context delineates what they mean. Therefore, if we have talked about the qualifications of guru previously, then this sentence means that smriti also describes the qualifications of a guru. If we have spoken about the regulative principles of society, then this sentence means that smriti also describes the regulative principles of society. If we have previously talked about life and death, then the smriti also describes the meditation upon life and death.

There are many lessons to be had here. First, four references to smriti, from a text which is understood as śrutī, means that the śrutī is not independent. Second, certain things like meditation on death are not found in śrutī, which describes the nature of Brahman; but they are found in smriti. Third, as we have discussed previously, Vedic texts have a progressive nature in which the higher truth is also described in the subsequent texts. Therefore, the relation between śrutī and smriti has the following three nuances—(1) sometimes śrutī refers to the smriti for additional details, (2) sometimes the śrutī refers to smriti to find those things that are not found in the śrutī, and (3) sometimes the śrutī refers to smriti to obtain a superior understanding that is absent from the śrutī.

Now, we can turn to the reference to smriti for the meditation on death. In the Bhagavad-Gita, Lord Kṛṣṇa makes two clear references to Himself as death.

Bhagavad-Gita 10.34:
mrtyuh sarva-haras caham
udbhavas ca bhavisyatam

I am all-devouring death, and I am the generator of all
things yet to be.

Bhagavad-Gita 11.32:
kalo 'smi loka-ksaya-krt pravrddho
lokan samahartum iha pravrttah

Time I am, the destroyer of the worlds, and I have come
to engage all people (i.e., I have come here to cause their
deaths).

God is everything, but everything is not God. Similarly, God is death, but death is not God. To understand this, recall our familiar analogy of mammal and cow. The mammal is in each cow, but the mammal doesn't reduce to the cow. Likewise, Kṛṣṇa is in death, as the cause of death, but He is not death alone. He is also life. In fact, Kṛṣṇa is both life and death, which means that He is living, and all life is a manifestation of Kṛṣṇa. But He is also renounced from everything, and, by that renunciation, He causes everyone to be separated from their bodies and material attachments. The death of the body is not death of the soul. It is only the separation of the soul from the body, and this detachment is forced upon us by the Lord's will. If we become attached to the Lord, then this detachment is not forced. In short, if we are attached to the Lord, then He is also attached to us, and we don't see the renounced aspect of the Lord. But if we are detached from the Lord, then we sometimes see His renounced aspect.

Kṛṣṇa is the embodiment of six qualities—knowledge, beauty, power, wealth, fame, and renunciation. The devotees of the Lord see everything as the manifestation of the Lord's knowledge, beauty, power, wealth, and fame. They see Him in everything, as the source of everything, and as the controller of everything. The non-devotees, however, don't see the knowledge, beauty, power, wealth, and fame as emanating from the Lord, as the Lord being immanent in everything, and the Lord being the controller of all these things. They think that these qualities are their qualities, that they are knowledgeable, beautiful, powerful, famous, and wealthy. To alleviate that illusion, the Lord comes as death. "You think you are knowledgeable, beautiful, powerful, famous, and wealthy? All right, you are no more." Now you lose everything that you thought was yours before. And you restart the delusion of acquiring them again. Therefore, the Lord is also death. For those who cannot see the Lord as knowledge, beauty, power, wealth, and fame, the Lord shows Himself as forced renunciation.

If you are not sure that God exists, and the material engagements seem very real to you, then God can demonstrate to you His existence in the form of death. Hence, for those who are overly attached to material life, the meditation on death is recommended. It is not contrary to the meditation on the Paramātma, the Universal Form, or the meditation on the names of the Lord. The difference is that in these meditations, we see the Lord as knowledge, beauty, power, wealth, and fame, but while meditating on death we see Him as renunciation. Death is the most severe kind of renunciation, and God is renunciation itself. Therefore, the vision of death approximates the vision of renunciation itself. During this life, we might lose some money, some property, some friends, some family, etc. These are renunciations but they are partial. During death, we lose everything. Therefore, death is a more complete vision of renunciation. As sure as death and taxes. Since death is sure, therefore, the Lord is also sure.

QUESTION

But it is sometimes said that the soul doesn't have to leave the body. The soul rather ascends to the Lord's abode without any change in the body. Therefore, it seems that death is not always certain. How do we reconcile that?

3.4.38 (463)

वशिषानुग्रहश्च

viśeṣānugrahaśca

viśeṣa-anugrahaḥ—the special benediction (of the Lord); ca—and.

TRANSLATION

And that (i.e., bypassing death) is a special benediction (of the Lord).

COMMENTARY

This body is not material. The purpose we use this body for is material. Matter and spirit are not different kinds of 'stuff'. Matter simply means the selfish use of the body, and spirit means the selfless use of the body. So long as we have selfish purposes, the purposes are always frustrated. And due to this frustration, we change our purpose. Then, as this purpose changes, we keep getting new bodies—to fulfill our new purpose. But if the purpose is fixed in a particular type of service of the Lord, then we don't need to renounce this body, because it fits our purpose. Hence, many devotees are elevated to the spiritual world in this body itself. That is because this body is not material or spiritual. It is an instrument and the instrument is neither good nor bad. The purpose for which the instrument is used is good or bad. So, if the devotee doesn't want to change the instrument, then there is no reason for the Lord to force separation from this instrument. That elevation with the body into the spiritual world is called a special benediction of the Lord in this sūtra. In short, this body is not temporary. It exists eternally, along with innumerably such eternally existing bodies. The body never changes; however, the soul changes the bodies.

When the soul has faulty purpose, then the Lord forces a change in the body. If the soul wants a different type of body to perform a different kind of service, then again, the Lord causes the change of the body. But if the soul doesn't want to change the body, and the purpose is not faulty, then the same body continues into the spiritual world. However, that body becomes eternal. This so-called disease, old age, and death are the soul moving from one body to another. There is an eternally healthy body, and there is an eternally sick body. But we don't have to go from sick to healthy and healthy to sick bodies. These changes are forced by the laws of nature and the Lord's will because we have faulty purposes. If the purpose is fixed, then the body is also fixed.

You don't use a hammer or a drill if you want to cut vegetables. In the same way, if your goal is fixed on some service, then the body doesn't change. The elevation with the same body—and bypassing death—is a clear refutation of impersonal doctrines about matter as illusion. Matter is not an illusion. It is an instrument. That instrument is always real, but the purpose is illusory. As this illusory purpose changes, the instrument to fulfill the purpose changes. But if the illusory purpose is destroyed, then the instrument is eternal anyway.

When the Lord appears in this world, He is not born into a new body. And when He disappears, then He doesn't die and get another body. These are false misconceptions propagated by the impersonalist to confuse people into thinking that enviousness and selfishness of the Lord can be spiritualized. So, the impersonalist says that the Lord is born, and He dies. When He is born, then He takes on a body. And then when He dies, He has no body. The fact is that the Lord has the same body always. And that is because the body is not material. One needs to know the science of matter, which the impersonalist doesn't. Without knowing this science, He creates a false theory of the soul. Hence, if matter is understood scientifically, then God's and the soul's bodies are also understood. And then we can know how matter is also eternal, just as the soul. However, the connection between the soul and matter is not eternal due to the faults in the soul's purposes. The Lord has no fault, so He has an eternal body. When the faults are corrected in the soul, the soul too has an eternal body.

QUESTION

But isn't it possible that certain purposes in the spiritual world cannot be fulfilled by the present body? Would we not need a different body for that?

3.4.39 (464)
अतस्त्वतिरज्ज्यायो लङ्गिाच्च
atastvitarajjyāyo liṅgācca

atah—therefore; tu—than; itarat—the other; jyāyoh—better; liṅgāt—from the body; ca—also.

TRANSLATION

Therefore, from the other (spiritual) body also better than (this body).

COMMENTARY

Even in this world, there are many kinds of bodies. Some bodies are better at swimming, some at flying, some at crawling, and others at walking. Some bodies have a better brain, other bodies have better hands and legs. Therefore, there is a superset of bodies found in the spiritual world, and a subset of that superset exists as the material world. As a result, in one sense, the material world is a part of the spiritual world, because the bodies here are a subset of the bodies in the spiritual world. In another sense, since the souls are rebellious to the Lord, the material world is said to be totally separate from the spiritual world. Being a part of the whole and being separate from the whole are different modes of describing the material world relative to the spiritual world.

Given the rebellion in the soul, most bodies in this world come with many limitations. Thus, most fish are unable to fly, and most birds are unable to swim. Even when some species can do both, their abilities are not on par with the best of the abilities in the other species. We also have two hands and two legs, which limit us to do only one or two things at one time. But in the Vedic scriptures, living beings with hundreds or thousands of hands are described. They can do hundreds of things simultaneously. This means that their bodies are superior to our bodies. But they are still called material—i.e., inferior bodies—because they are inferior to the best-in-class bodies with many more capabilities.

In this world, we get separate types of knives, but in the spiritual world, we can get many kinds of Swiss Army knives. Those are called 'superior' in this sūtra, after stating that the material body can also exist in the spiritual world. So, knives can go from this world to the spiritual world, and occasionally, some Swiss Army knife can be seen in this world. But mostly, the Swiss Army knives are found in the spiritual world, and hence, they are called 'superior'.

The superiority of the instrument is different from the superiority of the purpose for which the instrument is used. Since our purposes are inferior, we also generally get inferior instruments. But if the purpose is superior, then we can also obtain far superior instruments. With great power comes great responsibility. As we demonstrate responsibility, the power increases accordingly. Therefore, we get access to more powerful instruments by showing that we can handle the responsibility. If we cannot show that responsibility, then we lose the power. Therefore, most of the weak bodies are due to irresponsibility.

In this regard, the story of a mouse is narrated. A mouse approaches a saint and says: "I'm troubled by cats; they are trying to kill me; please help." So, the saint says: "OK, you become a cat." Then after some time, the cat comes to the saint says: "I'm troubled by dogs; they try to chase me away; please help me." So, the saint says: "OK, you become a dog." In this way, the saint gives him bigger and better bodies, until the body of a lion is obtained. Then the lion looks at the saint and says: "You appear to be quite tasty." And the saint then says: "Again become a mouse." So, this is the disease of the material world. We get some power, and we want more power. Then when we get enough power, we say: "God doesn't' exist". Then, God says: "Again become a mouse."

The bodies of the material world are limited because the moment one gets a more powerful body, he thinks he can challenge the Lord. Then the Lord makes him a mouse again. So, the progression to even better bodies is halted. But otherwise, all the bodies in the spiritual world can exist in this world.

Topic 10

QUESTION

You are saying that the body is not material, and the same body can exist in the spiritual world. You have also said that the devotion can exist in this world, and it exists in that world. So, if the intentions and the body are the same, the person's role must also be the same, because through that role one can fulfill their intentions using the body as an instrument. Then, if these things are the same, then why do we say that the spiritual world is different from the material world? How can the ingredients be the same and the result be any different?

3.4.40 (465)

तद्भूतस्य तु नातद्भावःजैमिनिरपि नियिमातद्रूपाभावेभ्यः

tadbhūtasya tu nātadbhāvaḥ jaiminerapi niyamātadrūpābhāvebhyaḥ

tadbhūtasya—on attaining that; tu—but; na—no; atadbhāvaḥ—ceasing from that; jaimineḥ—of Jaimini (is this opinion); api—also; niyama—rules; atadrūpa—not this form; abhāvebhyaḥ—due to the absence.

TRANSLATION

But on attaining that (a role in the spiritual world), there is no ceasing from that (the person's role); even Jaimini (thinks that) the rules (of this form) don't apply to the other form, due to the absence (of the rules and regulations).

COMMENTARY

The terms bhūta and bhāva cannot be applied to the body because it has already been established that the body can be the same in the spiritual and material worlds. Then what do bhūta and bhāva pertain to? They pertain to one's role, or the relationships to other souls. However, in these roles, the soul no longer has dharma or the rules and regulations that restrict one's activities.

A material society is characterized by rights and duties. Factually, nobody has any rights, other than what is given to them by their karma. But we all have a sense of entitlement to rights; when the entitlements are frustrated, we blame others and say—they did not perform their duties. We generally don't say that we did not have the karma to get our rights fulfilled. Now the question arises: When karma is finished, and we are not limited to the fulfillment of rights, do we still carry the sense of rights? That is, do we keep demanding others to do their duties? This sūtra rejects this conclusion. It says that there are no duties, which means that nobody is obligated to do anything for you. The next sūtra says that along with the dissolution of duties, even the rights are dissolved. So, these two sūtras are interconnected because rights and duties are two sides of the same coin—if someone else does their duty, then I fulfill my rights.

But doesn't this sound counterintuitive that the soul enters a perfect world, and still doesn't have any duties? Wouldn't this society collapse if everyone neglected their duties? This seems especially perplexing because the sūtra also states that having attained a role, nobody wants to give up that role. So, what is everybody going to do if not their duties according to their role?

The answer is that people do everything, but they are not required to do anything. The existence of rules means you are required to do something, and not doing it would invite a punishment, and doing it would invite a reward. But if we dissolve the duties, then doing the duty invites no reward, and not doing the duty invites no punishment.

Freedom from karma means freedom from rewards and punishments. But that freedom is possible only when we are also free from the duties—i.e., the necessity to behave in a specific manner. Therefore, the dissolution of duties is identical to the dissolution of karma (i.e., reward and punishment), which is identical to the existence of freedom.

The spiritual world is like working in a voluntary organization. You do your work because you want to do it, not because you are required to do it. If you work, you are not paid for the service—the service is voluntary. And if you don't work, then you are not punished—the participation is also voluntary.

The only rule for working in a voluntary organization is that you don't prevent others from doing their work. You are welcome to assist or help them, and you are equally welcome to outdo whatever they are doing. In short, you can do the same work they are doing, although in a better way. Therefore, entry into the spiritual world doesn't mean an end to competition. The devotees of the Lord can compete, and they can serve each other. The service means that a soul will assist other devotees to do their service better. And competition means that a devotee will do better service than the others. But a devotee never says: "You cannot do this". Nor does a devotee hinder other devotees from doing what they can do, especially if they can do it better than themselves. When some devotee tries to hinder others from serving, this becomes a sign of envy.

To understand liberation, we must understand karma and dharma—namely that dharma is duties, and karma is rights. Freedom from karma means freedom from rights. But as soon as we stop having rights, we must stop demanding duties from others. Therefore, rights and duties are dissolved simultaneously. The soul obtains his freedom, and that freedom means that he now acts voluntarily. This voluntary action can be to serve other devotees, compete with other devotees, serve the Lord, or even compete with the Lord. The Lord is not averse to competition. He enjoys winning as much as He enjoys losing. Just like if a father and son play some sport, then the father enjoys winning, and the father enjoys losing to the son. In fact, the father enjoys losing more than winning. This is because of the affection between the father and the son. In the same way, the soul too must enjoy losing as much as he enjoys winning. If both situations are being enjoyed, then there is no envy, although there is competition. The moment one enjoys winning and doesn't enjoy losing, there is enviousness. Under that enviousness, one loses focus on what one can do to win and starts focusing on what one can do to prevent others from winning.

Everyone in the spiritual world is gracious— (1) they like serving each other rather than competing, (2) if they compete, they want others to win, and (3) even if they want to win, they are never unhappy losing. Serving the Lord, competing with the Lord, winning against the Lord, and losing against the Lord are all equally pleasurable. This is the symptom of lack of enviousness.

Therefore, carrots and sticks are useful only in this world to align the rebellious soul. But there is neither carrot nor stick in the spiritual world. And yet, everyone does everything according to their capacity and desire, voluntarily. This voluntary system of service doesn't conform to the authority structures of this world, the use of power to subjugate, control, reward, and punish. Therefore, it is important for spiritual leaders to understand when authority must be used to correct mistakes and purify the mischievous soul, and when the voluntary spirit must be encouraged to let the soul go free and do the best that one can. If the mischievous person goes free, then they create havoc. And if the solemn person is subjugated, then the potential for advancement is lost. Only one who has understood both material and spiritual worlds can act like this.

Topic 11

QUESTION

If there are no rules and regulations of duties, then what about the rights? Does it follow that even the rights are dissolved along with the duties? Doesn't the soul fall from the spiritual world without the rights and duties?

3.4.41 (466)

न च आधिकारिकमपि पतनानुमानात् तदयोगात्

na ca ādhikārikamapi patanānumānāt tadayogāt

na—not; ca—and; ādhikārikam—the sense of rights; api—even; patana-anumānāt—due to no reason for a fall; tadayogāt—because of union with that.

TRANSLATION

And nor is there any sense of rights; there is even no reason for a fall (due the non-fulfillment of rights), because of the union with that (the Lord).

COMMENTARY

In the purport to the previous sūtra we combined the discussion of both rights and duties, although the previous sūtra spoke about the dissolution of duties and this sūtra speaks about the dissolution of rights. When the duties are dissolved, then nobody is required to do anything. If they are not required to do anything, then nobody else can demand anything from them. All actions are voluntary. Therefore, there is no dharma (duties) and there is no karma (rights). Everything is driven by the soul's free will. However, this free will is purified, so one acts voluntarily. But even if one acts, they have no expectation of getting anything in return—i.e., gifts, rewards, remuneration, or recognition of their actions. And since there are no expectations, therefore, there are no rights.

In the material world, the preliminary teaching is responsibility—i.e., you do your duties, if you want your rights. The next better teaching is sacrifice—i.e., do your duties even if you are not getting anything in return. Once responsibility and sacrifice are perfected, then the next better teaching is that you don't have any duties—i.e., you can work voluntarily, or you can abandon all duties. However, since the soul has already perfected responsibility and sacrifice, he doesn't stop working, if he can work. He is just not obligated to work.

The pure devotees of the Lord understand this voluntary system of service, arising out of love. Love is not demanded, and even if love has been offered, there is no expectation of reciprocation. The only request is that the opportunity to love is not taken away. This means that the pure devotee of the Lord only asks the Lord to allow him to serve the Lord. He doesn't demand that the Lord loves Him back, and he is not disturbed even if the Lord doesn't love him back. When such voluntary love is established, the soul becomes totally free of the system of rights and duties of this world, and that is called liberation. Therefore, by loving the Lord, liberation is automatically obtained, and there is no separate need for trying to become liberated before or after devotion to the Lord.

QUESTION

The freedom from rights and duties is also attained by the impersonalist who merges into Brahman, dissolves the separate identities and by the dissolution of separate identities, all the rights and duties are automatically dissolved. So, how is devotion to the Lord any better than impersonal liberation?

3.4.42 (467)
उपपूर्वमपि तु एके भावमशनवत् तदुक्तम्

upapūrvamapi tu eke bhāvamaśanavat taduktam

upapūrvam—the initial or first part; api tu—even though; eke—some; bhāvam—the existence; aśanavat—just like eating; tat—that; uktam—is said.

TRANSLATION

Even though the initial or first part of (the transcendental) existence (Brahman) is attained by some, it is called just like eating (without sharing).

COMMENTARY

When children grow up, sometimes they abandon their parents. They say: "It was your job to take care of me when I was a child. Now that I have grown up, I can do the job of taking care of myself. Hence, I don't need you anymore. Isn't it great that I'm no longer dependent upon your care?" The impersonalist has a similar stance. He was dependent on the Lord in the material world. The Lord provided the knowledge for his liberation, guided him to the correct spiritual master(s), and inspired him from within to pursue this path every time he fell away from the path. But having attained that position, he loses all gratitude for the Lord. He thinks that now that he has attained this position, he no longer needs the Lord. That is just like children who use their parents during childhood, obtain some education, get a job, and start living independently. Now, they think that they don't need the parents anymore, so they don't have to do anything for them. They don't realize that without their parents they would be nowhere. So, the person with such a selfish attitude is not considered the greatest. He may have become great by achieving liberation from the material world, but there are many levels of greatness. Having a high position is certainly great. But remembering where one came from, using whose help, appreciating their contribution to our greatness, and remaining indebted to them, is greater.

Topic 12

QUESTION

Does this mean that a liberated devotee abandons the rights and duties even within this world? How does he conduct himself upon liberation?

3.4.43 (468)
बहसितूभयथापिसमृतेराचाराच्च
bahistūbhayathāpi smṛterācārācca

bahiḥ—outside; tu—but; bhayathā—just like a shining planet; api—even; smṛteḥ—from the smriti; ācārāt—from custom; ca—and.

TRANSLATION

The liberated soul acts outwardly just like a shining planet even though (this is not required of him) and acts according to smriti and custom.

COMMENTARY

The Bhagavad-Gita 3.21 states the following about a great person's actions:

> yad yad ācarati śreṣṭhas
> tat tad evetaro janaḥ
> sa yat pramāṇaṁ kurute
> lokas tad anuvartate

> Whatever action is performed by a great man, common
> men follow in his footsteps. And whatever standards he sets
> by exemplary acts, all the world pursues.

If a devotee abandons duties and rights, then this world will descend into chaos because the other people who do not understand the spirit of voluntary action would stop performing their duties. Hence it is said that the devotee acts outwardly like a shining planet or a great man in society, illuminating the world with knowledge and correct behavior according to the smriti and the established customs. The devotee follows the rules of whatever social system is best suited to the world at present. It may be a system of distributed power, a system of hierarchical power, or an egalitarian system of individual power. In either case, he is a shining planet—i.e., an exemplar of how people must conduct their lives. The devotee is not bound by any of these systems, and he has no preference for any of these. And yet, he tries to set an example for everyone.

Thus, advanced devotees are seen to support and exemplify all such systems alternately. Sometimes they let people decide the right action according to their judgment—illustrating the principle of individual power to decide what must be sacrificed and what must be preserved. Then sometimes they say that everyone must behave according to the principles of Varṇāśrama—implying that there are rules, but they are different for different classes of people, for different genders, and for those in different stages of life. Then sometimes they say that everyone must follow a common set of rules such as doing certain types of activities, at certain times, in a fixed predefined manner, and the performance of these duties must be monitored by a system of checks and balances. And then they sometimes say that a devotee is not bound by any rules or regulations. For most people, these diverse types of instructions can be very confusing. And some people then pick up whatever model that they find convenient.

But if we understand how all these systems are available, but they don't apply to everyone, then we can decide which system must be applied.

Topic 13

QUESTION

But what happens when an unqualified person imitates the actions of a liberated soul? Isn't there are difference between following and imitating?

3.4.44 (469)

स्वामिनःफलश्रुतेरत्यात्रेयः
svāminaḥ, phalaśruterityātreyaḥ

svāminaḥ—the master, or the person making a choice; phala-śruteḥ—gets the results according to the injunctions of sruti; iti—thus; ātreyaḥ—Ātreya.

TRANSLATION

The master (or the person making a choice) gets the results according to the injunctions of the śrutī; thus, it has been stated by Ātreya.

COMMENTARY

Throughout the Vedānta Sūtra, we see many sages and great personalities being quoted. Then sometimes the pastimes of the Lord are cited and sometimes His words are cited. Sometimes logic and reason are employed. Sometimes practical experience is used. Sometimes one scripture refers to another and cites it as evidence. And in the previous sūtra, even worldly customs were referred to as exemplifying great behavior. Thus, we can see how what we call 'evidence' or pramāna, includes all these things. Sometimes it is what the Lord said. Sometimes it is how He acted. Sometimes it is based on what is stated in one scripture. But if something is not stated in some scripture, then we pick the reference from another scripture. Then sometimes it is the doctrine of one philosophical system. But sometimes these doctrines are overridden by another doctrine. And sometimes it is simply the opinion of a great personality.

Therefore, if anyone thinks that religion is a fixed set of rules, then they are mistaken. All these injunctions are true, but they are not simultaneously true. They don't apply to everyone, in all social roles, circumstances, places, or times. The advanced devotee doesn't depend on any of these things, but he uses all of them. Thus, a devotee may not necessarily cite scripture; he may also use reason and practical experience. Sometimes, he might use the established precedents of other great persons, and sometimes he might employ social customs. Finally, he is also totally free to state what is not present in any of these systems.

Therefore, when we study any of these statements or instructions, we must carefully resist the temptation to universalize them. The only universal statement is that the Absolute Truth is everything. But since everything is not the Absolute Truth, therefore, we must know the role, place, and time for everything. The problem is that most people think that if the Absolute Truth is everything, then everything is Absolute Truth. So, they take all these diverse injunctions and try to treat them as universal truths. They might cite some great personality, some scripture, some philosophical doctrine, or some social custom as evidence. But the existence of the evidence doesn't mean that it must be used here, now, for this person, in this specific circumstance, or this purpose.

As we have discussed, reality is modal, and these modes are always dominant and subordinate. This means that the number of universal truths is very limited. These include the claims that (1) God is the source of everything, (2) God is the purpose of everything, and (3) God is the controller of everything. Other than these three universal truths, all other claims are subject to time, place, person, role or situation, and purpose. One must know the modal nature of reality and what principle, instruction, or idea is dominant or subordinate in each situation. Unless this is known, everything else becomes a mistake.

A common mistake in this regard is blindly imitating the advanced soul. The previous sūtra said that the advanced devotee sets the example for the rest of the world, and *evetaro janah* is used to state how the common people can imitate the example set by a great person. But this sūtra rejects blind imitation and says that everyone gets the result according to the śrutī injunctions. The point is that we are not machines governed by rules and regulations. All these things are presented to broaden our mind, and familiarize us with the nature of truth, right, and good. But this familiarity is not a replacement for judgment and choice. What is choice? A choice is the decision about which principle is dominant or subordinate in a place, time, role, for a person, and a purpose. If we make mistakes in that judgment, then the consequences are ours.

Therefore, reading the scripture, the words and pastimes of the Lord, the instructions of great persons, and indulging in the use of reason and observation is essential to broaden our mind. But none of this produces a machine preprogrammed to follow the rules. When a person hasn't broadened their understanding, then obedience to some basic rules and regulation is better than speculating what the right choice is based upon incorrect or incomplete information. However, as one grows in their understanding, the role of choice and judgment increases. And ultimately, the soul is totally free to choose whatever he wants, subject to the condition that everyone is fully responsible for their choices.

The relation between choice and consequence means that there are contextual laws, and we are not totally free to do whatever we want. But since these laws are contextual, therefore, we must know the law in each situation. These laws are very easy in one sense—everything is produced by the domination of three modes. But it is also very hard because the dominant-subordinate structure changes in every situation. Therefore, one must first understand the philosophy of the modes, how they enter each other, to create numerous situations. Then we can study how great persons have acted in these situations. As this understanding is honed, we develop the ability to make good choices.

QUESTION

You seem to indicate that the situation or circumstance is not enough to decide what must be done. It is also a person's level of advancement that matters in such decisions. If that is the case, and we don't have a good understanding of our level of advancement, then how can we make good choices?

3.4.45 (470)

आरत्वजि्यमति्यौडुलोमःितस्मै हिपरकि्रीयते

ārtvijyamityauḍulomiḥ tasmai hi parikrīyate

ārtvijyam—the ritvik (priest or cleric); iti—thus; auḍulomiḥ

—Audulomi; tasmai—for that; hi—because; parikrīyate—performs on one's behalf.

TRANSLATION

Therefore, Audulomi states that we can consult a ritvik (priest or cleric) for that (i.e., difficult decisions) because (they can make choices) on your behalf.

COMMENTARY

If we are confused about the correct choice in a specific place, time, role, etc., then we can consult a person who knows how to make good choices. This consultation is different from imitation. People often ask: "What would you have done in this situation?" This question assumes imitation; namely, if I do what the other person has done, then it must be good. The earlier sūtra endorsed such a position because it is better than speculating. But ultimately this question is flawed because (1) one may not have the ability to do what the great person has done, (2) the effect of that choice may be different on the person who is asking vs. the person who is telling, and (3) the tendency to universalize may lead to the wrong conclusion about how the present choice must be always applicable. Therefore, one should not ask: "What would you have done in this situation?" One should rather ask: "What should I do in this situation?"

Note the progression in these sūtras. Initially, it was said that one must follow the great person. Then it was said that you cannot blindly follow the great person because you are ultimately responsible for your choices. And now it is said that if you are confused about what should be done, then you can consult a great person. This progression is important because if clerics are always consulted, then two other conditions are not satisfied: (1) the clerics may simply be preaching without practicing it themselves, and (2) they don't know that advice is tailored to the spiritual level of a person, and the advisor is implicated in the consequences of advice. The progression indicates that only a great person must be consulted for advice. Then, mundane greatness is of no value; one must know how different people must act differently in different situations, and a wrong advice implicates the advisor in the consequences of the actions.

In modern times, there are numerous so-called gurus who keep advising people on different things. There are motivational gurus who tell you to be motivated, but they never put their motivation into practice to achieve anything great. There are business consultants who advise people on business, but they have never run a business themselves. And there are people who become gurus without ever studying under the tutelage of an enlightened guru. In this age, simply the ability to use flowery language is considered a mark of education. Such false advisors must be immediately rejected. Then, there may be many people who have achieved greatness, and we can listen to their ideas about how they overcame obstacles, but that doesn't tell us what we should do. These people come on television talk shows and create a fandom, but they don't benefit anyone, because their situations are quite different from our situations. Their advice is not completely useless, but it is always of limited value to us.

After we eliminate the advisors who don't follow their own advice and the advisors whose advice is inapplicable to us, then we can seek the enlightened person who can tell us what we must do. Such people were called Brahmanas earlier, and they had a superior position in society because everyone consulted them for their day-to-day decision making. They are called ritvik here, or a person who acts on your behalf. In short, you don't ask a ritvik: "What would you have done in this situation?" You ask: "What should I do in this situation?" and the ritvik will put himself in your shoes and act on your behalf. He will advise you as if he was in that situation, which means he must understand your specific role, ability, and situation, and then provide appropriate advice.

Again, in this modern age, there are people who "follow" other great people, but they never ask the right questions: "What should I do?" They just like to be associated to great people, as that makes them feel great. Sometimes, they may ask impersonal questions such as the meaning of this or that statement in a scripture, but not how that statement applies to their lives. They just collect theoretical and irrelevant facts and ideas, without changing their life. By not asking the right questions, they don't benefit from the greatness of others. They just feel satisfied that they are "in touch" with greatness, without trying to apply the principles of greatness in their lives, and themselves becoming great. A good teacher must also carefully avoid such false fandom. Therefore, there are basic qualification for both seekers and advisers.

The adviser must be great, and spiritually enlightened, and the seeker must seek to apply that greatness in their life. If both these conditions are not met, then nothing great is achieved.

QUESTION

But we find it hard to even get the association of enlightened ritviks. What are the basic qualifications of a ritvik who can be consulted for advice?

3.4.46 (471)
श्रुतेश्च
śruteśca

śruteḥ—about the śrutī; ca—and.

TRANSLATION

(The ritvik must) also (be knowledgeable) about the śrutī.

COMMENTARY

This sūtra clearly states that we must seek advice only from those who are well-versed in the śrutī, or that which is spoken by the Lord, heard and spoken by the great personalities, and understood under the tutelage of an enlightened spiritual master. A Brahmana is the knower of Brahman. A person wearing a Brahmanical thread is not a Brahmana or a ritvik. In India, at present, we can find many pandits who perform various kinds of rituals and ceremonies. They are well-versed in many mantras and rituals. But they don't know anything about the Absolute Truth. They don't know that the goal of life is transcending the material nature, and they are themselves often quite materialistic. If they are not broadminded, how can they put themselves in the shoes of others, and advise them on their activities? Unless they know that the rules and regulations are different for people in different stages of spiritual progress, and they are different for people in different situations, roles, places, and times, how can they tell someone else what they should be doing in their specific case?

Giving and taking advice is not free of the consequence of choices. Hence, a ritvik is implicated if they give the wrong advice. And a seeker is implicated in choosing a wrong ritvik. Therefore, seeking and offering advice are not without consequences, and both parties are equally responsible for making the right decisions. Therefore, the seekers must be careful about the advisor that they choose, and the advisors must be careful about which seekers they can advise. It is not at all improper for an advisor to decline to advise, either because he thinks that he doesn't understand the situation, or he doesn't believe that the seeker will follow the advice correctly, or even the sincerity of the seeker. Likewise, a seeker can reject an advisor if they are not qualified to advise.

This sūtra is a clear rejection of so-called clerics and priests. Many such clerics and priests are presently involved in sexual abuse, accumulation of wealth, the pursuit of political power, or the enlargement of an idiotic fandom. It is possible that a devotee might sometimes sacrifice some rule to fulfill a higher rule. But if lots of these rules are compromised, and the compromise is not for a higher principle, or it is claimed to be for a higher principle but such principles are not achieved by the compromises, then one must reject such clerics and priests. Such decisions cannot be universalized; but they must be judged.

Topic 14

QUESTION

But I am not even able to judge who truly knows the śrutī, and who doesn't. There are so many people who claim to know the myriad scriptures, but they may not always be the true knowers. There are also many contradictory religions which say different things. How do we identify the true knower?

3.4.47 (472)

सहकार्यन्तरवधिःपिकृषेण तृतीयं तद्वतो वधि्यादवित्

sahakāryantaravidhiḥ pakṣeṇa tṛtīyaṃ tadvato vidhyādivat

sahakāryantaravidhiḥ—the differences in the rules or procedures of collective activity; pakṣeṇa—is a side or part; tṛtīyaṃ—a third one; tadvataḥ—just like; vidhyādivat—as in the case of the acquisition of knowledge etc.

TRANSLATION

The differences in the rules or procedures of collective activity are a third part (of the whole understanding), just like as in the case of the acquisition of knowledge, etc. (three parts are necessary to claim that one knows).

COMMENTARY

Scientific knowledge involves three parts or aspects—prediction, explanation, and justification. By prediction we mean the ability to say that "if you do this, then you will get this result". In modern science, this called state preparation and observation. Different religions or priests might tell people to do different things to get different results (or the same result). And these differences are often confusing. Therefore, prediction of outcomes based on our actions is considered an incomplete understanding. To make this knowledge more complete, we must seek an explanation of how a certain action leads to a specific result. For example, someone might say: The sun rises in the morning, which implies that if you observe the sky in the morning, then you will see the sun. But it is not enough to make that predictive claim. We must also explain how the sun appears in the morning and disappears in the night. Such explanations are constructed in modern science by speaking about the motion of the sun and the earth, postulating that motion is caused by a property called mass, which exerts a force on the earth due to the gravitational law. Such an explanation may sometimes contradict other explanations. For example, present gravitational theory is able to explain the motion of planets like earth, but it cannot explain the motion of galaxies (due to what is supposed to be dark matter) or the constantly increasing distance between the galaxies (due to what is supposed to be dark energy). But even assuming we obtained an explanation that doesn't suffer from all these discrepancies, we still cannot claim completely knowledge. This is because there may be alternative explanations that predict and explain the same phenomena. To be sure that our explanation is the best, we must also justify the explanation, or demonstrate that this is also the best explanation.

Therefore, knowledge progresses in three stages. At the first stage, we seek the consistency and completeness of predictions. This means that we can predict everything that will happen (completeness), and we will never predict anything that will not happen (consistency). At the second stage, we seek the consistency and completeness of explanations. This means that we can explain all the predictions (completeness), and no explanation of any prediction contradicts the explanations of other predictions (consistency). At the third stage, we seek the justification of these explanations. This is achieved if every explanation is found to be the best explanation (completeness), and the principles by which we consider one explanation the best explanation doesn't contradict the principles by which another explanation is judged to be the best (consistency).

Modern science is far from achieving these three goals. For instance, we don't have a theory that predicts everything that will happen, and everything that will not happen. There are theories that make predictions partially (e.g., the best current theory of matter—i.e., atomic theory—makes probabilistic predictions, but with a probability, something with a 50% probability may not happen for a hundred years, and then always happen for the next hundred years; therefore, you cannot say if it predicts what will happen and what will not happen). Then we have many theories which partially explain such partial predictions, but even these partial explanations are mutually incompatible with each other. For example, the prediction based on probabilities in atomic theory depends on the definition of an ensemble, but the same world can be divided into infinite number of ensembles, so the partial predictions have a partial explanation. Furthermore, the explanations of atomic theory involve non-locality, while the explanations of general relativity involve locality. Therefore, the explanations of partial predictions are both incomplete and inconsistent. Finally, even the partial explanations of partial predictions are partially justified by some chosen principle, but the justifying principles employed in one theory remain incompatible with the justifying principles in other theories. For example, the local explanation is justified by reduction, while the non-local explanation is justified by holism. Hence, even the justifications are incomplete and inconsistent.

This sūtra recommends a relentless pursuit for answers to determine if one truly knows. The true knower knows the relation between cause and effect. Such a true knower is also able to explain the reason why a cause becomes the effect. And finally, a true knower can justify this explanation as the best explanation. These explanations must expand horizontally—i.e., to diverse phenomena. And as we expand horizontally, we are also required to ascend vertically, because the explanation is deeper than the phenomenon, but the explanation is also a phenomenon explained by a deeper explanation. Thus, a diversifying tree-like hierarchy is constructed, in which every node in the tree is a prediction, an explanation, and a justification. Therefore, to convince oneself of whether one truly knows, one can employ a variety of tests of their knowledge. Also, we can learn the criterion for truly knowing, because unless one truly knows, he or she will always make bad decisions, which will then cause their suffering.

Most people believe that knowledge is only for some people. They don't understand that without knowledge, bad choices are made, and with bad choices one is entangled in misery. The panacea described here is that one can ask a true knower, which then leads to the problem of identifying the true knower, and that problem is not any easier than knowing oneself. Therefore, there is a progressive path in which one learns a few things from the teacher, applies and tests them, then learns more and applies and tests it again. To identify the teacher some guidelines are given, but they are not different from the guidelines of knowing oneself. However, since a teacher has better knowledge, he can teach the student the complete truth, through a gradual process.

QUESTION

If a teacher, guru, or ritvik has been found, and he is prepared to guide the seeker, then should the seeker always rely on the teacher's guidance or also develop the knowledge themselves to make the best decisions and choices?

3.4.48 (473)
कृत्स्नभावात्तु गृहिणोपसंहारः
kṛtsnabhāvāttu gṛhiṇopasaṃhāraḥ

kṛtsnabhāvāt—by attaining the whole truth; tu—verily; gṛhiṇā—those in the house; upasaṃhāraḥ—finish or destroy all that is secondary.

TRANSLATION

Verily, by a full understanding of the truth (of correct decision making), those living in the household can finish or destroy all that is secondary.

COMMENTARY

People living in households are pulled in many directions—earning a living, taking care of the family, maintaining the house, saving for the future, etc. A renounced person relinquishes all these responsibilities and has a much simpler focus on the ultimate aims of life. But a householder must juggle many different priorities. Unable to make the decisions, they might want a guru's advice on marriage, health, children, finances, etc. Gurus who have renounced the world may not be comfortable with such guidance, and it is sometimes not the best use of their stature. Thus, a householder can try to acquire the understanding by which they can make good choices and decisions themselves.

The fact is that everyone needs to learn the science of good decision-making. This is as true for householders as is for renounced people. And if one has learned this science, then one is automatically liberated. So, why wait for a stage of life to begin learning this science? Everyone can begin learning this science wherever they are. This sūtra states that if householders obtain a full understanding of the science of choices, then they can destroy all that is secondary, which means that they will be liberated from the difficulties of the world.

QUESTION

But we find that the knowers of truth do not easily disclose the truth to everyone. Meanwhile, those who don't know the truth tend to talk a lot. This creates confusion about the truth in the minds of most people because most people are attracted by the greatest amount of noise, rather than the truth.

3.4.49 (474)

मौनवदितरेषामप्युपदेशात्

maunavaditareṣāmapyupadeśāt

maunavat—just like one who is silent; itareṣām—to the others;

api—even; upadeśāt—teach the others.

TRANSLATION

Even those who are just like silent, teach (the truth) to the others.

COMMENTARY

The truth is very subtle, because every type of contradictory claim is true, although these contradictions are not simultaneously true. When truth is impersonalized, then we think that something true must be true for all persons, at all places, and always. In the West, this impersonalized truth is called 'universal truth', and everyone seeking truth is conditioned by this impersonalism.

But if we say that truth is that which is true for everyone, everywhere, and always, then conflicting claims cannot exist. The need to overcome the contradictions in the truth now creates three kinds of approaches to knowledge. The nihilist says that all these contradictions must be dissolved to produce nothingness, because in nothingness there is no contradiction. The impersonalist says the truth is beyond these contradictions, but since all diversity is contradictory, therefore, we must remove such diversities to attain the truth. The materialist says that there are many contradictory propositions, but only one such proposition is true, and we must prove one of these propositions through reason and experiment. The problem is that the contradictions appear in different people, places, and times, so, the rejection of a contradiction means the rejection of half the people, places, and times. Now, these opposing sides engage in endless arguments and counterarguments, as each side dominates alternately, but they cannot exist without their opposite, so the contradiction never disappears.

The real knowers of the truth are aware that voidism, impersonalism, and materialism are not the answers to the problem of truth. But everyone seeking this truth comes to the true knower with the assumption that the truth must be found in one of these three approaches. Thus, if you say that something exists, then the nihilist has a problem—because he claims that nothing exists. Then, if you say that whatever exists is different from the other existing things, then the impersonalist has a problem—because he claims that only one thing exists. Then if you say that many existing things are mutually contradictory, then the materialist has a problem because he says that contradictions cannot exist. The nihilist and the impersonalist nod in vociferous agreement with the materialist, since they too don't want contradictions to exist, although the nihilist wants to dissolve everything, while the impersonalist wants to dissolve diversity.

The problem is that people have a preconceived notion of reality, and they want to fit the knowledge within that conception. The nihilist wants the conclusion to be nothingness; the impersonalist wants the conclusion to be the dissolution of diversity; and the materialist wants mutually consistent diversity. Arguing with a nihilist, an impersonalist, and a materialist becomes hard, not because they are right, but because they are always talking about a universal truth. The universal truth is impossible. But people think that the alternative to this universalism is relativism, so if we give up universalism then there is no truth. Thus, the relativist also jumps on to the bandwagon of criticism of truth.

To know the truth, we must know the following: (1) everything that is ever possible is eternally true, as a possibility, (2) these possibilities are mutually contradictory so all possibilities are collectively contradictory, but they are not seen simultaneously, and (3) one side of the contradiction manifests at one place, in one person, and at one time. Therefore, the Absolute Truth—as different from the universal truth—is a person who originally exists a possibility; He expands into many persons at different places and times, so the possibility becomes real, but this reality is not self-contradictory, because the contradiction is always in a different person, place, or time. In short, if we are prepared to discard our impersonalist ideas about 'universal truth', and can embrace a personalistic 'Absolute Truth', then knowledge is both consistent and complete.

One who is completely satisfied by knowing the truth has no necessity to tell anyone about this truth. But they impart this knowledge to the humble person. The sign of humility is not just the preparedness to accept a description of the truth within the nihilist, impersonalist, materialist, or relativist doctrines. The prior necessity is to discard all these models of truth themselves. If one is prepared to make this change, then real knowledge can also be obtained. Therefore, the fundamental criterion for someone to know is to be a devotee. They may not be pure devotees, but they must have some inkling of devotion. With an inkling of devotion, a pure devotee can make them perfect devotees, and with that perfection in devotion, one can also obtain perfect knowledge. There is, however, no scope for perfect knowledge within nihilism, impersonalism, materialism, or relativism—or even their parent doctrine of universalism.

Topic 15

QUESTION

Even if someone is prepared to teach, we find that the process of learning is very long. There are too many difficulties, and most people abandon the process because of these difficulties. Why is the understanding of truth so hard, if everyone is supposed to know this truth, and perfect their lives by it?

3.4.50 (475)
अनावष्किुर्वन् अन्वयात्
anāviṣkurvan anvayāt

anāviṣkurvan—the activity of removing the poison; anvayāt—(establishes) from the connection (to the Absolute Truth).

TRANSLATION

The activity of removing the poison (automatically establishes) the connection (from the individual soul to the Supreme Lord—i.e., Absolute Truth).

COMMENTARY

We can see the progression through the last several sūtras. Initially, it was said that a cleric must be consulted—this seemed easy because we can just ask someone who knows. But the problem was: How do we identify such a person? So, then we discussed the qualifications of the cleric. But how many times can you ask someone? Every moment in our lives requires a choice or a decision. The practical difficulties in consulting someone at every moment led to the recommendation that we must develop this understanding ourselves. However, even to acquire this understanding we need a teacher. We are no longer talking about a cleric who will give us readymade answers to our questions. We are rather seeking a person who will teach us the truth by which we can decide ourselves. The problem is that the knowers don't reveal the complete knowledge easily. Therefore, it was said, they can reveal even though they mostly remain silent. But since they are generally silent, a person must exert on their own to extract the requisite knowledge from them. Now, we come to the problem of this sūtra, namely, that this process of extraction is long and hard. In response, this sūtra says that is hard because the poison is within us. When this poison is removed, then the knowledge is also automatically attained. Therefore, the hardship is not in the knowledge, but in the poison within.

What is that poison? As discussed in the previous sūtra, this poison takes many forms such as nihilism, impersonalism, materialism, and relativism. The process of freeing ourselves of this poison begins with the rejection of materialism—i.e., that we are only the body. If there is only the body, then there are no ideas, there can be no theories, and nothing can ever be known. The people who reject materialism, therefore sometimes argue for relativism—we have freedom, we can think and feel, but there is no universal truth; everyone must create their own truth. But relativism destroys society. Therefore, the person tired of relativism says that anything outside the self is an illusion, but since we are defined in relation to these things outside us, therefore, both the self and the other are illusions. Thus, arises the doctrine of nihilism. But calling the world and the self an illusion doesn't mitigate the suffering. Therefore, the person who rejected the self and the others, now says that the self and the other are identical. This is also the doctrine of impersonal unity or oneness. To attain this oneness, we must give up all desires and pleasures. By giving up material desires and pleasures, you can obtain freedom from suffering, but should freedom from suffering be also called happiness? Or, is happiness beyond the freedom from suffering? In short, suffering must be stopped, and happiness acquired?

The journey from materialism to relativism to nihilism to impersonalism is long and arduous because many types of poisons need to be removed. Once these poisons are removed, then the final step of knowing the Absolute Truth is very easy. In short, knowledge is not hard. What makes it hard is the poison within. Whenever truth is injected, it gets mixed up with the poison. The truth is then distorted, and often, parts of that truth are rejected. When these parts are rejected, then the truth gets weaker, and the poison gets stronger. To strengthen the truth, we must inject it again, to weaken the poison. So, the process is long because it necessitates a change in the person. Once that change has occurred, then knowledge is naturally obtained. Sri Chaitanya has termed this process as the 'cleansing of the mirror'. The soul is the mirror, but it is dirty. This dirt must be removed, and once it is removed, the reflection is clear. Therefore, knowing the truth is not constructing a picture of the truth piece by piece within a dirty mirror. The process is simply cleansing the mirror, removing the poison, purifying the mind and the senses, and destroying the infection.

This is a radical conception of knowledge in which the fault is not with the teacher, the books, or the philosophy. The fault is in the seeker. Most people have trouble grasping this idea, as they keep blaming the teacher, the books, or the philosophy—the teacher is not good enough, the books are contradictory, and the philosophy is hard. These conclusions are rejected in this sūtra.

In Western philosophy, there are three cardinal doctrines of the mind. The empiricists such as John Locke say that the mind is a blank slate. The idealists such as Immanuel Kant and Carl Jung say that the mind is preformed with all the ideals. And the psychoanalysts like Sigmund Freud say that the mind is forever dirty. If the mind is a blank slate, then there is no problem in knowing, because it is already clean. If the mind has all the ideals, then knowledge is simply knowing the ideals within. And if the mind is always dirty, then nothing can ever be known. Thus, Western philosophy closes all the doors to the purification of the mind—either the mind is blank, or the mind is already perfect, or the mind is forever dirty. In the first two cases, there is no need for purification. And in the third case, there is no possibility of purification. Therefore, people coming to Vedic philosophy from a Western perspective have a lot of trouble, because the basic premise is that you are dirty, and you must be cleaned, but nobody wants to accept that they are basically dirty and need cleansing.

Topic 16

QUESTION

The process of cleaning seems to be very hard, because the things that we are cleaning it with, may themselves be dirty. For example, if we say that we clean ourselves with knowledge, but all this knowledge is contaminated by the biases we already have, then this process of cleansing seems infinite. How can then we clean the mind before the perfection in knowledge is acquired?

3.4.51 (476)

अइहकिमप्यप्रस्तुतप्रतबिन्धे तद्दर्शनात्

aihikamapyaprastutapratibandhe taddarśanāt

aihikam—worldly; api—even; aprastuta-pratibandhe—in the unborn or the eternal restrictions; tat-darśanāt—from vision of that (the Lord) is obtained.

TRANSLATION

Even in this world, from the vision of that (the Lord) in the unborn or the eternal restrictions (i.e., the bounds of the Lord's love).

COMMENTARY

The term *prastuta* means that which has appeared, and when used alongside *aihikam*, which means worldly (or temporary), the meaning (by contrast) becomes that this world is temporary and the *aprastuta* must be eternal. We can also say that *aprastuta* is spiritual and *aikham* is material. In this case, this eternity and spirituality is combined with restrictions. Thus, we have come a full circle from the preceding sūtras where it was stated that the soul has no restrictions of rights and duties in the spiritual world. Before this sūtra, it was already confirmed that the body is not a restriction; it is merely an instrument for fulfilling the desire, and a different kind of body can be obtained to fulfill the desires. We even spoke about more capable bodies in the spiritual world. Therefore, after rejecting the body being a restriction, and then rejecting the restrictions of duties and rights, we are again speaking about restrictions.

What are these eternal restrictions? And why does the sūtra say that these restrictions can exist even in the material world? This restriction is not of a body or of duties and rights. These are the restrictions of love. They are eternally a possibility, and hence exist even in the material world. The love can manifest even while the soul is present in this world, so, the temporariness of this world doesn't impact the eternity of the love. Therefore, after saying the soul is free from rights and duties, this sūtra says that the soul is bound by love. In short, the Lord doesn't ask the soul to do anything, and the soul doesn't expect any reciprocation from the Lord. And yet, there is spontaneous activity. After stating, in the previous sūtra, that the soul must be purified, this sūtra says that if the loving devotion the Lord is established, then purification is automatic.

In short, the poisons of materialism, relativism, nihilism, and impersonalism are different manifestations of the deeper poison of the lack of love. If this love is not established, then the process of purification of the poison is very hard, because the poison simply changes different forms and one keeps moving from one kind of illusion to another. But if the love is established, then all kinds of poisons are destroyed, the soul is purified, and perfect knowledge is obtained. Therefore, the route to perfect knowledge is through devotion.

Topic 17

QUESTION

We have spoken about the difficulties in making the correct type of sacrifice; we have discussed the difficulties in Varṇaśrama; we have spoken about the challenges of a cooperative society; we discussed the difficulty in identifying the right teacher; we spoke about the difficulties in acquiring knowledge; and finally, we discussed the problems in removing the poisons in the soul. Is your final conclusion that devotion to the Lord solves all these problems?

3.4.52 (477)
एवं मुक्तफिलानयिमःतदवस्थावधृते
evaṃ muktiphalāniyamaḥ tadavasthāvadhṛte

evaṃ—in this way; muktiphala-aniyamaḥ—there is no rule that

restricts the attainment of liberation; tat-avasthā-avadhṛte—that situation or position is devoid of all the faults (namely, the poisons mentioned previously).

TRANSLATION

In this way (by acquiring the devotion to the Lord), there is no rule that restricts the attainment of liberation, and that situation (of loving the Lord) devoid of all the faults (namely, the poisons that were discussed previously).

COMMENTARY

Love of the Lord is the solution to all problems of knowledge, social organization, and the unhappiness within. If this love is absent, then we struggle through a difficult process of identifying the correct decisions, and due to lack of knowledge, we seek teachers who might be misguided. If this love is absent, then social organization becomes impossible because there is no higher purpose that binds people together; people may stay together if their pleasure is being satisfied; however, any discrepancy in their selfish pleasures produces conflicts. Without this love, the soul constantly suffers from the fear of loss and eventually of death; with every loss comes loneliness, and death brings the ultimate separation from everyone and everything that made us feel secure. Therefore, even though happiness can be achieved through the progress in knowledge, better social organization, or worldly love, these methods of achieving happiness are themselves not guaranteed without the Lord's love. Hence, no method works without the Lord's devotion, and every method can work with the Lords' devotion. Therefore, devotion is not contrary to the pursuit of knowledge, better social organization, or worldly love. However, the individual pursuits of knowledge, social organization, and worldly love are inherently flawed.

Therefore, one must always begin in devotion to the Lord. This devotion may not be initially perfect. But it can be perfected through the gradual progression in knowledge, social organization, and loving relationships. All these things are meant to improve the devotion. However, if they are separated from this purpose, then they are individually and collectively frustrated.

Chapter 4

This is the shortest chapter in the text, and it discusses the nature of death, what happens after death, how a soul enters a spiritual abode, and how the experiences of the spiritual world are similar or different to those of this world.

Section 1: This section discusses the nature of death, what is lost at death and what is preserved at death. We all know that our material body and its associated things are lost at death. The mind and intellect are also destroyed at death and we need to learn everything again. However, this section describes how spiritual progress made during the present life is not lost upon death. This includes both the advancements obtained by spiritual knowledge and spiritual activities. However, if the soul is liberated by devotion to the Lord, then the pending karma, which would have otherwise been reaped in future lives is destroyed. Thus, the material suffering and enjoyment are destroyed upon liberation, but the partial spiritual progress made within a life is preserved.

Section 2: This section discusses the differences between the Sāñkhya and Yoga systems of practice. On one hand, it is said that the mind controls the senses, and the senses control the objects. On the other hand, it is said that the mind and sense control can also be obtained by controlling the prāṇa. However, the section then describes that by this mind and sense control, one enters the nihilistic state of balance that existed prior to the creation of the universe. The spiritual state beginning with Brahman is said to be beyond the nihilistic state. The section then describes how the liberated soul upon death reaches a specific abode of the Lord being guided by the light emanating from the abode. This idea is then generalized to say that even yogis ascending to higher planetary systems, and the soul going to lower and hellish planets are also similarly guided by the light. In short, depending upon a person's qualification, they can see only those planets and places which they deserve in the next life.

Section 3: This section discusses the nature of yajñá or sacrifice. An extensive discussion is undertaken about why these sacrifices are performed through fire, and not through air or water. The reasoning is that only the procedures of fire sacrifices are convenient—i.e., the mantras of the fire sacrifice are shorter and simpler—whereas the procedures of air and water sacrifices are much more complex. The section then says that fire was chosen as the method of sacrifices after careful consideration, which means that the rituals described in the four Vedas aren't the only types of sacrifices. The conditions under which other types of sacrifices (e.g., through water and air) can be performed are described. Thus, the practicality of these sacrifices is taken into account, which underscores the fact that the Vedic knowledge is presented not just because it was imparted by the Lord, or is rationally understandable, or that it was converted in a textual form in a certain age, but also because it was practical. This practical knowledge is part of everything that is possible, some of which may be impractical. Thus, the pragmatic nature of the Vedic knowledge is established.

Section 4: This section discusses the state of pure devotion to the Lord. It is said the devotee has the body of pure cognition. Through this body, the soul has states of waking in which the devotee sees the Lord face-to-face, a body of dreaming through which the devotee sees the Lord through his imagination, and a body of deep sleep in which the devotee has a persona related to the Lord. The devotee is also said to feel separation from the Lord in the dreaming state, but this separation is not different from the union of the waking state. Finally, the section distinguishes the state of pure devotion from impersonalism, the idea that the soul merges into the Lord's body, that the soul is equivalent to the Lord, or that devotional experience is quite similar to the material illusions.

SECTION 1

Topic 1

QUESTION

It seems that whatever question I ask, you always come around to the same conclusion. It doesn't matter whether we discuss the nature of material reality, the structure of the universe, the nature of the body and mind, the question of right and wrong action, the process of social organization, the progression in knowledge, or the understanding of logic and meaning. You always give the same conclusion—namely, that the soul must be devoted to the Lord. Is it necessary to repeat this conclusion, even after we have already discussed it?

4.1.1 (478)
आवृत्तःःअसकृदुपदेशात्
āvṛttiḥ asakṛdupadeśāt

āvṛttiḥ—repetition; asakṛt—repeatedly; upadeśāt—from the teaching.

TRANSLATION

From the repeated teaching (of the ultimate conclusions in the scriptures).

COMMENTARY

In the beginning of Manu Samhita, which describes the rules for social order, Lord Viṣṇu is glorified as the creator of the world. In the beginning of Brihat Parāśara Hora, which describes the principles of astrology, Lord Viṣṇu is again glorified. Many Purāna, such as the Śrīmad Bhāgavatam, the Viṣṇu Purāna, and others, discuss the material creation, but describe Lord Viṣṇu to be its creator. In this way, personalism has been taught in every division of human knowledge which means that even if someone is studying non-transcendental topics, they are constantly reminded of the transcendental topic. Furthermore, as we have discussed, everything is inside the Lord, and the Lord is inside everything—as the original purpose. Therefore, we can study several subjects or topics, but before we start, we must ask ourselves: Why are we doing this? And the answer is the Lord. When we finish studying it, we need to summarize the subject, and we must then describe it as a branch of knowledge that describes one aspect of the Lord. And while we are studying it, we might often ask: How do we know? And the answer is that it was originally revealed by the Lord, subsequently accepted, understood, and tested by numerous others, and finally their understanding was sometimes weaved together with the Lord's instructions. Therefore, at the beginning, in the middle, and at the end, we always remember the Lord—as the purpose, as the cause, and the whole truth.

QUESTION

But how many times must this conclusion be repeated? Isn't it enough to say it once, and then focus our attention on the discussion or other things?

4.1.2 (479)

लङि्गाच्च

liṅgācca

liṅgāt—from the indicatory marks; ca—also.

TRANSLATION

(We can judge) from the indicatory marks (of happiness) also.

COMMENTARY

There is no topic other than the Lord. He is the whole truth, He is the cause of the partial truth, and He is the purpose of all the partial truths. The conclusion of knowledge is therefore understood in three ways. First, we can say that there are diverse subjects, but what is the conclusion of studying all these subjects? In short, why should I study anything, instead of nothing? And the answer is that we want to know the Lord. Second, we can say that now that we know the conclusion, why should I study any of the detailed subjects or topics? And the answer is that the Lord has many aspects, and we are simply studying the aspects of His persona. Third, we can ask: But why should I study all these aspects? And the answer is that we serve the Lord through these aspects.

If we don't know the whole truth to begin with, then the diversities cannot be reconciled. But if we know the whole truth, but without the diversities, then the whole truth is impersonalized. Finally, if we know the whole and the part, but we don't engage the part in the service of the whole, then the parts are relativized. Hence, there is no knowledge without the Lord. Without the Lord, we can obtain numerous mutually contradictory theories that cannot be reconciled. Or, we can destroy all variety to say that it is an illusion. Or, we can conclude that all that I know is simply my experience, and has no objective existence. All these are different kinds of ignorance. Truth is where when we can find the consistent and complete knowledge, which is variegated, and it is real. That kind of truth is impossible unless we understand the nature of the Lord.

Ignorance and delusion appear in many forms. As a result, the truth is unknown, and whatever is known is misused. This sūtra says that to destroy the illusion and the misuse we must constantly repeat the understanding of the Lord as the origin, purpose, and controller of the world. He must be known at the beginning, in the middle, and at the end. Whatever else is known, remains incomplete or incorrect unless the Lord is known, and harmful unless it is used in the Lord's service. By listening to these descriptions repeatedly, we can destroy the many kinds of poisons that exist within us. Once these poisons are destroyed, the complete truth is known, and the person is completely satisfied. This satisfaction then develops into the love of the Lord. And due to that love, the symptoms of happiness appear in the body. These symptoms have been discussed earlier, and this sūtra simply says that we must go on listening to these descriptions until the symptoms of happiness appear in our body.

Topic 2

QUESTION

What is the effect of repeatedly hearing these descriptions of the Lord?

4.1.3 (480)

आत्मेति तूपगच्छन्ति ग्राहयन्ति च

ātmeti tūpagacchanti grāhayanti ca

ātmeti—as one's own; tu—but; upagacchanti—come near; grāhayanti—desire to perceive; ca—also.

TRANSLATION

(By repeatedly hearing these descriptions) one starts considering the Lord as their own, they come near, and they desire to perceive (the Lord) as well.

COMMENTARY

Three effects of listening to the descriptions of the Lord are described here. First, one starts considering the Lord as their own; this consideration is establishing the relation to the Lord. Just like we consider our father, mother, spouse, friend, or children our own, in the same way, the devotee starts considering that the Lord is one's own. The Lord is no longer an alien concept or someone who created the world, or merely as someone great. We know of many ideas, but we don't consider them our own. We know of many great people, who may have done great things, but we don't consider them our own. Without that attachment, such people, things, and ideas come into our consciousness and go out of it. With an attachment to the Lord, a personal relationship is created. Second, as this relation is created, then one comes close to the Lord. This closeness is knowing the nature of the Lord, such as what He likes and dislikes, how He looks like, how He interacts with His devotees, and so on. Third, despite this knowing, there is an ever-greater desire to know more. This is generally in contrast to our ordinary relationships. For example, we might consider our parents our own, and we might also know them, or be close to them. But we don't constantly desire to know them more; familiarity breeds contempt, and there is a limitation to how much one wants to know the other person. But there is no limit to this knowing in the case of the Lord. By knowing something about the Lord, the desire for knowing the Lord even more automatically increases.

Topic 3

QUESTION

But what is the difference between seeing the Lord, and hearing the various descriptions of the Lord? You have earlier said that these two things are identical as they have the same meaning. But now you are saying that by hearing about the Lord, there is progression to seeing the Lord. So, it seems that seeing the Lord is better than hearing. What is the difference in the two?

4.1.4 (481)
न प्रतीके न हि सः
na pratīke na hi saḥ

na—not; pratīke—in the symbol; na—not; hi—because; saḥ—he.

TRANSLATION

(The Lord is) no longer known in the symbols because He is not (a symbol).

COMMENTARY

When you read a travelogue, then you see the symbols of the experience of travel. The meaning or experience of the travel is present inside the travelogue as meaning; however, the travelogue is different from the travel. The difference is primarily that the travelogue doesn't capture all aspects of the travel. But if you undertake the travel, then you can experience all these details first-hand. Nevertheless, if you haven't traveled to a destination, then you might still read about the destination through a tourist guide, a tourism brochure, etc. The information in the brochure or the guide is incomplete, but it is not false.

In the same way, the scriptures are like tourist guides and travel brochures. They give information about the destination so that you might be attracted to go there. Once you develop attraction, then you obtain the wherewithal to travel. During this preparation, you keep imagining how good that destination would be, by recalling the pictures and descriptions of the destination from the travel brochures and guides. But, if the destination is great, then the experience of the place exceeds all the expectations set by the brochures and guides.

This analogy is employed in this sūtra by stating that the scriptures are symbols of reality. The symbols are true, in the sense that there is a real destination. But these symbols cannot capture that destination completely. They are provided to attract the potential aspirant, just like travel brochures are provided by travel agents. Once you reach that destination, you realize that everything in the brochure also exists in the destination, but everything in the destination isn't in the brochure; hence, the experience exceeds the brochure by far.

This is the meaning of saying that in the beginning, one only reads the brochures—i.e., the scriptures. But ultimately, one also travels. The brochure is true because everything in the brochure is in the destination. But the destination is greater than what is described in the brochure. Hence, the brochure is a symbol of the destination, but the Lord is the destination. Therefore, for the advanced devotee, He is not merely known by books; He is also experienced directly.

Topic 4

QUESTION

But we go to so many tourist places, we enjoy for some time, and then we come back. How is the spiritual world different from other tourist places?

4.1.5 (482)

ब्रह्मदृष्टिःउत्कर्षात्

brahmadṛṣṭiḥ utkarṣāt

brahmadṛṣṭiḥ—seeing the Lord; utkarṣāt—from growing attraction.

TRANSLATION

From the growing attraction upon seeing the Lord.

COMMENTARY

We go to many tourist places, do many touristy things, and then get bored. A tourist attraction may be quite enjoyable, but there are people living in that tourist destination who are not as excited to be in that destination. In fact, the people living in that tourist destination may want to go to other tourist destinations. This sūtra says that once you reach that destination, you never leave because the attraction keeps growing. Therefore, those who are already living in that destination are not looking to go to other tourist destinations. The attraction to the destination keeps growing, so alternative desires don't develop.

Knowing the Lord is not like knowing our relatives where the knowing stops at some time because we know everything there is to know, and when everything has been discovered, then, complacency sets in, and the attraction declines. We might still like our relatives, but we are not constantly eager to learn more about them. Hence, the early stages in a romantic relationship are quite exciting because we are learning new things about a new person. But after some time, everyone settles into their knowledge, and the excitement wanes. Now, people go to other tourist destinations to rekindle their romance, hoping that a new place will bring something new out of them and the others.

But the spiritual world is not like that. The Lord is infinite, and there are always new things to be known about the Lord. As we learn new things, we act in different ways. And this difference in action reveals another side of a person which was previously unknown. Similarly, as we know more, the Lord knows that we know more. Therefore, He too acts differently, and then He reveals something that was previously unknown. Therefore, attraction creates additional knowledge, additional knowledge creates novel actions, and that novel action then increases the attraction, and the cycle perpetuates endlessly.

The spiritual world is therefore like an ever-expanding tree. The Lord is the root of the tree, but every branch, twig, and leaf is present in the root. The soul is a leaf in this tree, but as the soul learns more about the Lord, and then due to this knowledge, the leaf expands—the root becomes a subbranch of the leaf as the knowledge acquired by the leaf. Then the Lord knows about this expanded leaf, and that expands Him. Thus, the devotee learns about the Lord, then the Lord knows that the devotee knows about Him, then the devotee knows that that the Lord knows that the devotee knows, and so on. The new knowledge produces new actions and so the novelty is never finished. Due to this expanding mutual knowledge, the soul expands inside the Lord, and the Lord expands inside the soul. And as we know more, we are also attracted even more.

Topic 5

QUESTION

You are saying that there is growing attraction between the soul and the Lord, but doesn't this attraction mean that ultimately the soul and the Lord will merge into a single entity? Just like we might say that two bodies with mass are attracted to each other, and due to this attraction, they come close to each other. Then as they come closer to each other, then, the attraction increases further. Due to this increased attraction, they must come even closer. So, the result of this mutually increasing attraction, and the decreasing distance between the attractor and the attracted, must be that they eventually collapse into a single object. And that object would not have the distinction between the two.

4.1.6 (483)

आदत्यिादमितयश्चाङ्गे उपपत्तेः

ādityādimatayaścāṅge upapatteḥ

ādityādi-matayaḥ—the ideas of the sun etc.; ca—also; aṅge—as a part or subordinate member; upapatteḥ—because of logical deduction.

TRANSLATION

The ideas of the sun etc. (i.e., the other planets) are also said to be the parts or subordinate members (of the Lord's body) and this is understood as logical deduction (namely, how the whole divides into the parts; the part is called *upa* and the part is considered lower relative to the whole which is called *patti*).

COMMENTARY

This sūtra refutes the black hole doctrine of love. According to this doctrine—espoused by the impersonalist—the soul and the Lord are attracted, and then they come closer to each other; as they come closer, the attraction increases and the distance decreases; eventually the soul collapses into the Lord.

This sūtra cites the example from Vedic cosmology, where the planets like the Sun and the Moon circumambulate the polestar, where Lord Viṣṇu resides. These planets are attracted to the Lord, and their circumambulation is caused by this attraction. However, these planets don't collapse into the polestar. Rather, the Sun and the other planets remain 'lower' than the polestar. These planets are said to be aspects or parts of Lord Viṣṇu, and the Lord is the whole. Therefore, by worshipping these planets, one worships some aspect of the Lord. The polestar denotes the cosmic ego, and the Lord is the soul of that ego.

The Sun, specifically, is said to be the representation of the Lord's intellect, while the Moon represents the mind. The other five planets, namely, Jupiter, Mercury, Mars, Venus, and Saturn are representations of the five elements. The polestar resides at the center of the Nakṣatra, which are initially divided into four parts—representing the four moral principles—and then are further divided into seven parts, thus creating the 28 Nakṣatra. Collectively, these 28 Nakṣatra represent morality. This morality then serves the ego or the polestar, as the Nakṣatra circumambulate the polestar. The intellect or the Sun then serves the morality. The moon then serves the Sun. Finally, the other five planets serve the Moon. This 'service' is described in Vedic cosmology as the control of one celestial entity over the other entities. Thus, for example, the polestar causes the rotation of the Nakṣatra. The Nakṣatra then 'drag' the Sun, the Sun 'drags' the Moon, and the Moon 'drags' the other planets. Due to this dragging, three primary kinds of calendars and times are recognized in cosmology.

The first time is attributed to the Nakṣatra movement and is called the sideral calendar. The second time is attributed to the Sun's motion and is called the solar calendar. The third time is due to the Moon's movement and is called the lunar calendar. Then, there are five other calendars called *vatsar*, *anuvatsar*, *parivatsar*, *samvatsar*, and *idavatsar*, and are attributed to the motion of the five planets. In this way, Vedic cosmology describes time through eight calendars. Only the first three calendars are well-known today. Cosmological texts give detailed calculations of how the Nakṣatra drag the Sun, and the Sun drags the Moon, which are then used to compute the time in Vedic cosmology. The calculation of the other five types of calendars is not found today, but these are noted in the Śrīmad Bhagavatam. As a result, the effect of one planet on the other planets—which forms the basis of astrology—is not fully understood today, although this understanding can be extrapolated with some effort.

Now, we can come to the main point of this sūtra, which is that attraction between the soul and the Lord is not physical. It is not like the gravitational force in which two bodies come closer, the attraction increases, which brings them even closer, and ultimately, they collapse into each other. The impersonalist uses these analogies because there are numerous Vedic texts which describe devotion to the Lord, and the impersonalist is unable to deny their existence. So, he coopts these texts, and says that even by devotion the soul merges into the Lord. In short, even when the Vedic texts describe devotion to the Lord, the impersonalist interprets them not as love, but as a vehicle to merger. For the impersonalist, if the final state is merger, then devotion can be accepted.

But this sūtra clearly refutes this identity by stating that the planets like the Sun and the Moon are aspects of the Lord, they remain lower than the Lord, and their attraction causes them to circumambulate the Lord, rather than collapse into the Lord. This whole-part doctrine is semantic. The hand is a property of the soul, the hand has expanded from the soul, and the hand serves the soul. The term *upapatti* is used to indicate logical deduction. We have discussed the nature of logical deduction earlier; *upa* means the part and *pat* means falling. The part falls out of the whole, like a leaf emerges from the root in an inverted tree. The separation of the part from the whole then creates an attraction between the whole and the part—the purpose of the part is the whole. Due to this attraction, the part serves the whole but doesn't merge into the whole.

Therefore, if physical analogies of attraction—e.g., gravitational force—are used, then the result is a black hole in which the soul and the Lord are merged, and the distinction between the two ceases to exist. But if semantic analogies of attraction—i.e., the whole is the purpose of the part—are used, then the result is constantly growing attraction, without the part collapsing into the whole.

Topic 6

QUESTION

Some people also say that the Paramātma is situated in the heart so that the soul can merge into the Paramātma, and this merger is called yoga. Just like if two numbers are added, then the result is a bigger number. Once these numbers have been added, then we cannot distinguish between the two numbers. In the same way, when the union between the soul and the Lord has occurred, then we must say that the soul has been added to God, and the result is a bigger quantity called Brahman. After this addition, we cannot separate them.

4.1.7 (484)
आसीनःसंभवात्
āsīnaḥ sambhavāt

āsīnaḥ—sitting; sambhavāt—due to the possibility (of soul's liberation).

TRANSLATION

Due to the possibility (of soul's liberation), (the Lord) is sitting (in the heart)

COMMENTARY

The impersonalist says that the Lord in the heart is also a finite entity because He has a form, and everything with a form is finite. However, after all the finite entities have been merged, then the result must be infinite. Therefore, yoga or union is like a mathematical addition of numbers in which small quantities are added to a larger quantity, and ultimately, we obtain infinity.

The quantitative idea of addition is again a physical idea. But according to the whole-part theory, the whole is 1, and everything else is a fraction of 1.

In this regard, we can note that numbers are used in two ways— cardinally and ordinally. Cardinally, numbers are one, two, three, etc. Ordinally, these numbers are first, second, third, etc. We do not start counting from infinity and then proceed backwards to 1. We rather count from 1. The number 1 divides into parts, which means that 1 is the root of the tree, and the fractions of the number 1 are the trunks, branches, and leaves of the tree. This is also how numbers are counted in a binary, ternary, or any other system of counting. The main problem is that to count something, we require a *base* of counting. For example, if the base is 10, then we divide the whole into 10 parts, not infinite parts. Then we divide each of these 10 parts into further 10 parts, not infinite parts. By the successive application of this division, infinite parts are created, but the sum of these parts is not infinite. The sum of all these parts is still 1. Once these parts have been created, we can say that the whole is the first part, then there are 10 subparts, each of which has 10 further subparts, and so on. The cardinality of the parts—i.e., the total number of parts—is infinite. This cardinality can also be numbered as the first, second, third, etc. part. But the whole is still 1.

The Param Brahman is the idea 1, and the Paramātma is the symbol of the idea 1. Just like you can represent the idea 1 infinite times by typing the numeral 1, similarly, the Param Brahman is the singular idea of 1, but the representations of this Param Brahman are infinite symbols of this idea. Nevertheless, because the numeral 1 represents the idea 1, therefore, in one sense, they are non-different, and yet in another sense, the numeral 1 is not identical to the idea 1.

Now we come to the main point of this sūtra, which is that the numeral 1 appears as the representation of the idea 1, so that we can understand the idea 1. If this numeral did not appear before us, then how will we grasp the idea? The impersonalist thinks that Brahman is physically infinite. Infinity cannot have a form, so Brahman must be formless. But this claim can be countered by saying that Brahman is the idea 1, and everything else is either a fraction of 1, or the representation of the idea 1, or even the representations of the fractions of 1. The fractions of 1 are the properties of the Lord, and the representations of 1 are the symbols of the whole. We cannot equate the representation of the fraction to the representation of the whole. For example, a table is the representation of the idea table, which is a part of the whole truth. The sound Kṛṣṇa is also a representation of the whole truth. That doesn't mean that the word 'table' and the word 'Kṛṣṇa' are equally limited because they are both parts. Yes, they are both parts, but one symbol means the whole, and the other symbol means the part. So, unless we distinguish these symbols by the meaning, we will simply see them as parts, and then apply physical analogies of whole and part.

The Paramātma is indeed a part of Param Brahman, but He is also a representation of the Param Brahman. Physically, He is a part, and semantically He is the whole. He appears before the soul—who is both physically and semantically a part—to enable the possibility of the part knowing the whole. This appearance of the Lord as His representation doesn't equate Him to the soul.

Therefore, when we speak about yoga, we must not talk about adding two numbers to get a bigger number. It is about recognizing how the soul is a small meaning, the Lord is the full meaning, and how the partial meaning has manifested from the whole meaning and hence must serve the full meaning.

The soul and the Lord exist in three modalities—universal, contextual, and the individual. The universal modality is the meaning—the Lord is the full meaning, and the soul is a partial meaning. The individual modality is that the Lord is a person, and the soul is a person. And the contextual modality is that this part is related to the whole, and the part gets its meaning in relation to the whole. We cannot call something the leg of a chair, unless we also say that there is a chair. The legness of the part is understood only in relation to the whole. Therefore, the chair must appear before the leg, for the leg to know that it is a leg. If the chair doesn't appear in this way, then how can the leg know what it is? But when the chair appears, it always appears as a symbol of the whole. In short, in each leg of the chair, the whole chair is immanent as a symbol. This symbol has the same meaning as the chair, but it is not equal to the chair.

Even when the soul merges into Brahman, it is like a fraction of 1 collapsing into 1. It doesn't mean that 1/100th now became 1. It means that 1/100th doesn't know that it is 1/100th. This ignorance is also called liberation, because at least the 1/100th is not thinking that it is separated from the 1. However, it is regarded inferior to the situation when 1/100th knows that it is 1/100th, doesn't consider itself separated from 1, and doesn't think itself to be identical to 1.

QUESTION

Are there other ways in which we can support the distinction between the soul and the Lord? How can we know that we are the parts and not the whole?

4.1.8 (485)

ध्यानाच्च

dhyānācca

dhyānāt—on account of meditation (implying that); ca—and.

TRANSLATION

And on account of meditation (implying that we are not the whole).

COMMENTARY

The impersonalist claims that meditation is temporary. We meditate on the Lord temporarily, which then increases our attraction to the Lord. Thereby we come closer to the Lord, which then increases the attraction further, until we collapse into the Lord. But the devotees say that meditation is eternal. The meaning in our mind may be the same as the Lord. But the individual who knows the meaning is always individual. Our attraction to the Lord is that we want to know Him. And the closeness to the Lord is that we know Him better. But regardless of how well we know Him, we don't become the Lord. Thus, attraction constantly increases, as does the proximity. But this proximity is not physical; it is semantic. We know the Lord; we do not become the Lord.

QUESTION

Then, why is it said that the soul is 'fixed' upon liberation? You are saying that the Sun is moving around the polestar, but it is said the soul is fixed. How can the idea of fixation be reconciled with the idea of motion and change?

4.1.9 (486)
अचलत्वं चापेक्ष्य
acalatvaṃ cāpekṣya

acalatvam—immobility; ca—also; apekṣya—is relative to.

TRANSLATION

Also, immobility (or fixedness) is in relation to (the Lord).

COMMENTARY

Many physical ideas are being refuted successively; now, it is the turn of refutating the physical idea of motion. This physical idea says that if you walk from one room to another in your house, then your position is not fixed. Therefore, if the devotee is active—i.e., moving around—then this motion cannot be called a fixed state. And if it is not fixed, then it is temporary. Whatever is temporary must also be false because truth is also eternal. Therefore, anything that is moving cannot be called the truth. The flaw in this claim is the equating of two different ideas, which seem almost identical, although they are not.

These two ideas are *motion* and *change*. In the material world, motion is almost always accompanied by a change. But in the spiritual world, motion exists without a change. Unless we distinguish between the two, it seems that every motion is also a change, and that change would entail temporariness. To understand the difference, let us discuss the Vedic description of motion.

Space in Vedic philosophy is semantic. In this space, different types of things are in their fixed position. There is hence a location for a type of object denoted by your house, and another location for the type of object denoted by your body. Therefore, both your body and the house are in fixed positions. The soul moves in this space—from one body to another. However, the body and the house do not move—since each body is at a fixed location in space.

Then why do we sometimes say that I am close to the house, and at other times say that I'm farther from the house? This sense of proximity and distance is created by an interaction between the body and the house. When the interaction between the house and the body becomes stronger, then the two seem to be close. But when the interaction is weakened, then the two seem farther. Thus, without moving from their position, the body and the house come closer and go farther, and this change in proximity and distance is called 'motion'.

Hence, there are two distinct ideas that seem to be similar, but they are not the same. The idea of *change* pertains to the soul moving across bodies, and the idea of *motion* pertains to the interaction between the bodies, which creates the sense of proximity and distance. Change is when the body feels stronger or weaker, you feel hungry or full, you feel energized or sick, etc. According to Vedic philosophy, all these bodies are eternally present; however, the soul moves from one body to another. Thus, the body is changing as you get older. But the body is also changing as you feel sick or healthy, hungry or full, energized or tired. Some of these changes are reversible and some of them are not. On the other hand, motion is when this body seems closer to a house. This proximity of the bodies can occur when the body is hungry or full, energized or tired, sick or healthy. Therefore, both change and motion are needed.

In the material world, both motion and change occur one after another, and sometimes change is the cause of motion and sometimes motion is the cause of change. For example, if your body changes from a satisfied to a hungry body (which is change) then you move to get something from the kitchen (which is motion). In this case, the motion is caused by change. Similarly, you might see something tasty because you have come close to it, and that encounter with food can make you hungry. In this case, coming close to food (i.e., motion) is the cause, and feeling hungry (i.e., change) is the effect. In general, most changes cause some motion, and most motions cause some change. Owing to this fact, in this world, the distinction between motion and change is collapsed, and we start describing even the change in the bodies as motion. For example, a scientist will say that your feeling of hunger is the motion of molecules.

Now imagine that you are have been eating, and the food is so tasty that you will like to keep eating. But you cannot because after some eating, the body becomes full. In short, your eating is motion, and the body changes due to this motion. But it would be nice if there was only motion and no change. In short, if you could keep eating the tasty food, and the body would never be full.

This imaginary situation becomes reality in the spiritual world. You can go on eating, but the body will never become full. You can stop eating, but the body is never hungry. You can work constantly, but the body is never tired. It is the same body always. It doesn't become old or young, fat or thin, hungry or satisfied, weak or strong. However, this fixed body keeps interacting with other bodies, and comes close to them or moves farther away from them. As a result, in the spiritual world, there is motion, but without any change. Since there is no change (of body), therefore, we can say that the position is fixed. But because there is motion (of body), hence, we can also say that there are activities.

Thus, change can exist without motion—e.g., you can lie in your bed the whole day, and you will still become hungry. And motion can exist without change—e.g., a devotee can keep working and never become tired. A yogi conquers the change in the body, and despite living for very long, his body remains young. He may also conquer hunger and sleep as these are changes to the body. Ultimately, some yogis can transfer themselves to higher planets in the same body. They have motion, but they don't have change. The problem of this world is change—i.e., that we are born, and we die: the body changes. The problem is not motion. Therefore, in the spiritual world, the devotees can serve the Lord without changing their body, and that motion doesn't entail any change.

The impersonalist is unable to distinguish between motion and change. He says: if you are moving, then you are changing, and whatever is changing is temporary, therefore, any activity performed in service of the Lord is temporary. Similarly, meditation on the Lord is also a mental state, so it is temporary. He doesn't realize that by this meditation or activity, the changes end.

Therefore, the fixedness of the spiritual world refers to the lack of change, not the absence of motion. In short, you have an eternal body, but that body keeps performing activities. This fixed body has a fixed location in space. It is a semantic object whose meaning determines the location in space. However, this body then interacts with other bodies, and the stronger interaction brings two bodies close, and the weaker interaction causes them to move apart. In short, the proximity and distance of motion are produced due to an interaction. The interaction is caused by our consciousness, under the control of desire. In the material world, this interaction is also produced due to karma; so sometimes, we are forced to suffer, even though we don't want to suffer.

But in the spiritual world, the proximity and distance are produced because of one's desire. Hence, if a devotee desires to see the Lord, then the Lord is immediately there.

The Lord also has a fixed position in space—He is the origin of that space—and that origin is His body. And yet, He moves around, appears and disappears. By this motion, He doesn't change His body. It is simply motion, which is caused by His desire of interaction, which then creates proximity. Therefore, the proximity and distance are *effects* (of desire), rather than the *causes*.

Modern science inverts this idea and says if two things come close, then the force becomes greater, and then two objects interact strongly, and the result of that stronger interaction is faster motion. Thus, in the theory of gravitation, the force between two objects increases with decreasing distance, and with this increased force the speed of motion increases. Hence, the distance between two objects is the cause, the force between the objects is the effect, and the force makes the object move. In Vedic philosophy, the force of desire comes first. It then creates an interaction, which then reduces the distance, and that proximity then produces an experience. Therefore, we cannot ask: Can you show me God? This is because we are far from God. To see God, we must first come close to God. That proximity requires an interaction, which requires a desire. To see the Lord, we must develop a strong desire. That strong desire will produce an interaction with the Lord. That interaction will then reduce the distance to the Lord. And with that reduced distance we will see the Lord face to face.

If science adopts the semantic notion of space, then we will get two kinds of motion. First, there will be a motion of the soul across many bodies. Second, there will be stronger and weaker interaction between the bodies, which creates the experience of proximity and distance. In short, whatever science considers 'space' would no longer be a reality. It will simply be a phenomenal experience. The real space will be semantic in which the soul moves across bodies.

In summary, the devotee is fixed in relation to the Lord, but the devotee is also moving around the Lord. Likewise, the Lord is fixed in relation to the devotee, and yet, He moves around the devotee. This is the dance of the Lord with the devotee. But this dance is only motion; it is not a change of the body.

QUESTION

Does this mean that while meditating, we are factually close to the Lord? That we can see the Lord even in this body, as we develop a desire, which causes an interaction, which reduces the proximity and then creates a vision?

4.1.10 (487)

समरन्ति च

smaranti ca

smaranti—remembering (the Lord); ca—also (is a vision).

TRANSLATION

Remembering the Lord is also (the real experience of the Lord).

COMMENTARY

All materialistic theories of space are built upon our waking experience. But in Vedic philosophy, waking experience is understood based on the dreaming experience; the dreaming is understood based on the deep sleep; and the deep sleep is understood based on the transcendent state. Let's begin by understanding dreaming. While you are dreaming, your senses and the mind develop an interaction with a reality that is not interacting with the body. Since distance is created by an interaction, therefore, the reality you see in the dream is close to your senses and the mind, but far from the body. Factually, the body and the senses are equally far from the perceived object—during waking or dreaming. But during waking, the interaction is with the body, which then creates sensation and thoughts. And during dreaming, the interaction is with the senses and the mind. The effects of this interaction become visible in the body too—e.g., that your eyes might flutter during a dream—which means that the senses and the mind haven't left the body, and yet, you can see what the body can't.

If dreaming is understood, then the waking state is described in the same way. That is, whatever you are seeing, is not factually 'near' you. You have a human body, which has a type. And the computer, table, or chair, with which your body is currently interacting, have different types. The different meanings of the 'human', 'table', 'computer', and 'chair' etc.

constitute their position in the space, and the distances in this space do not change over time. And yet, these distant objects interact, create proximity, and then perception. Hence, when you dream of a computer, the process is the same as when you see the computer while waking. Both are caused by an interaction. That interaction is caused by the combination of guna and karma. Therefore, sometimes you are forced to see certain things, and sometimes you see because of your desire.

The deep sleep state is the combination of the guna, karma, and chitta, which lie dormant, and they are activated in the dreaming and waking state. Within this dormant state, there are further subdivisions, and the dormant gets reactivated slowly. Therefore, sometimes, a distinction between a 'manifest' and 'about to manifest' is made. This 'about to manifest' sometimes creates dreams, so people can sometimes see the future, sometimes the past, and sometimes just their fantasies, which are neither in the past nor in the future. The past is seen due to the chitta, the future is seen due to karma, and the fantasies are seen due to guna. When none of these are seen, then the state is called deep sleep, in which the guna, karma, and the chitta simply exist dormant.

With this understanding, we can appreciate the nature of meditation on the Lord. It is a desire for the Lord, which creates an interaction, then reduces the distance, and then produces an experience. The process of seeing is the same in both cases. When we meditate, the distance between our senses and the Lord is immediately bridged, proximity is created, and the Lord is hence seen.

If we don't understand ordinary vision, then we also don't understand the vision of the Lord. But if science is advanced to explain ordinary vision, then the same science applies to the vision of the Lord. The difference is simply that to see the Lord, we would have to change our desires. In short, if we desire strongly, then that strong desire will create an immediate perception. Therefore, the devotee rejects all doctrines about liberation. He says: the main point is to see the Lord, and that seeing is available here and now. So, where is the problem if I'm entrapped in a temporary body if I can constantly see the Lord? The Lord that I see in my meditation is not different from the Lord that anyone else is seeing in the spiritual world. My experience cannot be called 'dreaming' while their experience is called 'waking'. They are factually the same experience.

Ultimately, the body doesn't see. The vision is due to the senses and the mind. In the spiritual world, the vision is created through the body, and in the material world, the vision is created directly through the senses and the mind. Thus, the Brahma Samhita says that with the eyes anointed by the mascara of love, the devotee constantly sees the Lord in the heart. Notably, this mascara is not applied to the gross bodily eyes. It is applied to the subtle senses.

The senses are comprised of three aspects—emotion, relation, and cognition. The emotion is the desire to see, which exists as lust in this world. The relation is the ability of the sense to connect to the object being seen. And the cognition is the ability to represent the object's meaning within the sense. Therefore, when we see, the senses 'go out' to the object of seeing, and then they 'bring back' the essence of the object and represent it within the sense. This going out and coming back is due to desire. Hence, if the desire exists, then the senses can go out to the Lord, and then they can bring back the Lord. In short, we have only one business—to develop the desire for the Lord. The rest is all the mechanics of perception. One can learn about the mechanics and develop the understanding of how the Lord can be seen. But even if one doesn't know anything about this mechanics, but simply has the desire, the Lord is still seen. Therefore, both devotees—those who know the mechanics and have the love, and those who don't know the mechanics but have the love—are on par. The mechanics is not important, but one who knows the mechanics can convince others about how the Lord is seen. Those who don't have the faith in the Lord, can also learn this mechanics before they develop devotion to the Lord.

Topic 7

QUESTION

You are saying that the Lord can be seen in any place, any time, in any body, and other than the desire for the Lord, there is no special qualification?

4.1.11 (488)

यत्रैकाग्रता तत्र अवशिषात्

yatraikāgratā tatra aviśeṣāt

yatra—wherever; ekāgratā—singular focus (of the mind); tatra—there; aviśeṣāt—from the absence of a specific quality.

TRANSLATION

Wherever there is singular focus (of the mind), there (the Lord can be seen), from the absence of a special quality (of the place, time, body, or the role).

COMMENTARY

As we have discussed, there are various types of bodies and roles in this world. Some bodies are superior, and some are inferior. Some roles are higher, and the other roles are inferior. Some places are considered holy, while other places are considered unholy. Some of the times (such as early morning) are considered superior to the other times (such as late nights). But all these are ultimately mundane considerations. They are applied when the mind is impure. Under this impurity, some places and some times are helpful in thinking about the Lord. When the body is unhealthy, then it is hard to concentrate the mind, therefore, a healthier body is considered superior. In some roles, we get a better opportunity to understand the Lord, as compared to other roles.

However, ultimately, there is no restriction of place, time, body, or role. The only thing that matters is desire. If the desire is there, then other things can assist, but they cannot prevent; wherever there is a will, there is a way. But when the desire is not there, then other things are not useful. One simply makes varieties of excuses, and the situation is used to justify the lack of desire.

Topic 8

QUESTION

But if the devotee reaches the spiritual world, and can see the Lord face to face, does the process of meditation or remembrance cease to be relevant?

4.1.12 (489)

आ प्रयाणात् तत्रापि हि दृष्टम्

ā prayāṇāt tatrāpi hi dṛṣṭam

ā prayāṇāt—till death; tatra—then; api—even; hi—certainly; dṛṣṭam—is seen.

TRANSLATION

Till death (the Lord is seen in meditation) then (when the devotee reaches the spiritual world) even (though the Lord can be seen face to face in the spiritual world) certainly (He is also) seen in (meditations).

COMMENTARY

For a devotee, the Lord is not simply cognitive perception. The Lord is also the purpose of existence. If you have a goal or a purpose, you keep imagining various possibilities, and your mind is engaged in these thoughts. These imaginations are created when the senses and the mind contact a possibility, which is then experienced. Since the possibility is eternal, therefore, the imagination is not unreal. But the imagination is created by the devotee's choice, rather than the Lord's choice. However, when the Lord is seen face to face, then the Lord fulfills that fantasy and imagination by His will. For example, the gopis of Vṛndāvana imagine how Kṛṣṇa will steal their butter. They imagine how Kṛṣṇa will eat a little and waste a lot. Then they imagine the ensuing argument with the thief and the complaint to the thief's mother. Then they imagine how the mother will scold the thief, and the thief will deny everything. Then they imagine that when the mother wants to punish the thief, they will placate the mother. This is, in one sense, a total fantasy. In this way, by imagination, the gopis are constantly thinking about Kṛṣṇa. But all this imagination also comes true when Kṛṣṇa does the very same things that the gopis have previously imagined. In short, what was fantasy previously, now becomes a reality. The fantasy is conjured by the devotee, and the fantasy is fulfilled by the Lord. Therefore, in one sense, there is a difference between fantasy and reality—because the devotee creates the fantasy, and the Lord fulfills the fantasy. But in another sense, there is no difference between fantasy and reality because the fantasy is always fulfilled, and when it is fulfilled, it is just like it was previously imagined.

The creation of all these fantasies is the meditation. And the fulfillment of these fantasies is the reality. Entry into the spiritual world doesn't mean an end to the meditation—or the creation of fantasies. Hence, even though the Lord can steal the butter of the gopis, and hence He can be seen doing all these things, the devotees are also constantly meditating on the Lord doing these things. Hence this sūtra says that meditation is not merely something we do in this world. In the spiritual world too, there is constant meditation. Hence, there is no contradiction between fantasies about the Lord, and the Lord's reality.

Topic 9

QUESTION

You said that the devotee reaches the spiritual world after death. But isn't it possible that the devotee had unfulfilled karma from previous lives which must be suffered or enjoyed through subsequent births? How can the devotee reach the spiritual world upon death unless this karma has been finished?

4.1.13 (490)

तदधगिम उत्तरपूर्वाघयोरश्लेषवनिाशौ तद्व्यपदेशात्

tadadhigama uttarapūrvāghayoraśleṣavināśau tadvyapadeśāt

tat-adhigame—in that attainment; uttara-pūrva-aghayoḥ—the subsequent sins that were previously created; aśleṣa-vināśau—the destruction of that which is clinging (to the soul); tat-vyapadeśāt—that is stated everywhere.

TRANSLATION

In that attainment (the continuous meditation on the Lord is), all the previously created sins that have to be subsequently (endured), and all that is clinging to the soul is destroyed; this is stated everywhere (in scriptures).

COMMENTARY

The soul exists in the world due to a causal body comprising three aspects, called guna, karma, and chitta. The guna is all the material desires, which exist as habits in us. When the devotee develops constant meditation on the Lord, these desires are destroyed. However, there are still impressions from the past in the chitta, and the karma accumulated in the previous births. The destruction of that which is clinging to the soul refers to the impressions of the chitta. And the destruction of the sins created in the past (to be endured in the future) refers to karma. Therefore, if the desires are destroyed, then impressions of the past, and the karma produced due to the actions from the past are also destroyed.

Karma is described in three ways—*sañcita*, *prārabdha*, and *kriyamāna*. The term kriyamāna refers to that karma which is acting right now. The term prārabdha refers to the karma that was fixed at the time of birth and must be endured in this life. And the term sañcita refers to the karma that would be reaped in the future lives. Upon death, the kriyamāna and the prārabdha are naturally destroyed, for everyone. However, for the devotees, even the sañcita is destroyed, if they have developed unceasing meditation on the Lord.

According to the rules of morality, everyone must suffer or enjoy the consequences of their previous actions. However, devotion to the Lord goes beyond ordinary morality, and this is indicated by the fact that karma is destroyed if devotion has been developed. In short, the basic principle of moral consequence—i.e., tit-for-tat—is not applied to the devotees. The purpose of morality is to bring the soul to devotion. And once that purpose is achieved, then the means to achieve that purpose are not necessary anymore. Of course, it is possible that karma is destroyed without a person becoming the Lord's devotee—e.g., in case of Brahman liberation. It is also possible that a devotee begins the process of devotion but can't perfect it. Such devotees need to take birth again, and karma acts upon them in a way to help them attain the devotional goal. Therefore, the true purpose of morality and karma is not the soul's punishment, because then a devotee could never circumvent their karma. The true purpose is to help them attain devotion, after which karma becomes unnecessary.

This is an important distinction between impersonal liberation and devotion to the Lord. The impersonalist can be liberated only when all the karma has been destroyed, and he is reborn until this karma has been destroyed. The devotee, however, doesn't have to wait for all the karma to be finished. As soon as perfect devotion to the Lord is attained, the karma of future lives is destroyed. This also means that even for a devotee the present life may not be pleasurable, due to the prārabdha which was fixed at the time of birth. Similarly, if someone hasn't perfected their devotion, then the sañcita will cause their rebirth.

Topic 10

QUESTION

A devotee may have developed affections to other devotees in this world during their presence. Are these affections are also destroyed upon death?

4.1.14 (491)
इतरस्याप्येवमसंश्लेषःपाते तु
itarasyāpyevamsaṃśleṣaḥ pāte tu

itarasya—other than this; api—even; evam—in this way; saṃśleṣaḥ—embracing or attachments; pāte—at death; tu—but.

TRANSLATION

Other than this (i.e., karma, guna, and chitta) (the spiritual) embracing or attachments are but (i.e., not destroyed) in this way even upon death.

COMMENTARY

Spiritual aspirants often take a spiritual initiation from a guru. The guru may subsequently leave the body, and by the argument of the previous sūtra, where all impressions of the past (in the chitta) or attachments and desires (i.e., guna) are destroyed, it may seem that the guru forgets about the disciple after he leaves this body. This sūtra rejects that conclusion and says that the spiritual embracing or attachments are not destroyed. But what is a spiritual attachment? And how does it differ from a material attachment? A devotee loves the Lord, and thereby he develops attachment to the others who love the Lord. Such love is spiritual. On the other hand, there may be other people that love us, or we may love them, but that love is not because of the common love of the Lord. When the affection between two persons is caused by their mutual love of the Lord, then this affection is not forgotten. However, a devotee is kind, and loves everyone—including trees, birds, and animals—but this affection is not spiritual because it is not born out of their mutual affection of the Lord. This affection, which might exist between a devotee and their family, friends, neighbors, etc. is limited to this life, and is lost upon death. Likewise, if a disciple is not sincere, then the guru may have some affection for the disciple in this life, but that affection is just like the love for other people not devoted to the Lord. Just as the other affections are lost upon death, similarly, the affection for the insincere disciple is also lost when the guru departs. The relation to the guru is eternal for the sincere disciple, and it is temporary for the insincere disciple.

All disciples must therefore become sincere to the Lord because the relation between the devotees is based upon their shared love of the Lord. It is sometimes incorrectly said that because a devotee is attached to the guru, who is then attached to the Lord, therefore, merely by attachment to the guru one becomes attached to the Lord. This idea is partly false. For example, if a disciple has personal affection for the guru, and renders him personal service, but neglects the guru's instructions on how to serve the Lord, then, such a disciple has affection for the guru, but no affection for the Lord. Such kinds of affections abound in this world—people love their spouses, children, country, and pets. But all these loving relations are not due to their mutual love of the Lord, and such loving relationships are destroyed upon death. In the same way, loving the guru's body or serving him personally, while neglecting the guru's instruction to serve the Lord is a mundane understanding of love. This idea of love equates the love between a guru and a disciple to that between two ordinary people. All such relationships of mundane affection are destroyed at death, according to this sutra. The enduring relationship instead is based on mutual love of the Lord.

The relationship between a guru and a disciple is also broken if the disciple doesn't respect the guru. Fault-finding, second-guessing, questioning of the judgments, or disobeying the instructions of the guru are all good grounds for the guru rejecting the disciple. While a magnanimous guru can tolerate many difficulties in teaching a disciple, as the guru endures these problems, the disciple develops a sense of false entitlement and that worsens his attitude. If the solution becomes a problem, then the solution must also be abandoned. Therefore, the correct approach is that the guru should abandon the disciple.

Topic 11

QUESTION

You said that the karma of the previous lives is destroyed for a devotee upon death. What about the karma of this life? A devotee may have performed some sinful actions before becoming a pure devotee. Are these actions from the present life also destroyed if one becomes a pure devotee of the Lord?

4.1.15 (492)
अनारब्धकार्ये एव तु पूर्वे तदवधेः
anārabdhakārye eva tu pūrve tadavadheḥ

anārabdha-kārye—the karma that has not yet begun to bear fruit; eva—certainly; tu—but; pūrve—previous; tadavadheḥ—limited to that duration.

TRANSLATION

Certainly, the karma that has not yet begun to bear fruit (is destroyed) but the previous (actions of this life) are limited to that duration (of life).

COMMENTARY

Many of us may have come to spiritual life without a full understanding of right and wrong, and we may have performed sinful activities during the performance of devotional practices. If a person becomes a pure devotee, then even this karma is destroyed. This means that upon leaving the body, all past obligations—from the previous lives and this life—are finished, and the soul may not take birth again. The condition is that one must be a pure devotee, which means constantly remembering the Lord, including and up to the point of death.

As we have discussed earlier, death is a point of loss for most people, because they lose everything that they were previously attached to. However, for a devotee, death is a time of celebration since the laws that force a change of body—e.g., from childhood to youth to old age—don't apply after death.

Topic 12

QUESTION

What if someone has performed many actions for spiritual progress, but perfect devotion has not been attained? Are these actions also destroyed?

4.1.16 (493)

अग्निहोत्रादि तु तत्कार्यायैव तद्दर्शनात्

agnihotrādi tu tatkāryāyaiva taddarśanāt

agnihotrādi—the fire sacrifice etc.; tu—but; tat-kāryāya—actions for achieving that; eva—certainly; tat-darśanāt—from the understanding of that.

TRANSLATION

But (the progress made through) fire sacrifices, actions performed for achieving that, from the understanding of that, are certainly (not destroyed).

COMMENTARY

Whatever is done for material progress is always lost. For example, you may be wealthy in this life, but you may become poor in the next life. However, whatever is done for spiritual progress is never lost. Therefore, the level of progress attained in this life carries into the next life, and the subsequent progress begins from that level. Even in this life, every day's spiritual advancement begins from the advancement made on the previous day. If one realizes the gradual progression, then even without attaining the ultimate result, they also develop an unshakeable faith in the spiritual process. Through such realization, one can see a difference between material achievements which go up and down in this life, and spiritual achievements, which only increase with time.

Different people who come to spiritual life have different levels of conviction, attachment, and commitment. This difference can be attributed to the different levels of progress they have made in their previous lives. Thus, a child may be more advanced than an old man, and age is not a strict indicator of one's advancement. For example, Śukadeva Goswami was younger to his father and grandfather. However, he spoke on Śrīmad Bhagavatam, even as his father and grandfather listened in the audience. Therefore, from a social perspective, the elders are accorded respect. However, from a spiritual perspective, even a young person can be honored. Many people think that spiritual advancement is attained in old age, or that spiritual topics are for old people. But we see that some children are also attracted to spirituality from birth. Age only pertains to the body, but the soul is eternal, and its progression never diminishes.

QUESTION

But haven't you said that ultimately all these activities (like fire sacrifice) are not substitutes for devotion, thereby implying that they are somehow material? If the progress obtained by other material activities is lost, why is the progress obtained by actions other than Lord's devotion not lost at death?

4.1.17 (494)

अतो'न्यापि ह्येकेषामुभयोः

ato'nyāpi hyekeṣāmubhayoḥ

ataḥ—therefore; anya—other; api—even; hi—indeed; ekeṣām—is one; ubhayoḥ—both.

TRANSLATION

Therefore, (the purpose) of all the other activities is indeed one (i.e., the progression in spiritual life) even both (i.e., also living a better material life).

COMMENTARY

If you drive a car, then the purpose of the car is to take you to some destination. However, for that purpose to be achieved, the car must be functional. Therefore, the maintenance of the car, and keeping it functional, also becomes a goal. However, the maintenance of the car is the secondary goal, and the achievement of the destination is the primary goal. But let's postulate that someone indeed has car maintenance as the primary goal. To keep the car working and shiny, they need money. If the car wasn't taking one to a goal, that money must come from somewhere else. Now, that something else, which is used to earn money, which is then used to maintain the car, becomes the secondary goal. Hence, there are always many goals, but these goals become primary and secondary, or as we have called them, dominant and subordinate.

Similar statements have been made in the past, so to understand why this statement is novel, we need to recall the previous discussion, and then contrast the present sūtra to the previous ones. All the confusion arises from the use of two approaches—one bottom-up and one top-down. In the final analysis, the world is top-down, with its root in the Lord. However, we can reach the Lord by following a bottom-up process. Thus, many seemingly contradictory statements are made. First, we can say that only devotion to the Lord is important, and everything else is unimportant. Second, we can say that all yoga processes and systems of knowledge are useful if they are pursued as secondary goals for the primary goal of devotion. Third, we can say that knowledge, work, and mystical experience are the primary goal, however, to perfect these goals, we must acquire devotion to the Lord since they are otherwise imperfect.

In the first case, we reject everything else at the outset and focus only on the devotion to the Lord. In the second case, we employ some of the other paths as tools to attain the final goal. And in the third case, we pursue the individual activities for their own sake, but after attaining a certain level, we realize that further perfection requires devotion to the Lord; then, devotion is used as a tool for perfecting the other activities, but further progression requires even more devotion; slowly, by this process, ultimately, devotion becomes unselfish.

The discussion in the previous sūtras pertained to the first two cases—outright rejection, or the acceptance as a secondary goal. Now, it is being said that even if you accept the other things as primary goals, you still need devotion to the Lord to perfect that goal, because otherwise it will always be imperfect.

To illustrate these three approaches, let's apply them to the discussion about the relation between religion and science. First, we can say that since science is the study of matter, and our goal is devotion, therefore, we should not bother with science. Second, we can say that scientific knowledge can help us achieve devotion to the Lord, so it is a good secondary goal for attaining a primary goal. Third, we can also say that science is the primary goal, and the scriptures are studied, or devotion is pursued, as a method to perfect science. In these approaches, the Lord is the only goal, the primary goal, and the secondary goal. But they are all accepted as legitimate processes because eventually they lead to the same conclusion, although the latter two systems are slower.

Thus, some devotees see a contradiction between religion and science, and they reject science. Some devotees don't see a contradiction and they recommend the use of science for the purposes of devotion. And some devotees see science itself as the goal, and religion as the vehicle to achieve the goal.

The previous sūtras accepted the first two methods, and this sūtra accepts even the third approach. Here it is said that when genuine progress is made by those who perform other activities (e.g., fire sacrifices) this effort is not lost and one keeps trying to perfect that process and eventually attains the devotion to the Lord. Hence, even philosophers and scientists can come to the point of loving the Lord, even if they are only interested in philosophy and science to begin with. Throughout this text, we have illustrated the reason for this attainment: all knowledge remains either inconsistent or incomplete until the Lord is understood, because only in the Lord the diversity and contradictions are reconciled. Hence, if a seeker sets out with the intention of knowing the truth, they are eventually led to devotion to the Lord. The problem is that most times philosophers and scientists are not interested in the truth. They are more interested in name, fame, power, wealth, and enjoyment, rather than the truth. Under these forces, the truth is suppressed or distorted, and over time, one suppression and distortion is replaced by another. Such a person hence goes in circles rather than progressing toward the Lord. Therefore, all scientific activity that claims atheism as the goal is lost over time, because it goes in circles. However, the agnostic, who is receptive toward the truth, can become a devotee.

If you are climbing a hill, then reaching a higher point includes reaching the lower point. But if you are going around in circles, then whatever was previously achieved is also lost. Therefore, the hierarchical path is progressive, and the circular path is a waste of time. In this sūtra, the many practices recommended in the scriptures that take us to a higher truth are acknowledged. They must, however, be distinguished from activities that take us in circles.

When people worship the demigods to obtain material benefits, they generally go in circles—some good karma is obtained, enjoyed, and then lost. But one can also worship the demigods and say—they give us only a certain type of happiness, and I must also know about the source of all happiness. When a person asks such a question, then he is gradually elevated to higher and higher planetary systems, until he reaches the place of the Lord, and realizes that He is the ultimate truth. The people who are progressively elevated from lower to higher planets must be distinguished from those who are elevated temporarily and then fall back to their previous state. The process of progressive elevation is partly material and partly spiritual. The higher level includes the lower level, so nothing is lost even as one progresses, but the ultimate truth is eventually attained. This sūtra says that the 'one' is attained and 'both' are attained.

We can attain the 'one' by exclusively focusing on the 'one'. We can attain the 'one' by using the 'other' as a tool or method employed to achieve the 'one'. And we can also attain the 'one' by focusing on the 'other' but accepting the 'one' as the guiding light to perfect the attainment of the 'other'. All these processes are accepted while rejecting the focus on 'other' without the 'one'.

Topic 13

QUESTION

It is much easier to understand the progression with knowledge because it is easier to see that knowledge exists in an inverted-tree-like structure. It is harder to see how different kinds of activities can

also be called progressive. After all, all these actions are performed with our senses—e.g., hands. How do we say that some activity of the senses is superior to other such activities?

4.1.18 (495)
यदेव वदियायेति हि
yadeva vidyayeti hi

yat-eva—as surely; vidyaya—with knowledge; iti—thus; hi—certainly.

TRANSLATION

As surely with knowledge, thus certainly (with the other activities).

COMMENTARY

The actions of our hands are not physical. They also have meanings. Thus, some movement is cooking, some movement is typing, and some movement is driving. But apart from these meanings, there are higher-level meanings in the mind. Just like the senses of knowledge perceive properties such as color, taste, smell, etc. and the mind perceives the meaning—e.g., that this thing is a table, or this word means something—similarly, the meaning associated with activity is associated with a purpose. When you read a book, you first get sensations, then you get a meaning, then you judge if this meaning is true or false, and then you try to get the purpose. However, when you perform the actions, then the activity is directly linked to a purpose, and other meanings are invoked to determine if the actions will achieve the purpose. For example, if you are driving a car, then you must know that turning the wheel clockwise will turn the car to the right, that this turning will take you closer to the destination, etc. But you will not do any of these things unless you have a purpose in mind. Therefore, action is considered superior to knowledge, because many people read books, but very few of these readers translate this knowledge into real activity.

In the Bhagavad-Gita, jnana-yoga is described as the first step to yoga. Following this there is dhyāna-yoga, or meditation which is generally performed for some time during a day. Karma-yoga is superior to both these methods because it is performed for most of the time. Thus, you might acquire some knowledge by reading a book, but it is generally hard to accept it, because the mind is uncontrolled. Then as the mind is controlled, the knowledge is accepted, and one decides to do something about what one has learnt. In short, activity is produced only after some conviction in its efficacy. On the other hand, it is possible to perform these activities mechanically without knowing their true meaning and purpose. For example, most people perform fire rituals without knowing what they are doing, and the results obtained thereby.

Thus, in one sense, activity is superior to knowledge, because one acts after a conviction. In another sense, one might act without an understanding, so activity is considered inferior to knowledge. Only the context decides what is superior. In the Bhagavad-Gita, Lord Kṛṣṇa imparts knowledge which then leads to activity—i.e., Arjuna fighting the battle. Therefore, the activity is a progression over knowledge. However, because many people on the same battlefield were fighting without this knowledge, their activities are inferior.

The Kauravās were fighting because they wanted to enjoy their kingdom. Bhīśma and Drona were fighting due to the obligation to the Kauravās. Many warriors on the side of Pāndavas were fighting to uphold goodness over evil. And Arjuna was fighting simply because it was pleasing to the Lord. They have the same activity—i.e., fighting—but the underlying meanings are different. Hence, the same activity can be performed with different mental states. Likewise, different mental states can lead to different activities. For example, when Arjuna felt attached to his cousins and teachers, he refused to fight. Therefore, the same activity can be tied to different mental states, many activities can be tied to the same mental state, different mental states can result in different activities, and different mental states can also produce the same activity.

There is no hard and fast rule about whether an activity is higher or lower. But we can decide if the activity is superior or inferior based on the mental state. This allows us to say that the superiority or inferiority of both knowledge and action are based on the meaning. Once this equivalence is established, then there is no difference between knowledge and action. One may read a book and that reading is perfection if the knowledge is supreme. One may perform an action and that action is perfect if the person is thinking about the Lord.

Based on the mental state, we can determine if an action is superior or inferior. And this determination is based on the same principle by which we say that a book is superior or inferior. Therefore, if one performs a fire sacrifice with a higher meaning and purpose, then that activity is superior. Conversely, if one performs the same sacrifice without understanding the meaning or purpose, or the purpose is evil, then that same activity must be deemed inferior. Thus, by changing the meanings, we can progress by action, quite like knowledge.

Topic 14

QUESTION

But since these actions are performed with a goal or purpose in mind, isn't this activity considered selfish, and therefore, inferior to knowledge?

4.1.19 (496)

भोगेन त्वितरे क्षपयित्वा संपद्यते

bhogena tvitare kṣapayitvā sampadyate

bhogena—by enjoyment; tu—but; itare—of the other; kṣapayitvā—having exhausted; sampadyate—in the completion of the purpose of the activity.

TRANSLATION

But by the enjoyment of the (pleasure of) the other (the Lord), the results of the activity are destroyed (and) and completes the purpose of the activity.

COMMENTARY

The impersonalist believes that since purposeful activity leads to consequences, therefore, one must stop all activity. However, in this sūtra, this idea is rejected. The sūtra says that if we start enjoying the enjoyment of the Lord, then two things are attained— (1) we are enjoying and (2) there are no consequences. The impersonalist gets liberated—i.e., freed from the consequences—by sacrificing enjoyment. But the devotee destroys the consequences of actions without sacrificing the enjoyment. The distinction between mundane and spiritual activity is not in the activity; it is rather in the meaning of that activity. The mundane mind is occupied with the thoughts of impending selfish pleasure while the activity is performed. The spiritual mind is also occupied with the thoughts of the Lord's pleasure, and the thought also pleases the devotee.

We can call the pleasure obtained by pleasing the Lord selfish—after all, the devotee is enjoying. And we call this desire unselfish—because the devotee can also undergo bodily suffering if that pleases the Lord. The fact is that for a devotee, unselfishness dominates selfishness. In material life too, people proffer altruism because they know that if by their actions their relatives, friends, or countrymen are benefitted, then that benefit will also benefit them. So, they are not opposed to altruism, but the selfishness still dominates because the altruist will stop helping others if their happiness was sacrificed. Therefore, the material and the spiritual world are different because in the material world others are served as a byproduct of selfishness; but in the spiritual world, the individual happiness of a person is obtained as a byproduct of serving the Lord. If this inversion in causality is not understood, then we falsely equate lust with love. They are both desires, but the desire to love cannot be equated to lust.

SECTION 2

Topic 1

QUESTION

You are saying that there is no difference between knowledge and activity because underlying both is an intention or meaning in the mind, which determines whether the knowledge and activity are material or spiritual. How is this intention or meaning in the mind translated into a perceivable action?

4.2.1 (497)

वाङ्मनसि दर्शनाच्छब्दाच्च

vāṅmanasi darśanācchabdācca

vāk—speech; manasi—in mind; darśanāt—from being seen; ca—also; śabdāt—from scriptural statements; ca—and.

TRANSLATION

From the speech from scriptural statements also being seen in the mind.

COMMENTARY

Sāṅkhya philosophy recognizes five senses of action, and speech is first. Therefore, while this sūtra describes the nature of speech, we can apply this to the actions of the other senses of action as well, by extending this example. This example is easily understood because we speak after a thought appears in the mind. The conversion of a thought into speech involves four components: (1) meaning, (2) language, (3) effort, and (4) speech. We know that the same meaning can be expressed using different word from different languages, and thus language plays a key role in converting the meaning into words. Similarly, while speaking, we need some power to transform thoughts into words.

The words we speak in a language exist in a shared space of that language. When someone learns a language, they become familiar with that space, or they enter that space. By 'space' I mean a collection of dimensions. Each dimension is a meaning or a universal, and that meaning or universal is given a name. For example, there are universals like cow and mammal. In English, these universals are called 'cow' and 'mammal' and in German 'kuh' and 'säugetier'. The words 'cow' and 'kuh' are the individual expressions of the same meaning. Therefore, in one sense, the universal space is common for both languages. But when these universals are combined with the individual, a language-specific space of these universals is created. In this space, the meaning of each word is often defined by a contrast to other words in that language, which produces language-specific contextualized meanings, unique to a specific language.

The mind is a space in which (a) there are many dimensions of the universals, (b) these dimensions have different names, and (c) each dimension is related to some dimensions and not related to other dimensions. A thought in the mind is a linguistic object in this space. Just like when we place an object in a physical space, we describe it through coordinates such as $\{X, Y, Z\}$ or $\{R, \theta, \varphi\}$ or $\{\chi, \psi, \omega\}$ etc. In some cases, similar ideas have similar sounds across languages. In some cases, the same meaning is called by different sounds. And sometimes the different sounds also have different meanings. Once these dimensions are defined, then we create an object in this space using the same symbols. A thought is a linguistic encoding of meaning within the mind.

In Vedic philosophy, the sounds themselves have a meaning. For example, the sound 'Kṛṣṇa' means 'all attractive' and it doesn't matter what language you use, you can chant the name 'Kṛṣṇa' with the same effect. It may mean nothing in your language, but it has an objective meaning. This is because every meaning has an original name and a contextual relation to other names and meanings, which constitutes the original semantic space called śabda-brahman, whose dimensions are the letters of Sanskrit. These letters have three aspects—universal, individual, and contextual, or a meaning, a name, and a distinction to other meaning-names. We can create alternative languages by disconnecting these in their original form and connecting them in new ways. By this disconnection and connection, alternative languages are produced. However, there is never a situation in which we have pure meaning, without a name, and without a connection to other names and meanings, that contextualize the meaning.

Therefore, when this sūtra says that vāk or speech appears in the mind, it means that everyone thinks in some language. Thought is not pure meaning—i.e., something devoid of language. It is not pure speech—i.e., something devoid of meaning. It is the combination of a meaning, a name, and a relation.

Once the meaning appears in the mind, it expands further into two different, but related ways. These are called the expansions of knowledge and action. For example, you can use the word 'car' to describe a car, but if someone asks, "What you do mean by 'car'?" then you can explain the meaning in two ways. First, you can say that a car has this shape, size, color, etc. Second, you can say that it works in this way. Everything that looks like a car may not work like a car—i.e., move on a street. And everything that moves on a street may not be a car. Therefore, these two methods are employed to explain the meaning of 'car'. These explanations of the meaning are called its 'expansion'. Basically, the idea of car is expanded into something that we can perceive by our senses of knowledge, and something that can be used by our senses of action. Each such sense of knowledge or action is also a different space, and the mind combines these spaces to create a combined picture of the world we perceive and use.

The mind has a choice by which it creates dominant-subordinate structures. For example, sometimes we use the fact that people live in a building to say that the building is a house. At other times, we can consider the size of the building and say that it is bungalow. Then, we look at the garden around the house and say that it is a mansion. The choice of the mind is (a) how many facts it considers before formulating a meaning, and (b) which facts are given greater or lesser importance in formulating the meaning. Thus, if some facts are ignored, then the meaning is incomplete. And the dominant-subordinate structures create inconsistencies, which then result in a change in the selection or rejection of facts, followed by their reorganization in new dominant-subordinate structure.

The material mind either ignores some important facts or changes the dominant-subordinate structures to produce a false, wrong, or bad meaning. When the material mind expands into actions through the senses of action, then these incomplete, false, wrong, or bad meanings are expanded into improper actions. When the material mind uses the senses of knowledge to perceive, but ignores some facts, or organizes them incorrectly, then incorrect knowledge is produced. The spiritual mind, on the other hand, also neglects some facts and organizes the remaining facts with different priorities. And its action senses are also involved in converting this knowledge into activity. Hence, the false, bad, and wrong things must be filtered out, and whatever is remaining, can be organized with the purpose of serving the Lord. In short, the choice in the mind is used in many ways—initially to select facts, and then to organize the facts.

With this background, we can understand this sutra: It says that the mind is capable of perfect knowledge because the perfect knowledge of the scriptures can also appear in the mind. This 'appearance' is called darśan or seeing, and the term is also used for 'philosophy'. The Western idea of philosophy is 'love for wisdom', and it is practiced as speculation, question and answer, etc. In its best form, philosophy can be equated to anumāna, or thinking, imagination, and speculation. But the Vedic idea of philosophy 'vision' or 'seeing' in the mind. The entire universe, and even things beyond the universe, can be seen in the mind, and when the vision is true, right, and good, it is called darśana. The intellect decides if the vision is true; the ego determines if this is good; and the moral sense is responsible for deciding if the vision is righteous. These three instruments of judgment work along with the mind to determine darśana.

But besides this capacity for each mind to obtain the vision of that which is true, right, and good, there is another deeper meaning of darśana which is that it can appear in the mind *before* being expressed externally. A good example of such vision is that of Brahma who was given a darśana by the Lord in the mind by inspiring him to see the nature of the truth, right, and good. Brahma then expanded this into two things—the three Vedas called Rig, Sama, and Yajur represent the nature of truth, good, and right respectively, and form darśana. The fourth Veda called Atharva is the conversion of the truth, right, and good, into activities, which are described as ritualistic procedures. And the fifth Veda, which includes Purana, Itihasa, and Tantra, describe additional activities, pastimes, and procedures, by which common people can practice—and through that practice, understand—the nature of darśana or truth, right, and good.

Since the knowledge manifests from Brahma's mind due to the inspiration of the Paramātma in the heart, therefore, the knowledge subsequently encoded in the Vedas is transcendent, even though it is manifest as speech by Brahma (who is considered a soul—although an advanced and enlightened soul). It is however not considered Brahma's creation, because it is true, right, and good, and there is only one thing that is completely true, purely good, and perfectly right, and that thing is the Supreme Lord. All other things are partially true, partly good and bad, and partially righteous and unrighteous. Therefore, we can also say that darśana is nothing other the vision of the Lord in the mind. When the Lord appears in our mind, we can understand how He is the perfect truth, right, and good, then we have perfected our philosophical knowledge.

QUESTION

If the mind is spiritualized in this way, does it mean that the body is also spiritualized? What is the difference between spiritual and material bodies?

4.2.2 (498)

अत एव च सर्वाण्यनु

ata eva ca sarvāṇyanu

atah eva—therefore certainly; ca—also; sarvāṇi—all (senses); anu—subordinates or servants (of the mind).

TRANSLATION

Therefore, certainly all (senses) are subordinate (to the mind) as well.

COMMENTARY

Since the mind can select or reject the data or actions of the senses, and organize this data and actions in different priorities, therefore, the mind is said to be controller of the senses. Accordingly, the senses are said to be the servants of the mind. Of course, the senses can sometimes make the mind their servant. At present, most people say that we have no free will, and we are dragged by the demands of the senses. This means that they haven't realized the ability in the mind to control the senses. If you don't use it, you lose it. Once the senses become dominant, they start dictating to the mind what is higher or lower priority. This situation is described in the Vedic texts as the condition of a husband who has ten wives, and each wife (i.e., the sense) drags the husband (i.e., the mind) in a different direction, asking the husband to do her bidding. As the husband tries to please one wife, the other wives demand attention. So, the husband runs from one wife to another, trying to please the unhappy wives.

Therefore, the first step in spiritual life is that the mind must obtain mastery over the senses. However, even if this mastery is obtained, one doesn't necessarily become perfect. One just becomes a better materialist. Perfection also requires that the mind uses its choice to select what is important and neglect what is unimportant, and then prioritize the more important things over the less important things. The spiritualist and the materialist are distinguished by the truthfulness, rightness, and goodness of their choices. Therefore, above the mind is the intellect to judge the truth, above the intellect is the ego to judge the goodness, and the above the ego is the moral sense to judge the rightness. Just like the senses are serving the mind, similarly, the mind serves the intellect, the intellect serves the ego, and the ego serves the moral sense. Perfection means that this hierarchy is collapsed. In short, the mind only thinks the truth, right, and good, so these separate instruments of judging are not required. And the difference between the mind and the senses is not required because the sense act as servants rather than masters, and voluntarily relinquish their priority to the other senses when required. Arbitration between the senses is necessary when the senses are in conflict; however, when there is cooperation, arbitration is not needed. Similarly, the distinction between the senses and the soul is dissolved because there is no difference between eternal happiness and sensual pleasure, between knowing the full truth and perceiving the immediate facts, between performing the duty or simply doing what one feels like doing.

The differences between the moral sense, ego, intellect, mind, senses, etc. in the material world, are byproducts of various types of conflicts. To overcome these conflicts, these entities exist in a hierarchy, and the higher entity controls the lower entity and here the mind's control over the senses is described.

In the spiritual world, the 'mind' is the soul; the soul's three aspects are the three faculties of judging truth, right, and good. Each of these three aspects has two further aspects called knowing and action. And each of these two aspects has five further aspects known as the senses of knowing and action. In the final analysis, there is no difference between the soul, the mind, and the senses. These are simply understood as the parts of the whole, and the parts sometimes serve the whole, and the whole sometimes serves the part. This 'service' is simply one part becoming dominant over the rest of the parts, and the other parts becoming subordinate. Then, the domination of the mind over the senses disappears in one way, but since the 'mind' is the soul, it also persists in another way.

Hence, the soul is the three aspects collectively. The moral sense, the ego, and the intellect are the three aspects of the soul. The two aspects of these three aspects are the senses of knowledge and action. And five aspects of each of these two aspects are the five senses of knowledge and action. Since we cannot separate these aspects, therefore, we cannot say that the soul is different from the ego, moral sense, intellect, mind, the ten senses, or the body. And yet, since we can distinguish between these aspects, therefore, the 24 elements of Sāñkhya exist even in the spiritual world, but they are not different from the soul.

In the Śrīmad Bhagavatam, Lord Viṣṇu is described to have 24 different forms. In these forms, different aspects of the Lord are permanently dominant and subordinate. They appear as different incarnations of Lord Viṣṇu, displaying different qualities. For example, the Aniruddha form of the Lord is called the representation of the mind; from a material perspective, the mind is subordinate to the intellect, ego, and the moral sense. But from a spiritual perspective, the mind is everything. Therefore, the Aniruddha, or Paramātma, is sometimes described subsequent to Vasudeva (the representation of the moral sense or *sat*), Saṅkarṣaṇa (the representation of the ego, or *ananda*), and Pradyumna (the representation of the intellect, or *chit*). At other times, the Paramātma is said to be the full representation of the Lord within the heart of a living entity.

These descriptions indicate that the 24 elements of Sāṅkhya are not exclusively 'material' or separate from the study of the soul. They are also aspects of the soul, but when they become dominant or subordinate, different forms of the Lord are created. In fact, just as innumerable types of material bodies are created by the domination of these aspects, similarly, the Lord has innumerable forms. Finally, Lord Kṛṣṇa is described as the complete form in which any of these aspects can alternately become dominant or subordinate. In the Śrīmad Bhagavatam, therefore, He is described as the 25th form, and in Sāṅkhya, the soul is said to be the 25th element. The 25th element is the balanced state of the 24 elements, which means that the other 24 forms are aspects of the complete form. Hence, the study of 24 elements is in one sense the study of matter. In another sense, it is the study of the soul. In another sense, it is the study of the many incarnations of the Lord. And finally, it is also the Absolute Truth.

The text has so far discussed so many topics, including the material elements. As we approach the conclusion of the text, it can seem surprising that the discussion of mind, senses, prāna, etc. are being revived. Indeed, a mundane reading of the text would imply that after discussing the soul and the Lord, we are again discussing matter. But we are not. We discussed the nature of matter earlier. In the beginning of this chapter, we discussed the body in the spiritual world, and how it acts in relation to the Lord. And what we are discussing now is the details about the spiritual body, and its similarity to the material body. The same words are employed in relation to both material and spiritual bodies, in relation to our body and the Lord's body. Hence, the discussion can be interpreted alternately as matter, soul, or the Lord. This is the power of the personal description; if we establish the principles, then we can scientifically study the soul and God, like we previously scientifically studied the nature of matter.

Topic 2

QUESTION

If the mind is superior to the senses, then how does the mind control the senses? And why are the senses sometimes said to control the mind?

4.2.3 (499)
तन्मनःप्राणे उत्तरात्
tanmanaḥ prāṇe uttarāt

tat—that; manaḥ—mind; prāṇe—in prāṇa; uttarāt—subsequently.

TRANSLATION

That mind is subsequently (or further) controlled by the prāṇa.

COMMENTARY

As we have discussed previously, prāṇa is the power of choice, and this choice is effected as the dominant-subordinate structures. We have also spoken about the power of choice in the mind, which also creates dominant-subordinate structures. Therefore, there are two different systems of control described in the Vedic texts. In the Sāṅkhya system, the mind is controlled by the intellect, which is controlled by the ego, which is controlled by the moral sense, which is controlled by the soul. Therefore, if one has a strong sense of morality, then everything is subsequently controlled. In the Yoga system, all these elements of Sāṅkhya are said to be controlled by the prāṇa. One method of controlling the prāṇa is the control of breath. And once the prāṇa is controlled, then everything else, including the senses, mind, intellect, ego, and the moral sense, are also controlled. These two systems seem to be contradictory, but they are not.

To resolve this contradiction, we can recall how the Absolute Truth is divided into masculine and feminine aspects; the masculine is the will and the feminine is the power to fulfill that will. The 24 elements of Sāṅkhya are the expansions of power, and the prāṇa described in the Yoga system (which is also divided into many aspects) is the expansion of the will. Since power exists in the will, and the will exists in the power, a stark distinction between the two may not sometimes be made. But these can also be distinguished. We must also remember that the will can control the power, and the power can control the will. Therefore, in the Sāṅkhya system, morality controls everything else, including prāṇa. But in the Yoga system, the prāṇa controls everything else.

To understand this mutual control, we can think of a machine which works if it is fed with power. The 24 elements of Sāñkhya are, in one sense, like different machines. As they are fed greater or lesser power, they become dominant or subordinate. Since 24 elements of Sāñkhya are expansions of power, and they can command the will, therefore, the body is able to control the soul—in the material world. But that doesn't mean that the soul cannot control the body by exercising its will over the power. When the power controls the will, then Prakriti is superior and Puruṣa (the soul) is inferior. But if the will of the Puruṣa gains control, then Puruṣa is superior and Prakriti is inferior. Since both can control each other, therefore, they can both be both superior and inferior, or neither is permanently superior or inferior. Thus, the Sāñkhya and Yoga systems are not contrary, even though they describe different methods of control. They are only differing emphases on the masculine or the feminine aspects.

In the Vaishnava texts, the Sāñkhya system is given greater emphasis, and in the Shakta texts, the Yoga system is given greater emphasis. Thus, the role of prāṇa is relatively obscure in the Vaishnava texts, and more pronounced in the Shakta texts. In the Upaniṣad, there is an allegorical story about an argument between the different parts of the body. The mouth says that I swallow food, which is required for everyone else, so I'm superior. The hand says that I put the food in the mouth, so I'm superior. The stomach says that I digest everything from which the hand gets the power to put the food in the mouth, so I'm superior. In this way the argument goes on and remains inconclusive. Finally, the prāṇa says that each of the other parts are only involved in one aspect, however, I (the prāṇa) am involved in all the aspects. Therefore, I'm superior.

However, this story is incomplete, because the prāṇa is divided into many aspects. There are powers of ingestion, digestion, circulation, assimilation, and elimination. If we divide the prāṇa into many aspects, just like we divided the body into many parts, then, the superiority of the prāṇa cannot be established, just like the superiority of the other body parts could not be established.

Therefore, we must step away from notions of absolute superiority and inferiority and look at the problem from the perspective of masculine and feminine aspects. We have said that the soul comprises three aspects of relation, cognition, and emotion. But these aspects are also divided into will and power. The will aspect desires a relation, emotion, and cognition, and the power aspect fulfills that will. However, this description can lead to the mistaken idea that the power is inert, and the will is conscious. Hence, a nuanced understanding is that both masculine and feminine are persons, and they both have desire, will, or choice. However, these desires are different in the masculine and the feminine. As we have discussed earlier, the masculine is the want to be needed, and the feminine is the need to be wanted. Simplistically, the desires in the masculine and the feminine become different as wants and needs. This understanding helps us nuance our view of how the dominant-subordinate structures are created by choice—the choices are produced due to needs and wants.

There are many aspects of our material existence that exist as needs—e.g., sex drive, hunger, sleep, etc. There are also many aspects of our material existence that exist as wants—e.g., wealth, fame, power, etc. If one is struggling with needs, then the control of prāṇa through the Yoga process helps in conquering them. And if one is struggling with wants, then the control of the senses and the mind through the Sāṅkhya understanding helps in conquering them.

Often if needs are unfulfilled, then they transform into wants. For example, unfulfilled sexuality, sleep deprivation, or unsatisfied hunger, can transform into the desire for power, fame, and wealth. Indeed, many spiritual aspirants who control eating, sleeping, and sex, maniacally pursue power, wealth, and fame. Similarly, sometimes if wants are unfulfilled, then they can transform into needs. For example, people failing to obtain wealth, power, and fame can develop insomnia, eating disorders, hypersexual behaviors, etc. Therefore, there are no hard and fast distinctions between Yoga and Sāṅkhya, and both in combination or either of them alternately, can be employed by spiritual aspirants. As a result, Sāṅkhya and Yoga systems have traditionally been seen sometimes as aspects of one system, and sometimes as two closely related systems.

Topic 3

QUESTION
You have earlier said that the prāṇa is Lord's energy and work

according to His direction. You are now saying that the soul can also control the prāṇa. How do we reconcile these? Does prāṇa control the soul, or is controlled by it?

4.2.4 (500)

सोऽध्यकृषे तदुपगमादभिभ्यः

so'dhyakṣe tadupagamādibhyaḥ

saḥ—that (prāṇa); adhyakṣe—in the ruler (i.e., the Lord); tat—that (the Lord); upagama—submissive approach; ādibhyaḥ—the cause of approach etc.

TRANSLATION

That (prāṇa—the feminine energy) in the ruler (i.e., the Lord—the masculine) is the cause of the submissive approach toward that (the Lord).

COMMENTARY

We earlier discussed how the Lord is the origin of space, the soul is different points in space, and the connection between the origin and the different points in space is described as prāṇa. The same point is now repeated, although now with the nuance that the soul can also approach the Lord through prāṇa.

The origin of space is the masculine form of the Absolute Truth. The expansion of space is the feminine form of the Absolute Truth. And the soul within that space is expanded from the masculine, present within the feminine. This has been previously described as the Lord injecting the soul as His 'seed' into the mother through His glance. The soul is therefore a child or a part of both the masculine and the feminine—the masculine is the father, and the feminine is the mother. The mother controls the father and is controlled by the father. The child can also control the mother, but not in the way the father does. But it doesn't mean that the child is powerless. The child also receives the power of the mother, provided it becomes submissive to both the father and the mother. This submission is described in this sūtra by using the word *upagama*. The term *gama* means going, and *upa* means as a subordinate part. If the soul is arrogant, then the prāṇa doesn't work. But if the soul is submissive, then the child can approach the mother to seek Her help, to approach the father. As we have discussed, the desires in the masculine and the feminine forms are like wants and needs. If a soul approaches the Lord with a want, then he acts like the masculine. The Lord may agree, as this is also considered devotion, although not on par as when the soul develops a need. When the desire in the soul is like a need, rather than a want, then the soul acts like the feminine. In short, now, the soul is more a mother's baby rather than the father's child. The mother now controls the baby and gives the baby the power to approach the Lord with devotion.

Effectively, there are two kinds of devotional desires—wants and needs. The soul who has renounced the false boldness of the material world which desires independence, and now agreed to surrender to the Lord as His servant, is considered great. However, there is still some boldness in the desire, by which the soul acts masculine. This masculinity is expressed in the fact that the soul is attracted to the Lord's six qualities of knowledge, beauty, power, wealth, fame, and renunciation, and behaves like the prince who sometimes wants to sit on the throne of the king—not to replace the king, but just to feel what the king feels being the king. We have discussed earlier how this devotion is described as the five kinds of liberation—having the same form as the Lord, living in the same place as the Lord, enjoying the same power as the Lord, living in proximity to the Lord, or believing that everything meant for the Lord is also meant for the soul. The affectionate child of a king considers himself just like the king, although there is no malice or competitiveness with the king.

But the devotion of wants is distinguished from the devotion of needs. The neediness is not like the aspiration for knowledge; it is instead like the necessity for food. The soul who has renounced the wants and developed the need for the Lord is considered greater, because the soul has greater dependence on the Lord, and the Lord enjoys His chivalrous nature of wanting to be needed even more. Under the neediness, the feminine aspect becomes predominant.

Under boldness, the prāṇa controls the senses and the body (i.e., the parts) and the wants in the mind, senses, and the body are fulfilled by the mind. Under shyness, the mind, senses, and the body become the controllers of prāṇa.

This basic difference appears even within this world in two types of meditation. In the first type of meditation, the meditator is advised to withdraw the senses within by controlling the mind, and to stop the flow of thoughts in the mind by focusing on the self. In the second type of meditation, the meditator is advised to let go of all the attempt to control the senses and the mind, and just observe; this 'observation' is called the 'mindfulness' of the aspirant, and involves letting go of one's tendency to control, and become a passive observer. This passive observation involves identifying oneself with prāṇa, which is attained if one simply focuses on the breath going inward and outward.

The practices of mindfulness are predominant in Buddhism and the practices of mind control are predominant in Yoga. While the mindful practice helps in cessation of thoughts, the Yoga system doesn't consider this cessation a spiritual state. It is rather a state devoid of material influences. Thus, superior than the state of material wants and needs is the state where one has no want or need—the state without wants is called Brahman, and the state without needs is called the state of nothingness. You might not be hungry right now, but you can become hungry after some time. Therefore, the cessation of needs is considered temporary relative to the cessation of wants by which one acquires a body. Once the body is acquired, then it also brings needs, and whatever started out as a project of fulfilling one's wants through the body, now becomes a project of fulfilling the body's needs. Thus, in the material world, the soul starts out with the masculine tendency to dominate but becomes the servant of the body. Therefore, freedom from wants—which led to the body—is considered superior to the freedom from needs. This superiority is predicated on the fact that if we gave up the body, then we will also be free from the needs of the body. So, by getting the state without the wants, we will also get the state devoid of the needs. Hence arise the nihilistic doctrine in which the soul is devoid of all needs, and the impersonal doctrine of Brahman in which the soul has no wants.

Superior to these is the state in which one wants the Lord. And even superior to that state is one in which one needs the Lord. As we have discussed before, Vaikuṇṭha is the realm of boldness, and Goloka is one of shyness.

Śrīla Rupa Goswami, in his Upadeśāmrta, describes six qualities of a guru, by which the guru has become free of needs—i.e., the necessity to serve the mind, the senses, and the body. The six minimum qualifications of a guru are—freedom from the urge to speak (i.e., the urges of the senses of action), the urges of the mind, the urges of anger (i.e., the ego), the urge for tasty food (i.e., the urges of the senses of knowledge), the urge for hunger, and the urge for sex (which are the two main urges of the body). This is the first state of the soul beyond the material world, although it is the nihilistic state aspired for by the Buddhists. Beyond this freedom from material needs is the freedom from material wants or Brahman. Thus, the guru may not be liberated but must be beyond this world. Such a guru can guide others in the material world because he is not controlled by the necessity to serve the body. But he may not be qualified to take the soul toward Brahman, the wanting, or the needing of the Lord.

Thus, we find many kinds of seemingly contradictory statements ranging from the claim that prāṇa is only a mechanical process that doesn't lead to perfection, to the claim that the surrendering to the Lord, and being governed by His will is the highest perfection for the soul. Accordingly, the Shakta system is sometimes considered lower than the Shaiva and Vaishnava system, and sometimes, the Shakta system of devotion to the feminine is called the highest system. The fact is that in the material world, surrendering to the material power is the lowest process, and in the spiritual world, this surrender is the highest goal. Previously, the process of prāṇa was considered but called inferior. Now, this process is being recommended, after the recommendation of mind control. Therefore, the superiority of this method is recognized after stating it is inferior. If one understands the contexts, then both statements are considered true.

QUESTION

You earlier said that the mind is the controller of the senses and the body. Now you are saying that the mind can be controlled by the prāṇa. Does this mean that the senses and the body can also be controlled by the prāṇa?

4.2.5 (501)

भूतेषु तच्छ्रुतेः

bhūteṣu tacchruteḥ

bhūteṣu—the elements; tat-śruteḥ—that is stated by the śrutī.

TRANSLATION

The (five) elements (are controlled by prāṇa); that is stated by the śrutī.

COMMENTARY

Most of us think that to push a table or a chair, we must use our hands. Then we also think that the movement of the hands is caused by the brain sending a signal to the hand. Finally, we say that the signal is the movement of molecules. But what causes the molecules to move from the brain to the hand?

In atomic theory, a molecule exists in a 'stationary state', and it jumps to another 'stationary state' although the cause of that jump is not known. In classical physics, motion was caused by a force, but in atomic theory, that force (e.g., electromagnetism) only produces a stationary state. Then, since the molecule jumps from one state to another, there are potentially many states to which it can conceivably jump, and the next state of the molecule cannot be predicted thus. Therefore, according to atomic theory: (1) we cannot explain how a signal is sent, or (2) even why the signal goes to the hand instead of the legs.

In Vedic philosophy, as we have discussed before, there is a difference between motion and change. When we perceive the world, and the world seems close to us, then, the proximity is caused by a stronger interaction between our body and the world; therefore, we can see things very far, without ever moving. Then, when we act, the action is manifest from the senses as a possibility (which was preexisting in the senses), and the senses don't change. Therefore, it is possible to perceive and act without bodily change, and all these perceptions and actions are motions and interactions of the body. If all activity was like this, then we would never get tired—e.g., by pushing a table. Since we do get tired in the material world, therefore, the body is changing. This change is described as the conservation of energy. For example, there is some energy in us, and when we push a table, the energy is transferred to the table (or to the floor as heat). We must regain the energy, and without its presence, the body feels tired.

As we have discussed earlier, motion doesn't require energy conservation, because there is no energy transferred, unless, of course, it is change rather than motion. When change occurs, then one body disappears and the other body appears, and to prevent the conclusion that something becomes nothing, and nothing becomes something, we use the principle of energy conservation.

Thus, energy conservation means something else in Vedic philosophy. It means that the total number of possibilities in the universe is fixed. However, these possibilities are sometimes manifest and sometimes unmanifest. When the world goes unmanifest, then, according to modern science, energy would not be conserved, but according to Vedic philosophy the energy would exist in a potential state. In terms of modern science, we could say that the kinetic, thermal, radiation, and every other kind of energy has become 'potential energy', but you cannot observe the effects of such potential energy. Therefore, strictly speaking, the energy conservation principle would be broken at that time. Likewise, during the creation of the universe, the scientific principle of energy conservation would be violated, since the unmanifest state is not superhot like the claim in big bang, and yet the universe is produced from the unmanifest state, which (according to modern science) would seem to be the creation of energy. Thus, the scientific principle of energy conservation is rejected in Vedic philosophy, although the material energy is said to be eternal. This eternity rests upon the principle that all the possibilities exist, even if we don't see them. Once the principle of energy conservation is clarified, then we can discuss prāṇa.

The first role of prāṇa is in creation, maintenance, and destruction. Creation means manifestation; destruction means unmanifestation; and maintenance is preventing the manifest to become unmanifest. The need for maintenance arises because there is a natural tendency in the material energy to become unmanifest. So, keeping it manifest—e.g., preventing the tables and chairs around you from disappearing automatically—requires prāṇa. Classical physics believes that the manifest state is natural, but in Vedic philosophy, it is unnatural. It is as if the material energy is a reluctant creator of the world, and She would rather wind up the worldly business as quickly as possible, if it is not needed. Thus, even if something has manifested, keeping it manifest is due to prāṇa.

The second role of prāṇa is called revelation and hiding. Hiding means that every time you act, you lose some ability—e.g., you now feel tired—and this ability is transferred to another object and place, which is called revelation. In short, unlike the previous case where a possibility is manifest into an observation, in this case, something that was previously possible, now becomes impossible, and what was previously impossible now becomes possible. This revelation and hiding creates the modern principle of energy conservation, because we say that energy (or the power to act) disappeared from here and appeared in another place. The energy conservation was 'local' in classical physics, but it is 'non-local' in atomic theory. In short, energy can disappear here, and appear anywhere else. The appearance and disappearance are also due to prāṇa.

In summary, in the former case, the possibility is fixed, and it becomes manifest and unmanifest; and in the latter case, the possibility itself appears and disappears (and subsequently, it can become manifest or unmanifest).

In atomic theory, these two ideas are described as the 'collapse' of a wavefunction (when a possibility becomes reality) and the 'evolution' of the wavefunction (when something impossible becomes possible or vice versa). In the material world, the wavefunction evolves, so this world is called temporary. In the spiritual world, the wavefunction doesn't evolve, so it is called permanent. In short, when you push a table in the material world, you get tired. But by pushing the table in the spiritual world, you don't get tired. The evolution of the wavefunction is called the change in the body in Vedic philosophy. This change exists in the material world but doesn't exist in the spiritual world. Thus, the body becomes weak and strong in this world, however, the body retains its strength in the spiritual world—whether it is working or not.

Therefore, the brain pushing a molecule, which then pushes your hand, which then pushes the table, and then causes you to feel tired, is the evolution or the change of the body. The soul moves from one body to another. And this evolution of the body is described here as the effect of the prāṇa on the five material elements. Once the body changes, there is ability to act, and that ability can then be used to perform some work. The problem is only that when you work, you also get tired. In short, in general, motion (or the collapse of the wavefunction) produces a change (the evolution of the wavefunction).

In modern atomic theory, this connection between motion and change isn't made. So, the theory says that the wavefunction evolves, and then collapses on a measurement. The problem is that a measurement involves the transfer of energy. So, when a measurement is performed, energy must leak out of the system, and that leak would cause the wavefunction to evolve again. By not making this connection between collapse and evolution, the problem of consciousness is restricted to the collapse—it is said that consciousness collapses the wavefunction, but the evolution of the wavefunction is deterministic. There is some truth to this idea: Even if you don't work, you will still feel hungry and tired after some time. So, there is indeed an evolution even without an energy transfer. But hunger and tiredness come faster when we work. Therefore, the evolution and collapse must also be connected within a scientific theory.

These ideas remain obscure even in Vedic philosophy, because of the use of the terms 'creation' and 'destruction' vs. 'revelation' and 'hiding' which seem to mean the same, and yet they are not the same. Due to revelation and hiding, the material universe appears and disappears, and we lose old bodies and gain new bodies. This process of change doesn't exist in the spiritual world. Therefore, prāṇa doesn't effect the five elements by making the body older or younger. It still effects the five elements by manifesting their abilities—e.g., if you taste an apple, the flavor is manifest upon the contact with the tongue. But even if you eat the apple, the apple is not diminished. Hence, eating doesn't make the body fat, and not eating doesn't make the body thin. In this world, it is said that "you can't eat your cake and have it too". That is true for this world. But in the spiritual world you can eat your cake, and you will still have it.

Thus, in the spiritual world, there is day and night, and yet, it is said that time doesn't exist. This creates much confusion in people's minds, because how can we have time and yet not have changes? The short answer is that time causes motion but doesn't cause change. In this world, motion and change are tightly interconnected, so we are unable to distinguish between them. But if the transmigration of the soul is understood, then we would have to distinguish between the motion of the body in this life, and the change of body across lives. Then we will understand that much of what we call motion is mixed up with change even in this life, so, the body is changing even now. Then we can understand how motion can exist without change, and that would mean that the soul can have a body, that it can talk and eat, and yet, everything is eternal. All these things can be understood scientifically so we don't have to rely on 'faith'. However, we must have the intelligence to understand a different science.

QUESTION

However, one might say that prāṇa is only manifest in the living body, and it is not always seen in the inanimate things. Therefore, the inanimate things must be moving without the prāṇa. And hence we should try to explain the working of the world without prāṇa, and then the body also without it.

4.2.6 (502)
नैकस्मिन् दर्शयतो हि
naikasmin darśayato hi

na—not;   ekasmin—occasionally;   darśayataḥ—perceives; hi—certainly.

TRANSLATION

(The prāṇa is) certainly not seen occasionally (i.e., it is always seen).

COMMENTARY

As we have discussed in the previous sūtra, many things happen in this world without our choice. For example, we get tired after working, although nobody chooses to feel tired. Hence, the materialist says that if these things are happening automatically, then even the body must not be working due to our choice. Since we just said that the body is controlled by prāṇa, and prāṇa can be controlled by a choice, but we simply cannot wish away tiredness, therefore, even the purported control of the mind through the prāṇa must be false. In short, the argument of the occasional presence of prāṇa leads to total denial. Therefore, whatever is not our choosing, must also be explained due to prāṇa.

We can see that machines can work automatically, but they can also be controlled by our will. Thus, you can switch on power to a fan, and you can switch off a running fan. Once the fan has been switched on, we are not making the fan rotate by our will; it is automatically rotating due to the energy flow. Similarly, the prāṇa can work automatically, and it can be controlled by our choices or free will. While we are asleep, we are not aware of breathing, blood circulation, or digestion. In fact, we are not aware of these things even while waking. Therefore, the prāṇa indeed works without a conscious intervention. The question is this—How do we intervene in this automated working of prāṇa?

The short answer is that nature works through the alternating patterns of dominant-subordinate structures. One mode becomes dominant for some time, while the other modes remain subordinate. However, in the material world, after some time, a conflict between the modes is produced and the resolution of that conflict is that the other modes must be allowed to become dominant. The alternating periods of mode domination produce what is called the 'balance' of the modes, and nature automatically creates balance. Thus, whatever seems important right now, will one day become subordinated and will remain there for some time. Then it will return to domination and the previously dominant modes will be subordinated. This process of mode alternation also happens in the spiritual world; however, the change is cooperative rather than competitive. In short, the modes don't compete for domination and lose the battle for domination to become subordinate. They relinquish their position naturally.

The cause of mode domination in the material world is prāṇa—the power of the mode to dominate is obtained due to prāṇa. This prāṇa in turn works under the control of time, which moves the power from one mode to another. Similarly, by controlling prāṇa, the effects of time can be reduced or stopped. This mutual control of time by prāṇa and prāṇa by time is understood as the will of Śiva and Śakti. Time is the cosmic will, and prāṇa is the cosmic power. This will and power are ultimately vested in Śiva and Śakti and are controlled by their desire. The difference is that time is the masculine desire of wants and prāṇa is the feminine desire of needs. Therefore, some alterations occur because they are wanted, and other changes happen because they are needed.

When the soul does not consciously intervene in the body's working, the body works automatically due to the desires of Śiva and Śakti. Just because we do not choose to become tired, doesn't mean that nature is mechanical. Nature is working due to desires, although these might not be our desires controlling nature. Due to the automated working, karma is automatically manifest as opportunities, and ability is gained or lost (e.g., we become tired) automatically. Within these abilities and opportunities, we can exercise our will as well.

All such classic claims of contradiction between choice and determinism are based on flawed concepts of causality, where matter is a reality rather than a possibility, where everyone has access to everything, and nobody's opportunities are restricted. Once abilities and opportunities are taken out of the equation, then choices lose meaning, because you cannot choose to exercise an ability within a given opportunity. So, the role of prāṇa is that we can control our desires by prāṇa, but nature and time control the ability and opportunity. If we don't exercise our choices, then the abilities and opportunities evolve automatically. But if we use our choices, then we can take advantage of the ability and opportunity. Therefore, the so-called determinism of nature is also due to prāṇa and time and ultimately desires, but that desire doesn't create determinism. It creates abilities and opportunities, that we can use by our prāṇa.

Topic 4

QUESTION

What state is attained by the complete control of the mind and prāṇa?

4.2.7 (503)

समाना चासृत्युपक्रमात् अमृतत्वं चानुपोष्य

samānā cāsṛtyupakramāt amṛtatvaṃ cānupoṣya

samānā—balanced; ca—and; ā sṛti-upakramāt—from which the creation begins; amṛtatvam—immortality; ca—and; anupoṣya—not hungry.

TRANSLATION

(By the control of mind and prāṇa) one also attains the balanced state from which creation begins, which is immortal and not hungry.

COMMENTARY

In this sūtra, the nihilistic state of emancipation is described. The primordial state of matter is called pradhāna and it constitutes the balanced state of the three modes. In this balanced state, the dominant-subordinate structures of the modes don't exist. But when the soul is injected into pradhāna by the Lord's glance, then pradhāna creates prakriti in which the three modes are separated, and now they start producing dominant-subordinate structures, and pradhāna expands into a tree-like structure as the modes enter each other. This sūtra states that by controlling the mind and the prāṇa, this process can be reversed to the balanced state. The balancing means the absence of material cognition, emotion, and relation, and hence it is like a person in a dark room, with nothing to perceive, nothing to desire, and nothing to relate to. This is emancipation by the removal of everything other than the self, which means that there is self-awareness, but there is nothing else to be known. While the Buddhists aim for this state, their claim that it is nothingness is incorrect. The balancing pertains to the modes of matter, not to the modes in the soul. In short, even in the nihilistic state, the soul is not completely happy because there is a desire which is not being fulfilled due to lack of relation and cognition. The latter balancing is achieved in Brahman, when the desire is fulfilled by vectoring the desire to the self. Now, there is a self, there is a desire for self, a relation to the self, and the cognition of the self. Therefore, Brahman is superior to the nihilistic state because the nihilistic state is a dissatisfied state, but Brahman is satisfied.

Of course, even in self-awareness, the soul is not completely satisfied because the self is not the complete truth, and this incompleteness creates the desire to know something other than the self. Therefore, the soul can fall even from Brahman, although the possibility of a fall is reduced significantly.

The balanced state of the material modes is the *experience* of emptiness, not emptiness itself. It can be pleasurable relative to the material world, which is always conditioned by fear of three kinds—(1) the fear of loss, destruction, and death, (2) the anxiety that something bad will happen, within the anticipation of something good happening, and (3) the feeling of being oppressed by the world, even if one doesn't have the fear of death or the anxiety of something going wrong. A person who finds this world a burden wants to keep a distance from everything. That is achieved in nihilism. It is not the destruction of the self (although it is claimed to be so). It is also not the voiding of all experience—there is still awareness of the self. It is merely the voiding of the world.

The Buddhists claim that it voids the self because in self-awareness there is a difference and non-difference of the knower, known, and knowledge—all three are the self, and yet, they are different modes of the self. Factually, this is not a contradiction because one desires the self, focuses on the self, and then knows the self, alternately. Therefore, the denial by contradiction is also false. Similarly, the impersonalist claims that matter is inert, and Brahman is conscious, which is also false. Even to be self-conscious, one must desire the self; that desire requires a knower and it must be pointed toward a known. When the soul has dissolved its individuality, the knower and the known disappear, and hence, the knowledge of the self also disappears. It is merely existence without an awareness or experience. Therefore, if Brahman is defined as the dissolution of identity, then by definition, it must also entail the dissolution of self-awareness. Hence, there is a fundamental difference between the descriptions of Brahman in personalist and impersonalist philosophies. In the personalist philosophy, the soul is always an individual—even in Brahman—where he exists as self-awareness, but this self-awareness is free of the contradictions between the three aspects of the soul. The impersonalist instead says that there is no self, which means there should be no self-awareness. Therefore, if we follow the impersonal doctrine, then we can say that there is no self-awareness (which is false). Only when we say that the soul is eternally and individual can we say that the soul is self-awareness in Brahman. But this 'self' is incomplete, as it isn't aware of the whole truth (the Lord) and the other living entities (His parts). The "I" in Brahman is the balanced state of the soul's three modes, but this balance is temporary because the self is incomplete. Therefore, both nihilistic and impersonalist philosophies about the self are rejected compared to the devotion to the Lord, but they are superior to the material experience.

Topic 5

QUESTION

You have said that transcendence is spiritual experience. So, is the cessation of experience by mind and prāṇa control considered transcendence?

4.2.8 (504)

तदापीतेःसंसारव्यपदेशात्

tadāpīteḥ saṃsāravyapadeśāt

tat—that; ā apīteḥ—which has not entered (the supreme abode); saṃsāra-vyapadeśāt—from being described as the material world.

TRANSLATION

That which has not entered (the supreme abode) from being described as the material world (i.e., the experience of nothingness is not transcendence).

COMMENTARY

We have discussed how the soul can enter the spiritual world in the present body, therefore, the body is not material. Similarly, we have discussed how the spiritual world also has relationships, so these relationships are not material. The difference between material and spiritual is simply in the purpose in the soul. A fulfillment of selfish purpose and the selfish purpose that remains unfulfilled, are both considered material. The cessation of all purpose is better than selfish purpose, but it is still not considered spiritual. In this sūtra, the nihilistic state referred to by the previous sūtra is rejected as ultimate transcendence.

QUESTION

But you have said that the pradhāna is still beyond the material experience. So, it must be considered superior to material experience. In what way?

4.2.9 (505)

सूक्ष्मं प्रमाणतश्च तथोपलब्धेः

sūkṣmaṃ pramāṇataśca tathopalabdheḥ

sūkṣmam—subtle; pramāṇataḥ—as greater proof or evidence; ca—also; tathā—thus or in the same way; upalabdheḥ—because it is experienced.

TRANSLATION

There is also greater proof of the subtle (i.e., the soul) thus obtained by the experience (of the absence of the worldly experience).

COMMENTARY

In Cartesian philosophy, the certainty of other facts is established based on the certainty of the self. Our thoughts, sensations, or judgments can be false or hallucinatory but the self that has these hallucinations cannot itself be a hallucination. If the self is known with certainty, then it is possible to distinguish between true and false—e.g., that which leads to the permanent happiness of the self is true and that which leads to unhappiness, or oscillates between happiness and distress, is false. The materialist claims that even the experience of the self is matter, which means happiness and distress are nothing other than material states. Since matter has no purpose, therefore, happiness cannot be a goal, and unhappiness is not unnatural. Hence, one cannot distinguish between truth and falsity, and the existence of matter cannot be established. Every method of science is therefore flawed because you have no way of knowing that your experiments are not hallucinations, that your theories are not false.

This sūtra states that as one controls the mind and prāṇa, he can see that the self exists even when the material experience doesn't. In the experience of nothingness, the self is not voided. Therefore, by such experience, one can confirm that the self is different from everything else—namely, that it is not the body, that it is not defined by relationships, and that it is not enjoyment, or suffering. This realization is valuable as a counterargument to materialism.

QUESTION

So, you are implying that the observer is different from matter because there is a state in which the observer exists without material experience?

4.2.10 (506)

नोपमर्दनातः

nopamardenātaḥ

na—not; upamardena—by the destruction; ataḥ—therefore.

TRANSLATION

Therefore, by the destruction (of the body) (the soul is) not (destroyed).

COMMENTARY

Many people argue: Can you prove the existence of the soul? A common argument cited in the support of the soul is transmigration to a different body. But the skeptic now asks: How do I know the same soul goes to another body? After all, we have no recollection or memory of past lives. Then, sometimes we can cite examples of how some people do recollect their past lives, especially if they have died in unnatural circumstances. However, even this doesn't satisfy the skeptic. He might say: these are possibly aberrations of the brain that creates a memory. So, this sūtra offers another method—you can control your mind and prāṇa and enter the emptiness state. In that state, there will be no thoughts, or sensations, or judgments. But you can still experience the self-existence. In short, if you cannot rely on external evidence, or doubt its existence, then make an effort and void the mind and senses by prāṇa control, and you can confirm that you are different from all that is being experienced. Of course, most skeptics don't have the motivation or even the resilience to pursue such a process. But the process is open to anyone who wants to obtain such an experience.

QUESTION

But how can we know that the experience of the self during the void and the experience of the self during ordinary experience are the same self?

4.2.11 (507)

अस्यैव च-उपपत्तेः-एष ऊष्मा

asyaiva ca-upapatteḥ-eṣa ūṣmā

asya eva—certainly to this; ca—also; upapatteḥ—because of logical reasoning and conclusion; eṣaḥ—this; ūṣmā—heat.

TRANSLATION

Certainly, to this (the soul) also (attaches) this heat (i.e., the body) because of the logical conclusion (since it exists with and without experience).

COMMENTARY

The difference between the experience of the self during the experience of nothingness and the experience of the self during ordinary experience is "I" vs. "I am". By "I am" we mean three things— "I am this body and mind", "I am father and friend", and "I am happy or sad". During the experience of the void, the "I am" is destroyed because there is no cognition, emotion, and relation. But during worldly experience, the "I am" is defined through material cognition, emotion, and relation. Therefore, when the soul contacts matter, "I" expands into "I am". This expansion is based on two premises—(1) the soul and matter are separate existents, because the world can exist even when I don't exist (for the world), and (2) I can exist even if the world doesn't exist (for me). The interaction between the soul and matter creates an experience, and therefore, the experience is the conclusion obtained from the premises. If either of these two premises were false, then the conclusion would also become impossible.

As we have discussed earlier, premises don't lead to conclusions automatically. Rather, they first give rise to a question, and then, a conclusion is used to address the question. Therefore, if the soul's existence remains a premise and doesn't become a problem—e.g., you don't ask yourself: "Why do I exist?"—then there is no need for material contact. Similarly, if the existence of matter remains a possibility, and doesn't become a problem—e.g., "Why does matter exist?"—then even the material universe remains unmanifest. Our material experiences are the consequences of two premises converting into two problems. The soul develops the desire to enjoy the material energy, and the material energy develops the desire to control, manipulate, and delude the soul. Then, both these premises, which have now become problems, become the solution to each other's problems. The soul now tries to enjoy the material world, and the material energy enjoys the control, manipulation, and delusion of the soul.

Now, someone can say: How do we know that the "I am" in the world was previously the "I" outside the world? What is the evidence of the persistence of one's personal identity? Our sense of identity is founded on memory, and in the state of void, we will lose this memory, so we cannot recall the previous worldly experience, and without that recall, we cannot say that it is the same "I". The answer to that problem is that the absence of memory is not the only absence. The absence of the problem—which led to the contact—is the deeper absence. If we understand that the contact is caused by this problem, then the cessation of the problem is evidence enough that it is the same person. Therefore, the soul can know that it is the same individual within and without the body because the problems magnify in the body, and they are reduced without the body. Likewise, the problems of bodily experience change into the problems of existing without any experience. These problems existing within the soul, although their solution is in matter. By observing how one becomes happier without the bodily problems, and how suffers more due to the bodily problems, a person can know that the same soul exists within and without the body.

All of us have a desire for happiness because we have experienced happiness in the past. That recollection or memory of happiness is not due to the body but lies innate in the soul. As a result, everyone wants to live eternally, and happily. Where does that desire arise from? We don't see people living eternally and happily in this world. And yet, everyone is trying to be eternally happy. We don't accept unhappiness and suffering as a natural consequence of living. The reason for these discrepancies is that we don't completely rely on our material memories. We also rely on the spiritual memory of eternal happiness, which cannot be wiped out; we will never stop seeking eternal happiness.

Topic 6

QUESTION

But isn't it true that the soul forgets about the transcendental world when he enters the material world? If so, how can he remember the state without problems? And if he cannot remember, how can he establish continuity?

4.2.12 (508)

पुरतषिधादतिचेत् न शारीरात्

pratiṣedhāditi cet na śārīrāt

pratiṣedhāt—due to denial; iti cet—if it be said; na—not so; śārīrāt—due to the material body.

TRANSLATION

If it be said that the (memory of past lives or perfection) is denied in this body, (then we say) not so; it is (sometimes) due to the material body.

COMMENTARY

Many people say that we have no memory of the spiritual world. But then we can ask: Why are you trying to obtain happiness, order, righteousness, freedom, truthfulness, justice etc.? Shouldn't you be quite comfortable with suffering, chaos, deceit, injustice, bondage, and wrongs? What makes you aspire for perfection if you have no memory of perfection? If your experience is only about this world, and you have never seen perfection, why aren't you comfortable with it? The fact is that people aspire for perfection because they have seen perfection. This is especially true of the perfectionists. But even those who are not themselves perfect, or want to be perfect, still want others to be perfect. Every thief wants an honest accountant. Every cheater wants to receive a fair trial. Every murderer wants others to show him some mercy and kindness. So, whether we aspire to be perfect, or we expect others to be perfect, we have an inkling of perfection within us. That is the memory of past perfection.

The quest for perfection is the light in our life. However, in many people this light is dimmed, and they become lazy apologists for imperfection. They rationalize the imperfection in others, often simply to rationalize the imperfection in themselves. Until, of course, they face the sharp end of that imperfection in others directed toward them. Then, suddenly, their sense of perfection is revived, and indignation replaces complacency. Therefore, when a person suffers in their life, they develop a strong aspiration for perfection. Those who are relatively comfortable in their lives claim that there is no need for perfection, that perfection doesn't exist, or that we cannot define perfection because everyone has a different definition of perfection. The cure for this complacency is karma: when you suffer, then you will desire perfection. Then, you will dream of a world in which there was no crime, no pain, no injustices; a place where there is perfect love, freedom, and the opportunities to pursue happiness. How can this desire for perfection arise if there isn't a sense of perfection in us? Therefore, the dimming of the sense of perfection is not its complete elimination. It exists in everyone, but we think that we don't have to be perfect. But when we undergo suffering, then we realize that perfection is important even for us. In fact, one learns that their suffering is due to their imperfections, and the path of happiness is not in asking others to be perfect; it comes when we are perfect. The imperfect people will always exist; but we don't have to live with them.

QUESTION

But if everyone tends to forget the perfection upon the acquisition of the material body, then how can the recollection of perfection be revived?

4.2.13 (509)

सपष्टो ह्येकेषाम्

spaṣṭo hyekeṣām

spaṣṭaḥ—clear; hi—certainly; ekeṣām—in some.

TRANSLATION

(The sense of perfection is) certainly clear in some (people).

COMMENTARY

The claim that the memory of perfection is lost when one enters the material body is rejected in this sūtra. It is certainly dimmed in most people and may be completely hidden in some. But there are also people in whom the desire for perfection, the understanding of perfection, and the method to attain that perfection is clear. Many people simply desire perfection but don't know what that perfection is, or how it may be attained. Some people desire perfection and know what that perfection is, but don't know how to achieve it. Finally, most people are simply lazy to even try to know perfection or try to achieve it.

Perfection means unity, but there are three levels of perfection; sometimes they are called perfect, more perfect, and most perfect. The impersonalist who aspires for Brahman says that unity is opposed to diversity, and hence, it is obtained when we reject diversity. The personalist who aspires for Vaikuṇṭha says that unity and diversity are not contradictory; the main problem is that people of this world are lazy, stupid, and inept, and they keep doing things that against their best interest. If only they became enlightened about our best interest, then everyone will do the right thing, and the suffering will end. The term kuṇṭha means lazy, stupid, and inept, and Vaikuṇṭha means freedom from stupidity, laziness, and ineptness. Śrīmad Bhagavatam 7.5.31 summarizes this idea:

na te viduḥ svārtha-gatiṁ hi viṣṇuṁ
durāśayā ye bahir-artha-māninaḥ
andhā yathāndhair upanīyamānās
te 'pīśa-tantryām uru-dāmni baddhāḥ

They do not know that their selfish interest is certainly Viṣṇu. With false hopes, they consider the external world to be the meaning of life. Themselves blind and just like the blind (i.e., the leaders who are blind but pretend to be enlightened), they create false rules and regulations, even though they are bound due to the ropes created by the Lord.

So, the devotee who accepts diversity, and the laws created by the Lord, sees that his self-interest is in following these laws. He gives up all attempts to create new rules and regulations for people to become happy. He simply accepts the instructions of the Lord as the commandments to become happy.

Then, the personalist who aspires for Goloka says that even the selfish interest of our happiness is not perfect. Yes, it creates unity by accepting the Lord as an authority, but an even better perfection is if the Lord's happiness is the goal. Such a devotee pleases the Lord without desire for one's pleasure.

Accordingly, these three stages are called perfect, more perfect, and most perfect. This sūtra says that these ideas of perfection are not totally lost in this world. There are some people who have such varied ideas of perfection.

QUESTION

But in the present world, many of these ideas of perfection have been lost. How can we attain this perfection when we don't find such perfection?

4.2.14 (510)
स्मर्यते च
smaryate ca

smaryate—by remembering (the perfection); ca—also.

TRANSLATION

(Perfection can be attained) also by remembering (the perfection).

COMMENTARY

The knowledge of God exists because humanity desires perfection. However, the atheists claim that God is man's creation, and that they can create a perfect world through their rules and regulations. The result of atheism is that people with materialistic goals are produced. Once such goals are adopted as hallmarks of perfection, then lying, cheating, fighting, and killing become the means to attain such 'perfection'. Now, society descends into an abyss of imperfection but the rich and powerful, who haven't faced the sharp end of these imperfections themselves, continue pushing the false ideologies of perfection. Nature has a perfect arrangement to make them face the imperfections of the laws and regulations they have created. When one suffers endlessly, then one dreams of a perfect world again, free from such attempts at perfection.

This sūtra states that remembrance of the perfection leads one to perfection. How? If one thinks about perfection, their actions become perfect. And both due to the change in one's mind and in one's actions, the soul is transported to the world of perfection. Therefore, even if one is currently in an imperfect situation, one should constantly think about the perfect world. This thinking will make them perfect, and then transport them into a perfect world.

Topic 7

QUESTION

By thinking of perfection, does one reach the nihilistic state? Or does one go beyond the nihilistic state into the world that embodies the perfection?

4.2.15 (511)
तानि परे तथाह्याह
tāni pare tathāhyāha

tāni—those (thinking about perfection); pare—go beyond; tathā—in the same way (as those controlling the mind reach the nihilistic state); hi—certainly; āha—that is said.

TRANSLATION

Those (thinking about perfection) certainly go beyond (the nihilistic state) in the same way (as those controlling the mind and reach the nihilistic state); that is said (in the scriptures).

COMMENTARY

New bodies are acquired based on the mental state. Therefore, just as those controlling the mind and prāṇa stop the mind and end the sensations and thoughts, and hence reach the nihilistic state, similarly, those thinking about perfection engage the mind in this perfection and use the senses in the perception of perfection and perfect actions, and they reach the perfect world.

Many people performing meditation and controlling the body and the mind consider themselves superior to those who engage in the Lord's devotion. That conclusion is rejected here. If someone stops their mind, they reach the place devoid of all experience. But if someone engages their mind in thoughts about perfections, then they attain the Lord's abode which is the perfect place. Mind and sense control are harder because there is innate tendency in the soul to enjoy pleasure. Therefore, the control of mind and prāṇa is obtained with great difficulty, and yet, the result attained by this control is inferior to the result obtained by the devotees who constantly think about the Lord's pastimes.

Topic 8

QUESTION

What about those devotees who think about perfection in this world? Are they considered a part of the spiritual world or a part of the material world?

4.2.16 (512)

अवभागःवचनात्

avibhāgaḥ vacanāt

avibhāgaḥ—non-difference; vacanāt—from the statements.

TRANSLATION

From the statements (those thinking about perfection in this world) are non-different (from those thinking of perfection in the spiritual world)

COMMENTARY

As we discussed earlier, the gopis in Vṛndāvana think about how Kṛṣṇa will steal their butter, which is their fantasy. But then Kṛṣṇa also fulfills their fantasy, and therefore, that fantasy is also reality. Similarly, the devotees in this world can also think about various kinds of pastimes with the Lord. Kṛṣṇa may not appear immediately to fulfill these fantasies, but the meditation upon the Lord is not false. Nevertheless, because there is a difference between the fantasy and its fulfillment, therefore, the term non-different is used in this sūtra.

The implication is that thoughts about the Lord may seem to be fantasy right now, but when the devotee reaches the Lord's abode, those fantasies become real. Sometimes, the Lord also comes to this world to fulfill our fantasies. Whatever can be imagined, exists as a possibility, as part of the Absolute Truth. We do not create anything; we only access what already exists. Since it exists eternally, therefore, it is real. And yet, when it manifests, it produces greater pleasure. Still, since the soul chooses from that which exists eternally, therefore, the soul is the cause of the manifestation, just as the Lord is the cause of the fulfillment. Even in the material world, if someone makes bad choices, they become responsible for those choices, even as the Lord fulfills their desires due to karma. Thus, the principle of desiring a possibility, and that desire getting fulfilled by the Lord is the same in this world and the spiritual world. The difference is that in this world, the choices are unmindful of the Lord, and hence they are material. But when the choices become mindful of the Lord, then they are spiritual. Since it is possible to make the same choices in material and spiritual worlds, therefore, the devotees in both places are non-different.

Topic 9

QUESTION

If devotees in the material world are non-different, but not identical, to those in the spiritual world, how do these devotees reach the spiritual world?

4.2.17 (513)

तदोक्कोऽग्रज्वलनं ततुप्रकाशतिद्वारःवदियासामरथ्यात्
तच्छेषगत्यनुस्मृतियोगाच्च हार्दानुगृहीताःशताधिकया

**tadoko'grajvalanaṃ tatprakāśitadvāraḥ vidyāsāmarthyāt
taccheṣagatyanusmṛtiyogācca hārdānugṛhītāḥ śatādhikayā**

tat-okaḥ—that house; agra—foremost; jvalanam—illuminated; tat-prakāśita-dvāraḥ—the illuminated doors of that (illuminated house); vidyā-sāmarthyāt—according to the one's eligibility or understanding; tat-śeṣa-gati—moves toward upon the cessation of that (i.e., the body); anusmṛti-yogāt—based on the recollection of the union; ca—and; hārdānugṛhītāḥ—the heart being preoccupied or favored; śatādhikayā—that which is greater than hundred.

TRANSLATION

That house is the foremost illuminated; the doors (of the house) are illuminated; on the cessation of that (body) one moves toward (the house) based upon the recollection of the union according to one's eligibility or understanding (of the Lord). (The approach to the Lord's abode is possible if) the heart is preoccupied by that (pleasure) greater than hundreds (of material pleasures).

COMMENTARY

Many important points are made in this sūtra, which we should consider one by one. First, what do we mean by illumination? The material world is called 'darkness' because the real nature of things is hidden in this world. For example, you can see the body, but it is harder to know what someone is thinking, even harder to know what they believe in, even harder to understand their true intentions, and even harder to know their values. Since we cannot see all these things, therefore, people are able to cheat others by hiding their thoughts, beliefs, intentions, and values. The fundamental principle of a loving relationship is transparency. If we cannot be honest about who we are, then love may be based on deception, but it doesn't last. Therefore, illumination of the Lord's abode means that everyone knows everything about everyone. You cannot hide your true nature under a fancy suit or dress, pretending to be a devotee.

Second, there is a difference between the house and the door. Since we enter a house through the door, our true nature is discovered at the illuminated door. The owner of the house doesn't invite everyone in. Rather, He invites only those who meet the criteria for entering His abode. This means that every devotee cannot go to every abode. To go to an abode, one must have the qualifications necessary for the abode.

The arriving devotee is therefore screened at the door to check if they are qualified to enter that specific abode, and the illumination of the door means that nothing can be hidden from the screening process. In short, you cannot simply enter an abode by faking your qualifications.

Third, the Lord has many residences, each suited for the devotees in different moods and understandings of the Lord. A devotee is guided toward that specific abode that matches their understanding, and this guidance is based upon what they have experienced during their meditation. This means that the person who has no understanding of the Lord cannot reach any abode. But even if a devotee has some understanding, he must go to the abode that matches that understanding. The Lord displays many kinds of pastimes with his devotees. In some pastimes, He is the master, in others, He also acts like a friend, child, parent, or lover. Each such form or aspect of the Lord requires a different understanding of the Lord. So, there is a desire in the devotee about where he wants to go, and there is screening about the devotee's qualifications. This indicates a process of mutual acceptance. The devotee may desire to enter the intimate pastimes of the Lord, but unless he is qualified, he is not allowed. Similarly, the devotee may be qualified for certain abodes, but he may prefer to go to another abode. The abode is decided by the desiring and the deserving.

Fourth, we cannot go to the Lord's house unless the heart is freed from mundane desires and has experienced a pleasure hundreds of times greater than material pleasure. Unless this pleasure has been experienced, one would naturally remain more attracted to the mundane pleasures of the world.

Thus, four methods of screening are described here. We cannot depart for the spiritual abode unless we have freedom from mundane desires—we will go to another body suited for mundane enjoyment based on these desires. If we depart for the Lord's abode, we must know which abode we are going to arrive at, and that is possible only if we have a specific attraction to a form of the Lord based on prior understanding. Once we arrive at this destination, we will be screened at the door to determine if we are indeed qualified to enter that abode. And once we enter, everyone can see what we are thinking, feeling, intending, etc. because nothing can be hidden from others in the Lord's abode.

These descriptions clearly indicate that one doesn't go the Lord's abode simply by joining an institution, accepting a guru for fashion, wearing a fancy dress that shows renunciation, or other ways in which people are deceived in this world. Rather, one must be completely purified of material desires, have the attraction for a form of the Lord, be qualified to serve that form of the Lord, and then act according to those requirements along with everyone else.

Topic 10

QUESTION

If the devotee has the attraction for a specific form of the Lord, and desires to enter that specific abode, how does he find that specific Lord's abode?

4.2.18 (514)
रश्म्यनुसारी
raśmyanusārī

raśmi-anusārī—following the rays of light.

TRANSLATION

(The soul goes to an abode of the Lord) by following the rays of light.

COMMENTARY

If you want to go to a destination, merely having the goal of reaching that destination is not enough. You must also have a map to the place and should be able to follow the route on the map for a destination. Vedic cosmology describes the maps of the material and spiritual worlds. But even if you have the map, you still need to see the road signs that guide you to the destination. This sūtra describes the road signs to reach the destination. If you are traveling on a highway, you will often see the signs that indicate the distance and direction to a destination. The road signs to a destination are called the 'rays of light' in this sūtra. In modern science, light only has a frequency and a quantity of energy. But, as we have discussed earlier, these particles of energy also have meanings. Therefore, light is not meaningless; it always carries a meaning. The previous sūtra spoke about the innumerable abodes of the Lord, where a devotee goes according to their desire and qualification. However, a devotee may be qualified to go to many abodes, and he must choose one of the many abodes.

This choice is facilitated by the abodes advertising their presence by the light emanating from that abode. Every planet and star in the material universe advertises their presence by a light with a unique type of meaning, and these meanings are studied in astrology as having different effects on our lives. In the same way, the different abodes of the Lord advertise their light. The devotee then follows the advertisement to its source, which is called 'following the rays of light' in this sūtra. Thereby, he reaches the abode through the light.

We have all seen shopping malls with many kinds of stores which advertise their presence by a shining sign. The spiritual world is also like a shopping mall. You enter a mall if you want the thing that the store advertises, and if you are qualified to pay for what the store advertises (as we discussed in the previous sūtra, the doors of the Lord's abode check a devotee's qualification, so window shopping is not allowed). Thus, the spiritual world affords infinite pleasures, and there is choice for the type of pleasure that the devotee desires. By following the light from an abode, a devotee reaches one of the Lord's abodes.

QUESTION

But what if the devotee doesn't know about many abodes of the Lord, and their differences? How will he decide under the ignorance of these abodes? Is the choice of the Lord's abode made randomly or even under ignorance?

4.2.19 (515)

नशिनि इति चेत् न सम्बन्धस्य यावद्देहभावित्वाद् दर्शयति च

niśi na iti cet na sambandhasya yāvaddehabhāvitvād darśayati ca

niśi—the night or darkness; na—not; iti cet—if it be said; na—not; sambandhasya—according to the relationship; yāvat-deha-bhāvitvād—the type of body one has acquired; darśayati—(the soul is able to) see; ca—also.

TRANSLATION

If it be said (that the soul decides the abode) in darkness (we say) not so; whatever is not according to the relationship and unsuitable to the type of body one has acquired, is also not visible to the soul (for it to choose).

COMMENTARY

According to classical physics, light spreads uniformly in all directions, and therefore, we must receive light from every star and planet in the universe. However, according to atomic theory, light is only transmitted when the source and receiver are entangled. Thus, in classical physics, light is emitted as waves—and propagates equally in all directions. However, in atomic theory, light is emitted and absorbed as photons, which means that it is occasionally emitted and not to every destination. The contentious issue is whether can be emitted to every object in the universe (even occasionally). There are no good answers to this problem in atomic theory because we don't know how the source and the receiver of light are entangled. That explanation is provided in Vedic philosophy—we get to see something only if we have the requisite karma. Therefore, even in Vedic cosmology, the upper four planetary systems, the lower seven planetary systems, and the 28 hells are not visible to us. The influences on our life are controlled by the planets up till the polestar. Therefore, we can see things that are below the polestar—i.e., the parts of the zodiac (which cosmology calls 'galaxies') and the planets such as Mars, Venus, etc.

A similar principle is applied to the spiritual world in this sūtra by stating that not everyone sees every spiritual planet. Rather, these planets are seen according to one's relationship to the Lord, and the type of body one has. Notably, this means that not every type of body is found in every planet. The different relations and bodies constitute the devotee's 'deserving', and since the devotee deserves to enter these planets, therefore, the light from these planets reaches the devotee, to help him decide which planet he wants to go to. Hence, the decision is not totally random or blind. As we have said, the light has meaning, so one can obtain a description of the planet from the light. Therefore, the choices are informed, however, not every possibility is accessible for everyone.

Topic 11

QUESTION

Is this selective visibility of the Lord's abode unique to the spiritual world? Or can this also be applied to the transmigration in the material world?

4.2.20 (516)

अतश्चायने'पि दक्षिणे

ataścāyane'pi dakṣiṇe

atah—from this (we can understand); cā—also; ayane—moving; api—even; dakṣiṇe—southern.

TRANSLATION

From this (we can) also (know) even the southern movement of the (sun).

COMMENTARY

In Vedic cosmology, the Sun goes around the Meru mountain, and the orbit of the Sun is slightly higher on one side, and slightly lower on another side. As the Sun moves in its orbit, it goes upward for six months, and then downward for the next six months. The phase of upward movement is called Uttarāyana or northward movement. And the phase of downward movement is called Dakśhināyana or southward movement. The living entities who die during the Uttarāyana movement, are said to move to higher planetary systems. And the living entities who die during the Dakśhināyana movement enter the lower planetary systems, including hells. The Mahabharata describes how Bhīṣma fell to the ground due to Arjuna's arrows, during the Dakśhināyana phase. But he had his father's benediction to decide when he wanted die. So, he lay on a bed of arrows on the battlefield until the Sun turned toward Uttarāyana.

In the previous sūtra, it was said that the devotee ascending to the Lord's abode receives information only about those places that he is qualified to enter. This sūtra says that the same principle of selective visibility applies even to those leaving the body during the Dakśhināyana phase when the soul must enter the lower planetary systems according to his qualification for these planets. Similarly, from the narration about Bhīṣma, we can understand that the heavenly planets become visible to a soul based on their qualification. In short, if you are not qualified, then you cannot even see the planet's existence.

QUESTION

But there are also many yogis who ascend to higher planetary systems in this universe. Is their destination also determined by their qualification?

4.2.21 (517)

योगनिःपरतचि समरयेते समारते चैते

yoginaḥ prati ca smaryete smārte caite

yoginaḥ prati—regarding the yogis; ca—and; smaryete—in the type of remembrance; smārte—in the ritualized activities; ca—also; ete—these.

TRANSLATION

And, regarding the yogis, (the destination depends upon) these—the type of remembrance (meditation) and the ritualized activities (fire sacrifices).

COMMENTARY

This sūtra clearly spells out the role of guna and karma in the acquisition of the next body. Guna represents what we desire, and this sūtra refers to the guna as the type of meditation one performs—whatever one is meditating upon is what they are desiring. Karma represents what we deserve, and this sūtra refers to karma by the kinds of ritualized activities one has performed, as they lead to good karma. To enter a material planet, one needs both—i.e., one must be qualified to enter, and one must desire to enter. This is one of the differences between good and bad karma—bad karma doesn't give us the choice of whether we want to suffer (i.e., the suffering is forced) but good karma gives us a choice about whether we want to enjoy. Therefore, a person with good karma can renounce pleasures, but the person with bad karma cannot renounce distress. Based on one's qualification, the relevant places of destination are visible, and among those that are visible, one can choose where one wants to go.

For the person going to one of the many lower planetary systems, more than one planet can be visible if they indeed deserve to enter them. However, for the hellish planets, typically only one planet would be visible, which means that one doesn't have a choice about how the suffering must be endured.

In the spiritual world, there is no karma. Therefore, the definition of qualification changes—the qualification is the devotee's mood. There is a subtle difference between mood and desire. For example, the desire can be to see the Lord as a father, mother, friend, servant, lover, etc. But the mood is whether one feels that kind of emotion to enter such a relationship. Desiring and feeling are subtle distinctions within the emotional state of a person. The qualification is whether a person feels the emotion appropriate for the desire. In short, *being* a friend is not a designation of a friend; rather, one must *feel* the friend's emotion.

This idea can be understood by looking at ordinary relationships. For example, a couple can get married, because they want to get married. But they may not feel attracted to each other, although they want to stay in the marriage. In this world, people look at various things before they get married—financial security, good looks, family status, etc. The Lord doesn't see any of these. However, He doesn't enter a relationship if there are only wants and no feelings. If someone cannot develop the feelings that make a good relationship, simply wanting to have such a relationship is not adequate. Therefore, the qualification is not karma. The qualification is the capacity to experience a type of feeling.

SECTION 3

Topic 1

QUESTION

How does the performance of fire sacrifices lead to good karma? The creation of good karma is understandable if we think about action and consequence. But it seems strange that fire sacrifices lead one to higher planets.

4.3.1 (518)
अर्चिरादिना तत्प्रथितेः
arcirādinā tatprathiteḥ

arciḥra—fire sacrifices; ādinā—eating, offering or etc.; tat-prathiteḥ—that (the Lord) is celebrated.

TRANSLATION

By offering fire sacrifices, that (the Lord) is celebrated (or worshipped).

COMMENTARY

In the Vedic system, fire sacrifices have been performed for ages as a system to worship the Lord, as well as the demigods. The sacrifice involves throwing grains such as rice into the fire. However, before the offering is made, the thing being offered is imbued with a meaning by the chanting of the mantra. For example, a worshipper takes a pinch of rice in their hand, chants a mantra to imbue that rice with a meaning, and then offers the rice into the fire. The rice is held in the hand from the beginning to the end of the mantra, and then, rice is offered into the fire by chanting *svāhā* which means "I give myself to you". What is being given is not the rice, but the rice as a symbol of meaning.

The fire can also represent the Lord, or one of the numerous demigods. Therefore, the fire also must be symbolized as the mouth of the Lord or one of the many demigods. This is also achieved by chanting mantras, after lighting the fire, to invite the Lord or the demigods to be present in the sacrifice as the fire. Thus, just as the rice becomes a symbol of meaning, similarly, the fire also symbolizes a personality, and both are achieved by the chanting of mantras.

The person making the offering is the subordinate principle, and the person to whom the offering is made is the dominant principle. The rice and the fire are just symbols of the person making the offering, and the person receiving the offering. Thus, by throwing rice into fire, essentially, the worshipper offers himself to the worshipper, although the offering is made through rice and fire. When a person becomes a devotee of the Lord, then he offers himself directly to the Lord. Now, rice and fire are not involved as intermediaries. Therefore, the process of devotional surrender and the process of a fire sacrifice are very similar in principles, however, they are implemented in different ways.

Topic 2

QUESTION

But why fire specifically? Could it not be water or air? Why isn't an offering made into water or air also considered the celebration of the Lord?

4.3.2 (519)
वायुमब्दात् अवशिषवशिषाभ्याम्
vāyumabdāt aviśeṣaviśeṣābhyām

vāyum—air; abdāt—from water; aviśeṣa-viśeṣābhyām—from the non-specific and specific.

TRANSLATION
From non-specific to specific, from air to water.

COMMENTARY

The use of fire in a sacrifice—as representing the mouth of the Lord—raises some questions: Why fire? What not air or water? After all, we could just throw the grains of rice in the wind or into a body or water, after symbolizing them as the mouths of the Lord through a mantra. If fire can be symbolized to be the Lord's mouth, by a mantra, then water and air could also be symbolized in the same way. Then why aren't systems of air or water sacrifices found in the scriptures? Why are sacrifices always performing using fire, and not air or water?

A similar question could also have been raised earlier when it was said that the devotee is guided to the Lord's abode through light. One might wonder: Why light? Or, why seeing? Could it not be sound, touch, taste, or smell? Any of these can carry the information from a source to a receiver. For example, one could say that the devotee can be pushed to the Lord's abode by the pressure of air on the skin. Similarly, a devotee could be guided to the Lord's abode by aroma. So, given these alternatives, what is so special about seeing?

This sūtra says that air and water are too non-specific and specific (respectively). What does this mean? We have discussed earlier about how the meaning in the mind expands from a subtle to a gross meaning. The subtle meaning is abstract, while the gross meaning is detailed. For example, the idea cow is abstract, and the shape of the cow is detailed. The successive perceptions of sound, touch, sight, taste, and smell add further details to the previous perception. Thus, sound contains touch, sight, taste, and smell in unmanifest form, but in touch sound is manifest, in sight, touch and sound are manifest, and so on. Accordingly, the air element is a non-specific or abstract representation of meaning, whereas the water element is a specific or a detailed representation of meaning. Since fire is between air and water, therefore, it is more specific than air, and less specific than water. The purport is that the fire element is an optimum representation of meaning—neither too detailed, nor too abstract.

We must note that since the grains and the fire are symbolized by mantras, therefore, a more abstract symbolizing would require the utterance of fewer sounds, but they would also be more difficult to pronounce. We can call this more 'compressed' encoding of meaning. Likewise, a more detailed symbolizing would require many more sounds, however, they would also be easily pronounceable. We can call this more 'expanded' meaning. As an analogy, scientific laws are expressed succinctly through formulae, but the full meanings of these formulae are harder to understand. Conversely, to explain these laws, we can employ long-form descriptions, which are also easier to understand.

The problem of semantic condensation leading to difficulty in uttering and understanding the sounds is seen while studying Vedic texts. The Sanskrit of the four Vedas is incredibly hard, and that is because it is incredibly condensed. Vedic mantras, for example, employ sounds like 'grim', 'shrim', 'klim', 'hrim', etc. and there is practically nobody who understands what these sounds mean. As a result, the popular phrase 'mumbo-jumbo' is used—somewhat appropriately. However, these are not meaningless sounds; they are just highly condensed meanings. Then, the Sanskrit of the sūtra-based texts, such as the six systems of philosophy (including the Vedānta Sūtra), has an intermediate level of difficulty. As we have seen, the meaning of each word depends on the context of what has and has not been previously said; the same sentence, therefore, has different meanings depending on the context. Finally, the Sanskrit of the Purāna and Itihāsa is the easiest; they are like long-form narrations where every word has a dictionary meaning, and the meaning changes only occasionally based on the context. Therefore, we can easily quote these texts while teaching others. The sūtras must be memorized and used as mathematical formulae, which can be understood, but the understanding is not for everyone. Finally, the Vedic mantras must be perfected by pronunciation, rhythm, and meter, and quite often, there is very little to comprehend regarding their meaning.

To return to the main point, once we understand the differences between abstract and detailed expressions, and the associated difficulties with more condensed (a minor error drastically changes the meaning) and the more expanded (they will necessitate very long performances), then we can see how something between the condensed and expanded methods would seem appropriate—it is easily remembered, uttered, less prone to mistakes, and not very long. This sūtra essentially says that the fire format of sacrifices is chosen over air or water sacrifices since that makes the sacrificial performance more convenient.

Topic 3

QUESTION

But you are implicitly accepting that even water and air could be used for sacrifices—even though the performance of such sacrifices would be harder?

4.3.3 (520)

तडितोऽधि वरुणःसंबन्धात्

taḍito'dhi varuṇaḥ saṃbandhāt

taḍito—fire; adhi—after; varuṇaḥ—varuna; saṃbandhāt—due to the appropriateness.

TRANSLATION

After fire, varuna (water) (is accepted) due to the appropriateness.

COMMENTARY

In the previous sūtra, fire sacrifices were accepted due to their ease, however, others have not been rejected. Therefore, it is implicitly acknowledged that the mantras of the four Vedas could be different if they were to be used for air or water sacrifices. The four Vedas would be totally incomprehensible if the mantras were meant for air sacrifices, and they would be significantly longer if the mantras were meant for water sacrifices. This sūtra says that if one must perform other sacrifices, then the water sacrifices are more appropriate.

In short, instead of chanting mantras that are even more incomprehensible, it is preferred to chant mantras that are longer. This would naturally elongate the duration of the sacrifice. Similarly, the medium through which the offerings in the sacrifice reach their intended recipient would also change. Elements such as fire, water, and air have their own deities. In a fire sacrifice, the deity is called Agni (somewhat confusingly, the fire element is also called agni). In a water sacrifice, the deity is called Varuna (although in this case, the element is called apah or abda). Therefore, the previous sūtra could also be understood as referring to the demigod Agni, whereas this sūtra refers to the demigod Varuna.

Water sacrifices are not alien to Vedic culture, but their importance has been lesser. The offering to the forefathers, for example, is made in water, rather than in fire. Similarly, sometimes, the Sun is worshipped through water, rather than fire. Ultimately, these mediums of worship aren't very important. Greater importance is attached to the mantras, which are adapted for a medium.

Topic 4

QUESTION

Under what circumstances could one prefer an air sacrifice over the other forms of sacrifice (i.e., the water and fire sacrifices mentioned previously)?

4.3.4 (521)
आतविाहकिाःतल्लङ्गिात्
ātivāhikāḥ talliṅgāt

ātivāhikāḥ—faster than vehicle; tat-liṅgāt—due to the symbols of that.

TRANSLATION

Due to the symbols of that (meaning) being faster than the vehicle.

COMMENTARY

All Vedic mantras follow a meter, which are categorized by the length of the meter. Thus, there are meters that are 12, 18, 24, 30, 36, 42, and 48 symbols long (each successive meter has 6 extra symbols than the previous one). The maximum size of the meters is said to be 72 symbols, so the total number of meters is sometimes accepted to be 12. The simplest meter is called *dvāśa-ākshara* or 12 symbols long. For example, the mantra Om Namo Bhagavate Vāsudevāya is a 12-symbol mantra. The 12 phonemes in the above mantra are om-na-mo-bha-ga-va-te-va-su-de-va-ya, and since each symbol requires one unit of time, so, the 12 phonemes in the mantra require 12 units of time.

However, there can be some mantras in which the phonemes do not fit the individual units of time. An example would be a half-phoneme which requires half a symbol and therefore half the time needed for a regular phoneme. In such a case, two such half-phonemes could be combined to create a complex phoneme. But it is also possible that this half phoneme is followed by several full phonemes, and eventually a half-phoneme. If one looks at the wave patterns of mantras of such complex phonemes, then the pattern must change halfway through a time interval. This change can continue for several phonemes, until another half-phoneme is encountered, when the pattern returns to normal. To utter such a mantra, the tongue needs to change pattern halfway through the interval, utter each of the subsequent phonemes over two halves of two successive intervals, until the half-phoneme reverts the pattern back to normal. Due to the change of pattern halfway through the interval, twice the information must be encoded in that interval—once for each of the half-phonemes. This is when the symbol rate is seen to be twice as fast as the clock frequency.

When we encode information in any medium, the process is called modulating a carrier. The carrier has a constant frequency, and it is like the constant ticking clock in which you can insert one symbol per period. If the rate of transmitted symbols is slower than the carrier frequency, then a method called 'frequency modulation' is employed. If the rate of transmission is equal to the carrier frequency, then a method called 'amplitude modulation' is employed. And if the rate of transmission is greater than the carrier frequency, then a method called 'phase modulation' is employed. Phase modulation is basically changing a wave pattern within a single cycle of a wave. With advancing technology, modern circuits can fit anywhere between 2 to 64 symbols in a single cycle. For example, when 2 symbols are fit into a cycle, the method is called BPSK (Binary Phase Shift Keying) and when 4 symbols are fit into a cycle, then then the method is called QPSK (Quad Phase Shift Keying). When 64 symbols are fit into a single cycle, then the method of modulation is called 64-PSK. In all such cases, the wave form changes pattern multiple times during a single time cycle.

While chanting mantras, the goal is not to increase the data rate of mantras, so greater speed isn't for faster chanting. It is needed due to complex sounds which constitute a single phoneme, and yet are not simple phonemes. When mantras use complex phonemes, then the symbol rate is greater than the carrier frequency, and this sūtra says that all sacrifices that require such mantras should be performed through the medium of air, rather than water or fire.

We can see from these sūtras why most Vedic rituals are forbidden in the present age—the rituals are long and complex, our pronunciations are imperfect, we are unable to keep time and the rhythm, and, of course, we don't understand the meaning. Hence, in this age, only the chanting of God's names is suggested. Some of these names also involve complex phonemes. For example, the sound Kṛṣṇa contains a complex phoneme—kṛṣ—in which kṛ and ṣ are half-phonemes—but there are no restrictions to the chanting of the sound Kṛṣṇa. Therefore, we can surmise that the recommendation of this sūtra is that the air is the preferred method for complex phonemes, not the only method.

QUESTION

If the methods of water and air are sometimes accepted, why are the number of sacrifices based on the water and the air methods so limited?

4.3.5 (522)
उभयव्यामोहात्तत्सदिधेः
ubhayavyāmohāttatsiddheḥ

ubhaya—both; vyāmohāt—due to mental confusion; tat-siddheḥ—it is proven.

TRANSLATION

Both (the air and water methods) create mental confusion, it is proven.

COMMENTARY

The earlier sūtra indirectly implied that the sacrifices based on water and fire will be either too specific or too non-specific, and we discussed how they will either lead to very complex or very long pronunciations. If this wasn't clear enough, then this sūtra states explicitly that these methods lead to excessive mental confusion, and that has been established (perhaps by employing them). In short, the performance of fire sacrifices is not an accident, even though it sometimes seems mumbo-jumbo, and the method has been established after considering other methods, finding them too complex, and rejecting them.

QUESTION

You say that it has been proven, implying that other methods were employed, tested, and then rejected. But we don't find such descriptions in the śrutī. How should we understand their absence from these scriptures?

4.3.6 (523)

वैद्युतेनैव ततःतच्छ्रुतेः

vaidyutenaiva tataḥ tacchruteḥ

vaidyutena—certainly by the method of fire; eva—alone; tataḥ—thereafter; tat-śruteḥ—that (method) was presented as the śrutī.

TRANSLATION

(It was established) that by the method of fire alone (sacrifices should be performed) thereafter, that (the sacrifices) was presented as the śrutī.

COMMENTARY

In an earlier sūtra we discussed three claims about the origination of scriptures—(1) they were spoken by the Lord, (2) they were written at a specific time by an author, and (3) they can be rationally confirmed because they are logically expanded from the knowledge received from the Lord. Now, this sūtra adds a fourth method of experimental confirmation. It says that although the scriptures logically followed from the knowledge received by revelation, what we see as the śrutī isn't merely the revealed knowledge. Rather, that revealed knowledge was expanded into many forms (e.g., the rituals for water and air), then these methods were tested, and some of them were found to lead to mental confusion. Those methods were ignored, and only those that were found viable for the general population, and effective in producing the results, were presented as the śrutī. Again, the distinction between the śrutī and smriti can be dissolved through this distinction because the śrutī is not merely untested revelations. Rather, knowledge in a summarized form was revealed to Brahma, who then provided it to his sons, who then expanded this knowledge in many forms through logical inferences, tested the knowledge, and then presented the methods that work as the śrutī, while the other methods were discarded.

Topic 5

QUESTION

You are saying that the rituals were presented as śrutī after testing, and you have said that the śrutī is revealed knowledge. Generally, experimental methods are obtained after trial and error. But that doesn't square with the idea that the knowledge was also revealed. How do we reconcile these claims?

4.3.7 (524)
कार्यं बादरःिअस्य गत्युपपत्तेः
kāryaṃ bādariḥ asya gatyupapatteḥ

kāryaṃ—the rituals; bādariḥ—Bādari; asya—its; gati-upapatteḥ—the activities are produced by logical inference.

TRANSLATION

Bādari (says that) the activities in a ritual are obtained by logical reasoning.

COMMENTARY

When scientific knowledge is derived by trial-and-error, or speculation and experimentation, then we don't know upfront if a theory will work. Sometimes the theory works, and then we present it as truth. Sometimes, we find something working, and then we make a theory for it. But there is another approach for the formation of procedures and theories—we can start with the goal of what we want to achieve, find the position of that goal in the space of all possibilities, then compute the path to this destination in space, and finally convert this path into an activity and test whether it achieves the intended goals.

The problem today is that we don't know that there is a space in which all the possibilities exist eternally. We think that whatever we cannot see, also doesn't exist. So, we must first see its existence, and then we can form a theory about it. Or, whatever theory we formulate must be based on what we have already seen. Thus, all modern science is limited by what we can observe.

But the method of scriptures is not like that. It basically starts by asking: What are the different types of goals people might have? And, how can we achieve these goals? Then based on the knowledge of the Absolute Truth, they make logical inferences and identify the path from the present state to the goal, test that path as a procedure, and then describe it as a method of goal attainment. Thus, many scriptures provide detailed descriptions of reality, and other scriptures simply say that to attain this goal you must do this, live this kind of life, or perform these procedures. By producing a compendium of procedures—which are known as yajñá—the scriptures save people from the detailed investigation into the nature of reality before they fulfill their goals. However, since some people may be curious about how these procedures were arrived at, why they work, and what other procedures may be discovered using the same process through which the existing procedures were discovered, the scriptures also provide a detailed understanding of reality. Thus, the theoretical and practical aspects of the scriptures are interconnected. The practical aspects are for those who just want to attain some goals, without understanding the underlying details. They are like manuals to drive a car from one place to another. The theoretical aspects of the scriptures are the descriptions of a car's working.

This sūtra states that even the rituals were not derived by experimentation. Rather, one started out with a goal and found the method to achieve that goal. The goal-driven derivation is possible in a semantic reasoning system, so the term *upapatti* is used here. The difference is this. In an axiomatic reasoning system, we start with the premise and try to derive a theorem, but there is no way to determine if the method of proof is getting closer to a theorem or not. Therefore, the construction of a proof becomes a method by trial-and-error, and there are numerous conjectures in modern mathematics which remain unproven. However, in a semantic reasoning system, we start with the axiom, and we set the goal as the theorem's proof. And the system will then find the proof to the theorem automatically because it can determine if the proof is closer or farther from the theorem. In short, *upapatti* here means an automated theorem-proving system, in which the axioms are given, the theorem is the goal, and the proof is the path that connects the axioms to the goal. Once this proof is identified, then it can also be practically tested. The test would begin from the axioms, follow the path traced by the proof as a procedure, and finally construct the desired goal as the intended theorem. Thus, the methods of reason and experiment are identical—you can construct the desired object by a process, which you could theoretically derive earlier. Hence, there is no need to be amazed by such claims of deriving the rituals by logical inference. These things are imminently feasible in a semantic reasoning system—if the system is complete.

QUESTION

But how can we say that the theoretical methods of construction will produce the desired results? What seems to work on paper doesn't seem to always work in practice. Thus, we find that our plans often fail in practice, even though they seemed to be perfectly in order on paper. This is generally because in our planning we fail to foresee the situations that can thwart our plans. So, if you say that by knowing the procedure, we know the method of attainment, that seems to not take into account the many unforeseen causes of failure.

4.3.8 (525)

वशीषतित्वाच्च

viśeṣitatvācca

viśeṣitatvāt—from being just like the specifics; ca—also.

TRANSLATION

Also, from being just like (we know) the specifics.

COMMENTARY

If you want to reach a destination by road, you might start out with a roadmap on how to reach that destination. However, at some point in your travel, you might find the road is blocked or under construction. Then you retrace your steps on the map and find the next best road. Similarly, the procedures given in scriptures may not always exactly match the most suitable path to a destination. In such a situation, one can abandon the path, and take another path that takes us to the destination. Therefore, the door is open to such modifications—provided the main road is inaccessible. However, generally, if the main road is open, we would not try to create a path just for the sake of it.

In the same way, the scriptures provide some roadmaps to the destination, but it would be incorrect to suppose that every type of hurdle is anticipated in the scriptures. When such hurdles are encountered, then adjustments can be made. These adjustments should, however, not violate the moral principles, unless there is no other way. Just as meat-eating is recommended when one is dying, and there is no alternative path, similarly, the principle of the least amount of sacrifice to deliver the greatest amount of benefit applies. This sūtra states that by studying the specifics of the situation, we can also adapt the procedures to attain the goal. Therefore, there is a recommended path, which should work in most cases. But if it is not, then changes are acceptable.

QUESTION

But doesn't it mean that people may change all Vedic procedures by citing the specifics of their situation? How does one guard against such changes?

4.3.9 (526)

सामीप्यात् तु तद्व्यपदेशः

sāmīpyāt tu tadvyapadeśaḥ

sāmīpyāt—due to nearness; tu—but; tat-vyapadeśaḥ—that is stated.

TRANSLATION

But it is stated that (the alternative paths are selected) by their nearness.

COMMENTARY

We have discussed how a path is determined by the proximity to the destination—i.e., the shorter path to destination is preferred. In this sūtra, another restriction is applied, namely, that the alternative path (if it must be chosen) must be near or close to the path described in the scriptures. For example, if you are traveling to a destination, and you find a blocked road, you don't go back to your home and start on a completely different path. You rather find the smallest deviation from the predetermined path to bypass the current hurdle. In the same way, the adjustment of paths doesn't entail the invention of arbitrary new paths. Rather, these adjustments are subject to (1) hurdles being encountered, (2) the smallest necessary adjustment from the path, and (3) the goal still being reachable by the new path. What is small is further determined semantically, rather than physically. For example, just because a road is blocked, we don't drive through someone's house, just because it seems to be the shortest path. We rather find the nearest legitimate path. In the same way, we should aim for the nearest path, but also a legitimate path. In short, we should minimize the changes to the path, and not violate moral principles in selecting paths.

QUESTION

If we are still not able to find the nearest path or smallest change to complete the sacrifice due to hurdles in its execution, what should a person do?

4.3.10 (527)

कार्यात्यये तदध्यक्षेण सहातःपरम् अभिधानात्

kāryātyaye tadadhyakṣeṇa sahātaḥ param abhidhānāt

kārye-atyaye—on the completion of the sacrifice; tat-adhyakṣeṇa saha—along with the ruler of that (sacrifice); ataḥ param—therefore the supreme (Lord); abhidhānāt—due to bringing in close connection.

TRANSLATION

(If the hurdles encountered during a sacrifice cannot be mitigated by the nearest adjustment, then path selection must be based on the criterion that) upon the completion of the sacrifice, along with the ruler of that (sacrifice—e.g., a demigod), even the supreme (Lord) (also) comes closer (to the worshipper).

COMMENTARY

The Lord is the remedy to all problems. He can correct every mistake, and He can make every imperfection perfect. Therefore, this sūtra says that if you are struggling to find the correct path under the present circumstances, then think about the Lord, and what will bring you closer to Him. This is again not an endorsement for wanton disregard for rules and regulations. It is permissible when the prescribed path is not working, and when there are no easy alternatives (because each alternative may not be very near to the original path).

QUESTION

But the śrutī doesn't permit one to change the procedures. They are meant to be strictly followed by the practitioners or they don't produce results.

4.3.11 (528)

समृतेश्च

smṛteśca

smṛteḥ—from the smriti; ca—also.

TRANSLATION

From the smriti also (we can understand how to adjust the regulations).

COMMENTARY

An illustrative example of the adjustment of the rules and regulations is provided in the story of Maharaja Ambarīṣa, as narrated in the Śrīmad Bhagavatam. Maharaja Ambarīṣa was fasting for Ekādaśi while Sage Durvāsā arrives at his palace. Maharaja Ambarīṣa invites the sage to accept food at his palace, and after accepting the invitation, the Sage goes for a bath in the river Yamuna. After the bath, Sage Durvāsā sits in meditation and time passes by. Since the time for breaking the Ekādaśi fast is about to pass, Maharaja Ambarīṣa faces a dilemma. Should he break the fast by eating something to preserve the vow of Ekādaśi? Or, should he not break the fast until the Sage Durvāsā has eaten? It was customary in Vedic culture to feed the guests before the host eats, which is good moral principle, but not on par with the Ekādaśi vow. The guru of Maharaja Ambarīṣa advises him to break the fast by drinking water.

When Sage Durvāsā returns from his bath, he realizes that Maharaja Ambarīṣa has already taken water, and he becomes very angry. Under this anger, Sage Durvāsā pulls a clutch of hair from his head and throws it on the ground to produce a demon which would kill Maharaja Ambarīṣa. However, Lord Viṣṇu sends His Sudarśana Chakra to protect Maharaja Ambarīṣa. The Chakra kills the demon, and then pursues Sage Durvāsā, who runs everywhere for shelter, but is unable to find protection. Finally, Sage Durvāsā goes to Lord Narayana for protection, but the Lord says that He is unable to protect someone who has offended the devotee. Then, Sage Durvāsā returns to Maharaja Ambarīṣa and begs for his forgiveness. Meanwhile, a year has elapsed, and Maharaja Ambarīṣa is still standing in the same place for Sage Durvāsā to return so he can feed him, surviving just by drinking water. Upon seeing the grievous condition of Sage Durvāsā, Maharaja Ambarīṣa prays to the Chakra to become peaceful. The Chakra then stops burning Sage Durvāsā, and the glories of the Lord's devotees are revealed. The main point is that even if ordinary people are offended by our actions, if the Lord is pleased, then these offences are disregarded. Therefore, the Lord's pleasure is the supremely beneficent goal of our lives.

QUESTION

But many people consider the rules of the śrutī to be higher than the descriptions in the smriti. They say that obedience to the rules and regulations is essential, and without such rules, the results of the sacrifice are not obtained. What should be the answer to these claims that contradict the smriti?

4.3.12 (529)

परं जैमनिःमुख्यत्वात्

paraṃ jaiminiḥ mukhyatvat

param—the Supreme Lord; jaiminiḥ—(says) Jaimini; mukhyatvāt—on account of that being the primary purpose (of the sacrifice).

TRANSLATION

(Even) Jaimini says that the Supreme Lord is the main purpose of the Vedic sacrifices (so who else is qualified to claim a higher position for rules?).

COMMENTARY

Many arguments about the temporarity of the Vedic rituals have been offered in the previous sūtras. First, it was said that these rituals have been derived from the Absolute Truth by logical inference. Second, it was said that in the process of derivation, many rituals were abandoned as they created mental confusion. Third, it was stated that often there are difficulties in following these procedures, and the procedures can therefore be adjusted if that brings the worshipper closer to the Lord, and examples from smriti can be used as affirmations of this principle. However, if someone still insists that the rules of śrutī must be upheld, then the sūtra cites the example of Jaimini—the foremost proponent of these rituals—and states that even he accepts the Lord to be the supreme.

The conclusion is that the rules and regulations are prescribed to help people if they want to achieve certain outcomes and to prevent people from behaving arbitrarily. But all such principles are subordinate to the Lord's pleasure. Whenever possible, these regulations must be strictly followed, and the least amount of deviation was prescribed earlier. But, ultimately, the only inviolable principle is that the Lord is satisfied by the performance of all such rules. When a religious practice blatantly disregards these regulations, then it falls victim to immorality. On the other hand, when a religion blindly follows these regulations, then it becomes fanatical and superstitious. Therefore, both blind obedience and blind disregard for these regulations are considered unacceptable.

QUESTION

Since you mention Jaimini, you are accepting the Mīmāṁsā philosophical system as a valid method of concluding the Lord being the supreme as well?

4.3.13 (530)
दर्शनाच्च
darśanācca

darśanāt—due to the philosophical systems; ca—also.

TRANSLATION

(The Lord can be accepted as the supreme purpose) due to the philosophical systems (demonstrating the purpose as the supreme) as well.

COMMENTARY

Matter can be controlled by choices, but choices need to be regulated. This regulation comes to us as rules of social order, the organization of objects into functional structures, and even the formation of institutions and societies. Apart from being good for life here, these regulations have a purpose—to become free of all regulations. When the soul is purified of material contaminations, then he learns how to use his freedom responsibly. The impersonalist says that we never get rid of rules of regulations unless we merge into Brahman. Therefore, the regulations of scriptures must be mandatorily followed. The personalist says that one is free of these regulations when one has learned to use their freedom responsibly. What is responsible use of freedom? It is the recognition that everything was created by the Lord and must be engaged in His service. When the soul acts responsibly, then the rules and regulations don't apply. As we have discussed earlier, even in this world, society can be egalitarian—i.e., everyone can act responsibly, without being bound by rules and regulations. Since most people don't act responsibly in this way, therefore, a hierarchical system of organization is prescribed in which the responsible classes have greater freedom and the irresponsible classes have less freedom. But when society degrades to a point where nobody acts responsibly, then the hierarchy is flattened to a system in which nobody is free of rules and regulations.

Therefore, rules and regulations are not permanent; they are prescribed to bring a person to the point of responsible action. As one starts acting responsibly, the rules can be reduced, and ultimately, eliminated totally. The freedom from rules and regulations, rights and duties, rewards and punishments, is the highest goal of life. The rules are mandatory for the irresponsible people, but they are optional for the responsible people. The responsible people follow the rules not because they are bound by them, but because these rules get the best results. But when they do not get the best results, then they can be selectively applied, modified, or completely rejected. Thus, a philosopher should ask: What is the purpose of rules and regulations? Is it merely obedience to the rules? Or do we get out of the rules when we begin acting responsibly?

In Sāñkhya philosophy, the world comprises objects, rules, and purpose. The objects are organized by rules, and the rules are chosen by the purpose; the body is an object, the mind constitutes the rules, and the soul is the purpose. A more advanced understanding is that the purpose is in the soul, but the soul is not the purpose. Similarly, in Mīmāṃsā, the rules and regulations are meant to achieve a purpose—nobody accepts the idea that rules are self-justified.

QUESTION

Some people say that the fact that these can be adjusted based on time, place, and situation, means that such rituals and procedures are basically a method of entrapment to engage the mundane mind toward progressive activities, but ultimately, all such rituals must be considered delusional activities.

4.3.14 (531)
न च कार्ये प्रतपित्तत्यभसिंधिः
na ca kārye pratipattyabhisaṃdhiḥ

na—not; ca—and; kārye—in the actions; pratipatti—the rules and regulations; abhisaṃdhiḥ—deliberately deceptive.

TRANSLATION

The rules and regulations in the actions are not deliberately deceptive.

COMMENTARY

The impersonalist oscillates between opposite extremes, trying to justify his untenable positions. At one end, he says that the rules must be strictly followed, and he criticizes devotees if they adjust the rules for serving the Lord. However, if someone asks them: If your rules are so sacrosanct, then why are they different from one scripture to another? Then, the impersonalist says that all the rules and regulations are yet another form of māyā or delusion. The central point of impersonalism is to deny the existence of an eternal purpose. Without a purpose, you must make opposite claims—(1) there are just rules without a purpose, or (2) if the rules are contradictory, then they must be illusory.

The devotee instead says that the contradictory rules are different prescriptions for different people. The man suffering from fever must apply a cold patch, and the man suffering from cold must apply a hot patch. The hot and cold is contextual, variable, and temporary; the goal is singular—good health. Therefore, there are no universal rules. However, there are good contextual rules—e.g., that cold needs a hot patch, and fever needs a cold patch. The rejection of universality of the rules is not the rejection of even the contextually good rules. Finally, as the context changes, even these contextual rules must be adapted. For example, someone suffering from both cold and fever needs to sit in a fresh, open, and airy atmosphere, because fresh air equally counteracts both cold and heat. The rigid application of rules won't produce health; and the rules and regulations are important only because they lead a person to health.

Therefore, both extremes of universally applying rules, and treating all rules as illusions, must be rejected. Universal acceptance and rejection must be replaced by a contextual acceptance and rejection, with the choice of the rule in each context driven by a singular purpose—the restoration of health.

Topic 6

QUESTION

So, do you recommend blind obedience and blind rejection of rules?

4.3.15 (532)

अप्रतीकालम्बनान्नयतीति बादरायणःउभयथाऽदोषात् तत्क्रतुश्च

apratīkālambanānnayatīti bādarāyaṇaḥ ubhayathā'doṣāt
tatkratuśca

a pratīka-ālambanāt—by not taking shelter of symbols; nayati—
the leader; iti bādarāyaṇaḥ—so says Bādarayana; ubhayathā—in both
cases; adoṣāt—from absence of faults; tat-kratuḥ—does that (which
pleases the Lord); ca—and.

TRANSLATION

Bādarayana says that the true leader by not taking shelter of symbols (i.e., the rules and regulations), in both cases (i.e., whether the
rules are followed or not), due to having no fault does that (which
pleases the Lord) also.

COMMENTARY

In every society today, there is a battle between those who demand
more regulation, and those who demand less regulation. Those
demanding more regulation say that the people are misbehaving, so
they must be controlled by rules. And those demanding less rules say
that when people are given freedom, the best results are produced.
The devotee of the Lord rejects both extremes. He says that if one is
devoted to the Lord, then whether the rules are followed, or they are
rejected, there is no fault, because these rules are merely the symbols
or representations of a higher purpose. If the purpose is fulfilled, then
the rules and regulations are not themselves sacrosanct. This stage of
devotion, however, is fully cognizant of the laws of moral action. If
this principle is blindly imitated by an ordinary person, then they are
implicated in the consequences of their actions, which causes them to
suffer and enjoy. This is because an ordinary person whimsically picks
whatever rules he likes and rejects whichever rules he doesn't. The
sole criterion for deciding upon rules is his convenience. The devotee,
however, picks the rules and regulations based on the Lord's pleasure.

QUESTION

To determine what will please the Lord requires a person to fully know the Lord. How can one decide what to do unless they know the Lord?

4.3.16 (533)

वशिेषं च दर्शयति

viśeṣaṃ ca darśayati

viśeṣaṃ—the qualities (of the Lord); ca—also; darśayati—sees.

TRANSLATION

(The devotee) also sees the qualities (of the Lord).

COMMENTARY

This sūtra rejects the whimsical selection of rules and regulations by one who doesn't see the Lord or understands what pleases Him. An impersonalist subordinates our free will to rules and regulations. The anarchist subordinates the rules and regulations to our free will. But a devotee subordinates our free will to the Lord's free will. In short, the devotee learns to act just like the Lord would act in each situation. By acting just like the Lord, the devotee becomes non-different from the Lord. Since the Lord is not implicated by karma, similarly, the devotee is also not implicated by karma. But to act in this way, one must intimately know the Lord and ask: How will He act in this situation?

By this constant remembrance of the Lord and meditating upon Him to decide what we need to do, the devotee begins to see the Lord. Thus, by trying to act just like the Lord one gains an understanding of the Lord, and by this understanding, the he acts like the Lord even more. Thus, as soon as someone reposes their faith in the Lord, both their knowledge and actions improve—better actions lead to better knowledge, and better knowledge leads to better actions. This cyclic process of improvement is different from a blind acceptance and blind rejection of rules. It is about being non-different from the Lord.

SECTION 4

Topic 1

QUESTION

Does this mean that the Lord's devotees are authorized to create rules and regulations for society, even if they are different from the scriptures?

4.4.1 (534)

संपद्यावरि्भावःस्वेनशब्दात्

saṃpadyāvirbhāvaḥ svenaśabdāt

saṃpadya—having attained; āvirbhāvaḥ—the manifestation of emotions (of the love of the Lord); svenaśabdāt—from that which is called his own.

TRANSLATION

(Those) having attained the manifestation of the emotional state (of the love of the Lord) from that which is called his own (personality) (are also qualified to propound rules and regulations for the general masses of people).

COMMENTARY

A devotee leads the world in three ways— (1) by explaining the nature of the Absolute Truth through scripture, reason, and observation, (2) by becoming the example and embodiment of this understanding, and (3) by propounding the rules and regulations for others who want to attain the same state. Many people may explain this understanding partially and imperfectly, and they are themselves not the perfect embodiments of this understanding. They are not considered qualified to prescribe the rules and regulations for the others.

Only one who has attained the emotional state of love of the Lord is described in this sūtra as being qualified to become leader, who can prescribe rules and regulations. Others are qualified to teach the understanding of the Absolute Truth, and practice this understanding themselves to become the perfect embodiments of the understanding. However, in general, they should refrain from trying to propound rules and regulations for others. This is mainly because there are innumerable injunctions about what must be done, and these injunctions apply to different people, places, times, and circumstances. Which rule and injunction applies to which person, in which place, time, and circumstance, needs a profound understanding of all four. When rules are misapplied or universalized, then the ultimate aim of achieving the Lord's love is missed, even if some temporary benefits may be attained by the application of rules.

The spiritual master is one who is expert in adjusting the injunctions for a person, in a time, place, or situation. And the qualification of the spiritual master is that he must have attained the emotional love of the Lord. Anyone else who pretends to be a spiritual master, and prescribes faulty rules and regulations, also becomes implicated in the consequences of such flawed rules.

QUESTION

Does this mean that one cannot understand the scriptures on their own, since they contain many contradictions applicable to people in different situations, and only a devotee of the Lord is qualified to decide what to apply?

4.4.2 (535)

मुक्तःपरतज्ज्ञानात्

muktaḥ pratijñānāt

muktaḥ—liberated; pratijñānāt—from the promises (of this world).

TRANSLATION

One must be liberated from the promises (of the world).

COMMENTARY

The rulers of this world are themselves bound by rules. They may bend the rules of a nation or society to their wishes, but they cannot escape the laws of karma. The devotee is not bound by these laws; he is not even interested in obtaining power or mastery over material nature. He gives the rules and regulations for the benefit of people, so that they may attain a similarly liberated state. Therefore, he is also free from enviousness and fear—i.e., the worry that someone might attain the same position tomorrow as I have it today. Therefore, the regulations are not for subjugating people; they are for elevating them and bringing them to the point where all regulations cease to be meaningful.

QUESTION

This state of a person in which he is not bound by rules, but gives the rules for others, and yet follows the rules himself to set an example, seems contradictory. In one sense, the rules are rejected; in another sense, they are propounded; and in another sense, the propounder himself follows the rules that he has propounded. So, by following his rules, he seems to be bound by the rules he has propounded, which is contradictory to being free from all possible rules.

4.4.3 (536)
आत्मा प्रकरणात्
ātmā prakaraṇāt

ātmā—the self; prakaraṇāt—on account of the context.

TRANSLATION

The self (is only bound) by the context of its existence.

COMMENTARY

Being bound *by* circumstances is not the same as being bound *to* circumstances. Being bound to a circumstance is due to karma and being bound by circumstance is due to dharma. A liberated soul accepts the bounds imposed by circumstances as dharma, but he is not bound to the circumstance due to karma. Furthermore, the rules and regulations of this world are contextualized to a role, but not contextualized to the time, place, and person. For example, a court judge can render judgments on other people, but he is not allowed to change the rules based on different people. The previous judgments are used as precedents in courts to claim that if this was done to that person at a previous time and place, then the same principle must be reapplied now. In short, the rules and their applications tend to be universalized across times, places, and persons, and the freedom to contextualize these rules is taken away. The devotee is free from such universalization. Even when he breaks the principles that he himself upheld in other places, times, or toward people, he is not bound by karma. Thus, he identifies the best dharma for a place, time, and person.

Topic 2

QUESTION

Doesn't the definition of the dharma in relation to a context (or a socially constructed identity) entail that the self is not truly an individual entity?

4.4.4 (537)

अवभागेन दृष्टत्वात्

avibhāgena dṛṣṭatvāt

avibhāgena—non-different; dṛṣṭatvāt—from being seen like that.

TRANSLATION

(The self and the others) are non-different, from being seen like that.

COMMENTARY

Even when a soul is situated in a relation to others, the primary relation is to the Lord. In this relation, each part performs a different function; however, they serve a common goal. Just like the interest of the hand is not different from the interest of the legs, but the work of the hand is different from the work of the hands, similarly, each person is different and non-different. Due to the commonality of their interest, the individuals are non-different, but because they perform different functions, they are different. A materialist or an impersonalist predicates the difference between individuals based on their different bodies, but the devotee states that with the difference in bodies also comes an identification with the body as the purpose of existence. Thus, people develop a different purpose, which gives rise to competition and conflict in this world.

The materialist says that this competition must be regulated by rules, and the impersonalist says that the individuality must be dissolved. But the devotee says that the different bodies are not a problem—they are only instruments of capability. The rules and regulations are not fundamental—they are guidelines of how the instruments must be used. The differences of instruments and appropriate uses can be reconciled if the purpose is shared. Now, the common purpose becomes the identity and the bodily uniqueness becomes the difference. Since difference and identity exist simultaneously, therefore, each person is non-different from the other: the body is different, but the purpose is identical. Hence, the difference between the individuals need not be dissolved, and the differences need not lead to conflict. The reconciliation of the purpose is superior to materialist diversity and impersonalist unity. Since both principles of diversity and unity are rejected, therefore, 'non-difference' is used.

Topic 3

QUESTION

Isn't the principle of non-difference, by the attainment of common purpose, also seen in this world, when people gather in institutions and societies for a common purpose? If so, how is the devotee's non-difference better?

4.4.5 (538)

बृराह्मेण जैमनिःउपन्यासादभिर्यः

brāhmeṇa jaiminiḥ upanyāsādibhyaḥ

brāhmeṇa—those with the qualities of Brahman or Brahmanas; jai-miniḥ—(so says) Jaimini; upanyāsādibhyaḥ—on account of the narrations etc.

TRANSLATION

According to Jaimini (even in this world the dissolution of the difference between self-interest and other interest) is found in the Brahmanas (since the Brahmanas act in other's interest) according to narrations (about them).

COMMENTARY

A selfish person thinks that even if someone is helping them, it must be for their selfish reasons. Similarly, a selfish person thinks that if someone is criticizing them, then it must be due to their selfish reasons. These are the goggles through which most people see, and they classify others into selfish friends and selfish enemies. The advice of a selfish friend is distrusted, and the criticism of a selfish enemy is disregarded. Thus, people live within their bubbles of distrust and see the Brahmanas and devotees through the goggles of that distrust. If a Brahmana gives them advice, they don't think how it can benefit them, but how it must be benefitting the Brahmana to give such advice. If the Brahmana criticizes them, they don't think how they are hurting themselves, but why the Brahmana should hurt them. It is impossible to correct such misperceptions; the person with red goggles will see the world red. With such goggles, the cooperation of a Brahmana is equated to the sectarian alliances of selfish people, and their competition is equated to the drive for materialistic domination. Hence, mundane people cannot benefit from the advice and criticism of a Brahmana because they cannot distinguish them from the others. They are so comfortable living in the dark, that they consider any sign of light as an oncoming train.

Only when these goggles are removed, then one sees that some things are red, and some are not. But removing such goggles itself means progressing in realization. This sūtra says that it is possible to distinguish the Brahmanas from mundane cooperation and competition through some distinguishing marks. Two such qualities are the perfection of knowledge and renunciation.

QUESTION

But many qualities of the Brahmana are found in ordinary people. Many people may have some knowledge and renunciation. Then, what is the difference between the semi-knowledgeable and renounced vs. the devotees?

4.4.6 (539)

चतितिन्मात्रेण तदात्मकत्वादतियौडुलोमिः

cititanmātreṇa tadātmakatvādityauḍulomiḥ

citi-tanmātreṇa—the body of pure cognitive ability; tat-ātmakatvāt—because that being its true nature; iti—thus; auḍulomiḥ—Audulomi (states).

TRANSLATION

(The difference between the Brahmana and the liberated soul is that the liberated soul) exists in the body of pure cognitive ability because that is the soul's true nature; such is the (viewpoint or statement) of Audolomi.

COMMENTARY

The Brahmana is one who knows the difference between the soul and the body, and by that distinction, many types of material ignorance and attachments are destroyed. But the destruction of this ignorance and attachment is not the same as the acquisition of the Absolute Truth and attachment to it. Therefore, the Brahmana is superior to the materialist because the materialist doesn't know that he is different from the body. The devotee is also superior to the Brahmana because he not only rejects the material identity but also establishes the spiritual identity. In this spiritual identity, the soul has a body of pure cognition, which is different from the material body. This is indicated by the term *citi-tanmatrena* which means the pure quality of cognition. And this body is not different from the soul, which is indicated by saying that this body is ā*tmakatvāt*, which means the true nature of the self. The impersonalist argument is also refuted thereby because there is a body, and that body is the nature of the soul. As we have discussed before, the soul is the 'mind' with three aspects of cognition, relation, and emotion, and the senses are subdivisions of this mind. The parts are not separate from the whole, and yet, the parts are not the whole. Therefore, the soul has all the sensations, and yet, these senses are not separate from the soul. The Brahmana doesn't have such a fully developed body. He can see that he is different from the body, but he relies on the body for perception. The devotee has transcended this body and obtained another body. Thus, the devotees are superior to the Brahmanas, which are superior to the materialists. Meanwhile, the ideologies of impersonalism are false.

QUESTION

In the material world, we can understand that the soul has a body to perceive. But you are now saying that even in the liberated state, the soul has a body and various types of perceptions through the senses and the mind. Does this not create a contradiction between the bounded and liberated states?

4.4.7 (540)

एवमप्युपन्यासात् पूर्वभावादविरोधं बादरायणः

evamapyupanyāsāt pūrvabhāvādavirodhaṃ bādarāyaṇaḥ

evam—thus; api—even; upanyāsāt—on account of the narrations; pūrvabhāvāt—due to the former qualities existing; avirodhaṃ—there is no contradiction; bādarāyaṇaḥ—(so says) Bādarāyaṇa.

TRANSLATION

Thus (with a pure cognition body), even (in the liberated state) according to the narrations (about the devotees), due to the previously existing qualities (of perception), Bādarāyaṇa states that there is no contradiction (in this).

COMMENTARY

The impersonalist argument for the rejection of cognition arises from the fact that this cognition comprises of opposites such as hot vs. cold, bitter vs. sweet, big vs. small. Since these opposites cannot be reconciled, therefore, they cannot constitute Absolute Truth. And if this perception is not giving us the Absolute Truth, therefore, it must be an illusion. The mistake in this argument is that these opposites are simply potentialities, and they manifest one by one, at different places, in different relations, and with different persons. When they exist as potentials, the contradiction doesn't exist. When they are manifest, then, they are never manifest in the same place, time, person, and relation. Therefore, the contradiction never arises. However, since these things exist in this world, so, the completeness of knowledge requires that they exist in the Absolute Truth as well. The impersonalist trades completeness for consistency and says that because there are contradictions, therefore, the Absolute Truth must be devoid of variety. But the devotees say that the Absolute Truth is not contradictory, despite manifesting all the contradictions. So, with the dissolution of the problem of contradictions, the argument for their reconciliation is unnecessary.

Thus, the devotee also has a body with all perceptive faculties, which then perceive contradictory qualities. These qualities are parts of the Absolute Truth, and the devotee sees the connection between these parts and the whole. Just like we might see two faces of a coin, and we know different aspects of the coin by this perception, similarly, the devotee perceives all these qualities and simply considers them different aspects of the Lord. Each aspect is known through a different desire, and a different relation, therefore, the Lord is never completely known. But this perspectival knowledge is not considered an illusion or ignorance, because we are not forbidden from experiencing other aspects. We just don't experience them simultaneously. And this lack of simultaneity arises due to the modal nature of reality. In short, modalities solve the problem of contradictions, while accommodating variety. The impersonalist solves the problem of contradictions by rejecting all variety. Therefore, the modal solution to the problem of contradictions is better than the impersonalist solution (in which all the variety exists in a balanced state of possibility).

Topic 4

QUESTION

You have described so many methods of spiritual attainment, but

in each of these methods there are some difficulties. For example, there are difficulties in understanding the scriptures, in finding the right spiritual master, in performing the various processes for spiritual understanding, and in deciding the right course of action in each case. Therefore, none of the paths is trivially achieved. What is your recommendation in the face of such difficulties?

4.4.8 (541)

संकल्पादेव तु तच्छ्रुतेः

saṃkalpādeva tu tacchruteḥ

saṃkalpāt—through will; eva—only; tu—but; tat-śruteḥ—scriptures say.

TRANSLATION

But only by (a strong) will (is transcendence achieved); this is the verdict of the scriptures.

COMMENTARY

Any serious practitioner of spiritual life knows that the process is extremely difficult. There are many allurements of the world. There are uncontrolled desires. The mind and the body are not strong. It is not easy to understand the scriptures. The application of the scriptural principles is not easy. Meanwhile, the mind and the body are suffering in this world due to the previously produced karma. Under these situations, most people give up spiritual pursuits.

In the Bhagavad-Gita, Lord Kṛṣṇa states that out of thousands of men, one aims for perfection. Out of thousands of men aiming for perfection only one gets liberated. And out of thousands of such liberated souls, only one knows the Lord completely. If we take the lower end of these numbers, and if we say that there are about 7 billion people on this planet, then the best-case estimate would be less than 7 people on this planet would attain spiritual perfection.

A million out of a billion people take some interest in spirituality. While almost everyone has some religious affiliation, most of the people have no spiritual interest. A few million people in this world have some interest, and these people come from all walks of life, all religions, places, and social statues. When these million people endeavor for perfection, perhaps a thousand people get liberated. Thus, we can expect that a thousand souls on this planet will likely not be born again into a material body—most of them will dissolve their identity and enter Brahman, although they are likely to fall again into this world. Then, one out of the thousand liberated souls will obtain an understanding of the Lord. Such a soul will not return to the material world. Notably, this calculation applies only to humans, not to the other species like trees, plans, animals, birds, etc. If we count them too, then spiritual perfection is even rarer.

As a contrast, there are over 2000 billionaires in this world; so, it is a thousand times easier to become a billionaire than it is to attain spiritual perfection. Of course, a billionaire is created due to good karma. But spiritual perfection is not limited by karma; everyone can attain it. However, that doesn't mean that everyone will attain it. The requirement is simply a strong will. If this strong will exists, then the Lord directs the soul's actions from within the heart. But the Lord doesn't force anyone to do anything, and He doesn't interfere with a soul's free will. Therefore, if someone doesn't have a strong will to attain the spiritual perfection, then they will remain those who never tried seriously, or those who tried but failed, or those who tried and succeeded partially.

QUESTION

Why do you place such a great emphasis on the soul's free will? Can't the soul be pushed by others toward spiritual perfection? Aren't religious institutions trying to push many people toward such perfection in modern times?

4.4.9 (542)

अत एव चानन्याधिपतिः

ata eva cānanyādhipatiḥ

ata eva—for the same reason; ca—also; ananyādhipatiḥ—(the soul is said to be) without a ruler or lord (i.e., he is considered to be independent).

TRANSLATION

And for this very reason (of the free will being the most important), (the soul is said to be) without a ruler or a lord (i.e., he is considered free).

COMMENTARY

The injunctions of the scriptures are available to everyone, but they are not a substitute for effort. In modern times, people complain about lack of time, but it is not a lack of time; it is only a lack of will. Similarly, they say that it is hard to control the mind and the senses, but it is also a lack of will. Most people are afraid of failing, and hence they are afraid of trying. They are unable to take the hardship needed to attain the perfection of life, so they remain in the cycle of birth and death. Some people even complain that they have no free will—that they are controlled by the circumstances! All these are symptoms of tamo-guna under which a soul becomes conditioned to easy happiness, with the emphasis on 'easy'. As tamo-guna rises, charlatans appear to show people an easy path. Under rajo-guna, people endeavor, but only if results from their actions are seen. So, under rajo-guna people enthusiastically begin spiritual life, but if quick and immediate results are not obtained, then they go back to their earlier life as fast as they had come. Then, under the mode of sattva-guna, a person has the capacity to tolerate difficulties to obtain long-term gains. Therefore, if one begins spiritual life under sattva-guna, then they can sustain it over time.

Thus, a spiritual master doesn't just recommend a spiritual process, but also the method by which one can be elevated to sattva-guna. Methods of such elevation include giving up intoxication, meat-eating, illicit sex, and gambling, waking up early, maintaining routine, etc. These practices don't lead to spiritual advancement. However, they increase sattva-guna, which is necessary for one to persist in spiritual life. Many people think that these practices are themselves spiritual progress, but they are not. They are simply healthy, clean living, which is neither necessary nor sufficient for spiritual progress, but it is recommended to maintain sattva-guna. Once life is regulated in this way, then a person can perform spiritual activities, like chanting the Lord's names, worshipping the deity, meditating upon the Lord, and reading the scriptures. Under sattva-guna, one makes faster progress, because the mind has been regulated. The difficulty is that most people are so immersed in tamo-guna, that they don't want to change their lifestyle. Without developing sattva-guna, even if they read scriptures, they misunderstand everything. Even if they practice some meditation, their minds are constantly distracted. Since they don't make spiritual progress without sattva-guna, they blame the process and reject it quickly.

Therefore, this sūtra says that nobody can push you if you don't want to push yourself. As people are pushed, they become resentful. Even if a teacher tries to educate them, they argue with the teacher and blame the teacher for the difficulties. They resent the fact that knowledge is difficult, its application is even harder, and persisting on this path for a long time is the hardest.

Studies on sportspersons have shown that the most successful sportspersons aren't the most talented, the strongest, or those with the most resources. They rather have the quality of being able to get up after a fall and try again. This requires will. Thus, even material success comes to a person who endeavors consistently. The same principle applies to spiritual pursuits. The difference is that the spiritual pursuits are longer than material endeavors. Therefore, for a material endeavor, one must give up laziness and replace it with passion—i.e., the belief that by endeavoring one will get results. For spiritual pursuits, one must even give up passion, because the results are not immediate. The hare and the tortoise story is relevant in this context. The hare is passionate; he runs and then sleeps. The tortoise is persistent; he doesn't have the best resources, the greatest talent, or the most strength. But he persists and eventually wins. In the case of humans, persistence requires a high level of sattva-guna. Hence, the lazy people never get started in spiritual life, because they keep looking for excuses about how the hardship can be avoided by shifting the blame on something else. The passionate get started, but soon, they go back to sleep.

Many people make some effort initially, after which they settle into a comfort zone. They think: I'm making some effort, so that should be sufficient, right? Wrong. Effort means a constant striving toward greater perfection. When we settle into a comfort zone, that's where we remain. Spiritual progress is not measured by the quantitative output. It is measured by the qualitative change in a person. This change is in our control and cannot be forced by anyone. Therefore, the soul is lord and master of his destiny. It also means that the soul is alone in this journey—nobody is coming to save you unless you want to save your-self. Lordship comes with the responsibility for the right decisions.

Topic 5

QUESTION

But if someone doesn't have the strong will for spiritual per-fection, how can they acquire it? How does one develop a stronger desire for perfection?

4.4.10 (543)
अभावं बादरिःआह ह्येवम्
abhāvaṃ bādariḥ āha hyevam

abhāvaṃ—absence; bādariḥ—Bādari; āha—says; hi—certainly; evam—in this way.

TRANSLATION

(The feeling) of absence; Bādari says that in this way (by feeling the absence) one certainly attains (a stronger desire).

COMMENTARY

The antidote to the comfort zone is the feeling of absence of the Lord. Most people who don't aspire for spiritual life don't feel this absence. They think: My life is mostly okay; I have these things today, and I will have those things tomorrow, and in this way, I will live my life comfortably. This sense of comfort is the symptom of tamo-guna. One doesn't realize that the human life is obtained by great difficulty, and it is not to be wasted upon things that can be obtained in other lives too. The sense of comfort is produced by thinking that whatever exists with me presently is going to exist with me permanently. Thus, one might think that their wealth is going to grow, that their family will remain with them, etc. Hence, when someone loses their wealth, their loved ones abandon them in times of trouble, or they face other kinds of betrayals, then they realize the futility of the material life. Then they aspire for transcendence.

This aspiration is missing the perfection. In most people, it comes only when the material support system disappears, and one is left alone. In that state of loneliness, one cries for the Lord, and promises to never forget Him. But as soon as some comforts are obtained, one forgets the Lord immediately.

Therefore, mother Kunti prays to Lord Kṛṣṇa to keep sending her difficulties because under those difficulties the Lord is never forgotten. This sūtra says that one must replace their feeling of comfort by desperation, separation, and longing for the Lord. A strong will is not developed by the possibility of big achievements. Most people know that if they work hard then they might achieve great things. But they don't work hard. Why? Because they are comfortable in their present life. Those who are endeavoring (even under a mode of passion) have an inner burning desire; they think that the world is meaningless for them, and they must create some form of meaning to make their lives bearable. This kind of burning desire is necessary even for spiritual endeavors. Therefore, Lord Chaitanya states the following in the Śrī Śikṣāṣṭakam:

> yugāyitam nimeṣeṇa
> cakṣuṣā prāvṛṣāyitam
> śūnyāyitam jagat sarvam
> govinda-viraheṇa me

"O Govinda! In your separation, each moment seems like a yuga. Tears are flooding my eyes like rain, and the whole world seems empty."

The philosophy of nihilism was earlier refuted in many ways. But in this sūtra, the philosophy of nihilism is also accepted. This nihilism is created by the feeling of separation from the Lord. The nihilist says that the world doesn't exist, that we are all alone in this world, or whatever exists is meaningless and we must give it meaning. The devotee accepts this ideology of meaninglessness without the Lord. His life is unbearable unless it is connected to the Lord's service. Such a devotee endeavors not because he wants to achieve anything. Rather, he endeavors simply to fill the emptiness created otherwise. When a devotee develops this constant sense of separation, then the Lord is immediately obtained. Therefore, the highest goal of life is to develop the sense of separation. It is a madness, but it is also the highest purpose of life. If this separation is established in the heart, then the Lord is not forgotten even for a moment.

The mode of sattva-guna also creates a comfort zone. It brings peace and tranquility in a person's life, and because the mind and the senses are no longer hassled toward futile pursuits, a person starts enjoying a life of peace. For this reason, sattva-guna is not considered a spiritual state. Rather, the state of desperation and emptiness is considered a spiritual state. But this desperation is not the pursuit of material gains; it is not the pseudo-happiness of laziness; and it is not the sense of comfort obtained under mental peace and tranquility. The spiritual journey is long because one must elevate themselves from laziness to passion, from passion to tranquility, and from tranquility to desperation.

Each stage of progression is hard, because the next step in spiritual progression is the very opposite of the previous step. Thus, the lazy person finds it hard to be passionate. A passionate person finds it hard to be tranquil. And the tranquil person finds it impossible to be desperate. Indeed, some people might equate tranquility with laziness, and passion with desperation. As a result, the devotees endeavoring for the Lord—because they find the world meaningless otherwise—are often equated to other passionate people, and the impersonalist says: Why don't you become more peaceful and tranquil? Why are you so agitated? Only someone who knows the full spectrum of progression realizes the difference between the states, and which state is higher than the others.

QUESTION

How do you characterize the feeling of absence of the Lord? What is the experience of meaninglessness, and what are the symptoms of this feeling?

4.4.11 (544)

भावं जैमनिःविकिल्पामननात्

bhāvaṃ jaiminiḥ vikalpāmananāt

bhāvaṃ—the feeling (of absence); jaiminiḥ—Jaimini; vikalpaāmananāt—due to (devoid) of alternatives, these do not enter the mind (as thoughts).

TRANSLATION

According to Jaimini, under the feeling (of absence), all the alternatives (of material enjoyment) do not enter the mind (and cannot be thought of).

COMMENTARY

The feeling of absence and meaninglessness is also experienced by a depressed person. Depression is the state of tamo-guna attained due to the failure of the attainment of rajo-guna. If we are frustrated in love, or other material achievements, then we fall into depression. In the depressed state, there is an active conflict between tamo-guna and rajo-guna. Anxiety is the preliminary stage of depression, and under anxiety, there is a paralysis caused by tamo-guna, and a hyperactivity caused by rajo-guna. As the condition progresses, one suddenly feels hungry and then loses appetite. The body gets stiff due to tamo-guna, and feverish due to rajo-guna, and both these conditions create pain. If one tries to cool the body, then stiffness increases; if one tries to heat the body, then the fever grows. Thus, the illness can be prolonged and incurable.

The way out of such a state is mild activity that produces small wins. Big things that require tremendous efforts, and the results which will arrive after a significant delay, cannot be performed during this state. Similarly, activities that don't produce a sense of achievement will push a person further back into depression. Hence, a person suffering from depression should not try to entertain themselves out of the problem, because there is no self-worth in it. Cooking a meal, cleaning the room, or paying bills, creates an immediate sense of accomplishment—i.e., it feeds the rajo-guna, and the sense of self-worth increases. Similarly, small activities, when no activity is being performed, also feeds rajo-guna. As rajo-guna becomes dominant, then tamo-guna is naturally subordinated, and the conflict between these modes subsides. One now becomes capable of doing bigger things. Such practical tips are often useful even for practicing devotees who may be struggling with various problems in their life.

These three modes exist even for advanced devotees. The devotee first feels separated from the Lord. To overcome this separation, the devotee performs activities satisfying to the Lord. Then by the achievement of results in such activities, the devotee feels satisfied. But this sense of satisfaction doesn't last. Rather, the sense of separation returns, the devotee acts for the pleasure of the Lord, and then again feels satisfied by the Lord's satisfaction. In this way, the modes keep cycling, and nothing other than the Lord is remembered.

QUESTION

When a devotee is imbued by this sense of separation from the Lord, then what does he do? What are his actions under the mental state of emptiness?

4.4.12 (545)

द्वादशाहवदुभयविधं बादरायणोऽतः

dvādaśāhavadubhayavidham bādarāyaṇo'taḥ

dvādaśāhavat—like the twelve-fold sacrifice; ubhayavidham—in two ways; bādarāyaṇaḥ—Bādarayana; ataḥ—therefore.

TRANSLATION

Therefore, Bādarayana says that (the devotees act) just like the twelve-fold sacrifice in two ways (i.e., serving the masculine and feminine forms).

COMMENTARY

During the reign of Svayambhuva Manu, there was no qualified person to become Indra, and therefore Lord Viṣṇu appeared as Indra, and He was then known as Yajna. He along with His wife—Lakshmi, who is called Dakśinā—had twelve sons named Tosha, Pratosha, Santosha, Bhadra, Śānti, Idaspati, Idhma, Kavi, Vibhu, Svahna, Sudeva, and Rocana. These twelve expansions represent the ten senses, the mind, and the ego. As we have noted earlier, our body comprises masculine and feminine aspects—the elements of Sāñkhya constitute the masculine aspect, and the prāṇa energizing the senses, mind, ego, etc. is the feminine aspect. In this sūtra, the term *dvādaśāhavat* or the twelve-fold sacrifice indicates the twelve parts of a sacrifice, and the term *ubhayavidham* or the two-fold practice, denotes the masculine and feminine aspects. They are a single family, but the parents are two-fold, and the children are twelve-fold. The constitute the entire perceptual apparatus of experience. The names of the children of Yajna and Dakśinā denote various kinds of happiness or satisfaction. Essentially, Yajna and Dakśinā unite to create happiness.

Now, this sūtra says that the devotees are just like the twelve-fold division of the two-fold practice. In short, they dedicate their mind, senses, and the ego to the Lord and His consort. Sometimes they want to serve the Lord, and sometimes they need the Lord. The sense of needing is the feeling of separation. The sense of wanting is the desire to serve. And the sense of satisfaction is the meeting of the want and the need—the Lord is obtained through His service. From this meeting, a new need is created, which then transforms into a want, which then meets the need, and the cycle repeats endlessly. Yajna is the person who is offered, Dakśinā is the offering for Yajna, and their union is the children. It is understandable if these things are not immediately clear. We can understand them to the extent that we can, and by experience it can become clearer.

QUESTION

You are saying that the devotee feels separated from the Lord. Then you are also saying that the devotee is united with the Lord. How do we reconcile this simultaneous separation and union? Doesn't it sound contradictory?

4.4.13 (546)

तन्वभावे सन्ध्यवत् उपपत्तेः

tanvabhāve sandhyavat upapatteḥ

tat-abhāve—in His absence; sandhyavat—just like union; upapatteḥ—it follows or is reasonable.

TRANSLATION

It follows that in His absence (one feels) also just like the union.

COMMENTARY

As we have discussed before, space is semantic, which means that there are three kinds of proximities and distance. The first type of proximity is similarity of meaning, and distance is dissimilarity of meaning. When this similarity is created, then the possibility of knowing the unknown is produced, and one becomes qualified to know. Once a person has become qualified, then he can interact with that reality and the qualification and capability to know is converted into an experience. Finally, the interaction to that reality is caused by our desire, and when the desire develops, then we are emotionally proximate.

Thus, everyone can experience the Lord through a desire, interaction, and qualification. In this sense, when these are present, the Lord is ever-present. And yet, the difference is that when we see the Lord in this way, He is not visible to others, although the possibility of this interaction is eternal. Then again, when there is meeting, then the interaction is also visible to the others.

Hence, there is a difference between meeting and separation, and there is no difference between meeting and separation. Both meeting and separation are produced by the same process, although the separation creates private experience, and the meeting creates experience accessible even to others. Therefore, the term *sandhyavat* is used here, which means 'just like union'. It is not the same as meeting, and yet, it is not different from the meeting. The key point is that missing the Lord, finding the world empty, and then seeking the Lord, creates the same type of experience as when the Lord is face-to-face. It just remains our personal experience and is not known to the other devotees.

QUESTION

Then what happens if the soul reaches the spiritual world and finds the Lord face-to-face? How is that different from the experience of separation?

4.4.14 (547)
भावे जाग्रद्वत्
bhāve jāgradvat

bhāve—in attainment (of spiritual world); jāgrat-vat—just as in the waking state.

TRANSLATION

In the attainment (of the spiritual world, where the Lord is seen face-to-face), (the experience is) just like waking state (i.e., public experience).

COMMENTARY

This sūtra makes the distinction between the feelings of separation, and the meeting with the Lord face-to-face, even more explicit by comparing these two as dreaming and waking. During dreaming, we see a reality, which is eternally possible, but others don't see it. Then during waking, we can see the same reality, and others can see it too. From the perspective of an individual, there is no difference between waking and dreaming—everything that is experienced in a dream can also be experienced during waking, and vice versa. And yet, the dream experience is private, while the waking experience is public. Thus, while the devotee is in the material world, he experiences the Lord due to separation, but the experience is private, and it can be compared to dreaming. Then when the devotee reaches the spiritual world, the same experience becomes public.

Topic 6

QUESTION

But if you say that the devotee's experience is just like a dream, then someone can say that it is not acceptable unless there is public evidence for it. I understand that God cannot be seen by everyone, but what is the evidence that the devotee is seeing the Lord? Can this seeing be known by the others?

4.4.15 (548)

परदीपवदावेशःतथा हि दर्शयति

pradīpavadāveśaḥ tathā hi darśayati

pradīpavat—like a lamp; āveśaḥ—seized by frenzy or imbued with the emotion; tathā—similarily; hi—certainly; darśayati—is seen.

TRANSLATION

Like a lamp (illuminates the world), similarly, imbued with the emotion (of the love of God), (the devotee) is certainly seen (to illuminate the world).

COMMENTARY

We previously discussed the argument from hallucination, which the impersonalist makes, and presented an argument against it: Even if the devotional experience is like a hallucination, what is wrong with that if it is permanent and blissful? This sūtra presents another argument against the claim of hallucination: we cannot see what the devotee sees, but we can find the evidence of that seeing, namely, that the devotee illuminates the world by his presence.

The material world is ignorance about the truth, right, and good. We don't see the truth because we think that matter is devoid of meaning; that is merely exists, but it doesn't tell us anything, it has no purpose, and it was produced randomly. With such ignorance, we are also unable to formulate consistent and complete theories about the world, but under ignorance we relegate the problem to the future. Then, as the meanings are taken out of reality, then the notions of right and good are either completely rejected or relativized to individuals. Thus, whatever an individual considers good, is good for him. And whatever a group of individuals consider right in a society is right for them. By disregarding the righteousness, people are entrapped in karma and they suffer endlessly, but they are unable to claim that pain and suffering is good.

The devotee alleviates this ignorance in many ways. First, he explains the nature of truth, right, and good. Second, he tells people how to elevate themselves to the truth, right, and good. Third, he demonstrates this elevated state through his own life. The explanation of truth, right, and good is the theory. The method of attaining this truth, right, and good, is the practice. And his life is the empirical evidence obtained by following the theory and practice.

An impersonalist is unable to explain even the nature of truth, right, and good. According to him, the self exists, but this existence has no meaning or purpose. This is like saying that the sentence "the sky is purple" exists, but we don't want to know if it is true, whether it should be spoken, and what happens when it is spoken. The materialist and impersonalist philosophies are nearly identical in the sense that both accept existence, although the former is existence with variety and the latter is existence without variety. That dissolution of variety doesn't constitute the answers to the questions of truth, right, and good. It is merely the dissolution of such questions themselves. Impersonalism is like a teacher shaming a student for asking good questions—because he doesn't know the answer. When this shame overwhelms the soul, he commits spiritual suicide. And by that suicide the questions of truth, right, and good cease.

Only a devotee has the answer to the questions of truth, right, and good. He also knows how to attain it, and he shows the perfection of such attainment in his life. Of course, the blind cannot see the light shining in their face.

QUESTION

You have described the waking and dreaming states of the devotee. What about the deep sleep state? Does that state also exist for the Lord's devotee?

4.4.16 (549)

स्वाप्ययसंपत्तत्योरन्यतरापेक्षम् आवष्कितृं हि

svāpyayasaṃpattyoranyatarāpekṣam āviṣkṛtaṃ hi

svāpyaya—in deep sleep; saṃpattyoḥ—with the wealth of (absorption in the Lord); anyatara-apekṣam—any expectation or relativity; āviṣkṛtam—covering being removed; hi—certainly.

TRANSLATION

In deep sleep, with the wealth of (absorption in the Lord), any expectation or relativity is certainly uncovered (i.e., the covering is removed).

COMMENTARY

The deep sleep state constitutes the personality or identity of the soul. We have discussed in the introduction how this personality is divided into five parts—(1) what I like, (2) what I can know, (3) what I can do, (4) where I exist, and (5) when I exist. Each such aspect of the personality also has a negative component—(1) what I dislike, (2) what I cannot know, (3) what I cannot do, (4) where I don't exist, and (5) when I don't exist. For a devotee, this personality changes into the following five aspects—(1) what the Lord likes, (2) what the Lord wants me to know, (3) what the Lord wants me to do, (4) where the Lord wants to me to stay, and (5) when the Lord wants me to stay. This is the wealth of absorption in the Lord. Then, with this wealth, all expectations of what I like or dislike, what I want to know or not know, what I want to do or not do, where I want to stay or not stay, and when I want to stay or not stay, are dissolved. Everything is reposed in the Lord's will. And with this reposing, the relativity of various opinions—i.e., that everyone wants something different—is dissolved. So, the wealth of the soul is not fame, power, money, knowledge, beauty, or renunciation. The real wealth is that the soul is surrendered to the Lord. This wealth is not separate from the self; it is also the soul's persona.

The dreaming state is manifest from the deep sleep state, which means that our persona creates the desires, fantasies, and apprehensions which are manifest in dreams. The same persona is then manifest during the waking stage. The difference is that the manifestation of the persona in dreams is conditioned by the senses, mind, intellect, ego, and moral sense, which have been developed in this life (although influenced by the unconscious of the past lives present as our persona). For example, humans will almost never see themselves as dogs or cats in a dream. Even if they have had other bodies in the past, they will always see themselves as what they are in the present life. If such identity is not yet developed, then there are no dreams. For example, newborn children have dreamless sleep because their senses are undeveloped, although they have an unmanifest persona. As a child grows up, the senses begin to develop, and babies begin to have dreams. In these dreams, they often move their body and make some sounds, which is an indication that the dream is mostly sensual. As the child develops further, the dreams have increasing mental component, and so you can try to interpret these dreams because now they have meanings. The dream experience, however, is not constrained by opportunity because you can go anywhere, see anything, and do anything.

The waking experience is constrained by opportunities created by karma—you cannot go everywhere, cannot see everything, and cannot do everything. In summary, the dreams are the expression of the unconscious persona through the constraint of the present body, and the waking experience is the same unconscious persona constrained by the present body as well as the opportunities afforded to the body at a given time.

The devotee also has an unconscious persona which is manifest as dreams or remembrance of the Lord, and then waking or face-to-face encounters with the Lord. When the dreaming and waking don't exist, the persona still exists.

Topic 7

QUESTION

You have answered all my questions, but I want to discuss some alternative viewpoints. Can you clarify them for me? My first question is: You have accepted that an impersonalist state is also transcendental, although it is not the highest perfection. How is the impersonal liberation attained by someone?

4.4.17 (550)

जगद्व्यापारवर्जम् प्रकरणात् असंनिहितित्वाच्च

jagadvyāpāravarjam prakaraṇāt asaṃnihitatvācca

jagadvyāpāravarjam—rejecting the worldly business; prakaraṇāt—caused by different situations; asaṃnihitatvāt—due to as if not invested; ca—and.

TRANSLATION

By rejecting the worldly business that is produced by different situations, and (doing them) as if one is not invested (in the results of actions).

COMMENTARY

The soul's bond to the world is created by guna and karma. Guna means the desires and habits of enjoyment, and karma means the consequences of the actions produced due to these desires and habits of enjoyment. Accordingly, liberation from the material world is also obtained when both guna and karma are destroyed. In this sūtra, the method of destruction is explained as a two-fold process. First, the person rejects the businesses of this world in various types of situations. For example, such a person is not interested in solving the problems of world hunger, in creating a more prosperous or opulent society, or in educating people about the nature of this world. This is notable because many people aspiring for Brahman fall back into altruistic or charitable activities which are meant to improve a person's life in this world. Such activities are rejected in this world. Second, the person may perform some deeds for the bare sustenance, but even those actions are performed in a disinterested manner. Therefore, whether the results are obtained, the person remains equanimous. By the rejecting of all forms of worldly goodness, the person obtains freedom from guna, and by performing whatever little needs to be done with disinterest, he consumes the previously ordained good or bad karma, and doesn't create new karma. In short, utter disinterest is the recipe for getting to Brahman.

QUESTION

It is sometimes said that upon liberation, everyone becomes qualified to interact with the Lord, and then they have a direct interaction with the Lord. This seems contrary to the mood of shyness, but even in the mood of boldness, is the Lord known directly by everyone, or only by His intimate servants?

4.4.18 (551)

परत्यकषोपदेशादतिचेत् न आधकिारकिमण्डलस्थोक्तेः

pratyakṣopadeśāditi cet na ādhikārikamaṇḍalasthokteḥ

pratyakṣa-upadeśāt—from the teaching of direct experience; iti cet—if it be said; na—not; ādhikārika—qualified; maṇḍalastha—situated in a circle; ukteḥ—it is said;

TRANSLATION

If it be said that (the Lord is) directly perceived due to the teaching, (we say) not so; (He is known) only through those qualified to be situated in His circle; thus, it is said.

COMMENTARY

In many egalitarian religions, the equality of the soul is taught. It is said that the hierarchy of this world is an artificial creation, and this creation is exploited by the priests. Therefore, we must flatten society and treat everyone equally. This equality is supported on the principle of the souls being equal.

This sūtra however states that the Lord is supreme, and He has His inner circle of devotees. But this inner circle is also based on qualification. Therefore, the more qualified devotees know the Lord intimately, and the less qualified devotees know about the Lord through this inner circle. When a new devotee is introduced to this inner circle, it is through the recommendation of another devotee who is already in the inner circle of the Lord. Those in the inner circle make this introduction if they consider the devotee qualified to be in the Lord's inner circle. Therefore, the doctrine of equality is accepted in the sense that everyone can enter the Lord's inner circle. But it is also rejected on the principle that only those most qualified enter this circle, whereas the others know about the Lord through this inner circle. In short, the Lord doesn't immediately reveal Himself to everyone. He does, however, reveal Himself upon a pure devotee's recommendation. Therefore, it is said that the worship of the devotees is as good as the worship of the Lord because that mood of humility and graciousness is important to enter the inner circle of the Lord's personal devotees.

QUESTION

Some people say that the Lord has a form, but the soul becomes a part of the form and merges in the Lord. So, they don't deny that the Brahman has a form, but they reject the separation of the soul's identity from the Lord.

4.4.19 (552)
वकिारवर्तचि तथा हि स्थितिमिाह
vikāravarti ca tathā hi sthitimāha

vikāra-avarti—that which is not covered by distortions; ca—and; tathā—in the same way; hi—certainly; sthitim—situated; āha—the scripture declares.

TRANSLATION

(Just as the Lord) is not covered by distortions, in the same way, (the devotee) is also certainly situated (free of distortions); thus, the scripture declares.

COMMENTARY

Impersonalism is not a new ideology; it is has existed for thousands of years, and it changes forms. In the simplest form, neither the soul nor God have any form; they are not even separate individuals. In a more sophisticated form, God has a form, but the soul is within God, so he is not recognized as a separate individual. In an even more sophisticated form, the soul and God are separate, but they are equivalent; just like a lamp can be used to light other lamps, but once they have been lit, all the lamps are considered equivalent; in the same way, this impersonalist argues that upon liberation we all become God.

In this sūtra, the second type of impersonalism is being refuted by saying that the soul indeed has a form separate from the Lord, but this form is not an illusory or distorted form. Illusion and distortion are almost identical ideas in Vedic philosophy because illusion is created from the Absolute Truth by distorting and hiding parts of the truth and presenting that distorted and partial truth as the whole truth. Therefore, that illusion is also real, and a part of God, but it is not the whole truth, because it was created by hiding other parts. Therefore, when the term *vikāra-avarti* is used, it means that the soul doesn't have the tendency to distort, and he is not covered by any distorted ideas.

The implication is that the separated existence of the soul from the Lord is not like the illusion found in this world in which each person considers themselves to be the center of the world and entitled to exploit other living entities. The knowledge of truth means that the Lord knows He is the Lord, and the soul knows that he is the soul.

Thus, the cessation of illusion isn't the cessation of individuality. It is simply the end of the pretentious idea of being God.

QUESTION

Some people say that the Lord is only known through the scriptures, and every other method of knowing must be rejected. However, you have outlined other methods of knowing through reasoning and practical experience.

4.4.20 (553)
दर्शयतश्चैवं परत्यक्षानुमाने
darśayataścaivaṃ pratyakṣānumāne

darśayataḥ—sees; ca—also; evaṃ—thus; pratyakṣa-anumāne—in direct experience and inference.

TRANSLATION

(The devotees) thus also sees the Lord in direct experience and inference.

COMMENTARY

This is by far the main source of conflict between science and religion. The religious fanatic says that the words of scriptures cannot be understood by ordinary people and therefore they must be accepted based on faith. The scientific fanatic says that everything must be understood through *my* senses and rationality. Factually, both positions are wrong. The words of scriptures can be understood rationally and empirically, but it requires an advanced form of intelligence that goes beyond the measurement of instruments, and takes into account sense perception, thoughts in the mind, the judgment of truth, right, and good in the intellect, moral sense, and ego, followed by the understanding of the unconscious personality, then the soul which chooses this personality, and then the Lord who is the standard for judging the truth, right, and good. When the world is reduced to the numbers produced by measuring instruments, then both theoretical and empirical knowledge becomes severely incomplete. Thereafter, if the incomplete view is presented as the whole truth, then atheism is created. Similarly, if religions are unable to explain the details about perception, thinking, judging, choosing, and the ideal choices, then they become fanatic, and they attribute the absence of insight as the virtue of divine revelation.

This sūtra says that there is no contradiction between religion and science because the Lord is also understood through reason and experience. However, this is not a gratuitous license for speculation. Notably, modern science claims to employ the methods of reason and experience, but the main method of modern science is speculation. Thus, so many papers are published not because they are proven—rationally or empirically—but simply because they are *novel*. Keeping this in mind, we should not confuse reason and observation with speculation about truth. In short, the standards one applies to religion, namely that it should be rationally and empirically confirmed, must also be applied to science. The fact is that today these rigorous standards are only applied selectively. Thus, both science and religion indulge in reckless speculation, and speculating on truth has become the primary benchmark for an intellectual.

If speculation is rejected, and rigorous standards of reason and observation are applied, then, religion is not limited to the study of scriptures. Indeed, one of the measures of spiritual advancement is that a deep acquaintance with the truth enables a person to apply that truth in any context and field of study. Therefore, the proficient devotee can apply the understanding of truth without referencing the scriptures. This might seem ludicrous to novices in religion who want to see scriptural references for every type of claim. But as we have seen, the scriptures are so numerous and mutually contradictory, that without practical expertise we cannot apply them correctly. One who knows how to apply them doesn't check a book every time there is a decision to be made. He rather employs reason and experience to decide which injunction applies when. Thus, reason and experience are hallmarks of proficiency in scriptural knowledge, and those with such proficiency can also present an understanding of the Lord without referencing the scriptures—i.e., through reason and experience.

QUESTION

Some people say that once the soul enters the Lord's abode, and acquires a body just like Him, then the soul must be considered

equivalent to God. Thus, in some religions, there are many souls, but they are also just like God.

4.4.21 (554)
भोगमात्रसाम्यलिङ्गाच्च
bhogamātrasāmyaliṅgācca

bhogamātra—only for enjoyment; sāmya—equality; liṅgāt—from the body; ca—also.

TRANSLATION

Also, from the body similar to the Lord, which is meant only for enjoyment.

COMMENTARY

Under *sārūpya mukti*, the liberated soul gets a body just like the Lord in the Vaikuṇṭha planets. Similarly, in other forms of liberation, a devotee might live in the same place as the Lord lives, have the same opulence as the Lord, or even enjoy all those things that the Lord enjoys. This, as we have discussed, is like a king's son sitting on the king's throne. The son considers the father's property his own and enjoys everything just like the father. But the son doesn't become the king thereby. In the same way, the Lord controls everything, and He delegates His power to the soul to let the soul experience His power. The Lord's graciousness should not however mean that the soul is factually the Lord.

For example, when you receive guests in your home, you welcome them in various ways, ask them to sit, while you run around to serve them. Does that mean that the guest is the host, and the host is the servant of the guest?

Many people understand the language of power, but they don't understand the language of love. In many religions, God is described as the most powerful person, thereby instilling fear of God in the soul. Once this fear is instilled, then love is deemphasized. So, people think that if they go to God's abode, then either they will merge with God, or if they are separate from God, then they must continue to fear His power. Since this fear is undesirable, therefore, the spiritualist tries to find ways to destroy the fear. But how can we give up fear of the most powerful person? It must be that we become as powerful as God. This type of contortionist thinking is the result of the doctrine that God is the most powerful, and the relation between the soul and God is based on His power. In short, if God was not powerful, then there would no reason to love Him.

This sūtra however says that the relation between soul and God is for enjoyment. The soul gets a body like the Lord so that he can see, touch, and hear the Lord. This similarity doesn't make the soul equivalent to the Lord.

QUESTION

Some people say that although the personal abode of the Lord exists, it is also as illusory as the material world because it has numerous qualities. For example, they might say that since the Lord is infinite, and yet He takes a finite form to enjoy with the devotee, therefore, this finitude is itself an illusion. But the Lord accepts this illusory state, which is inferior to the infinite state.

4.4.22 (555)
अनावृत्तःशब्दात् अनावृत्तःशब्दात्
anāvṛttiḥ śabdāt anāvṛttiḥ śabdāt

anāvṛttiḥ—no covering; śabdāt—due to scriptural declaration.

TRANSLATION

(There is) no covering (in the spiritual world) thus is stated in scriptures.

COMMENTARY

We have now come to the end of Vedānta Sūtra, and now we attack the central problem of why people think that the Lord doesn't have a form. The problem is that the whole seems to have the same size as the part. From a physical perspective, the Lord's abode is bigger than the Lord, and the Lord resides within the abode. Since the abode is bigger than the Lord, therefore, how can we say that the abode was previously a part of the Lord? Similarly, there are infinite other living entities who have the same size as the Lord, and some of them might even be taller or bigger than Him. So, how can these bigger bodies be said to be a part of the Lord? All doctrines of impersonalism begin from the problem of size, and how to fit the universe into a person. Since this problem cannot be solved in physical thinking, therefore, it is said that God is infinite, and whatever is infinite cannot have a form. Or, even if God has a form, the universe still cannot be a part of the Lord, because how can such a big universe be compressed into the body of a person who has the same size as us? Finally, if everything is accepted to be part of a person, then the universe is called a hallucination projected out of a person; the person is finite, the hallucination is infinite. In this way, many bad ideas are the result of physical thinking.

But none of these bad ideas work, and every time these ideas fail, we can try to patch them, or go back to the original problem of size, which arises from physical thinking. The solution to this problem is to give up physical thinking and adopt semantic thinking. The form of the Lord is not physical. He is rather the original idea of knowledge. This knowledge has many parts or aspects, which are parts of His body. When these parts are subdivided, the world is created, and this sub-division is called His expansion or renunciation. Each such expanded part was previously within the Lord, so these expansions are also His property; this is called His wealth. The Lord controls these expansions, so His control over the creation is called His power. Finally, the expansions are created due to a purpose of enjoyment, so the purpose exists in each part, and this presence of the whole in the part is called His fame that is all-pervasive.

The central problem in all religious philosophies is that they speak about God's wealth, power, fame, and beauty, but they don't speak about the origin of these things—knowledge. Once knowledge is ignored as the origin of everything else, then wealth, power, beauty, etc. are construed physically. Then we start thinking: How can all this wealth, power, beauty, and fame reside within a person, and be created from the person? In short, how can you fit the universe inside God's body? From this difficulty arises monotheism in which the world is created ex nihilo, impersonalism where God doesn't have a form, nihilism where nothing at all exists, and materialism where only matter exists. The idealists speak of knowledge, but that knowledge is without a knower or a known. Can we really say that knowledge exists when there is no knower? For that matter, how can knowledge be true, if it doesn't correspond to a known? Therefore, the existence of knowledge alone doesn't solve any real problem.

When we speak of semantic thinking, we are simply saying that wealth, power, beauty, and fame are manifestations of knowing, which exists in three aspects—knower, known, and knowledge—of the Supreme Person. When the Supreme Person knows Himself, then knowledge is manifest due to His knowing. This knowledge includes other knowers, knowns, and knowledge, as its parts. But, since everything arises from knowing, therefore everything is semantic. The beauty, power, wealth, fame, etc. should not be treated as substances, forces, shapes, and sizes. Semantic thinking means that the Absolute Truth is jñānam-advayam or non-dual knowing in which the knower, known, and knowledge have not been separated, the diversity has not been created, and whatever we call the manifest world rests within the Supreme Person.

Once this semantic thinking is adopted, then the Supreme Person is understood as the word 'universe' from which the universe has expanded. Once the universe expands, then the word 'universe' seems to be a part of the universe, and the impersonalist now says that the universe has covered the word 'universe' therefore the covering must be an illusion. However, the impersonalist doesn't say that although light expands from the Sun, therefore, the light must be a covering of the Sun, and therefore, the real Sun must be that which doesn't emit light. The problem is terminology. Is light the covering of the Sun—implying that the Sun is somehow constrained by the light? Or is light the expansion of the Sun—implying that the light was previously in the Sun? Clearly, the Sun is smaller than the space in which its light expands. So, why can't that be the basis of understanding why the Sun is finite, the light expands to a much larger space than the Sun, and yet, this light previously existed in the Sun?

The Gayatri mantra says—*Tat-Savitur Vareñyaṃ*—or the Sun is the husband of the light and is married to light. The light is a part of the Sun, the consort of the Sun, and yet different from the Sun. The same principle applies in this case. The Lord is the master of His creation since the creation is His energy; She was previously within the Lord, and now She has expanded from the Lord. This sūtra makes this point succinctly—there no covering because it is an expansion. If we change the word from 'covering' to 'expansion', then everything becomes clear, and the various kinds of bad contortionist ideas are also rebuffed.

INDEX